Fourth Edition

Adolescence

A Social Psychological Analysis

HANS SEBALD
Arizona State University

PRENTICE HALL
Englewood Cliffs, New Jersey 07632

Library of Congress Cataloging-in-Publication Data

Sebald, Hans.
    Adolescence : a social psychological analysis / Hans Sebald. —
4th ed.
      p. cm.
    ISBN 0-13-006008-9
    1. Adolescence. 2. Teenagers—United States. I. Title.
HQ796.S423 1992
305.23'5—dc20   91-20469
                                        CIP

To Don Royer, my tutor at Manchester College, in gratitude; my friend ever since, with affection.

Acquisitions editor: Nancy Roberts
Editorial/production supervision and
   interior design: E.A. Pauw
Cover design: Mike Fender
Prepress buyer: Debra Kesar
Manufacturing buyer: Mary Anne Gloriande

©1992, 1984, 1977, 1968 by Prentice-Hall, Inc.
A Simon & Schuster Company
Englewood Cliffs, New Jersey 07632

Printed in the United States of America
10 9 8 7 6 5 4 3 2 1

ISBN 0-13-006008-9

Prentice-Hall International (UK) Limited, *London*
Prentice-Hall of Australia Pty. Limited, *Sydney*
Prentice-Hall Canada Inc., *Toronto*
Prentice-Hall Hispanoamericana, S.A., *Mexico*
Prentice-Hall of India Private Limited, *New Delhi*
Prentice-Hall of Japan, Inc., *Tokyo*
Simon & Schuster Asia Pte. Ltd., *Singapore*
Editora Prentice-Hall do Brasil, Ltda., *Rio de Janeiro*

Contents

PART II   ADOLESCENCE AND PERSONAL DEVELOPMENT

PART III ANTECEDENTS OF ADOLESCENCE: THE SOCIAL MATRIX

Preface

This book discusses adolescence as an individual as well as a collective phenomenon. On the individual level, it focuses on the adolescent's reaction to the urban-industrial conditions that have created an environment in which social roots are uncertain and personal identity is vulnerable. This aspect of the discussion is a social-psychological analysis. On the collective level, the book focuses on adolescents' attempts to compensate for uncertainty and vulnerability by engaging in subcultural or even countercultural behavior. This aspect is a sociological analysis. On both levels, adolescent behavior can be understood as a groping struggle—often anguished and drawn out—toward maturity, adulthood, and a stable identity.

In the course of portraying adolescence, I favor an interdisciplinary approach, which includes sociological, psychological, educational, anthropological, and family-life material, plus the occasional use of popular sources.

A full examination of adolescence must be both *analytical* and *comprehensive*—analytical in the sense of showing the causes and consequences of adolescence, and comprehensive in the sense of describing the broader sociocultural context in which adolescence thrives. The text divides this task into five parts:

1. Setting the stage by introducing basic concepts and definitions and providing a historical perspective to the subject.
2. Describing the nature of personality dynamics during the adolescent period.
3. Analyzing the causes of adolescence as they are embedded in the social and cultural matrix of urban-industrial society.
4. Describing the consequences of adolescence as individuals express themselves in compensatory collectivities, ranging from subculture to counterculture.
5. Discussing a range of challenges and social problems strongly associated with adolescents.

The last chapter provides an overview, which highlights the major ingredients of the book, and presents adolescence as an unavoidable crucible of democratic society.

While most readers of this book are probably college students, it is equally well suited for the layperson. This book is not written in academic lingo by professors for professors, but is a straightforward analysis in plain English. Parents who are not in the mainstream of academic life should therefore find it intelligible and helpful.

The book is a guide through the tangle of social and psychological circumstances that have created and now perpetuate adolescence. The route of this journey is reflected in the structure of the book, which provides students with insight into a lifestyle barely outgrown, educators with a systematic introduction to the characteristics and needs of modern youth, and parents with an understanding of the often disconcerting behavior of their offspring.

This is the fourth edition of *Adolescence: A Social Psychological Analysis.* Since the publication of the first edition in 1968, much has changed. Vehement uprisings of restless youth have shaken American society, indeed most of the Western world. Adolescence, as an ingredient of postindustrial society, has become a permanent fixture. The mass media have clamorously claimed more powerful positions in the socialization of the young; new sexual moralities have come and gone; patterns of drug use and abuse have shifted; roles, especially women's, have undergone changes; and colorful New Age movements have soothed many of the weary survivors of the counterculture. This edition reflects these changes.

The material on the counterculture has been reduced, for this upheaval is now part of American history; new attitudes and concerns of young Americans have replaced the once widespread militant resistance against what was then labeled the Establishment. A largely "me"-oriented new generation of adolescents has evolved during the 1980s and early 1990s.

A renewed attempt is made to portray adolescence as the expression of an expected style of behavior that forms a normative stage in the life cycle of modern Americans, indeed of almost all modern urban-industrial people.

Hence there will be less emphasis on the "problem approach" and greater adherence to an objective structural-functional analysis.

This type of analysis of adolescence allows inclusion of positive aspects, as, for example, altruistic volunteerism and creative and artistic achievements by young people who are using their freedom from the restraints of adult roles to explore their personal talents. I am frequently impressed by the quality of musical or dramaturgical performances that can be seen on American high-school campuses, let alone on college campuses. The inner dynamics of adolescence can undoubtedly express superb sublimations.

This volume reflects a continued awareness of the deep-reaching impact of the mass media, especially TV; their effect on personality development can hardly be exaggerated. Renewed emphasis is placed on the dynamics of the modern socialization process, including a reexamination of role expectations, or the lack thereof. Two interesting styles of raising boys and girls are compared: Momism and Dadism.

Further changes from the previous edition include restructuring the material throughout the book. Previously lengthy chapters have been broken up to form new chapters, thereby creating clearer divisions between topics and more manageable limits to discussions. The restructuring resulted in sixteen chapters, which lend themselves as convenient outline for a semester's course.

In addition, the new edition received the usual improvements in style and a thorough updating of figures and statistics.

Finally, a new chapter has been added about some of the challenges that adolescents level at society. Chapter 15 examines the high-school dropout, the inhospitable world of work for the young, sexuality and the teenager, pregnancy and the teenage girl, and teenage drug use.

The preface is also the place to acknowledge contributions. I very much appreciate the help of Karen Y. Murray, who generously provided insight and new ideas. Thanks is due to the reviewers of this and previous editions as well: Marvin R. Koller, Kent State University; John M. Dettoni, Fuller Theological Seminary; Bruce L. Warren, Eastern Michigan University; Alan Krasnoff, University of Missouri—St. Louis; Barbara A. Goodnight, University of North Carolina—Charlotte. Professor Koller's kind and sensitive remarks were particularly appreciated.

Thanks is also due to Nancy Roberts, senior editor at Prentice Hall, and her assistant Pat Naturale: both have smoothed the road to the book's production. Special appreciation is due to Liz Pauw, who with great care guided the book through the various stages of its production; her dedicated midwifery kept birth defects at bay.

Hans Sebald

1

Focus and Definition

ADOLESCENCE

Adolescence is an invention of modern civilization. It lacks the universality and naturalness that are innate to such statuses as childhood and adulthood. The societies affected are almost always urban-industrial countries, and hence if we want to understand the genesis of this modern occurrence we must scrutinize the typical conditions of industrial—particularly post-industrial—life. Somewhere within these conditions lies the answer to the question: Why adolescence in our time?

American society has been the prototype of an adolescence-troubled society. As Kenneth Boulding noted: "This is the first society that has ever segregated its youth."[1] The analysis of adolescence throughout this book is therefore most appropriately based on the American experience. Cross-cultural references are introduced only with the intention of deepening our perspective and helping us understand the adolescent conditions and symptoms found in our country.

KENNETH BOULDING SEGREGATED YOUTH

The phenomenon we call adolescence is probably the most generic explanation for what is going on among young people today. It is assumed that adolescence underlies a good part, if not the vast majority, of modern

[1]"A Conversation with Kenneth Boulding," *Psychology Today*, 6 (January 1973): 87.

youthful activities and expressions. Defense of this assumption requires examination of a field of complex interaction, and we shall try to identify in it the *causes* and the *consequences* of adolescence.

Since the causes are embedded in a myriad of urban-industrial conditions, only a number of the major ones will be selected for scrutiny. Identifying the consequences will lead to the youth subculture, a collective attempt at alleviating the difficulties of the adolescent experience. Basically, adolescence is an existential condition deeply felt by the individual. The collective phenomenon is the subculture that emerges as a consequence of adolescence. Only if this relationship is clearly understood can we recognize the essentially compensatory nature of the youth subculture—or even counterculture. The logical beginning of the analysis is therefore a discussion of precisely what adolescence means.

DEFINITIONAL DIMENSIONS

During the late twentieth century, adolescence has *historically* "matured" to become a legitimate part of the life span. This does not mean, however, that it is an esteemed part or a well defined part. Rather, adolescence's moratorium on clarity of expectations is seen as an unavoidable phase. In a way, society now *expects* to find in adolescence poorly defined expectations and corresponding behavior. This expectation invites self-fulfilling prophecy and may well reinforce what we call adolescent behavior. It sounds like a paradox, but postindustrial conditions have evolved a structure of the life span within which we allow for a phase that expects confused expectations. Hence, adolescent behavior has become *normative* and is no longer considered random or unstructured. Adolescents are expected to reflect storm and stress, to be rebellious, and to have a subculture of their own.

The life span theory has been advanced by Glen H. Elder, Jr., who defines it as a "concern with the description and explanation of age-related behavioral changes from birth to death."[2] Accordingly, adolescents should be viewed in the light of their relationships to other phases of the life span. This text will try to keep this in mind. If this approach at times presents adolescence as if it were an isolated phase, it admittedly does so as a heuristic measure, i.e., in order to bring the portrait of adolescence into sharp focus, adjacent statuses must necessarily recede into a subdued background.

An additional problem in portraying adolescence deals with the spatial distribution of adolescence. Since adolescence typically is an urban phenomenon, what about rural youth? Depending on family background, adoles-

Handwritten margin notes: EXPECT ROLE OF ADOLESCENCE IN AMERICAN SOCIETY; HEURISTIC; URBAN PHENOMENON

---

[2]Glen H. Elder, Jr., "Adolescence in the Life Cycle," in Sigmund E. Dragastin and Glen H. Elder, Jr., eds., *Adolescence in the Life Cycle* (New York: Wiley, 1975), pp. 1–22. Glen H. Elder, ed., *Life Course Dynamics* (Ithaca, NY: Cornell University Press, 1985).

cence is still a matter of degree for American youth. Hence portraying adolescence in temporal or spatial isolation creates certain violations of the true picture. This is the curse of working with an "ideal type" definition. Wherever possible, the reader will be alerted by modifications inserted in the discussions. With these caveats in mind, we will take a closer look at the definition of adolescence and identify six dimensions:

The Sociological Dimension

The word "adolescence" is derived from the Latin *adolescere,* which means "to grow into maturity." Since reference to growth is nonspecific, it could apply to physiological, psychological, or social growth. It is therefore necessary to agree on a more specific meaning. Adolescence in the *sociological* sense refers to the experience of passing through a phase that lies between childhood and adulthood. Historically it was thought of as a discontinuity of statuses, but now is better thought of as a *status with uncertain and diffuse guidelines,* engendering equally uncertain and diffuse behavior. In short, it means social existence without a clear blueprint for behavior.

The social scientist looks at the adolescent as going through a period of ambiguous role expectations. The young individual often cannot decide whether a situation calls for acting as a child or as an adult, and he or she frequently suffers uncertainty in relation to the adult world—the Establishment, as it is sometimes scornfully called. This confusion does not arise in relation to his or her peer group. In fact, adolescents evade uncertainty through involvement in the group activities of their agemates and by relying on the standards of the peer group, hence forming a youth subculture estranged from the larger society.

The intensifying circumstances that make American society the epitome of an adolescence-troubled society include the extraordinarily long period between defining an individual as a child and as an adult. Further, there are no distinct rituals signifying the termination of childhood and entry into adulthood. Many societies have such specific rites of passage, and anthropologists believe that they provide guidance to the individual and serve as an integrative function for society.

The Psychological Dimension

The purely sociological approach does not complete the portrayal of the adolescent experience. It illuminates only the social aspect. The *psychological aspect* deals with the crisis of identity. The sociological and psychological definitions complement each other insofar as they call attention to the principle that an undefined social situation will have a corresponding repercussion in the personality of the individual who goes through it. It calls to mind a special meaning of the old adage that "no man is an island." Sociologists adhere to the theory that a vacuous or inconsistent sociocultural environment is a poor bet for the development of a stable identity, whereas a clearly defined and consistent sociocultural environment is prone to yield a stable identity.

Erik H. Erikson's concept of *identity crisis* has been considered to be of as much relevance to our epoch as the problems of sex seemed to be to Freud's.[3] The concept deals with the relationship between what a person appears to be in the eyes of others and what he or she feels he or she is. It refers to the dynamics of the search for an inner continuity that will match the external social conditions. The reference was first used to explain a type of breakdown of inner controls observed among psychiatric patients. Similar control disturbances were found in young persons suffering from conflict and confusion. Gradually, the term *identity crisis* acquired a normative connotation and was applied to adolescents in general. As used by Erikson, *crisis* does not mean a breakdown or catastrophe but rather a "crucial period" when development must move one way or another and when stable reference points in and around the young person must be established. Generally, the identity concept focuses on the integration of a number of important elements—such as capacities, opportunities, ideals, and identifications—into a viable self-definition.

Adolescents differ in the pace with which they establish an identity. Some may formulate a limited identity too early in order to avoid further confusion. In Eriksonian terms, such an early identity formation is called "identity foreclosure," and is usually due to parental ascription. Many delay such crystallization, are for many years incapable of a clear formulation, and exist in a psychosocial moratorium during which they try out various identities.

Certain developmental tasks complicate the identity struggle of adolescents. They include the necessity of the young to learn new ways of behaving, to acquire new ideas about themselves and other people, and to make important decisions that will affect the rest of their lives. Developmental psychologists emphasize how important it is that the young learn to master these tasks during their teen years. For example, Robert J. Havighurst felt that healthy unfolding of the personality demands mastery of the following skills, knowledge, and attitudes:

1. Accepting one's physique and learning to cope with a masculine or feminine role.
2. Forming new relationships with agemates of both sexes.
3. Realizing emotional independence from parents and other adults.
4. Achieving assurance of economic independence.
5. Selecting and preparing for a vocation.

[3]Erik H. Erikson, *Identity: Youth and Crisis* (New York: W. W. Norton, 1968).

6. Developing intellectual skills and concepts for carrying out the general civic responsibilities of an adult citizen.
7. Desiring and achieving socially responsible behavior.
8. Preparing for marriage and family responsibilities.
9. Cultivating values in harmony with a realistic and scientific world picture.[4]

While Havighurst's nine developmental tasks have been traditionally accepted as important or even natural, his reference to the learning of masculine/feminine role differences is no longer uncritically accepted by all people as necessary or "natural." Many modern Americans would prefer to substitute a new developmental task: the necessity for the young to develop communicative skill. Such skill, it is thought, would enhance young people's individualities, help them to accept others' individualities, and enable them to engage in more sensitive social relationships. Presumably, individualistic development, safeguarded by communicative ability, would be preferable over restrictive role learning. The extent to which such substitution will indeed be accomplished is a story to be told by future historians. In either case, the process will be most demanding—whether it means learning a role or learning communicative skill. At this time, gender-differentiated role learning is still pervasive.

The Physiological Dimension

The problems presented by developmental demands are intensified by *physiological* changes that occur during the earlier part of adolescence. This period is characterized by rapid biological growth. During pubescence, the changing proportions of the body tend to cause poor coordination, and the maturing of the endocrine system sharpens sexual interest. The young must learn to adapt to these biological changes. Within a relatively short time they find themselves endowed with primary and secondary sex characteristics and have reproductive capability. However, society discourages the enactment of these capabilities, insisting on postponement of their expression.

The Legislative Dimension

Even a general *legal* declaration of adulthood is only partially sufficient to end adolescence. Although 1971 federal legislation enfranchised the eighteen-year-old, the new political privileges do not necessarily abolish other conditions of nonadulthood. For example, the initial reaction to the federal legislation, when twenty-nine states lowered the drinking age, has been

---

[4]Robert J. Havighurst, *Developmental Tasks and Education* (New York: Longmans, Green, 1952), pp. 30–55.

reversed since then and at least twenty states have reconsidered and raised the drinking age back up by one to three years.

5 The Economic Dimension

There is another abrogation, albeit an informal one, of full adulthood after age eighteen. What about the millions of young Americans who are between eighteen and twenty, and even older, enrolled in colleges and universities, and who are *economically* dependent on parents, relatives, and loans? Is it not a mark of adulthood to achieve a balance between production (making a contribution to the division of labor) and consumption? Many, if not most, young Americans who attend institutions of higher education have not achieved symmetry between giving and taking. They are still being nurtured and receive support and care without making an equivalent contribution. *Full* adult status, although only informally and not necessarily legally, is tied up with a balance between producing and consuming. Being a full-time student after age eighteen is often a moratorium on full adult status. Allowance must of course be made for individuals using savings that are the result of their productive statuses and that are now used to balance the score. Participation in higher education under such circumstances does not disturb the production-consumption balance. Students who work as well as attend school to finance their studies likewise achieve balance and maintain adult status—at least with respect to the economic criterion.

The legislation declaring eighteen-year-olds responsible adults has nevertheless introduced greater clarity. For example, the tradition of educational institutions playing the *in loco parentis* role has been curtailed, and college students have achieved a modicum of independence.

The Traditional Dimension

In many societies, additional criteria bear on the definition of full adulthood. We are dealing here with informal *tradition*. For example, in a number of societies a man may assume full adult responsibilities only after he has a full-grown son. In other societies, such as traditional rural Greece, a young man must spend about ten years arranging his sisters' dowries before he is considered a man. Among Irish peasants, a son is not considered a mature adult until his father finally retires.

These, then, are the major elements that signal the termination of adolescence:

MAJOR ELEMENTS THAT SIGNAL END OF AD.

1. Sociologically, terminating the unclear child/adult interim.
2. Psychologically, completing a number of developmental tasks and achieving a modicum of consistent identity.
3. Biologically, achieving physiological maturity.

4. Legally, reaching the age limit specified by law.
5. Economically, becoming self-supporting and maintaining a balance between production and consumption.
6. Traditionally, when informal customs lift the last restriction on adult privileges.

This list illustrates that there are various dynamic ingredients in the adolescent experience, all of them interrelated and culminating in a confounding experience. From a theoretical point of view, no agreement has been reached as to the relative importance of the various factors. Also, these variables are not conterminous; that is, each follows its own course and expires at different times. We may therefore speak of *degrees* of adolescence, or, conversely, of adulthood. For example, the onset of puberty normally signals the entrance into adolescence. This would set the modal entrance age at between twelve to fourteen years for girls and thirteen to fifteen for boys. But the termination of adolescence is not so readily determined. There are no objective physiological indicators signifying the termination. While economic independence, stable employment, and marriage are adult indicators, they do not necessarily indicate psychological maturity. Moreover, the psychological and sociological meanings of such achievements must be viewed within the traditions of a given sociocultural environment. In tribal societies, the transition from childhood to adulthood may be swift, and adolescence is merely a brief interval that is clearly terminated by an initiation ritual. However, in American postindustrial society this transition is exceedingly protracted, and no specific rite of passage tells the young when he or she is an adult.

As has been mentioned above, in a strict legal sense adulthood in the United States is reached at eighteen years of age. At that age, full civil rights usually become available to young Americans. These privileges pertain to, among other things, voting, driving, drinking, employment, marriage, concluding contracts, criminal justice, and so on. (As mentioned above, state and local statutes still defy uniformity about age levels.) But in a social-psychological sense, the termination of adolescence cannot be judged on the basis of chronological age. While the years of adolescence used to be fourteen through eighteen, in the late twentieth century these years start earlier and extend into the twenties, and many young Americans remain adolescents until they are thirty.

The criteria for this assertion are embedded in at least two interrelated processes. Adolescence terminates *psychologically* with the establishment of realistic and relatively consistent patterns of dealing with internal conflicts and the demands of the social and physical environment. It terminates *socially* when the sociocultural environment yields sufficient consensus to declare the individual an adult. The progress of the two processes does not necessarily run in a one-to-one relationship, since one may precede the other. It is possible, for example, that a person has established realistic modes of problem solving and is socially still not defined as an adult; and, vice versa, an individual may have entered adult status according to the general socio-cultural definition but may still be lacking in realistic patterns of problem solving. If the degree of inability to cope with the environment exceeds a certain limit, society can withdraw the status of adulthood from the individual regardless of chronological age and declare him or her mentally incapable. Such a person usually is placed under the supervision of a special institution, such as a mental hospital. However, psychological and social development are expected to coincide and produce a normally functioning young adult by the late teens.

Natural growth processes do not occur in distinct stages. Humans show considerable arbitrariness in defining life stages. They seem compelled to establish a stable structural order to facilitate social predictability and communication. In reality, life is a *continuous process,* and adulthood is the result of irregular and variable maturation that began with the fusion of the ovum and the sperm. It is, therefore, an arbitrary and heuristic practice to subdivide the period of adolescence into preadolescence, early adolescence, and late adolescence.[5] Whether these divisions contribute to the overall understanding of the adolescent phenomenon is doubtful. Nonetheless, such divisions may be of clinical value for counseling teenagers at specific phases of their development.

It has been said that an adolescent is one who if not treated as an adult acts like an infant. There is truth in this aphorism: if role expectations are poorly defined—as they are during adolescence—the resulting confusion may induce a youngster to resort to one of the adjacent roles, either that of the adult or the child. Either alternative—as unfitting to the situation as it may appear—constitutes relief from an anomic situation and provides a form of reaction. This, of course, is merely a situational solution. In general, decision making during adolescence is a most difficult process because the child's familiar forms of responding to a situation are no longer judged to be adequate, and new response patterns have not yet been developed.

DEFINITIONS: JUVENILE, YOUTH, TEENAGER

The nomenclature for labeling young Americans often leads to miscategorizations. It is therefore advisable to distinguish among a number of references that are often improperly used as synonyms for *adolescent.* They are *teenager, youth,* and *juvenile.* Some of these terms capture certain aspects of the concept of adolescence, but more often they exclude essential qualities and include peripheral connotations.

---

[5]E. B. Hurlock, *Adolescent Development* (New York: McGraw-Hill, 1949).

Juvenile

A striking example of blurring distinctions comes from the writing of Eric Hoffer, who used *juvenile* and *adolescent* interchangeably.[6] Accordingly, both references center on persons, young or old, who are confused by change—*any* type of change. While it is true that an essential aspect of adolescence deals with drastic change, sharpness of focus is diminished when the concept is applied to all types of change. The concept should be reserved for one specific process: the change from child to adult. Hoffer's liberal application of the concept of adolescent to Pope Julius II, various heads of state, and the Ku Klux Klan loses the analytic benefit that a scientific concept holds.

The term *juvenile* should be limited to matters of youthful law violations and enforcement, as in juvenile delinquency, juvenile court, juvenile detention center, juvenile officer, and so forth.

Youth

The term *youth* refers to the broad and nonspecific "younger generation," including children, adolescents (in certain societies), and young adults. The concept is practically universally applicable, since all societies normally have a younger generation. Since adolescence is not necessarily a universal phenomenon, and some societies have youth but no adolescents, the two terms are not interchangeable. There are many societies, however, in which youth and adolescents are merged. These are the industrialized societies. The society typically free of adolescence tends to be rural or tribal. Its youth—younger generation—makes the transition from child to adult status without the adolescent interim.

To complicate matters, some social scientists ascribe a highly specific meaning to the term. Kenneth Keniston, for example, studied the increasing numbers of young men and women who experience a particularly delayed entry into full adult status.[7] As he saw it, they moved into an emergent stage suspended between adolescence and adulthood. He called this stage "youth," and applied it to the eighteen-to-twenty-six age category. The reason for defining a postadolescent/preadult period was seen in the need to label the segment of America's young that consists of highly talented, affluent, and educated young people who defer entry into sociological adulthood. Presumably, these young adults are psychologically mature and meet the psychological criteria of adulthood: identity is resolved, capacity to work established, proficiency in a love relationship proven. However, they have not yet made commitments to the primary social institutions, such as marriage, family, and

---

[6]Eric Hoffer, "An Age for Juveniles," *Harper's* (June 1965).
[7]Kenneth Keniston, *Young Radicals* (New York: Harcourt Brace Jovanovich, 1968).

vocation. Hence, prime sociological characteristics of adulthood are lacking. While the great majority of young Americans move directly from adolescence to adulthood, these young individuals prolong experimentation with life's possibilities and their personal potentialities. The typical environments in which their activities unfold are college, graduate school, and, mostly in the past, the countercultural movement. Their identities are tied up with a generation and not with a tradition. The generations succeed each other quickly—as anyone over thirty-five has learned through rebuffs experienced when seeking association with youthful causes. Keniston called this phenomenon "youth culture"; Theodore Roszak called it the "counterculture."[8]

The significance of referring to Keniston's conceptualization is to make the reader aware of varying definitions. While Keniston's explorations produced insights, his choice of terminology could have been more felicitous. Retaining more descriptive terms for these eighteen-to-twenty-six-year-old Americans would increase the clarity of reference. The young adults who choose an extended moratorium could be more accurately described by such labels as "young adults," "young intelligentsia," "revolutionaries," members of the "New Left," "countercultural people," "dissident students," "young radicals," "older adolescents," and so forth—the choice of term depending on the particular nuance the communication means to accentuate. The term *youth,* as commonly used, has an inclusive connotation and should not be misappropriated for a highly specific segment of the younger generation. It is used throughout this book with the simple chronological denotation that is in harmony with common English language usage.

Teenager

The term *teenager* is probably the most widely used word referring to young people in American society. While its denotation refers to an age bracket, its connotation suggests stereotypical behavior. There is also the connotation of collectivity, of subcultural quality, suggesting that teenagers exist as a group rather than as distinct individuals. It is this latter connotation that is of sociological significance, since it purports to explain teenage behavior in terms of peer group norms.

The meanings ascribed to *adolescent* and *teenager* are closely related. Referring to a person as an "adolescent" means that we emphasize the peculiar interim between the statuses of child and adult; referring to a person as a "teenager" calls attention to age and the tendency to associate with peers and subcultural activities. Adolescence actually leads to the behavior typical of teenagers, since that behavior compensates for situational uncertainties.

---

[8]Theodore Roszak, *The Making of a Counter Culture* (Garden City, NY: Doubleday, 1968).

Before we leave the matter of definitions, a few remarks should be made to put the discussion in its proper perspective. First, definitions must be understood as more than mere communicative labels. They reflect our particular view of reality and, at the same time, have the ironic property of reinforcing what we perceive as real. This means that our definitions tell us something about the way we think, categorize, and consequently behave. For instance, a somewhat one-sided view is presented by Joseph Kett, who thinks that "adolescence was essentially a conception of behavior imposed on youth, rather than an empirical assessment of the way in which young people actually behaved."[9] Admittedly, scientists are not immune to imposing their biases through seemingly objective definitions, and there is probably little reason to exempt the sociological definitions of *youth* and *adolescence* from this danger. Quite possibly we have invented labels and definitions because they appear plausible but actually are afflicted with bias. As a result, we risk the danger of responding not to stimuli but rather to our definitions of stimuli. This may sound pedantic; yet unless we constantly check empirical conditions, we may lose ourselves in abstractions that have no real referents.

APPROACHES TO STUDYING ADOLESCENCE

If losing oneself in abstractions were the only problem, it would have small consequence besides paying professors salaries for engaging in mental gyrations. But the problem is deeper. Definitions *act* on the persons labeled, making them meet our biases and expectations. In the case of *teenager*, for example, our definition (1) tells us how we perceive them and what kind of reality-view we have, (2) predicates the way we treat them, and (3) consequently elicits a reaction and style of behavior that, in a sense, fulfills our prophecy. The point may be exaggerated here—we hope! The purpose for doing so is to alert the reader to the possible tricks language in general and definitions in specific can play.

What can be done to control these tendencies? In the context of this book, I try to observe a number of safeguards against the definitional trap:

The interdisciplinary approach. The behavioral sciences have been notorious in their subdivided and separate search for concepts, theories, and hypotheses. Various disciplines have divided up the person as if he or she consisted of discrete faculties; the results of this cognitive dissection have been incomplete and unreal portrayals of people. Throughout this book, an

---

[9]Joseph F. Kett, *Rites of Passage* (New York: Basic Books, 1976), p. 327. Also see Benjamin Whorf, *Language, Thought, and Reality* (New York: John Wiley, 1956), and Clyde Kluckhohn, "Culture and Behavior," in *Handbook of Social Psychology*, vol. 2, ed. Gardner Lindsey (Reading, MA: Addison-Wesley, 1954).

effort is made to merge sociological, psychological, anthropological, and some biological data to produce a fuller picture of the adolescent experience.

Examination of a wide variety of data.   Many books in the social sciences are written by professors for professors and limit their exploration to theories propounded by colleagues. An attempt will be made to modify the sacred ritual of academic inbreeding by including "secular" sources, such as non-professional magazines (for example, *Seventeen*), travelogues, news reports, letters by teenagers, and so on.

Cross-cultural illustrations.   To a remarkable extent we all are victims of the limited perceptual repertoire of our cultural background. Cross-cultural investigations are important to alleviate cultural myopia. Such studies have repeatedly demonstrated that our narrow frame of reference has a way of institutionalizing our own distortions of the truth. Throughout this book I shall make use of cross-cultural illustrations, although the main thrust of the analysis is directed toward the United States.

The structural-functional approach.   Basically a method of analysis, this approach starts with the scrutiny of certain conditions and then, as objectively as possible, looks for their consequences. Thus adolescence is seen as a consequence of a constellation of circumstances (to be explored in Part II). This approach frees the writer from searching for adolescent "problems" and negative aspects of this period of life.

To refer to certain aspects of adolescence as problems is of course understandable, since each stage in life has its unique problems. But we must also recognize aspects of adolescence that are positive. For example, adolescents have the opportunity to wait and grow. During this time, young individuals can make the best of a variety of experiments in lifestyle, education, and reflection. They have a chance to develop unique, independent, and integrated identities. To fully understand this point, it would be helpful to contrast the typical American adolescent with nonadolescent youth in other societies (or perhaps other times) and recognize the quality of life that emerges from the divergent lifestyles. The positive aspects of the adolescent moratorium might then become more apparent.

SUMMARY

Adolescence must be understood as an analytic concept with a number of important dimensions. The sociological dimension has a social-structural focus and is interested primarily in the so-called status discontinuity between childhood and adulthood. The psychological dimension is concerned with the development of personal and social responsibility, often referred to as "maturity." It focuses mostly on the concept of identity or, in this context, the crisis of identity. The legislative dimension consists of the laws specifying legal status according to age brackets (and the corresponding rights and obligations that go with them) and, in our case, deals with the age set for legal adulthood. The economic dimension weighs the balance between consumption and production, assuming that a normal adult creates symmetry between the two. The physiological dimension has to do with the somatic development of the individual, particularly his or her reproductive maturation. The traditional dimension deals with customs that tell people when a member of the community has reached adulthood. These customs are not necessarily legally enforced, but are nonetheless powerful demands as to what a person has to achieve in order to be able to claim adulthood.

The terms *juvenile, youth,* and *teenager* gain in clarity when *not* equated or confused with the term *adolescent.* Each has its own specific meaning and connotation, quite separate from the more analytic term of adolescent.

2

Adolescence: Its Time and Place in Civilization

Prior to and throughout the Middle Ages, children passed directly into the adult world between ages five and seven. The "younger generation" was hardly a recognizable concept. Barbara Tuchman's study of medieval conditions found that if children survived to age seven, their childhood was more or less over and they were treated as miniature adults.[1] Medieval artists appeared to be ignorant of what children even looked like, habitually portraying them as small adults. One twelfth-century painting illustrating Jesus' injunction to "suffer the little children to come unto me" shows Christ surrounded by a dozen undersized men. Schooling was of minimal importance and rarely extended into the teens. Teenagers of the Middle Ages sometimes made history at an age when modern teens are still going to high school. For example, Edward, the Black Prince, was sixteen when he triumphed at the Battle of Crécy; Joan of Arc was seventeen when she took Orléans from the English; and Ivan the Terrible was the same age when he commenced to make his name as the "Terrible" and had himself crowned czar of Russia. Work, in a strictly adult environment, came early. This rapid

---

[1]Barbara Tuchman, *A Distant Mirror* (New York: Knopf, 1978). Also see for comprehensive treatment Philippe Ariés, *Centuries of Childhood* (New York: Knopf, 1962).

transition from childhood to adulthood was the norm prior to the Industrial Revolution and resembled the custom of primitive societies, in which children become full-fledged members of the tribe in one painful and often hazardous initiation. This swift transition compressed or even abolished the confusion and terror of stepping into adult life.

HISTORICAL ASPECTS: FROM AGRICULTURAL TO INDUSTRIAL CONDITIONS

The certainty and swiftness of this transition gradually faded with the rise of the Industrial Revolution. Increasing urbanization and industrialization resulted in a slower and more ambiguous passage into adulthood. Greater concern for education and the occupational training of youth became evident. Most young people who lived in towns and cities went through apprenticeships, which prepared them for trades in the context of the guild system. Increasing numbers of young people traded the rural setting with its simple, observable work patterns for the urban milieu with its complex division of labor. This change divorced the place of residence from the place of work, and the working adult became progressively less visible to the young. A need evolved for formal education and vocational training, which in turn gave rise to new institutions. Concomitantly, ambiguity shrouded the status of the individuals who found themselves in the postchild and preadult phase which today we call adolescence.

With increasing industrialization, European societies developed a curious nostalgia about bygone pastoral days that were presumably more healthy and beautiful. As if to compensate for spreading industrial slums, Romanticism evolved. Romantics focused on children, and feared that the latter's assumedly pristine souls would be adversely affected by urban-industrial conditions. Society gradually accorded children their own activities. For the first time literature was created solely for the young by such nineteenth century writers as Charles Dickens and Lewis Carroll. As parents began to see children's play as a natural, even educational activity, toys began to appear in artists' paintings, and children were shown in more informal and playful poses.

The romantic sentiment was particularly strong in England. Jean-Jacques Rousseau, in *Émile* (1762), declared humans good by nature but saw them as being corrupted by urban civilization. The Frenchman's writings and sojourn in England nurtured the English sense of protection toward children. It was in England, the front runner of the Industrial Revolution, where the conditions for such concern were ripe. They were dramaturgically demonstrated by various literary works, as, for example, Dickens' *Oliver Twist* (1838), an entertaining mixture of melodrama and realism showing the grim existence of street urchins in the big cities. Therefore, not surprisingly, England was the first nation to introduce compulsory education of children (1878). At that point, industrialization had progressed sufficiently to produce the first real indications of adolescence. Discontinuity between child and adult statuses became noticeable, with the causes rooted in the changing economy and technology (shifting from agriculture to industry) and in a new cultural attitude toward children. It was deemed necessary to protect children from death, sickness, adult sexuality, and the assumed immorality of the city.

Many historical documents portray early industrial conditions and the plight of the urban young. Lord Thomas B. Macaulay, for example, wrote about the London of the late seventeenth century:

> When the evening closed in, the difficulty and danger of walking about London became serious indeed. . . . Thieves and robbers plied their trade with impunity: yet they were hardly as terrible to peaceable citizens as another class of ruffians. It was a favorite amusement of dissolute young gentlemen to swagger by night about the town, breaking windows, upsetting sedans, beating quiet men, and offering rude caresses to pretty women. Several dynasties of these tyrants had, since the Restoration, domineered over the streets. The Muns and Tityre Tus had given place to the Hectors, and the Hectors had been recently succeeded by the Scourers. At a later period arose the Nicker, the Hawcubite, and the yet more dreaded name of Mohawk.[2]

Macaulay easily convinces us that there was much youthful villainy in earlier times. There is a striking similarity between adolescent gang activities in large modern cities like New York, Chicago, and Los Angeles and the actions of youthful gangs in London almost 300 years ago. This casts doubt on the justifiability of the perennial complaint of many adults who negatively compare the youth of our day with the youth of previous generations. These complaints frequently conclude that youth has never been more degenerate than at present. Such reminiscing is more sentimental than factual. Socrates, nearly 2400 years ago, talked in a fashion that one finds repeated ever since— and one that possibly antedated him. He referred to the children of his time as being infatuated with luxury, behaving with bad manners and with disrespect for authority, and as being tyrants of their households.

While complaints about the behavior of the young appear timeless, they reached a crescendo during the Industrial Revolution. It was that era that convinced every major industrial society that it had a youth problem. Consequently, as Edgar Z. Friedenberg has pointed out, young people were given the "colonial treatment," which included (1) the attempt to persuade them to abandon their "barbaric" ways, (2) the assumption that they had no traditions of their own, (3) the conviction that they were economically dependent, and

---

[2]Thomas B. Macaulay, *History of England*, vol. 2 (Boston: Houghton Mifflin, 1899), p. 81.

the corresponding efforts to keep them that way, and (4) the failure to provide an adequate job market for them.[3] Children were safekept in schools—more for custodial than for educational purposes; in other words to keep them off the streets. Industrialized societies began to insist on segregating their young, on shutting them away from realistic life. Over generations, such practices created an artificial environment, a moratorium on adult life. Introduction of compulsory education in early industrial society thus constituted the chrysalis that eventually hatched into modern youth's subculture with its separate values, rebellion, and dissidence.

English—or, for that matter, *general industrial*—conditions, laws, and lifestyle were reflected in the New World, and American society of the mid-nineteenth century manifested typical youth problems. Reports concerning gang violence during the middle of the last century have a striking resemblance to today's headlines. The only difference seems to be that the names of the gangs are different. In 1857 the *New York Times* printed articles concerning the activities of New York City gangs with such names as the Dead Rabbits and the Bowery Boys. It was even necessary to call out the state militia in 1857 to squelch the street fighting between rival gangs and reestablish peace.[4] New Orleans, likewise, reported the activities of teenagers who roamed the streets beating, stabbing, and robbing innocent citizens.[5]

The influx of immigrants into the United States during the early 1900s did nothing to reduce the adolescent phenomenon. Anomie and marginality tinged the struggle of the immigrants' first-generation American children. While immigrant parents continued to draw their identity and response patterns from a background in the Old World, their children could choose between the values of their Old World oriented parents and the demands of American society. Choosing and adjusting was not easy for the young of various ethnic minorities. Ernest W. Burgess and Harvey J. Locke illustrate the youth problem of immigrant families using the example of an Italian family:

> . . . The third son is in Leavenworth: He is an original "42" [a notorious criminal gang that was located on the West Side of Chicago]. He finished two years of high school. At this point his family moved only about three blocks but into the midst of the "42" gang. Here the boy picked up delinquent cronies, cultivated new pleasures and habits, became delinquent and ended up as a big-time

---

[3]Edgar Z. Friedenberg, *Coming of Age In America* (New York: Random House, 1965). Also see John R. Gillis, *Youth and History: Tradition and Change in European Age Relations, 1770–Present* (New York: Academic Press, 1981); Paula Fass, *The Damned and the Beautiful: American Youth in the 1920s* (New York: Oxford University Press, 1977).

[4]Reported in David Gottlieb and Charles Ramsey, *The American Adolescent* (Homewood, IL: The Dorsey Press, 1964).

[5]Ibid.

robber, the accomplice in professional stick-ups, the pal of notorious, big gangsters. There was nothing the family could do to save the boy.[6]

Another social movement that aggravated the problem of adolescence in the United States was rural-urban migration. In the early decades of this century, there were conspicuous indications that uprooted rural youth had to make difficult adjustments to city life. One such adjustment involved becoming accustomed to less parental supervision and fewer family obligations. Former farm youths found themselves financially and morally independent. Many observers—then as well as today—judged such rural-urban migration dangerous and undesirable. City life was viewed as incompatible with the "wholesome" living seen as necessary for youth. Here is an example of this concern:

> One has only to compare the broken, bent, and depraved youth of the city with the honest and firm farm child to see what evil the city offers. On the farm the young person learns to respect work and to disregard evil influences. The air about him is fresh and he does not breathe the stench of the factory or narcotics. He can take pride in the accomplishments of his work and the pleasures of his family. In the city, youth are always subject to the wicked . . .[7]

The adjustments demanded of exrural youth living in urban centers are not necessarily problems of the past. As the evidence indicates, these problems are timeless and exist in the United States today. Youths with farm or rural-slum backgrounds who have migrated from Appalachia to the big cities of the Midwest are current examples. The following statement, made in 1910, could be easily applied today and would describe contemporary situations in such cities as Columbus, Cleveland, Philadelphia, and Indianapolis, all of which receive an influx of youth from the hills of Kentucky, West Virginia, and Tennessee:

> Never before in civilization have such numbers of girls been suddenly released from the protection of the home and permitted to walk unattended upon city streets and to work under alien roofs; for the first time they are being prized more for their labor power than for their innocence, their tender beauty, their ephemeral gaiety . . .
>
> Never before have such numbers of young boys earned money independently of the family life, and felt themselves free to spend it as they choose in the midst of vice deliberately disguised as pleasure.[8]

[6]Ernest W. Burgess and Harvey J. Locke, *The Family: From Institution to Companionship* (New York: American Book, 1945), p. 124.

[7]"Annual Report of the Ohio State Board of Agriculture," *Agricultural Record*, 1912, p. 476.

[8]Jane Addams, *The Spirit of Youth and the City Streets* (New York: Macmillan, 1910), pp. 5-6.

While value judgment inherent in the statement tends to obscure the technical aspects of the sociological process, the report nevertheless succeeds in conveying a picture of the situation.

In sum, the historical sketch shows that adolescence is not a newcomer to our era. It has been growing along with increasing urbanization and industrialization—in the United States as well as elsewhere. In essence, when the agricultural way of life gave way to the urban-industrial lifestyle, simple social structure was jolted and a fissure developed between childhood and adulthood. This fissure has become ever wider; indeed, it has developed into a gap.

POSTINDUSTRIAL CONDITIONS

While the industrial society produced the plain and simple adolescent, postindustrial society has created whole armies of adolescents with causes (or pseudocauses). To understand this development, a description of postindustrial conditions is in order.

Economic and technological progress can be divided into three sequential types: (1) agricultural, (2) industrial, or manufacturing, and (3) service-oriented, or postindustrial. Although most economic systems include a mixture of the above, they can be distinguished by their emphasis on a particular economic-technologic style. As societies become industrialized, an inevitable trajectory manifests itself. An ever-increasing proportion of the labor force concentrates on manufacture, and, as national incomes rise, there evolves an ever greater demand for services. Service orientation is established when the majority of the labor force no longer works in agriculture or manufacturing but in services like health, recreation (including entertainment, tourism, sports, mass media, etc.), research, education, government, transportation, the military, finance, and trade. Most countries in the world, especially in Asia and Africa, are still dependent on their raw labor power and natural resources. Russia and some of her satellite nations, Japan, and most of Western Europe engage the majority of their labor forces in industry and the manufacture of goods.

The United States has been the first nation in history to shift the greater portion of its labor force to the provision of services. In 1970 this proportion amounted to 60 percent and by 1990 it had risen to over 70 percent. To select just one example from the pool of services, there are about 3 million civilian employees in charge of running the vast federal bureaucracy of this country. In addition, there are state, county, and municipal government employees, comprising the single largest salaried group in the United States.

Daniel Bell's definition of *postindustrial society*[9] has been widely accepted among social scientists, despite its misleading choice of word, since we are obviously *not* living "post"industrial. On the contrary, our industrial complex has developed to the extent where goods can be manufactured in such expedient ways so as to assure their abundance—meaning elimination of the scarcity that was a principle of preceding economic systems. Methods have improved productivity to the point where a huge industry can be run by relatively few workers. The ultimate of scientific industrialization, the manufacture of "intelligence" through computers, enables a radical cutback in the number of employees and creates dispensable labor. This adds to the reason why a society is able to shift attention to service: it can shift labor surplus to this sector. In fact, the various services are industrialized themselves. The health industry, for example, includes medical research centers, government supervisory agencies, hospitals, physicians' associations, drug firms, and so on. Retention of the industrial mode of manufacture and rendering service in our age is the reason Alvin Toffler, in *Future Shock*, preferred the more plausible expression *super-industrial society* to describe late twentieth-century American society.[10]

The rise of the postindustrial system is a historical turning point. If we have failed to visualize this clearly, it is due to its gradual emergence and to the blind spots we develop toward what is closest and most immediate to us. Other Western societies are on the verge of turning into postindustrial service-oriented systems, with resultant changes in social relations and power structure imminent as well.

Cultural elements primarily affected are those related to the Protestant ethic: the notion of hard work, deferred gratification, and constant reinvestment of the fruits of one's labor. Since scarcity of goods has been drastically reduced by the use of advanced industrial means and since such reduction is accomplished by relatively few workers and relatively easy work, the old work ethic receded under the onslaught of state-of-the-art automation that created the ethic-eroding impression that work may someday be eliminated, that machines will eventually take over society's chores. John Galbraith proclaimed during the 1970s: "The greatest prospect we face is to eliminate toil as a required economic institution."[11]

Alas, the celebration of victory over toil was premature. The elation was induced by temporary economic updraft and the belief in the success of the War against Poverty during the 1960s and 1970s. It was particularly the young of the counterculture who experienced the impression of victory—not only

---

[9]Daniel Bell, *The Coming of Post-Industrial Society* (New York: Basic Books, 1973) and *The Cultural Contradictions of Capitalism* (New York: Basic Books, 1976).

[10]Alvin Toffler, *Future Shock* (New York: Bantam Books, 1971), p. 491.

[11]*Time*, "Is the Puritan Work Ethic Going Out of Style?" October 30, 1972, p. 96.

because they indeed had won astounding political victories, but also because they were the beneficiaries of various generous government programs providing grants and loans. Until the late 1980s, young people could devote their time to formal education relatively easily because they could draw from a variety of grants, loans, and welfare supplements. Policy makers even discussed the feasibility of every American citizen receiving a guaranteed annual income.

A turning point in Federal welfare and aids programs came in 1987 when the U.S. Senate unveiled a tight Family Security Act replacing the generous spending policies of previous years. Ironically, the main proponent for the limited welfare spending was Senator Daniel Moynihan who, a decade earlier, had introduced the idea of the guaranteed annual income.[12]

During the early 1990s we witnessed the emergence of hardships for the younger generation that its parental generation—the youth of the counterculture years of the 1960s and 1970s—had not known. It appears now to be much more difficult than a generation ago to achieve certain items of the American dream: an education, job/career security, and a number of material amenities that had been taken for granted one and two generations ago. Here now is a generation that had started out with their parents' philosophy of entitlement—being naturally entitled to an education, a workplace that is not merely economically secure but also psychologically rewarding and satisfying—but now faces public policy reversals more in line with a nearly bygone American rugged individualism than with entitlement philosophy.

The economic hardship is not the only problem the young are facing. They are aware of a number of disasters they have inherited from the older generation: dwindling natural resources, increased destruction of the ecosystem, widespread drug abuse, crime, poverty, and a population growth outpacing social programs. Suddenly, the young people of the 1990s realized that these problems were created for them by the older generation, who were materialistic, irresponsible, and insatiable consumers. Young people of the last decade of the millennium seem to be confused about it all: they grew up with stability, security, and the comforts of "good times" and naturally expect the same. It appears, at least from the vista of the early 1990s, that the predominant reaction of the young is privatization, a withdrawal to the pursuit of completing an education and eking out a career in an uncertain world.

Whether these new hardships will combine to have a rejuvenating effect on the old Protestant ethic remains to be seen.

Besides these changes in cultural attitudes, postindustrial conditions involve a number of important *social-structural* changes. One concerns the need to reduce the labor force. This is manifested by the educational institu-

---

[12]Walter Shapiro, "Tough, Tightfisted and Traditional," *Time*, August 3, 1987, p. 19.

tion playing a custodial role and expanding the adolescent experience as long as possible, and by early retirement that increases the need to entertain and care for the "elderly." Perhaps the most important alteration in the social structure has to do with increasing specialization. Modern roles isolate individuals by defining for them extremely limited modes of behavior. Life becomes largely a positional experience, with limited opportunities to interact on a casual and general-cultural basis. While the incumbent of the position may find a modicum of personal identity—a positional identity—and thus a compensation for the anomic nature of the general culture, he or she also experiences a notable degree of isolation.

Other changes in human relationships deal with the ascent of technological experts, who have profound influence over national policymaking. Theodore Roszak painted a vivid picture of the rule of the experts and their "objective consciousness," which is, in effect, the new technocracy of America. Related to this change is increasing government control over the goals of science. Government control of science is a corruption of a process that traditionally was apolitical. While government used to represent ideology—the emotional and the expressive—science dealt with the instrumental and calculative. As the government began to assume custody of the technical, it became a technocracy whose high priests were the scientific experts. This shows up the anomic nature of late twentieth-century America: a preoccupation with the mastery of instruments but a poverty of values concerning their application, a characteristic of a society emphasizing instrumental norms and neglecting basic cultural values.

Into what roles do the different economic-technological systems cast their young? In a typical agricultural society we find *youth* but no adolescents; in a typical industrial society we find *adolescents*; and in the postindustrial society we have *adolescents* and a *youth subculture*, which, in its advanced metamorphosis, can become a *counterculture*.

Postindustrial society, then, has widened the distance between child and adult statuses. While the gap and the structural conditions that created it already existed in the plain industrial society, the gap widened and the conditions intensified in postindustrial society. Major *structural conditions* responsible for this gap are: (1) Long periods of education, partly necessitated by the need for extensive preparation for the complex urban-industrial structure, and partly by the custodial function of the educational institution to delay youth's entry into the labor market; (2) separation of the location of work from domicile, making adult work invisible to the young; (3) highly specialized division of labor; (4) youth's considerable share of affluence; (5) relatively high social and geographic mobility to which young individuals are exposed. (Chapter 4 will elaborate on these conditions.)

In addition, some new cultural emphases accentuate the adolescent experience in the United States. Large numbers of young Americans expect society to provide a career and lifestyle that is both economically secure and psychologically rewarding. The attitude can be summed up as the "philosophy of entitlement," referring to the development of a pervasive feeling that one is entitled to all sorts of material and psychological benefits and that the provision of these benefits is the responsibility of society.

The implementation of this responsibility was to be social reform, social equality, and a more equitable distribution of power, wealth, and status. Most of these demands and efforts were at the core of the counterculture and provided material for varying interpretations. Writers like Theodore Roszak, Jack Newfield,[13] Philip Slater,[14] Charles A. Reich,[15] and to some degree Kenneth Keniston[16] arrived at an optimistic interpretation of youth's unrest and dissidence. They saw their rebelliousness directed against the broken promises of authority and the insensitivity of the American system. Roszak was particularly vocal in dignifying youthful resentment and interpreted it as a countermanifesto against technocracy. In his classic, *The Making of a Counter Culture,* he described what he felt are the insidious ingredients of modern American society, in which impersonal technocracy rules the lives of its members. These conditions have presumably dulled and dehumanized Americans. Roszak believed that youth has risen against technocratic tyranny, attempting to introduce sensitivity, humaneness, and mystique to life. While this attempt may very well have been sincere, it abated and by the early 1970s the countercultural movement had lost momentum.

The argument of these writers, that our materialistic and technologized culture is responsible for the rise of youthful dissent, is tenuous. Western societies have been materialistically oriented for hundreds of years. Technological innovations must have appeared overwhelming to people of every epoch, but there was hardly a youth countermovement to contend with as well. Thus the roots of dissent are at best only partly explained by this argument, and the significance of the period of moratorium is brought back into focus.

My point is that the adolescent phase affords the *time* and the *collectivity* enabling the young generation to offer new ideas and express dissent and criticism. Again I am proposing to reduce the explanation of a significant element in modern society to the concept of adolescence.

Evaluators of gadfly adolescence can be roughly sorted into two opposing camps. There are those who feel that the dissenting adolescents have nothing much more than a vacuum hiding behind impressive slogans and

---

[13]Jack Newfield, *A Prophetic Minority* (New York: Signet Books, 1966).

[14]Philip Slater, *The Pursuit of Loneliness* (Boston: Beacon Press, 1970).

[15]Charles A. Reich, *The Greening of America* (New York: Random House, 1970).

[16]Kenneth Keniston, *Youth and Dissent* (New York: Harcourt Brace Jovanovich, 1971). The inclusion of Keniston in the category of writers who render an optimistic value judgment of youth's activism should be modified. Keniston, unlike the others, bases his opinion less on intuition than on empirical studies.

quasiplatforms; that their contributions are largely immature and can even be destructive; and that they generally refuse to join adult institutions and to work in any substantial sense toward the betterment of society. These inter-preters list a number of negative aspects they feel are associated with youth-ful activism, such as unwise drug use, refusal to work, and delinquency and crime. A few of these writers do recognize *some* positive contributions on the part of adolescents, but they disagree with the wholehearted positive inter-pretation offered by Roszak, Newfield, and others. It's not so much *what* they say that is in dispute but what they *do not say* about the destructive aspects of adolescence.

In the opposing camp are those who emphasize that youthful causes have substance and that youth's dissent grows out of honest and yet-unfet-tered perceptions of societal ills. From a sociological point of view it can indeed be said that rebellious adolescents constitute dynamic elements in society and function as stagnation-preventing catalysts. When considered within the progress-oriented ethos of our Western civilization, these effects can be interpreted as a positive function.

CROSS-CULTURAL APPEARANCE OF ADOLESCENCE

The theory that industrial or postindustrial conditions have a characteristic effect on young individuals in any country is supported by cross-cultural examples. In the industrialized world we are witnessing various expressions of adolescence — some of them in the form of harmless fads, some in the form of delinquency, and some in the form of serious efforts to advance social change. This section presents an international sampling of youthful stirring that puts the discussion of American adolescence into universal perspective.

England has experienced an upsurge in youth-style and adolescent-gang activities since the middle of the century. It began with the elegantly dressed but often aggressive Teddy boys of the late 1950s. They were followed by the gentle Mods and the tough Rockers in the 1960s, forming opposing camps. The Rockers derived their name from rock 'n' roll, which the Mods rejected for what they thought were more refined styles. Mod was short for "modish" and "modernist." Rockers wore black leather and rode powerful motorcycles. Mods went for stylish clothes, long hair, high-heeled shoes, and motor scooters. Each group defined the other as the out-group, and each was visibly identifiable, forming a ready target for the other. Significant of English teenagers is their remarkable affluence, which they use to acquire their subcultures' material identifications in terms of "in" clothes, scooters, and motorcycles.

During the late 1960s and early 1970s, England made its contribution to the international hippie movement. Similar to the American counterparts, English hippies drew antagonism from the Establishment, mostly on account of appearance. Large contingents of bearded and drug-using British flocked to such favorite grounds as the Netherlands, where they found greater tolerance in Amsterdam's Vondel Park than in London's Hyde Park, and along the beaches of the Mediterranean. These English youths assumed a moratorium on adulthood by experimenting not only with lifestyles but also with life-locations. Many of them oscillated between wanderlust and academic pursuit—periodically returning to school in England and elsewhere in Europe.

Besides the activities of generally nondelinquent teen subcultures, juvenile delinquency has sharply increased in England—a typical trend for most European countries of the past few decades. The most extreme expressions were reported from London, where organized groups engaged in violent behavior that was obviously normative for the group and functioned to reinforce in-group sentiments.

Among the gangs were the Skinheads of the 1970s, who recruited primarily from lower-class neighborhoods and were responsible for initiating a new style. These teenagers, mostly boys, shaved their skulls, dressed in oversized workpants held up by thin, red suspenders and wore hobnailed, steel-toed boots, which they used as weapons to kick and trample. Some grew their hair a trifle longer and identified themselves as Suedeheads. Skins and Suedes were lineal descendants of the Rockers and specialized in terrorizing hippies, homosexuals, and immigrants from the Orient. Extensive Skinhead violence prompted mass demonstrations by Pakistanis in front of No. 10 Downing Street. Police were prompted to confiscate bootlaces and suspenders of suspicious Skinhead packs on the theory that it is difficult to kick if one's boots are flapping and trousers sagging.

The sadistic Skinhead style gave impetus to the sadomasochistic Punk style in the late 1970s, a style that assumed international dimensions and became noticeable in the United States by the early 1980s. Its initially rather crude British form transmuted into a more sophisticated style in America and, at least for specific subgroups, filled the want of style created by the demise of the mod and the hippie styles. American Punk, dubbed "the hippies' revenge," attracted mostly disturbed teenagers, who substituted sadomasochistic symbolism and mock violence on the dance floor for actual violence in the streets. A spin-off from Punk during the 1980s was New Wave, reintroducing bizarre mod styles, expressing less violence, and separating itself from Punk.

The early 1990s have seen a resurgence of Skinhead activities; this time as much in the United States as in Europe, and ever increasingly tinted with militant racism. Even the reunified Germany of 1990 experienced Skinhead violence as one of its first major delinquency problems.

Germans refer to their normative adolescents as *Teenagers,* an addition to the German vocabulary accepted as if it were of perfect Teutonic origin. The word has been incorporated into regional dialects and, for example, is often used in Bavaria with an added *l* to produce *Teenagerl,* suggesting a diminutive version of teenager. However, an unfavorable image of teenager is reinforced by the frequently antisocial conduct of German adolescents. Destructive conduct is not necessarily the domain of delinquent gangs, but is often the by-product of nondelinquent teenage fads. In the 1960s, when Britain's Rolling Stones performed in West Berlin, the aftermath of the performance included a rampage by teenage fans that cost the city $150,000 in damages.[17]

Excesses of teenage fads proclaim the existence of an adolescent collectivity. But they fail to leave a lasting imprint on society's social structure and institutions. Other segments of the youth population leave a more serious impression. For example, West Germany's students have manifested their moratorium on adulthood with particular force. Caught in the margin between family background and adult status in a complex industrial society, they have demanded more say in the environment in which they spend many years of their lives. During the 1970s, hardly a campus escaped their riotous demands. There were strikes, occupations of buildings, the taking of hostages, marches, sit-ins, and destruction of government property. The demands concentrated on obtaining a voice in structuring the curriculum, hiring and firing of faculty, distributing funds, and arranging various campus facilities. In addition, international matters, particularly the Vietnam War, played an important role in student protests. In 1973, for example, students stormed Bonn's city hall, smashing furniture and looting official files, to protest the visit of South Vietnam's President.

The Vietnam War had added a rationale to youth's outbursts the world over, but after its termination in 1972, an apparent paucity of causes created a lull in youthful activism throughout most countries. The lull came to an end in most European countries when new political and social concerns arose during the early 1980s. A new cause, uniting hundreds of thousands of young European protesters, came with the Reagan administration's abrupt and unilateral announcement in 1981 that it intended to deploy advanced nuclear weaponry on European soil. The announcement created, virtually overnight, a new peace movement and caused European youth to rush to antiwar and anti-American rallies in numbers not seen since the Vietnam War. Other concerns stirring up young Europeans, as well as their American peers, focused on nuclear power generators and their dangers to human life and the ecosystem.

One cause that degenerated into violent activism before as well as after German reunification was fueled by housing policies in big cities such as Berlin. Young people, many of them students and rootless adolescents, illegally occupied condemned residences, staged mass demonstrations, and

---

[17]UPI report (Berlin, September 17, 1965).

marched into planned battles against police. While many of the participating youths were sincerely motivated by social concerns, many participated out of nihilistic hostility against an anomic moratorium that prevented them from being meaningful members of a prosperous society. Indeed, alienation had driven a number of adolescents to the point of totally rejecting their society — a rejection based on irrational hatred without the benefit of ideology or coherent philosophy (thereby differing from political terrorists). These blindly destructive youths were called *Chaoten* and their professed purpose was to create as much chaos in society as they possibly could.[18] The fact that such a label came into existence tells us about a new phenomenon: the ultimate manifestation of nihilistic adolescence that holds no stock in the adult world. Although the majority of activist youths were not necessarily violent themselves, they protected the *Chaoten* at demonstrations and in street fights by forming protective phalanxes around them whenever the police charged or attempted to reach these usually masked individuals. It is a telling symptom of a civilization lopsided with adolescents when masses of young people choose to side with deliberate chaos-makers rather than with law and order.

The lull was broken in the United States during the 1980s by several political and social innovations. Among them were the reintroduction of draft registration for young men (which had been suspended after the Vietnam War), the administration's cutting of student loans and grants, and the government's overtures toward interfering with rebel movements threatening the status quo of a Central American country. Each of these events caused protests, rallies, and demonstrations. However, compared with reactions to the government's earlier Vietnam policy, the responses were mild-mannered.

The lull was more or less reintroduced during the early 1990s when, with the cessation of the civil war in Nicaragua, U.S. involvement in Central American conflicts abated and increasingly stringent economic conditions attracted the more personal and pragmatic concerns of American youth. Even the U.S. military action in the Persian Gulf region in 1991 did little to disturb their privatized attitudes, modifying them, however, by a tinge of patriotism.

France's adolescent problems were expressed in terms of the *blousons noirs* and *teenagers*. The latter term — again an untranslated innovation from American culture — was frequently branded by patriotic Frenchmen as an undesirable example of "Franglais," the intrusion of English words into French. The opponents of such innovations object to them on the assumption that with the introduction of English words, "*l'American* way of life" was also introduced, since new concepts stimulate new behavior patterns. Their analysis was correct — the typical teenager as we know him or her in the

---

[18]"Widerliche Auswüchse," *Spiegel*, August 17, 1981, pp. 31–32.

United States has become a way of life in France. The country also experienced a share of the countercultural uprisings that swept through Western Europe and North America during the late 1960s and early 1970s.

In Sweden there is concern about the *raggare* (alienated, subcultural youths) and Swedish young people in general. As Swedish society perplexedly stands by, their young people manifest rising rates of alcoholism, drug abuse, and suicide. It seems as if it were part of the old "Scandinavian puzzle." The youth of one of the world's most advanced and secure countries, protected by social welfare practices of every imaginable sort, are listless and desire to immigrate to other countries where they believe opportunities would challenge their wits and life would not be regulated to the point of boredom and meaninglessness.

Austrian society watches with consternation as boys and girls abandon yodeling and dirndls and turn to music and clothes that signal belonging to the subculture and recession from the Establishment. The older generation condescendingly calls them *Halbstarke*, "half-growns."

Australian society is confronted with growing numbers of adolescents who have formed, as in America and Western Europe, a distinct collective power vis-à-vis the Establishment.

Uninhibited symptoms of adolescence have erupted in the world of erstwhile Communism. Ever since the end of the Cold War in 1990, the new freedoms in Eastern Europe have included freedom to create or be part of a youth subculture. Just as in Western societies, industrialization had progressed to create discontinuity between child and adult statuses, and although Communist governments had tried hard to fill this interim, exploit it for their ideological goals, and create a national youth organization, their programs have ultimately failed to capture the young. Instead of internalizing ideological doctrine, the young preferred to imitate Western styles, especially those that sprouted from Western teenage subculture. Particularly avid imitators of Western styles were and still are called *stilyagi*, "style chasers," in Russia. Initially, the black market supplied such things as teen garments and rock 'n' roll records and tapes that were not available on the regular Russian market. During the mid 1970s, the Soviet government relented and realized the economic advantage of manufacturing their own blue jeans and teen-music records. The new freedoms also include hirsute freedom, and the previously frowned-upon long hair for Russian boys has become a common sight in the era of *glasnost*. In a sense, the Soviet Union has opened the door to the world of teenage subculture.[19]

Besides teenage subcultural styles, Russia is troubled by serious delinquency. News reaching the West indicates widespread adolescent drinking,

[19]Kitty Weaver, *Russia's Future: The Communist Education of Youth* (New York: Praeger, 1983).

assaults, rapes, and other delinquency among urban Soviet youth. The scope of delinquency is illustrated by the decision of various cities to impose curfews on teenagers, prohibiting them to be on the street after 9:00 p.m. In 1974, the Supreme Court of the Soviet Union called for "unwavering struggle against hooliganism."

A more significant indicator of adolescence is less visible and deals with the drawn-out period during which Soviet youth must prepare for positions in the industrial complex. Soviet sociologist Alexandre Kotlyar reported widespread dissatisfaction among Soviet youth, who felt that the industrial positions they had entered did not match the professional qualities they had achieved in institutions of education. As a consequence, young workers change jobs twice as often as do their fathers.[20] To remedy the situation and prevent later disillusionment, a program initiated in 1981 in the Ukraine required medical students to take internships. As an almost immediate consequence, 60 percent of the interns decided that they had chosen the wrong profession.[21]

It is true that Communist authorities have succeeded in curbing the "perennial student syndrome" (young people excessively extending the period of their education), but at the same time pay dearly for it. By means of a centralized system, they strictly enforce a *numerus clausus*—a Latin phrase meaning *allowing only limited numbers*—which regulates how many students are allowed to major in certain fields. Unlike the United States, Soviet authorities plan and project future societal needs for professions, and admit students to majors accordingly. For example, applications for majoring in medicine, biology, psychology, teacher's education, and architecture far exceeded the figures allotted for majoring in these areas in Russia as well as in East Germany during the early 1980s. Unlike previous years, no substitutions, even in related areas, were permitted.[22] Such regimentation avoids prolongation of the educational process and prevents unemployment after graduation, but it is hard on individual desires. As a consequence, young people's career satisfaction and general happiness is as much endangered in Communist countries as it is in Western ones.

However, this control of students' choices cannot be declared a Communist excess because the same centralized control has been enforced for decades in West Germany, and has been continued in reunited Germany. For example, the central government office for controlling enrollment in the various fields of study decided to close all enrollment possibilities in the area of business management beginning with the 1991 summer semester—a mea-

---

[20]Agence France-Presse (Geneva, November 1974).

[21]"Moscow Beat," *World Press Review*, 29 (April 1982), p. 14.

[22]"Numerus Clausus," *Mitteilungen,* Deutscher Akademischer Austauschdienst (*DAAD*), Bonn, March 1982, p. 2.

sure prompted by students' demands far exceeding adequate study facilities.[23]

The need for this regulation has been explained in similar ways in the West and in the East: (1) To avoid the kind of disabling pressure on the limited facilities of academic or training institutions that is created by allowing excessive numbers of students to enroll in certain fields. In other words, the policy tries to prevent substandard education brought on by overcrowding; and (2) to avoid having students major in fields that prove to have no future after completion of their education or training, because of a lack of demand for such careers or jobs. Here again we see a similar method of controlling the market by central government in the capitalist West as well as in the Communist East (or in whatever is left of it).

The centralized *numerus clausus* control is in sharp contrast to the educational policy in the United States, where students have nearly unlimited choices as to their majors, but also bear the risks as to whether future market conditions will accommodate them.

With the end of the Cold War and the general debacle of Communism as a politically viable system, just about all Eastern European nations have relented on their previously stringent measures to suppress and curb Western influence on their young. With minor differences, the authorities of Poland, Czechoslovakia, Hungary, Rumania, and Bulgaria have abandoned restraints and now resignedly stand by watching the younger generation join full-throttle Western mainstream teenage styles and behavior. What once was labeled "Western decadence" has become tolerated behavior, indeed has turned into new sources of lucrative commercial exploits. These formerly Communist and rather puritanical societies now experience a rapid merger of teen-subcultural lifestyle with capitalist enterprise. Gone are the days when East German authorities tried to suppress discotheques or, failing that, at least tried to impose Communist-approved musical tastes safeguarded by government-selected disc jockeys called—with Teutonic cumbersomeness— *Schallplattenunterhalter*. Gone are the days when—as in the 1970s—a special barbershop was set up in the Bulgarian capital where police force-sheared the locks of Western-style-imitating teenage boys they hauled off the street.

Of course, such phenomena as styles of hair and music merely scratch the surface of adolescence as a growing societal phenomenon. The more serious aspects are hidden in the constantly extending period of education and training to prepare for a place in the increasingly industrial lifestyle.

Adolescence has evolved also in non-European societies that have developed an industrial potential. In the Far East, for example, China, Japan, and Taiwan have undergone adolescent stirrings. Japan has achieved indus-

---

[23]"Erneut Numerus Clausus," *Mitteilungen,* Deutscher Akademischer Austauschdienst (*DAAD*) Bonn, November 1990, p. 14.

trialization to the point of postindustrial conditions, and the moratorium on adulthood has become a way of life. Concern was aroused by indications of an astonishingly high degree of youthful alienation from the economic and political system. A 1973 survey of Gallup International, which included responses from 22,000 eighteen- to twenty-four-year-old Japanese, Americans, English, West Germans, Brazilians, French, Yugoslavs, Swedes, Filipinos, Swiss, and Indians found Japanese youth's dissatisfaction and alienation to be the highest. Only about 10 percent answered "yes" to the question "Do you think your government protects the welfare and rights of the people?" Figures from other countries ranged from 30 percent in France to as high as 83 percent in West Germany. The study also showed that young Japanese were less interested in religion, had fewer close friends, were more inclined to believe that human nature is evil, and were less interested in kindness to others than youth in other countries.[24] Youthful crime in Japan has jumped over 10 percent during the early 1980s, with juveniles accounting for nearly half of all criminal offenders. Violence on school grounds increased over 40 percent during this time, and most of the crimes were directed against teachers.[25]

It seems to have been reserved for the Japanese society to escalate teen styles to their most ostentatious representation. On a typical Sunday afternoon, Tokyo's Harajuku district is jammed with teenagers in search of a lifestyle of their own, one that defies Japanese tradition. There is a multitude of shops with such exotic names as Octopus Army, Short Kiss, and Good Day House—all bringing Western (mostly American) teen styles to Japanese youth. Lifestyles for sale provide a sophisticated spectrum of subtle Western nuances from which to choose. "There are button-down collars and plaid pants for the preppie look, floral prints and batiks for the Third World look, tennis and soccer equipment for the ultra-fit look. One store sells nothing but Batman gear for the Caped Crusader look."[26] Japanese teenagers are highly sensitive to fluctuations in style and do their best to keep up with the various *bumu* (Japanese for booms, referring to what is "in" at the time), as they may change from Hell's Angels mode to the Italian casual to *Amekaji*, the American casual. American design seems to remain the base, favored for its comfortable and functional look and guaranteed by the innocuous inside label promising "Americanized as hell as well as originality." What exactly this is supposed to mean is probably lost in the translation, but it nonetheless convinces the buyer that it is enormously important. It goes without saying that *bumu* are also genuine business booms. Designers and manufacturers

---

[24]*New York Times*, August 5, 1973, p. 12.
[25]"Education: Japanese Students Are Driven by Shiken Jigoku," *Time*, March 15, 1982.
[26]"American Casual Seizes Japan," *Time*, November 13, 1989, p. 106.

have rushed to cash in on *Amekaji*, suggesting and symbolizing the Japanese dream for American-style freedom, openness, and individualism.

The political, economic, and industrial development of Taiwan has given similar rise to adolescence. Most notable are the *tai-paus*, gang members with largely middle-class backgrounds who have formed a subcultural environment within which they develop an identity. Over 100 *tai-pau* units have been identified, each with its own name and fiercely loyal following. Their activities are nonutilitarian and merely serve to maintain group solidarity. Delinquent behavior—like gang fighting, assaults, car theft, truancy, and police teasing—is to be understood in this light.[27]

Even from Communist China, long a repressive stronghold of Socialist purity, have come unmistakable signs of youthful upheavals. One of the most notable of these shook the country on June 4th, 1989 and is known as Beijing's Tiananmen Square Massacre. It claimed the lives of unknown numbers of dissenting young Chinese, mostly students, demonstrating for democratic reform.

In addition, China is plagued by wave after wave of juvenile delinquency, admittedly amounting to a national problem and explained by officials as a consequence of such urban conditions as overcrowding and unemployment. The president of China's Supreme Court announced in 1982 that a fourth of the inmates of Peking's prisons are under eighteen. A high proportion of murderers, thieves, rapists, drug traffickers, and racketeers are juveniles. For example, "in Hokiang a band of delinquents were convicted of 96 felonies: burglaries, robberies, rapes, and a bank robbery in which 60 people were held hostage." Officials try to stem the tide of Western influence that threatens, particularly in urban areas, to give impetus to subcultural behavior among the young. Referring to Western music and dance styles, authorities have not merely chided young Chinese for performing "vulgar dances to unhealthy music in dimly lit rooms," but even arrested and jailed a score of them in an attempt to halt the spread of "bourgeois culture."[28]

Today's China faces a dangerous dilemma: if the government relents and gives more democratic freedoms to the young, they surely will continue to demand more. If they clamp down on the burgeoning youth movement, future protest and upheaval will be just as inevitable.[29]

The list of countries experiencing adolescence includes most, if not all, urban-industrial nations. The above examples illustrate what can happen in a society with a division between generations.

The country internationally viewed as the prototype of an adolescence-

---

[27]You-Yuh Kuo, "Identity-Diffusion and Tai-Pau Gang Delinquency in Taiwan," *Adolescence*, 8 (Summer 1973): 165–70.

[28]"Chinese Juveniles," *World Press Review*, 29 (April 1982): 10.

[29]Associated Press, Peking, November 23, 1986; and "A Day in the Life of China," *Time*, October 2, 1989, pp. 30–79.

troubled society is the United States, and many observers of the international scene regard the American teenage subculture as the cause of the development of the various vernacular versions. It is undoubtedly true that American youth has had "form-inspiring" influence on youth in other societies through the mass media, which have effectively permeated international boundaries. However, it is questionable whether the American influence is *responsible* for the youth movements that are springing up everywhere in the world. It is more accurate to say that similar social and cultural conditions have arisen in these societies and that these are responsible for the development of adolescence.

The development of adolescence is basically due to (1) a finely divided division of labor, which produces a very technical and complex social structure, and (2) the failure of a culture to provide its members with a compelling ideation that would result in a strong identity and a feeling of purpose. The combination of these two variables, one having to do with the nature of the social structure and the other with the weakness of the culture, form the requisite and sustaining conditions for adolescence.

The nature of American social structure and American culture is probably more adolescence-inducing than that of most societies. A social structure that produces discontinuity between the status of the child and that of the adult would cause only minor forms of adolescent expression *if* the culture were able to compensate for the ensuing structural vagueness; that is, if the culture were able to infuse a sense of identity and meaning into the interim between the two statuses. The assumption is that in a typical urban-industrial environment the interim between child and adult statuses is usually unstructured and consequently lacks the type of meaning and identity that evolves from a definite career or from a goal-oriented apprenticeship. The burden of providing meaning during these interim years falls therefore on the overall ethos of the culture. If the culture fails to compensate for the social-structural limbo, adolescence is bound to express itself.

It is interesting to observe the progress that many of the developing nations have made toward the urban-industrial lifestyle and the concomitant development of juvenile and adolescent problems. Normally, adolescence is a symptom of a well developed and relatively affluent society. If this is true, many of the rural and semiurban societies may anticipate the development of adolescence along with technological maturation.

THE QUESTION OF UNIVERSALITY OF ADOLESCENCE

While it is true that a high correlation exists between urban-industrial conditions and the growth of adolescence, the correlation is not absolute. To understand the exceptions, it is necessary to recognize the interaction between *social-structural conditions* and *cultural forces*.

Structural conditions are found in institutional structure, group affiliation, authority hierarchy, socioeconomic stratification, and the division of labor, all of which form the basis of human relationships. For adolescence to evolve, the social structure, especially the division of labor, must be complex enough to exact a long transition from child to adult status. In sum, it requires the combination of two basic causes to produce adolescence: (1) social-structural discontinuity and (2) cultural anomie, a sort of societal normlessness that leaves it up to the individual to cope with social situations and to develop his or her identity on a more individualistic basis. If one or the other of these conditions is absent, typical adolescence cannot develop, as will be seen in some examples.

Adolescence can be curbed, or possibly altogether avoided, if a society provides a compelling and convincing ideology or religion for its members and succeeds in indoctrinating the young. The most reliable and lasting social-control mechanism is the internalized fervor and conviction that become part of the "conscience." Little or no external enforcement is needed to obtain firm adherence to cultural norms and values once people have internalized them as convictions. If a society succeeds in implanting an identity that rises above the narrow frame of social-structural arrangements and creates a feeling of meaningful belonging to a cultural tradition, symptoms of adolescence will be minimal.

This minimization is especially noticeable where a specific youth program is designed to infuse ideological directives. As a result, the void created by the structural interim between child and adult statuses is filled with meaning. The feeling of belonging to the general culture and the exposure to specific youth programs create an identity in the young regardless of the interim existence between childhood and adulthood. The young individual obtains the status of a meaningful and vital member of society and cannot be classified as adolescent.

Some examples in recent history illustrate the ideological compensation for adolescence-inducing urban-industrial structures. The *Hitler-Jugend* of Nazi Germany, the *Pioneers* and the *Komsomol* in the Soviet Union, the *Freie Deutsche Jugend* (FDJ) in the former East Germany, and the *Red Guard* in China were organizations that successfully combated the urban-industrialized conditions that produce adolescence.

Reference to these historical events is not to be interpreted as an endorsement of totalitarian systems that convert adolescents into cooperating and goal-oriented members of society. The purpose of presenting these situations is to elucidate the structural-functional principle that assumes that if certain cultural dimensions prevail, certain behavioral consequences follow. The German, Russian, and Chinese examples depict modifications of the generalization that adolescence is a universal trait of modern urban-industrial societies.

But these examples are historical examples and refer to situations that have lost ideological purity and have acquired adolescent symptoms. As noted earlier, subcultural and delinquent youth-activities have increased in Russia, while youth's ideological commitment appears to have decreased since the Stalinist era. Nevertheless, for millions of Soviet youths between the ages of fourteen and twenty-eight, the Communist Youth League, or *Komsomol*, still provides a tangible environment in which they receive guidance, fellowship, and a sense of belonging.

The historical example of East Germany, which used to be one of the Soviet Union's staunchest satellites, is of particular significance to social scientists. First, because it accomplished one of the most thorough eliminations of adolescence as urban-industrial societies go. It modeled its national youth, *Freie Deutsche Jugend*, after Russia's *Komsomol* and succeeded in organizing and indoctrinating a large segment of the country's young people. Along with that, it developed a parallel state-run youth movement, *Gesellschaft für Sport und Technik* (GST), the Society for Sport and Technology, which achieved a membership of about 650,000 and represented almost a third of the nation's fourteen- to eighteen-year-old population. The GST functioned primarily as a paramilitary training environment in which boys and girls learned to drive jeeps, shoot, operate radio transmitters, and parachute. These organizations cleverly provided activities for the young that would surely be attractive and fascinating to youngsters anywhere in the world. Once captivated through such exciting activities, they became receptive to ideological indoctrination. Both organizations were financed and tightly controlled by the government, had colorful monthly publications, and held members to an oath of absolute obedience.

The GST's responsibilities included an emphasis on athletic fitness, and their Spartan program proved so successful that the relatively small country of about 17 million walked away from several Olympic games with more medals than the USA.

Second, it illustrates, in an almost paradoxical fashion, that even an adamant regime like East Germany could not suppress youthful dissent. Evidently not even decades of trying to indoctrinate and organize the youth of the nation were sufficient to overcome their desire to join the free world. They played a major role in the demonstrations and agitations that caused the Wall to come down in 1989.

Third, the 1990 reunification of the two Germanys provided sociologists with a rare macro-case study of two sets of national youth merging into one society and trying to achieve common ground. It is important to keep in mind that after World War II East Germany's population had abruptly changed from Nazi totalitarianism to Communist totalitarianism; its young were absolutely unfamiliar with the democratic lifestyle and did not know how to function in a free society. In a sense, the young of both German societies had to undergo an acculturation process that, predictably, was weighed in favor of the West German cousins, but not without conflicts and frustrations on both sides.

In totalitarian societies, the political philosophy of the state imposes an identity on the younger generation that neutralizes social-structural features containing status-discontinuing potential. Youths in this type of situation do not have a moratorium on identity or commitment. Their commitment is a product of contrivance and persuasion; their identity a carbon copy of mass identity; and their individuality lacks the eventual benefits that come with the struggle of learning personal judgment—an essential part of the adolescent experience. Rather than facing adolescence, the young in these societies are relegated to a socially approved and well organized position such as the "youth of the nation" or "youth of the leader."

To achieve and maintain the mass position, the totalitarian leadership employs a range of stratagems including uniforms, marches, songs, slogans, pageantry, hero worship, oratory, and paramilitary games and plays. Many a national leader (for example, Hitler) showed intuitive skill as a social psychologist in manipulating and inspiring masses of young people. The well defined status of youth created clear standards, predictable behavior, and rights and obligations that were, or had to be, respected by the community. This public status alleviated, if not eliminated, the crisis of discontinuity between the status of the child and that of the adult. As a result, there was an absence of the adolescent symptoms and expressions so typical of the more democratic societies.

Because of modern urban-industrial youths' intense need for clear identity, they can easily fall prey to demagogues' promises, charismatic leaders' calls to action, and the various appeals of "the true belief." The development of many totalitarian regimes was possible because a leader or a power elite had success in winning the enthusiasm and loyalty of the nation's adolescents. Psychiatrist Maurice N. Walsh feels that the rise of Nazi Germany was possible partially because of the National Socialists' success in indoctrinating the nation's adolescents:

> It is a mistake to assume that the Nazis gained control in Germany solely by means of brutality and terror. No one who knows Germany can believe such a myth. Control was gained by seduction, and seduction of adolescents was a powerful tool in preparing the young Germans, through the Hitler Jugend, for their sacrifice in the coming war. Seduction of many of their parents was also carried out, but the older generation is never so easily seduced as is the younger. The reasons reside in the emotional instability of the adolescent, who is passing through a critical period in his emotional life and development.[30]

[30]This article first appeared in *The Humanist*, March/April 1967, and is reprinted by permission.

Pitirim Sorokin's classification of types of societies, or the specific phases through which most societies pass, may be helpful in this context.[31] A society with a salient ideation will find it relatively easy to extend a consistent and logically integrated identity to every member of the social system, even though the immediate social-structural position may lack clarity. This lack of structural specificity may not even be noticed or found disturbing, since the overall cultural identity and the feeling of belonging are ample compensation. Belonging to a national movement may be perceived as a position in its own right—the position of being a member of the totalitarian society. This membership enables the young to satisfactorily answer the question "Who am I?" The situation during the Middle Ages exemplifies the point. Millions of people would have answered the basic question of identity by saying: "I am a member of the Church" or more basically: "I am a child of God." The "true believer," who feels that he or she is a child and envisages a powerful "Father," possesses an identity as strong as or even stronger than any specific social position that he or she could ever occupy.

In effect, the tenets of the religio-cultural ethos were sufficiently meaningful to involve the believing member regardless of social differentiation factors, such as age, position in the division of labor, or socioeconomic status. In an *ideational* society, the central creed offers identity and belonging at any phase in the life cycle of the individual.

But societies do not remain forever in the ideational phase. Sorokin's theory holds that the subsequent stage is the *idealistic* period, during which the previously unambiguous creed breaks up into factions. The religious character of the ideation proliferates into philosophies that are more this-worldly than other worldly. The Renaissance marks the idealistic phase of Western civilization and the weakening of the ideational forces that could have functioned as a check on the development of adolescence. The cultural forces that had extended basic identity lost persuasiveness.

The idealistic period is followed by the *sensate* period, which, according to theory, includes the present. The unified cultural credo has declined, if not disappeared altogether, and rather than being concerned with ideational precepts we are now intent on satisfying immediate sensate cravings. Priority of values and ideas is determined by material and pleasurable results. Cultural norms and values have become nonspecific and allow increased individual freedom. This individual freedom has been held responsible for our current anxiety about, and confused searching for, identity. *The most striking sociological effect of this loss of basic cultural identity is the burdening of the social structure with the demand for an identity that is no longer available from culture.* A shift in identity-genesis has occurred: what the general culture can

---

[31]Pitirim A. Sorokin, *The Crisis of Our Age: The Social and Cultural Outlook* (New York: Dutton, 1941).

no longer provide is now expected from specific social positions. This means that members of contemporary society depend more strongly than ever before on a social position for identity. The specific role of a given social position, be it that of an auto mechanic or a physician, has become the core of identity.

Cut off from such social-structural anchors, adolescents tend to suffer problems of identity. Distress symptoms can be observed among the youths who have not yet chosen an occupation and among retired persons who are no longer actively involved in their identity-reinforcing occupation. However, unlike adolescents, the latter can at least draw on an identity associated with years in a given occupation.

Finally, the universality of adolescence in urban-industrial societies can also be challenged on the intranational level. In large modern societies the heterogeneity of the population allows for enclaves within which the young can remain relatively unaffected by the adolescence-inducing elements of the larger society. Not all American teenagers experience the same degree, or for that matter any degree, of adolescence. Young people who experience relative immunity to adolescence usually belong to such ethnic, racial, religious, or socioeconomic groups as the Hutterites, Amish, American Indians, and upper socioeconomic stratum. While the Amish and the Hutterites are nearly totally free of adolescence, the other groups experience adolescence in varying degrees and styles.

While the thrust of this book aims at identifying the typical adolescent experience of the American middle class, deviations from this norm are acknowledged and examined elsewhere.[32]

SUMMARY

Adolescence as a collective phenomenon is nearly universal in the modern world. Some countries exhibit it to a greater degree than others, usually depending on their degree of urban-industrial development. There seems to be a direct correlation between the degree of urban-industrial advancement and the extent of adolescence. Therefore, adolescence should not be described—let alone explained—as an exclusively American characteristic that has spread to other countries, but rather as an outgrowth of certain social and cultural conditions that can be found in many societies today.

Causal conditions of adolescence include the structural disruption of

---

[32]The limits of this book preclude treatment of the diversity of the adolescent experience, and the interested reader is advised to consult specialized works on racial, ethnic, and other minority groups, as, for example: B. Eugene Griessman, *Minorities* (Hinsdale, IL: Dryden, 1975); Elton Long, *American Minorities* (Englewood Cliffs, NJ: Prentice-Hall, 1975); Dale S. McLamore, *Racial and Ethnic Relations in America* (Boston: Allyn & Bacon, 1980).

the child-to-adult progression and a weak cultural idiom. Only when the two conditions coincide can adolescence develop.

Historically speaking, juvenile delinquency is not new. Chroniclers of all ages have commented on this particular youthful problem. However, it was not until the onset of the Industrial Revolution that the social structure made for discontinuity between the statuses. Likewise, it was not until the Renaissance that the ideational forces of medieval Christendom weakened. As a result, the social structure became a more effective source for identity than the general culture.

In the few cases where totalitarian states succeeded in indoctrinating youth with compelling convictions, the social-structural void between statuses was filled with meaning and purpose, and adolescence was prevented. However, in most contemporary urban societies teenagers find themselves in an ill-defined interim: adolescence.

3

Adolescence: Its Time and Place in Personality Development

A social psychological analysis of adolescence must never forget that two parties are involved: on one side is society, if not civilization, and on the other side is the individual. The parties do not always share identical interests, goals, and needs, but they are intricately interrelated. An investigation aspiring to completeness must attend to both. In the preceding chapter, the societal and civilizational setting was brought into focus. The present chapter shifts levels of examination and focuses on the individual's personality processes as they take place during the adolescent phase of his or her life span. While this appears to be an abrupt change of level, it is justified by the fact that societal and personal realities fail to manifest themselves in identical ways. Hence I feel that both parties must be introduced at the beginning of the book.

Among the major processes that occur in personality development are the learning of roles and the crystallization of a personal identity. The stirring of these intimately intertwined elements is at its most intense during adolescence, and this chapter discusses processes that go into the making of the human personality.

The frameworks for referring to personality can range from the biolog-

ical to the sociocultural. Gordon W. Allport surveyed the professional literature and extracted fifty different definitions of personality.[1] They can be
grouped into sociological, biological, psychological, juridical, or cultural categories. For example, E. Faris proposed a sociocultural definition by calling
personality "the subjective aspect of culture." Ernest W. Burgess held that
"personality is the integration of all the traits which determine the role and
status of the person in society. Personality might therefore be defined as
social effectiveness." C. H. Prince thought of personality as "the sum-total of
all biological innate dispositions, impulses, tendencies, appetites, and in-
stincts of the individual, and the acquired dispositions and tendencies—
acquired by experience." Arnold Gesell saw personality as "the pervasive
superpattern which expresses the integrity and the characteristic behavioral
individuality of the organism." Allport added that "personality is the dynamic
organization within the individual of those psychological systems that determine his unique adjustment to his environment."[2]

These illustrations show that the concept of personality has been used
to emphasize appearance, traits determining status, individual uniqueness,
sum totals of innate or acquired traits, impulses, dispositions, style of life,
adjustment to environment, and the subjective aspect of culture. Since the
concept can refer to literally any type of human behavior and is a concern of
behavioral scientists of different disciplines, diversity is inevitable. It is hardly
possible to synthesize all definitions currently in use. Rather than asking *what*
personality is, it might be more fruitful to first determine *which aspect* of
personality is to be discussed. In spite of the wide terrain covered by the
concept of personality, there are a few basic assumptions generally accepted
by social psychologists:

PERSONALITY AS SOCIAL PRODUCT

The aspects of personality in which a social scientist is primarily interested
are those that are socially learned. The etymology of the word *personality*
suggests learned behavior. It is derived from *persona* which, in Latin, refers
to the theatrical mask used by Roman actors in Greek dramas. Allusion to
"actor" implies that personality is a product of the social setting, of the social
"stage," and not of some biogenetic process.

---

[1]Gordon W. Allport, *Personality: A Psychological Interpretation* (New York: Holt, Rinehart
& Winston, 1973).

[2]Ibid., pp. 25–54.

PERSONALITY AS PROCESS

Personality is continuously affected by new social experiences, so that many behavioral scientists consider it more realistic to think of personality in terms of process than in terms of completed product. One of the reasons American sociologists are critical of Freudian theory is its heavy emphasis on personality as a product of childhood experience. Sociologists prefer to think of personality as an ongoing process, constantly patterned and repatterned by social and cultural stimuli. The facile sociological view of personality as a carbon copy of the sociocultural surrounding contrasts with the orthodox psychoanalytic view of personality as the end product of childhood years. Neither view is trustworthy, and the truth probably lies somewhere in the middle.

The findings of one of the very few longitudinal studies ever done on this issue supports the Freudian view. Between 1966 and 1974 the Institute for Social Research at the University of Michigan followed 2000 young men from tenth grade until five years after high school. During that period, researchers conducted five data collections to detect changes in attitudes, aspirations, and self-concepts. Marked differences in self-concept were found between persons who achieved educational and/or occupational success and those who were failures—*but* "these differences were largely in place by the tenth grade." Graduate students' high self-esteem simply mirrored their good self-image as high-school sophomores. Similarly, the poor self-image of the dropouts had existed before they abandoned school. The study also discredited the assumption that education has a powerful socializing effect on students. Racial attitudes are a striking example: "Our study found that racial attitudes were already set by the 12th grade. Something that was supposed to be the effect of college was really set before."[3]

Another theory that would ruffle the feathers of those sociologists stubbornly entrenched in purely social explanations of personality development was advanced by Harvard psychologist Jerome Kagan whose research findings convinced him of the operation of innate tendencies in personality development. Unlike most social scientists, Kagan believes that the formation of the conscience proceeds largely independent from external sources and is molded by parents to only a minor degree. Says Kagan: "I think that *all* children, provided they have an intact nervous system, know before they are three that hurting another is wrong. We can expect a conscience of every child. We don't have to build it in. All we have to do is arrange the environment so they don't lose it."[4]

---

[3]"Dogmatic Teens, Entrenched Attitudes at an Early Age," *Human Behavior*, October 1978, p. 32.

[4]Quoted in John Leo, "Lessons in Bringing Up Baby," *Time*, October 22, 1984, p. 97; also see Jerome Kagan, ed., *The Emergence of Morality in Young Children* (Chicago: Chicago University Press, 1987).

It seems that certain grand theories never go out of style. Kagan's idea is reminiscent of Jean Jacque Rousseau's romantic theory of the innateness of goodness in all human beings—until evil city existence destroys it.

PERSONALITY AS DEVELOPMENTAL PHASES

While psychologists largely agree that personality development does not occur in one big step but rather through certain phases, the specific division, labeling, and interpretation of these phases differ widely. (Compare the differing theories of Sigmund Freud, Carl Rogers, Erich Fromm, Jean Piaget, Erik Erikson, and others.)

It is primarily for exemplification that we continue with Kagan's ideas. Kagan is quite specific in his interpretation of typical adolescent symptoms, which the literature has described as *Sturm und Drang* (stormy and restless behavior), and thinks that they result from innate processes. But he does not hold responsible a genetic program (unlike G. Stanley Hall in his famous evolutionary theory, as we will see in Chapter 6); neither is he referring to hormonal upsets, as many other theorists would propound. Rather he is suggesting a developmental stage in which cognitive processes undergo an inner demand for consistency and integration. Accordingly, the turmoil of puberty is a symptom of brain development, signaling that "when you become an adolescent, you become cognitively able for the first time to evaluate the consistency of the beliefs you hold. You automatically detect inconsistency, and that creates uncertainty."[5] In sum, Kagan thinks that the tension of typical adolescence is mainly due to this cognitive conflict and not to hormones upsetting and exciting the young individual.

Since the elements of this adolescence-symptoms theory largely deal with material learned and encountered in the course of social interaction, this part of Kagan's theory may reconcile him to most sociologists.

Another approach to understand personality development was taken by Abraham Maslow's theory of hierarchical needs. According to Maslow, human beings exhibit a hierarchy of needs, and their fulfillment must proceed from primary physiological needs (for example, hunger, thirst, temperature control) to secondary needs (safety, protection, stability). After these come needs for affection and social belonging. Beyond these needs are those for self-esteem (success, competence, and independence). Maslow suggested that there is another group of needs he called "metaneeds" or growth needs. They include the need for knowledge, justice, and beauty. Metaneeds are not

---

[5]Ibid.; also see Jerome Kagan, *Unstable Ideas: Temperament, Cognition, and Self* (Cambridge: Harvard University Press, 1989).

hierarchical like the basic needs, that is, one can be substituted for another. But they cannot be satisfied before basic needs are satisfied. However, both types must be satisfied, or psychological maladjustment arises. Maslow believes that the healthy individual progresses from the fulfillment of one need to the next, steadily moving toward self-actualization. A supportive environment is imperative for achieving need fulfillment and resultant self-actualization.[6]

Piaget's theory that all experience is organized by intelligence is another notable example of the idea that personality has discrete developmental phases. Children construct and constantly revise their models of reality, and do so in a regular sequence. Mental growth, according to Piaget, proceeds through four major stages. During the first two years of life, the child is limited to the comprehension of only physical objects. For about the next four years, the child is preoccupied with symbols and the learning of language. Starting around age six, the child comprehends abstractions, masters numbers, and understands relationships. Finally, starting at about thirteen years, the youngster begins to understand purely logical thought and can analyze his own thinking processes. With that ability comes the understanding of double messages contained in irony, satire, double entendre, and aphorism. In explaining human behavior, Piaget would rank midway on the nature-nurture continuum, since he allowed for innate structuring and for biological timing of developmental abilities.[7] Hence he is not sociology's favorite personality theoretician.

PERSONALITY AS GESTALT

Normal behavior does not consist of unrelated fragments and discrete processes. Separate acts are parts of a response system integrated in a manner lending continuity and meaning to behavior. Gestalt emphasizes the meaningful integration of behavioral elements, using the concept of *Prägnanz* to denote major structural features that offer direction and orientation.

Principles of Gestalt theory help us to understand why persons perceive the world—events, other people, themselves—the way they do. Rather than evaluating each experience as if it were a brand new one, we order it into our personality system according to already established major mental categories: *Prägnanz* dimensions. These dimensions are basic assumptions derived from interpretations of (mostly early) experiences in life. Once *Prägnanzes* are

---

[6]Abraham Maslow, *Motivation and Personality* (New York: Harper & Row, 1970), and *Toward a Psychology of Being* (Princeton, NJ: Van Nostrand, 1968).

[7]Jean Piaget, *The Origins of Intelligence in Children* (New York: International Universities Press, 1952), and *The Grasp of Consciousness: Action and Concept in the Young Child* (Cambridge, MA: Harvard University Press, 1976).

established, further experiences are sorted into them. The basic underlying principle of Gestalt is that human beings desire consistency and meaningful integration of experiences. Apparently that is somehow related to our longing to see meaning and order in our life.

The implications of this mental process are highly significant; they can explain why persons once holding certain prejudices will continue to support them, often, if necessary, by selective perception and distortion; they can also explain certain types of communication—or, rather, miscommunication. Persons looking at one and the same data or empirical event literally see different things because they interpret them according to different *Prägnanzes*.

Adolescence has a peculiar significance on *Prägnanz* formation or confirmation. It is the time when the basic childhood *Prägnanzes* have to be reevaluated as to logical consistency, empirical verifiability, and moral validity. This is one of the toughest mental tasks a person can ever confront. And because it is so tough—requiring relentless, logical thinking and the hard work of restructuring attitudes—many adolescents never complete the task and continue to carry unrealistic childhood perceptions and imaginations into adulthood. Once this step is taken, the chances of restructuring *Prägnanzes* later in life diminish markedly and, if attempted, become ever tougher, because more and more accumulated interpretations in each *Prägnanz* will have to be reexamined and reassigned. Rather than subject oneself to confusing and laborious reordering of basic attitudes, the individual will usually try to defend and justify the old *Prägnanzes*. Hence, restructuring important elements in one's personality after adolescence becomes rare.

PERSONALITY AND PHYSIOLOGICAL PREREQUISITES

The development of personality is severely impeded if an individual's brain functions are damaged, unbalanced, or undeveloped. The abnormality can be defined as retardation, feeble-mindedness, or mental illness. Since our perspective is social-psychological, physiological processes are outside our focus and will be discussed only insofar as they are subject to cultural interpretation or as they play an important role in interpersonal relations.

PERSONALITY AND THE PRIMARY GROUP

The type of social interaction in which the young individual is enmeshed is of utmost significance to personality formation. If, for example, the primary family environment is disturbed, or partially or totally absent, virtually indelible marks will be impressed on the personality. Kingsley Davis reported on the case of Isabelle, an illegitimate child, who had lived in seclusion with her deaf-mute mother until she was nearly seven years old. When she was discovered, her behavior was that of an unsocialized animal. She had not learned language and could make only inarticulate sounds. At first it was thought she was feeble-minded. However, after careful training, Isabelle was able to progress, join the public school system, and achieve normalcy.[8]

A similar case of a "wild" child came to the attention of social scientists in the 1970s. They tried to rehabilitate "Genie," but succeeded only partially. It appears that if childhood years are not utilized for language development, a certain brain capacity atrophies and later teaching attempts will not rehabilitate it entirely.[9]

Such extreme cases are rare, and presented merely to make a point. There are less extreme instances in evidence every day. For example, subtle personality deficiencies can develop in the thousands of orphans and parent-neglected children who grow up in institutional homes resembling more a secondary than a primary group environment. Observations in the Junior Village at Washington, DC revealed that institutional youths suffer from anonymity and fears of abandonment. Educators believe that adult-child verbal exchanges are needed at an early age if the children are to learn the fundamentals of language. However, because the institution was not only crowded but also segregated by age, the two-year-olds could only speak with other two-year-olds. These conditions caused regressions in language skill and physical accomplishments.[10]

A New York study compared children in foster homes who had spent the first two to three years of their lives in an institution with children whose total experience had been in foster homes. The study found that children placed in foster homes after a period of institutional rearing evidenced greater problem behavior than children with complete foster-home experience. Institutionally raised children were found to be less secure, less proficient in entering into relationships, emotionally retarded, and often destructive and cruel without apparent cause.[11]

Another study showed that institution children had great difficulty in adjusting to foster homes. Compared with children who were placed in foster homes immediately after birth, institutionally raised children were more frequently replaced because of problem behavior. "Deviant" and "strange" behavior were the most common reasons for the replacement of such children, while similar symptoms were rare in the exclusively foster-home group.

[8]Kingsley Davis, "Final Note on a Case of Extreme Isolation," *American Journal of Sociology*, 5 (March 1947): 432–37, and "Extreme Isolation of a Child," *American Journal of Sociology*, 45 (January 1940): 554–65.

[9]Maya Pines, "The Civilization of Genie," *Psychology Today*, September 1981, pp. 28–34.

[10]J. W. Anderson, "A Special Hell for Children in Washington," *Harper's*, November 1965, pp. 51–56.

[11]William Goldfarb, "Infant Rearing and Problem Behavior," *American Journal of Orthopsychiatry*, 13 (April 1943): 249–65.

The problems leading to replacements in the institution group can be categorized into (1) aggressive, hyperactive; (2) bizarre and disoriented; and (3) emotionally unresponsive. In addition, institution children displayed greater speech deficiencies, more serious school difficulties, and more frequent mental retardation. The researchers concluded that institutional children tend to remain limited in their intellectual and emotional progress by a fixation on the more primitive levels of abstraction and conceptualization.[12]

Many studies support these findings, maintaining that removal of the primary group environment, normally represented by the family, tends to be detrimental to the personality of the young.[13] Since group environment is so highly instrumental in forming personality, the group's imprint can be traced to even less extreme cases of deprivation than those of institutional children. Research has shown delinquency rates and divorce rates later in life to be significantly higher for children whose family environment has been disturbed by separation or divorce.[14]

IDENTITY: MORATORIUM, DIFFUSION, AND MULTIPLE *PERSONAE*

The core of personality is self-perception and the answer to the fundamental question, "Who am I?" This question directly challenges the person's identity—in fact, predicates it. It is a question that can be examined on at least two levels: (1) On the personal, psychological level, and (2) on the social, if not civilizational, level. The psychological examination dwells directly on an individual and limits itself to his or her self-perception, possibly including the history thereof. The sociological examination explores the larger social and societal processes that influence identity formation, trying to show how societal conditions pattern identity processes in such a pervasive manner as to produce similar identity residues in members of society. This is the search

---

[12]William Goldfarb, "The Effects of Early Institutional Care on Adolescent Personality," *The Journal of Experimental Education*, 12 (December 1943): 106–29.

[13]See R. A. Spitz, "Anaclitic Depression: An Inquiry into the Genesis of Psychiatric Conditions in Early Childhood," in *Psychoanalytic Study of the Child* (New York: International Universities Press, 1946); Lauretta Bender and H. Yarnell, "An Observational Nursery," *American Journal of Psychiatry*, 97 (March 1941): 1158–74; and D. Beres and S. J. Obers, "The Effects of Extreme Deprivation in Infancy on Psychic Structure: A Study in Ego Development," in *Psychoanalytic Study of the Child* (New York: International Universities Press, 1950), pp. 212–35.

[14]William J. Goode, "Family Disorganization," in *Contemporary Social Problems*, ed. Robert K. Merton and Robert A. Nisbet (New York: Harcourt Brace Jovanovich, 1961), p. 549, and *The Family* (Englewood Cliffs, NJ: Prentice-Hall, 1982), p. 166. Daniel Amneus, *Back to Patriarchy* (Ithaca, NY: Cornell University Press, 1979), p. 18. Michael E. Lamb, "Paternal Influences and the Father's Role," in John Keating, ed., *Social Psychology 82/83* (Guilford, CT: Dushkin, 1982), pp. 68–73.

for possibly endemic features in the identity Gestalts—a search in harmony with the goal of sociology to validly generalize. The following discussion explores these two approaches and relates them to the adolescent phase in the life cycle. Erik H. Erikson, in the context of ego-psychoanalytic theory, believes that the development of identity is the distinctive psychosocial task of adolescence.[15]

The Psychological Approach

James E. Marcia's definition of identity refers to "an existential position, to an inner organization of needs, abilities, and self-perceptions as well as to a sociopolitical stance."[16] He links this definition to four basic identity statuses: (1) Identity achievement refers to individuals who have mastered a decision-making period and have self-chosen pursuits and ideological goals; (2) Foreclosure pertains to people who are also committed to occupational and ideological positions, but whose decisions were made for them by parents and other authorities. They show little evidence of going through or having gone through a "crisis." (3) Identity diffusion is experienced by youth who have no set occupational or ideological orientation, regardless of whether or not they went through a decision-making period. (4) Moratorium describes persons struggling with occupational and/or ideological issues and being in an identity crisis. The typical identity statuses experienced during adolescence in America are moratorium and identity diffusion. In line with the life span theory, enactment of these two statuses, or a mixture thereof, is virtually expected of young Americans today. A host of personality characteristics of these statuses were discovered by psychological research, and some examples are presented here.[17]

Typical emotional symptoms of identity diffusion and moratorium are anxiety and low self-esteem. Moratorium youth, predictable from their "in-crisis" position, are the most anxious and foreclosure youth the least anxious. Identity-diffused teenagers displayed the widest discrepancy between self-concept and the concept of how others perceived them. Identity development seems to be correlated with the development of moral reasoning, and it was found that youth with a more definite sense of identity had a clearer sense of ethics and empathy than identity-diffused individuals. In the area of intellectual performance, identity-achieved individuals showed better study habits and achieved higher grades than individuals in other identity statuses.

[15]Erik H. Erikson, "Identity and the Life Cycle," *Psychological Issues*, 1 (1959), Monograph #1; *Childhood and Society* (New York: Norton, 1963); *Identity: Youth and Crisis* (New York: Norton, 1968).

[16]James E. Marcia, "Identity in Adolescence," in Joseph Adelson, ed., *Handbook of Adolescent Psychology* (New York: Wiley, 1980), p. 159.

[17]Ibid., pp. 159–87.

A study of college dropouts showed that identity-diffused students usually dropped out because of low grades, while identity-achieved individuals left for more positive and self-initiated reasons. Moratorium individuals and identity-diffused individuals frequently manifest divergent traits, probably because moratorium individuals had a higher sense of identity. For example, in terms of cultural sophistication (interest in art, music, and literature), the moratorium individuals were clearly superior. The Eriksonian hypothesis that intimacy ability depends on a stable identity has been substantiated by research disclosing that identity-diffused persons score lowest on intimacy scales and are least self-revealing in intimacy tasks.

Studies have also revealed interesting gender differences: (1) In contrast to men, the level of identity diffusion among college women was as great in the senior year as it had been in the freshman year; that is, women showed less evidence of a regular progression toward identity achievement. (2) Among moratorium youth, boys appear to be engaged in an inner struggle to free themselves from their mothers' influence (if not domination). In general, moratorium youth seem to be less willing to give in to their parents than individuals in other statuses. (3) Identity-diffused boys seem to come from families with active mothers and passive fathers; identity-diffused girls come from families with the pattern reversed. (4) As a general rule, the primary concerns of most adolescent girls are not with occupation and ideology, but with the establishment and maintenance of interpersonal relationships. On the other hand, boys aim at life decisions that frequently lead to interpersonal conflict with family and authority. Experiencing such conflict often is an identity-confirming event for boys, but not for girls. Girls tend to see themselves as having failed if they do not succeed in establishing the all-important relationships and, hence, conflict proves confusing and stunting to their identity process.

While these separate psychological studies do not yet add up to a complete portrait of the adolescent identity status, they at least give us an idea of what is going on during that phase.

The Sociological Approach

This approach to the understanding of identity dwells on the larger sociocultural conditions and, in its social-psychological slant, tries to identify how these conditions impinge on the personality. Sociologists assume that personality in general and personal identity in particular are influenced by our reference groups, significant others, and the roles we derive from our cultural heritage. The crucial point at which all these influences converge and culminate is the guiding principle of personality: the basic identity. The personal identity is the agent that must be known, or at least sensed, before actions, reactions, and motivations of a person can be understood.

Adolescence is the time when the basic question "Who am I" is asked with unrelenting force and insistence and when reference groups, significant others, and roles are avidly scanned in an attempt to derive a meaningful answer. Hence, the answer intimately depends on these social and cultural involvements, and the unique nature of the involvements contributes to the unique nature of the individual personality. If, then, we want to make sense of modern adolescents and understand their identity, or relative lack of it, we must examine the nature of these sociocultural conditions.

The *traditional* social psychological theory of the process of identity formation contains a number of assumptions. It maintains, first, that identity is a holistic phenomenon that normally is relatively integrated and is grounded in a few fundamental precepts held by the person; second, that clarity and comfort with which an individual views him- or herself depend on how clear and free of conflict the important sociocultural conditions were to which the youth was exposed; and third, that a person's behavior patterns are thoroughly influenced, if not determined, by how the person perceives him- or herself. If the sociocultural conditions surrounding the young during the period of socialization do not add up to a unitary lifestyle without inconsistency and conflict, then failure to produce a unitary identity is anticipated. Such failure used to be judged as "pathology" of both the social environment and the personality troubled by ongoing identity crisis.

Earlier writers, concerned with the relationship between social interaction and personality formation, made an understandable assumption of their time; namely, that the various roles a person carries out are compatible. James M. Baldwin, Charles Cooley, George H. Mead[18] and others took as their point of departure the small community where a member was known as a total person and whose actions exhibited logical and ethical coherence. These notions of personality growth presupposed the small-town environment characteristic of nineteenth-century America, where the primary group was the consistent and almost exclusive influence on the development of the social nature of the individual. These early social psychologists described the rise of the social self as the process of taking over integrated sets of attitudes by way of role playing, role taking, and internalization of the "generalized other." The product of this process was normally an integrated personality system.

Although contemporary social psychologists usually agree with the logic of this learning principle, they believe that since the social environment has undergone significant structural changes, the process and product of personality development have also changed. The typical socialization environment of the urban-industrial era is no longer the small, intimate community where

---

[18]James M. Baldwin, *Social and Ethical Interpretations in Mental Development* (New York: Macmillan, 1897); Charles H. Cooley, *Human Nature and the Social Order* (New York: Scribner, 1902); and George H. Mead, *Mind, Self, and Society* (Chicago: University of Chicago Press, 1934).

a basic set of values and norms was the orienting force; it is now the anonymous city, with compartmentalized positions and roles no longer uniformly coordinated by a value premise. The typical member of modern society no longer develops a uniform outlook on life, but rather learns situational ways of solving problems. Absence of an overall personality premise is related to what psychiatrists have come to define as "problems of identity." Since role performances normally have formative impact, absence of coherence among the roles an individual enacts can result in lack of sufficient *Prägnanz*, the integrative quality of personality. Uncertainty about one's place in life has a concomitant reflection in one's self-perception.

Max Lerner sees modern Americans engaged in intense search for models and called the symptoms of this groping the "neurosis of the ego."[19] Lerner assumes that this type of mass neurosis is a novel symptom of Western people and quite different from previous mass problems. A previous endemic neurosis of Western civilization was the "neurosis of the id and the superego," which arose primarily from the patriarchal family setting in Europe, with its strict values and discipline, causing widespread repression of personal desires. In other words, while the causality of the modal European neurosis lay in patriarchal authoritarianism prompting various types of repression, the more recent American problem lies in the lack of models and compelling convictions.

The reason for the lack of personal models can be traced to the nature of modern social structure, which contains discrete and almost mutually isolated sets of interaction. Performing on various and often incompatible "stages" of social life has been described in terms of "off-stage" and "on-stage," "team," "script," "front," "audience," and "performance." These terms of the theater can easily be translated into social-structural concepts, such as positions, private vs. public, group, role, social behavior, the public, and role enactment. Use of dramaturgical imagery paints a vivid picture of modern persons as multi-*personae*, as opportunists, supersensitive to every ephemeral demand in the social environment.

Life in society is described as analogous to an infinite array of different "stage plays" where every social situation calls for its own script and character. The individual who is the character must keep one set of motives secret from the other. He or she compartmentalizes not only conduct but also the *reasons* for it. There is always a different audience; there is always a different set of actors; and, finally, there are always different goals and different motivations. The purpose of the performance is to influence others and gain success. This is usually done cooperatively by a team under the management of impressions. Hence, according to a number of modern sociologists, in lieu of the

[19]Max Lerner, *America as a Civilization* (New York: Simon & Schuster, 1957), pp. 694–97.

concept of the self as an autonomous moral agent or as the humanistic person of taste, the self is now viewed as an opportunistic agent observing, at best, purely discretionary rules.

It is easy to see that according to the traditional theory most modern youths suffer from lack of unitary identity, since the sociocultural environment in postindustrial America is not unitary and integrated. What are some of the modern features that cause the lack of unitary environment? One trait, ubiquitous in the lives of nearly all young Americans, is the mass media, especially television.

Most characters of the mass media exert influence on development of personality traits in an extremely situational fashion; that is, they depict situations that are often unrealistically isolated from the overall life context of the person portrayed. Limited character portrayal is responsible for a novel type of learning. Instead of presenting a holistic "significant other," whose various actions follow logically from basic values and norms, enabling generalization and prediction about other possible actions, the mass media present characters who exhibit behavior forms applicable to only a specific situation. In effect, the model depicts only a *situation* and not a total person. A child continuously exposed to the mass media tends to adopt such situational styles of problem solving and, as a result, may come to exhibit incompatible behavior forms. In crisis situations the youth may recall a style of problem solving that was shown by the hero or the successful villain of the mass media, and he or she may be induced to act accordingly. Hence the manner of solving a problem in one moment may be logically and morally incongruent with the manner of solution in another moment, since they are not derived from a common premise. The overly influenced youth, who has only minimal live models, tends to have no common premise but only unrelated stereotypes by which to determine solutions.

In a sense, the youth behaves like a different person in each situation, and the question of who the "real" person is becomes hypothetical. The youth is equipped with a number of different *personae*, which can change from situation to situation with no one *persona* more important than any other.

Lest this type of individual be confused with an abnormal or mentally disturbed person, it should be emphasized that reference is being made to the normal member of society, very much the same sort of person whom David Riesman described as the other-directed personality, who presumably is the prevailing personality type in modern American society.[20] Professor Riesman described this typical member of society as a gregarious creature, highly sensitive to the opinions and ideas of other people, constantly scanning the social horizon with a "radar screen" to pick up acceptable modes of

---

[20]David Riesman, *The Lonely Crowd* (New Haven: Yale University Press, 1950).

conduct. Ultimately, dependence on other-directedness creates a social atmosphere where actions are defined more by social sensitivity than by premises.

It would be misleading to suggest that other-directedness is the sole product of the mass media's characters and models. An equally prolific source of multiple *personae* is the social structure. Youth living in a modern urban-industrial environment are ensconced in a social structure that patterns life into discrete multipositional segments, thereby producing a world view that reflects confusion and conflict. For example, as members of the family they are expected to respect parents and to conform to a way of life that is partially obsolete in the light of what they learn in school. In their religious congregations they are taught dogmas and assumptions that are difficult to reconcile with scientific training and understanding. When they enter occupational positions, they are expected to interact differently with superiors than with colleagues. In sum, the different environments—family, job, school, church, peers, and military—call for different manners and values. In a sense, these different environments call not only for different behavior, but virtually for different persons.

Traditional social psychological theory is largely obsolete and a more flexible model of modern identity formation is needed. Actually, the revision might be more radical than that—perhaps *any* theory of identity has become superfluous and has lost applicability.

This is exactly what sociologist Erving Goffman argued: a style of social interaction has arisen that no longer requires—or could even profit from—a unitary identity.[21] The new interactional mode is *situational performance.* Such performance is too transient to be couched in terms of roles, since the concept of role connotes consistency and permanence. By 1982, when he died, Goffman had exhibited an increasing tendency to get away from the old labels and interpretations that suggested a simpler and more unitary lifestyle. Starting in this first book, *The Presentation of Self in Everyday Life*, Goffman used the language of the theater to describe the multi-"stage" life of modern urban persons. In his earlier writing, Goffman agreed with sociologist Robert E. Park, who felt that most social behavior consists of role playing and of following a consensual script and that "it is in these roles that we know each other; it is in these roles that we know ourselves."[22]

In his subsequent writings, Goffman deemphasized role as the prompting device for behavior, and moved "appearance" and "interpersonal manipu-

---

[21]Erving Goffman's most important works pertaining to this question include: *The Presentation of Self in Everyday Life* (Garden City, NY: Doubleday, 1959); *Interaction Ritual* (Garden City, NY: Doubleday, 1967); *Strategic Interaction* (Philadelphia: University of Pennsylvania Press, 1969); *Relations in Public* (New York: Basic Books, 1971); *Frame Analysis: An Essay on the Organization of Experience* (Cambridge, MA: Harvard University Press, 1974); *Forms of Talk* (Philadelphia: University of Pennsylvania Press, 1981).

[22]Robert E. Park, *Race and Culture* (Glencoe, IL: The Free Press, 1950), p. 249.

lation" to center stage. He called his data-gathering methodology "observations of a participant witness of contemporary urban America," and proceeded to describe what he thought was the prevailing mode of modern social interaction: the face-to-face interaction in daily settings. Contemporary Americans, he felt, put a premium on mutual manipulation under protected and consensual ground rules. These rules use body language and social ritual—eye contact, regard for personal space, ceremonies of apologies and explanations, vocabulary of embarrassment, and ceremonial profanities—more than abstract principles to govern the ubiquitous and ephemeral encounters in public life (*Relation in Public* and *Interaction Ritual*). Goffman reminded us of the myriad calculative, gamelike elements in our mutual dealings, which manifest themselves in even the shortest-lived encounters (*Strategic Interaction*). Governed by unspoken and unwritten understandings, these "games" are carefully polished front-stage performances (meticulously prepared by impression management) that testify to humans' need to maintain social appearances. Goffman was convinced that by looking at these sociological aspects we can derive greater understanding of modern humans than by examining purely psychological attributes.

In *Frame Analysis* and *Forms of Talk*, Goffman went much farther than in his previous writings and suggested that we are always putting on performances even in situations where we believe we "are ourselves." To explain these behavior patterns in terms of the old role concept would constitute a bias in the direction of wholeness and authenticity, which is not at all contained in such behavior. What is really taking place is a series of one-person shows that pragmatically change according to the contingencies of the various situations. Apparently, Goffman came to the conviction that "real life activities" are nothing but dramatic realizations—which means that there is no substance behind the show. Goffman was thus saying that we all wear social masks, and if we take off one mask, we will not discover a real self but only additional masks. This implies that the nature of the *situation* determines the character of the self.

The interpretation of humans as "appearances" rather than abiding selves or consistent identities is partly supported by other social scientists. Erik Erikson has argued that "ego identity" is not a fixed entity but rather a dynamic process that continues throughout the life cycle.[23] Growth and change of identity are related to a person's affiliations and identifications. Since in our modern age such external influences are subject to turmoil, identity processes have become labile. In recent writings, Erikson has downgraded the value of these groups, referring to them as dangerous "pseudospecies" that maintain their own uniqueness by dehumanizing others. Each of these groups enforces a "normalcy" that may, in fact, be pathological.

---

[23]Erik H. Erikson, *Life History and the Historical Moment* (New York: Norton, 1975).

The most outspoken proponent of Goffman's brand of the "new look" social psychology is Kenneth J. Gergen, who feels that the traditional assumption, that a firm and coherent sense of identity is necessarily a measure of normalcy, is an obsolete bias standing in the way of taking a fresh and unencumbered look at postindustrial interaction as it actually is.[24] The maintenance of a rigid, unidimensional identity would prove highly dysfunctional in our society; it would impede the smoothness and expedience with which flexible and pragmatic "appearance"-oriented modern humans interact and satisfy their needs. In fact, the old rigidity with which the traditional social psychologist predicated healthy and happy human beings would render them stifled and unhappy. Perhaps the old emphasis on "identity" has become a forced question that artificially conjures up some kind of imagined need to perpetuate the concept.

In sum, we have thus two theoretical interpretations of the relationship between modern social interaction and the personality system: the traditional one, upholding a unitary identity as a measure of normalcy, and the new multi-*personae* theory, rejecting the old rigidity and seeing functionality in the new flexibility. The impact of modern social interaction (with its ingredients of multiple and inconsistent reference groups, significant others, and roles) on adolescents can therefore be interpreted in two ways:

1. According to the traditional theory, a holistic identity is of paramount significance, and modern social interaction is seriously stunting its growth. The impact of situational character portrayal via the mass media and the diverse and discrete "stage lives" of people enmeshed in modern social structure have aggravating effects on adolescence. If adults suffer identity problems from the influence of such compartmentalized and ephemeralized social situations, how much more must adolescents, who are intensely involved in the process of identity formation. If identification situations, positions, and roles are isolated from each other, situationally defined, and often incompatible, isomorphic reflections become noticeable in the personalities of the young.

Situational definitions make learning difficult because the young individual can generalize only minimally and must learn the "proper" style for each separate situation. To accomplish such situational adroitness requires a longer period of learning than the simple and old-fashioned specific-action-follows-general-premise style of learning. Adolescence can become a lifelong condition if a young individual is unable to find a common denominator, a basic premise for specific behavior, among or beyond the multiple *personae* that modern society demands from him or her. For most adolescents, performing multiple characters will be a confusing problem of identity.

[24]Kenneth J. Gergen, "Multiple Identity: The Healthy, Happy Human Being Wears Many Masks," *Psychology Today*, 5 (May 1972): 31–66.

2. According to the new multi-*personae* theory, the question of identity may well be a white elephant inherited from a bygone era that does not apply to modern society. Humans involved in a postindustrial system must rely on communicative and interactional skills and not on rigid principles. In essence, personality development has become part of the activities of the marketplace, of the web of "strategy of success" within the manipulative process of interpersonal relations. Goals, norms, roles, and definitions fluctuate from one social situation to the other, and identity has lost its functionality. The modern person has become a *persona dramatis* — an actor of many scripts.

The problem of adolescents lies therefore more in learning skills to eliminate interpersonal friction than in learning basic roles and principles. Rather than integrity, adolescents must learn sensitivity; rather than proceeding by chart and principled plan, they embark on their life-journeys equipped with "social radar" that will tell them situational circumstances and help them to circumnavigate barriers and dangers.

Perhaps this novel type of human interaction is already visible in the relations between the sexes. Rather than proceeding according to traditional sex-role definitions, many young Americans embark on a course of interaction relatively unfettered by sex stereotypes and try to come to terms with each other on an individualistic level.

The future of identity formation, with which adolescence is so intimately associated, depends largely on which theory will prove to be true. At this time prognosis is difficult. Perhaps, indeed, we are facing the emergence of a new type of *Homo sapiens*, one who is conditioned by the postindustrial system to be skillful, communicative, and more concerned about practical problem solving than about how basic purposes and principles should pattern the world.

SUMMARY

In spite of confusion about the definition of *personality*, there is consensus of its social, processual, phasic, and *Gestalt* nature. In addition, development of normal personality depends on physiological prerequisites and adequate care in human group environment.

The question of identity formation as the core process of personality presents extraordinary difficulties. Traditional theory emphasized identity as the stabilizing, guiding, and integrating function of the person. Its stability depends, however, on the stability and consistency of the social environment. Concern has been expressed that this environment has become fragmented and inconsistent, thus effecting an isomorphic repercussion in the individual's identity. The characters of the mass media as well as the nature of modern social structure, with its multipositional life situations, induce modern humans to act in terms of isolated sets of social interaction. The various "scripts" and ethics that are part of modern social existence tend to endow the individual actor with multiple *personae*. This has repercussions for the person's identity, since the basic question "Who am I" demands a unitary answer.

A more recent social-psychological formulation deemphasizes the importance of identity and ascribes greater importance to the learning of communicative and interactional skills. Humans are thought of as functioning more efficiently without the rigidity of traditional roles. Adolescents, therefore, would do better to concentrate on learning skills rather than rigid principles.

The future will show which theory earns greater credibility. Future generations of adolescents will either display greater identity confusion or will adjust to the new "games" of social interaction that require less "script" and more intuition.

There is an escape hatch open to the young: they can get away from some of the confusion and conflict by seceding to subcultures with norms and values that lend temporary orientation.

4

Adolescence: Its Time and Place in Social Development

Growing up in a modern urban-industrial society has become a complex venture; traditional ideas social scientists and psychologists have held about the socialization process are largely anachronistic. In a sense, modern *Homo sapiens* no longer is in control of a unitary personality system, but must be understood from the perspective of a number of social-psychological concepts. Some of the major ones are discussed in this chapter.

REFERENCE GROUP

While it is true that the young child depends heavily on an immediate group environment for physical survival, this does not mean that a young person, once he or she has learned how to relate to abstract ideas and images, must remain on the relatively primitive level of relating only to physically present persons. People's effort to understand themselves and their universe is not limited, although highly influenced, by membership groups. *Direct* physical contact with other persons is not necessary to absorb ideas, philosophies, and religions. An actual example is that of a young man with no social connections to Greeks or corresponding ethnic subgroups in the United States, who decided to embrace Greek Orthodox Christianity. His decision was based not on social interaction but entirely on reading and abstract reflecting.

This example illustrates the difference between the reference group and the membership group. Human ability to abstract can free them from face-to-face interaction for information and acquisition of values. The concept of reference group was developed mainly to define the process whereby individuals derive norms and values without necessarily being in physical contact with those persons holding the emulated view. Normally, however, most of a person's membership groups also function as reference groups. In the cases where the two groups do not coincide, serious conflicts may arise for the person involved in both.

The relationship between adolescent behavior and reference groups is complex. Modern urban-industrial environment offers youth a heretofore unknown number of potential reference groups, and value derivation can proceed through ubiquitous images and models presented in the mass media. As a result of the diversity of reference groups, the adolescent's personality development is beset with a number of complications:

Shifting reference groups. A significant aspect of adolescence is the gradual shift in orientation from teenage standards to adult norms and values. Usually, the adolescent has no choice but to ultimately accept adult behavior patterns.

Multiple reference groups. Often because of personal preference, but more often because of mandatory conditions, the adolescent is involved in a number of membership groups, which usually constitute reference groups at the same time. Examples of such combinations for the adolescent are family, school, church, and peer group.

Sebald and White's 1980 study found teenagers divided on reference groups and unevenly aligned with peers and parents. Suburban high schoolers clung to their peers' advice on matters of whom to date, which clubs to join, how to dress, choice of hobby, and reading material. Only 10 percent or fewer of the teenagers would turn to parents in these matters. (This was particularly true of boys; significant boy-girl differences are mentioned in Chapter 12.) On the other side, approximately 50 percent sought parental guidance in matters of choosing a career, going to college, and how to spend money. Comparison with 1960 data shows that this juxtaposition has sharpened and nearly polarized, with teenagers of the 1970s and 1980s drawing distinct demarcation lines as to which issue belongs to which reference group.[1]

---

[1]Hans Sebald and Becky White, "Teenagers' Divided Reference Groups: Uneven Alignment with Parents and Peers," *Adolescence*, 15 (Winter 1980): 979–84.

Conflicting reference groups.   Multiplicity of reference groups frequently leads to conflict. Most conflicts stem from the clash between standards of the peer group and those of the parents. Peers represent a powerful reference group, and researchers have found that the clique's expectations often take precedence over norms and values held by family and adults. "The clique, then, acts as a protective structure which may oppose and evade adult authorities and sanctions."[2]

James S. Coleman, studying high school youth, found considerable conflict when a teenager had to choose between standards of peers and demands of parents.[3] The researcher presented the subjects with a hypothetical situation, asking them what they would do if they were asked to join a particular club to which they had always wanted to belong but at the same time were faced with a request by parents not to join. The response pattern of the students depended on the type of community in which they lived. Responses, gathered from ten different schools, had between 45 to 80 percent of the boys and 60 to 85 percent of the girls stating that they would probably or definitely not join the club against their parents' wishes. Greatest regard for the parents' demands was shown in the smallest school, in "Farmdale," a rural community; the least regard was apparent in "Executive Heights," a large suburban school. The four schools in which 70 percent or more of the boys preferred the parents' advice and the three schools in which 80 percent or more of the girls chose the parents as reference persons were located in smaller, nonurban communities. The schools in which girls and boys were least willing to conform to parents' ideas were two suburban schools, "Newlawn," a working-class suburb, and "Executive Heights," an upper middle-class suburb. The findings indicate that in "Farmdale" and "Marketville," the two smallest schools in a predominantly rural area, teenagers enter adult responsibilities earlier and are more familistically oriented, while in "Executive Heights," adolescents assume adult responsibilities later and remain more peer-oriented. These differences between a small farm community and an upper middle-class suburb illustrate the differential influence of the adolescent reference group. "Executive Heights" reflects a style of life that is spreading in the United States. "Farmdale" and "Marketville" reflect a more familistic style that seems to be gradually disappearing.

Conflicting reference groups tend to interfere with the formation of a unified and unambiguous self-conception. A young woman, for example, on being accepted into a sorority, may yield to informal pressure and develop modes of conduct like smoking and social drinking that would cause her family's disapproval. Another example would be the conflict experienced by a teenager simultaneously involved in a delinquent gang and in a family of law-

[2]Ernest A Smith, *American Youth Culture* (New York: Free Press, 1962), p. 9.
[3]James S. Coleman, *The Adolescent Society* (New York: Free Press, 1963), pp. 138–40.

abiding parents and siblings, or the conflict caused by holding membership in a religious congregation and at the same time being a member of a delinquent group.

Unclear reference groups.   A majority of modern youths experience difficulty in deciding between different, and often incompatible, reference groups, and are frequently torn between them, unable to clearly identify with any single one. This inability to identify completely with any reference group tends to thwart the formation of a clear and stable identity. In a sense, the social environment functions as a mirror showing the person an image of her- or himself. The powerful influence of social repercussion on the person's identity or "self" has been widely accepted as a basic principle of social psychology.[4] If social images are blurred, distorted, or markedly divergent, personality formation will probably reflect these ambiguities.

SIGNIFICANT OTHERS

One might insist it is not groups and their standards but rather individuals and their attitudes that significantly influence attitudes. Social scientists, in an effort to capture the meaning of this relationship, have suggested the concept of "significant other." H. S. Sullivan[5] first coined this concept and believed that significant persons have decisive influence on the perception (including self-perception) of the socializee. Robert K. Merton also tried to conceptualize this influence and suggested the term "reference person."[6] However, the term can be taken to imply volition, consciousness, and choice of reference on the part of the socializee—an assumption that would limit the application of the concept. The concept of significant other does not convey such limitations and thus allows for a greater variety of types of socializer-socializee relationships.

Those having the greatest impact on personality development are parents. Parental behavior constitutes a potential model for role learning. Since many roles can be learned only by observing others, observability of role enactment is important. In cases of general roles, such as the feminine, masculine, and marital, role taking is largely an informal and unconscious

---

[4]George H. Mead, *Mind, Self, and Society* (Chicago: University of Chicago Press, 1934), p. 164; Charles H. Cooley, *Human Nature and the Social Order* (New York: Scribner's, 1902), p. 184; and Alfred R. Lindesmith, Anselm L. Strauss, and Norman K. Denzin, *Social Psychology* (New York: Holt, 1977), pp. 312–48.

[5]As reported by Dorothy R. Blitsten, *The Social Theories of Harry S. Sullivan* (New York: William-Frederick Press, 1953), pp. 74–75.

[6]Robert K. Merton, *Social Theory and Social Structure* (Glencoe, IL: Free Press, 1957), pp. 302–04.

process. Specific roles, such as professional ones, are learned more formally and consciously.

Generally, the young acquire their role perceptions by unconsciously internalizing norms and values reflected by the behavior of models. The importance of this social psychological process can hardly be exaggerated, since role perceptions form the core of one's identity. It is the internalized roles and their degrees of clarity and meaningfulness that make up one's identity. It follows that individuals who are expected to exemplify certain roles possess an immense influence and, to a large extent, bear responsibility for role behavior of the next generation. Role learning and role transmitting may be influenced or disturbed by acts of commission and/or acts of omission. Acts of commission refer to definite instances exhibiting role behavior, such as exerting parental authority, engaging in adult work, and carrying out adult responsibilities. Acts of omission imply absence of exemplification of role behavior, as, for example, chronic father-absence affecting the child. Failure to provide role models is of concern to many behavioral scientists, since role confusion may arise when important norms are neither formally taught nor informally visible.

Children are highly dependent on their parents' example in acquiring sex role and marital role. These role concepts are part of the cultural heritage; that is, they are *learned* ways of behaving and thinking. In many modern societies, the norms that distinguish between masculinity and femininity are no longer as distinct as they were. Vagueness in sex-role definitions and decreasing visibility of parental models have contributed to problems of identity. Young males in the American middle class seem to be particularly vulnerable to the effects of cultural anomie and father-absence. The traditional family—characterized by patriarchal authority, familistic attitudes, and domicile-work combination—has almost vanished in favor of the modern equalitarian family, which emphasizes individualism over familism. Father-absence from the home has become frequent, and the young male has little or no opportunity to observe his father at work. Home life, *at least from the boy's perspective*, has become matriarchal.[7]

Social scientists have disputed the Freudian distinction between love-object and identification-object, preferring to view the relationship between infant and mother as identification and not as love.[8] Thus, learning cultural norms of masculinity necessitates a shift from the original identification-object—mother—to a culturally more acceptable identification-object—father, or some other adult male image. This is not necessary for the girl. As several social scientists have pointed out, the young female has an initial

[7]Talcott Parsons, "Age and Sex in the Social Structure of the United States," *American Sociological Review,* 7 (October 1942): 604–16.

[8]Orvall H. Mowrer, *Psychotherapy: Theory and Research* (New York: Ronald Press, 1953).

advantage in progressing toward appropriate sex-role identity.[9] The boy faces a more precarious situation for, if he does not make the shift of identification early enough during childhood, it may be difficult for him to achieve a masculine identity. Father-absence complicates the shift in identification, and the boy finds himself learning his role more by trial and error than by consistent imitation. As a result, boys more than girls seek and obtain instruction outside of the family and tend to identify with a general cultural image, or with the male *position* in general, while girls identify with the mother as a *person* and not with an impersonal image or position.

Social scientists seem to agree that physical absence of the father, or presence of a father not providing a clear role model, impedes the development of such traits as independence and achievement orientation.[10] Boys lacking adult role models develop more dependent and submissive personality features. In contrast, father-dominated socialization promotes assertive traits in young males.[11]

A word of caution: these traditional assumptions and findings must be reconsidered in the light of at least two major developments. First, progress made by the women's liberation movement has modified the traditional role definitions and stereotypical behavior. Hence, future social-psychological research may come up with different findings, necessitating modification of theory. Second, increasing power and scope of exposure to mass media, particularly television, constitute a change in socialization patterns that calls for modification of the conventional assumption that physically present role models are irreplaceable. For example, studies have found little evidence that father-absent boys are more feminine, dependent, and less aggressive.[12] It is possible that mass media heroes increasingly function as objects of identification.

---

[9]Daniel G. Brown, "Inversion and Homosexuality," *American Journal of Orthopsychiatry,* 28 (April 1958): 424–29; David B. Lynn, "Learning Masculine and Feminine Roles," *Marriage and Family Living,* 25 (February 1963): 103–5; and David B. Lynn, "The Process of Learning Parental and Sex-Role Identification," *Journal of Marriage and the Family,* 28 (November 1966): 466–70.

[10]Talcott Parsons and Robert F. Bales, *Family, Socialization and Interaction Process* (Glencoe, IL: The Free Press, 1955); Urie Bronfenbrenner, "Socialization and Social Class Through Time and Space," in *Readings in Social Psychology,* ed. Eleanor E. Maccoby, et al. (New York: Holt, Rinehart & Winston, 1958), pp. 400–25; and Paul S. Ullman, "Parental Participation in Child Rearing as Evaluated by Social Deviates," *Pacific Sociological Review,* 3 (Fall 1960): 89–95.

[11]Lois W. Hoffman, "The Father's Role in the Family and the Children's Peer Group Adjustment," *Merrill-Palmer Quarterly,* 7 (April 1961): 97–105.

[12]Hans Sebald, "Parent-Peer Control and Masculine-Marital Role Perception of Adolescent Boys," *Social Science Quarterly,* 49 (September 1968): 229–36; Alan J. Crain and Caroline S. Stamm, "Intermittent Absence of Father and Children's Perception of Parents," *Journal of Marriage and the Family,* 27 (August 1965): 344–47; and Joan McCord, William McCord, and Emily Thurber, "Some Effects of Paternal Absence on Male Children," *Journal of Abnormal and Social Psychology,* 54 (May 1962): 361–69.

CULTURE AND ROLE LEARNING

Humans are role-learning animals. They lack innate knowledge or feeling as to what their roles are to be and must rely on culture to provide blueprints specifying how to behave in certain places in the social structure. To achieve role skills takes years of effort, persuasion, and even coercion. Much of what is taught meets with initial resistance, for it thwarts the child's natural impulses. Freud expressed a social psychological principle when he said that the id forces must be replaced by the superego, meaning that the unrefined hedonistic approach to gratification must be replaced by culturally acceptable behavior.[13] The time during which this conversion to cultural standards takes place is turbulent and involves emotions of love and hate, conflict and anxiety, rejection and acceptance. Personality emerges not on the basis of the autonomous *action* of the organism, as orthodox instinctivists maintain, nor solely on the basis of the *reaction* to external stimuli, as many behaviorists claim, but on the basis of *interaction* with other individuals.

The human obligation to learn positional blueprints applies even to the most basic roles, such as the sex roles. It would be a misconception to equate biological maleness and femaleness with learned masculinity and femininity. Cross-cultural studies reveal that perception of masculinity and femininity depends on cultural definitions. Each culture postulates values and norms, defining actions and interactions of males and females.

Role definitions are premises from which specific actions and reactions can be deduced, thus allowing prediction of behavior. Role premises and their application in everyday life therefore become integral parts of the social order—in fact, the *foundation* of social order. For the sake of social order, it does not matter greatly *how* the role premise is formulated, just as long as there is consensus. The variety of formulations is exemplified by natives on some Polynesian islands who virtually reverse Western concepts of masculinity and femininity. Men tend the hearth and the children, while females perform the more strenuous outdoor work.

Definitions often change over time, especially in dynamic urban-industrial societies. Many qualities looked on as strictly masculine or feminine fifty years ago are not considered so today. Such changing conceptions invalidate instruments of behavioral scientists that try to measure sex-differentiation criteria. Examination of one of the earliest (1936) sex-differentiating instruments, the M-F (masculinity-femininity) inventory,[14] shows that many items are no longer relevant in determining masculinity or femininity. Cultural conceptions have been modified—generally in the direction of more diffused

---

[13]See Sigmund Freud's discussion of the repressive and often frustrating aspects of group life in his *Outline of Psychoanalysis* (New York: Norton, 1949), pp. 19, 121.

[14]Lewis M. Terman and Catherine C. Miles, *Sex and Personality* (New York: McGraw-Hill, 1936).

standards. One researcher found that in order to devise a valid and reliable instrument applicable today, more than one-half of the test items of the original M-F inventory would have to be discarded or modified.[15]

Learning to interact in terms of social roles is probably the most important function of socialization. To achieve adequate social participation, the young must internalize role prescriptions as cognitive and affective predispositions; that is, they must look at the world in certain ways and experience certain prescribed emotions. A young boy thus comes to see manliness in terms of courage and physical prowess and experiences profound emotional reactions should he be asked, for example, to wear girls' clothes. However, in order to perform any social role adequately, the boy must also be familiar with the other social roles in his environment. Understanding this network of interacting roles has been conceptualized as the "generalized other."[16] Personality grows concomitantly with role understanding. In fact, internalization of roles is almost synonymous with growth of personality, and internalized roles with which one identifies form the core of one's personality, the "self."

To avoid the mistake of looking for sameness of personality features where two individuals have internalized the same roles, it must be emphasized that a role is characterized by *personal* meaning and by the place it occupies among the other internalized roles and attitudes. The perception of one's role is a *Prägnanz*—and as all Prägnanzes, is highly personalized. The motivation it commands in a particular personality will not be the same as in other personalities. Thus the uniform role requirements are modified by idiosyncracies. For example, the role of girl in a given society is part of the cultural blueprint, but the role internalization of any particular girl is a specific variant and more than just a mirror image of the blueprint.

Another way of looking at the process of role internalization is through a theory describing the relationship between social structure and the personality system as *isomorphic interpenetration*.[17] The theory assumes that cultural norms interpenetrate both the personality system and social structure. In the personality system these norms manifest themselves as motivations, and in the social system they are known as role expectations attached to positions. In an "ideal-type" society, motivations and roles are isomorphic; that is, both exhibit themselves in the same form.

However, "ideal-types" seldom exist in reality. In American society there is considerable confusion concerning the specifics of male and female roles. For example, roles prescribed for college women tend to be contradictory. One study, dealing with college coeds, found that some attitudes necessary

[15]Sebald, "Parent-Peer Control."

[16]Mead, *Mind, Self, and Society*, p. 154.

[17]Talcott Parsons, "Psychology and Sociology," in *For A Science of Social Man*, ed. John Gillin (New York: Macmillan, 1954).

for a woman to successfully play the "feminine" role tended to interfere with her performance in the role of "modern" woman with emphasis on efficiency, independence, and self-assertion.[18] At times it is the independent "modern" female who will chafe under the pressure to conform to the "feminine" pattern, while at other times family and college will thrust the "modern" role on the girl. Generally speaking, American culture confronts the young female with powerful challenges to excel in competitive endeavors and to adopt techniques identical to those of the male. Later in life, however, the very success in meeting these challenges can cause frustration. Psychiatric opinion maintains that the early-learned habit of competing with the opposite sex can cause sexual and marital maladjustments as competitive attitudes are carried into the realm of sexual relations.[19]

The American teenager's task of learning basic roles is complicated not only by absence or rejection of visible models, but also by vagueness of role definition. Vague role concepts seem to be related to at least two conditions: (1) Parents suffer from "cultural lag" and have difficulty in conveying role definitions that fit the technological and social environment of their children. (2) The general culture is nonspecific, emphasizing personal choice.

In sum, the American ethos of individual freedom acts as an agent of uncertainty, leaving the young without clearly differentiated sex-role definitions, requiring them to take extra time to search for clarity. The matter of changing roles applies most acutely to today's young women. Their roles are undergoing more alteration than any other role, and this phenomenon merits additional discussion.

CHANGING SEX ROLES

Traditionally, American society, as most societies, has upheld polarized images of male and female, each with contrasting attitudes and behavior. But postindustrial conditions have challenged these images. Modern science and technology have affected the traditional division of labor between the sexes and brought about a reconsideration of thinking in terms of two essentially different lifestyles. The women's liberation movement feels that there is neither biological nor social justification for dividing humanity into feminine and masculine categories. The movement gained momentum to the point where many young Americans, especially young women, abandoned stereotypical role behavior.

---

[18]Mirra Komarovsky, "Cultural Contradictions and Sex Roles," *American Journal of Sociology*, 52 (November 1946): 184–89.
[19]Bruno Bettelheim, "Growing Up Female," *Harper's*, October 1962, pp. 120–28.

What is happening in essence is a modification of age-old cultural blueprints, according to which previous generations have patterned their interaction, and inauguration, at least during the transitional stage, of a pronounced degree of interpersonal anomie.

Reference to a "transitional stage" raises the question of what the end (or next) stage will be. In other words, what will be the nature of human interaction after the typical sex-role interaction has been abandoned or radically modified? The answer emphasizes a nonsexist style of *human* interaction expected to replace a sex-stereotyped lifestyle. Some find this starkly individual-centered prospect utopian, while others defend it only as feasible and necessary.

Whatever the future, at this time there is a significant eroding of the traditional stereotypes. Sex-role blueprints have become blurred, and prediction of a person's behavior on the basis of gender is no longer as reliable as it used to be.

This is particularly true for the female role. Role limitations and expectations have been vastly liberated for the girl and the woman, but not for the boy and the man. The male role has remained virtually unchanged and still reflects rigid and stereotypical norms of behavior and appearance.

A striking example has been—and still is—the reaction by the adult society toward "unmasculine" hairstyles of boys. Their ponytails, braids, or simply long hair caused more furor during the counterculture years than any other style or fad that emerged among the teenagers. Antagonism against boys' hirsute deviations has never died down. In 1990, school officials in Bastrop, Texas, daily sequestered an eight-year-old boy into a 10 by 13 foot isolation room, where he was taught by substitute teachers; additionally he was banned from gym classes and from eating in the cafeteria. His offense: refusal to cut his seven-inch ponytail. His parents appealed to the school board to lift the confinement, but it refused to discontinue the disciplinary measure on the basis that it violated the dress code. A state district judge supported the school's decision whereupon the parents threatened to take the case to the U.S. Court of Appeals. Their contention: "If girls are allowed to wear their hair long, boys should be too."[20]

Ludicrous as the case may appear on the surface, it tells us something of sociological significance: (1) Deviation from the traditional masculine role is unacceptable. (2) The vehemence of persecution with which male deviations are met have no parallel in the disapproval, if any, of female deviations from the traditional role.

Boys and men have felt the effects of the changes in the female role. As a result, they have had to reorient themselves, more subconsciously than

[20]"Education," *Time*, December 3, 1990, p. 57.

consciously, toward the female role in general, and their girlfriends, lovers, spouses, and other female associates in specific. The reorientation is unfortunately often combined with a good deal of confusion, sometimes resulting in frustration and even hostility.

There are a number of areas in which liberated female behavior has become noticeable. One interesting area deals with competition between men and women. Traditionally, the female tried to understate her intellect and tone down "success" when compared with men. Psychologists termed this attitude "fear of success." Presumably this fear was motivated by fear of deviating from the cultural blueprint, which stressed noncompetition and nonaggression vis-à-vis men. Traditional sex roles had tasks divided in such a fashion that competition was minimal. Postindustrial conditions, however, have brought the sexes closer together in career possibilities and allowed men and women to compete against each other.

Two related studies explored role diffusion and the connected anxieties in a sample of medical students in the 1960s[21] and early 1970s.[22] Whereas the earlier study found that 65 percent of the women had "fear of success" as compared with 10 percent of the men, the more recent study (using the same variables and the same school) found, somewhat puzzlingly, an unchanged percentage of the women but now 77 percent of the men afflicted with achievement anxiety. Details of the study disclosed, however, that the nature of "fear of success" was essentially different between the sexes. While for women the motive to avoid success was in both studies primarily based on the fear of experiencing social rejection or being found unfeminine, for the men the motive was primarily the questioning of the value of the achievement per se, especially in regard to academic and professional success. This type of anxiety had not been found in the 1965 study. Since the follow-up study was conducted in 1971, at the height of countercultural agitation, the heightened sense of questioning the traditional masculine role, the old career definition, and materialism in general may well have been reflected in the phenomenal increase in men's fear of success.

The philosophical base for men's fear of success was apparently still solid after the counterculture years. A late 1970s study supported the earlier findings of women's fear being based on personal-relational considerations, while men's fear was more abstract and philosophical. The latter feared their

---

[21]Matina Horner, "The Motive to Avoid Success and Changing Aspirations of College Women," in *Readings on the Psychology of Women*, ed. J. Bardwick (New York: Harper & Row, 1972), pp. 62–67.

[22]Lois W. Hoffman, "Fear of Success in Males and Females: 1965 and 1971," *Journal of Consulting and Clinical Psychology*, 42 (June 1974): 353–58.

lives might become one-sided and unfulfilled and that they might sacrifice humanitarian concern for self-advancement.[23]

Woman's fear of success was more narrowly based and dealt with fear of affiliative loss, specifically with the fear of being rejected by peers. These peers were mostly female associates (roommates, friends) and so, unlike males, anxiety arose more from same-sex in-group relations than from female–male interaction or competition. This finding introduces a sour note to the hopes of the women's liberation movement since serious obstacles to the free unfolding of talent are apparently generated *within* the female peer group and not necessarily (at least not directly) from the outside by a male group. It seems the Trojan horse of the women's movement is their own in-group.

That women's fear of success is no longer (if it ever was) determined by overwhelming concern as to how they might appear to men is illustrated by Mirra Komarovsky's longitudinal study comparing attitudes of the 1950s with those of the 1970s. In response to the question "When on dates how often have you pretended to be intellectually inferior to the man?" 32 percent reported "very often," "often," or "several times," 26 percent reported "once or twice," and 42 percent said "never" in 1950, as compared with 15 percent, 30 percent, and 55 percent respectively in 1971.[24]

Indeed, a study in the early 1980s discovered a new trend in which men, *not* women, tended to more often play "dumb" and knowingly underplay their intelligence and knowledgeability. The findings showed that more men than women underplayed their intelligence in almost all situations, including interactions with friends, strangers, bosses, coworkers, dates, and children. Understating was most common among persons with more education and high-status careers.[25]

This finding radically deviates from results of previous studies, in which women were consistently found to fake inferior capabilities. Further research is needed to establish whether this indeed is a reversal of a gender-differentiated attitude and whether it is perhaps a sort of male "reaction formation" to changes in women's roles.

[23]Phoebe K. Schnitzer's study reported in *Human Behavior*, August 1977, pp. 51–52. Another study, surveying 20,000 teenagers, corroborates that girls indeed are consistently more interpersonally and affiliatively oriented, have more empathy for their friends, and place greater emphasis on sociability; Daniel Offer, Eric Ostrov, and Kenneth I. Howard, *The Adolescent: A Psychological Self-Portrait* (New York: Basic Books, 1981), pp. 75, 95f.

[24]Mirra Komarovsky, "Cultural Contradictions and Sex Roles: The Masculine Case," *American Journal of Sociology*, 78 (January 1973): 873–84, and *Dilemmas of Masculinity: A Study of College Youth* (New York: Norton, 1976).

[25]Michael Hughes and Walter G. Gove, "Playing Dumb," *Psychology Today*, 15 (October 1981): 74.

Yankelovich's national survey corroborated the trend visible in the above-mentioned studies. For example, the traditional image of what it means to be a man seems to have undergone a change in the eyes of young adults. The old emphases on "good masculine looks," "physical strength," and "being handy around the house," come in last in a list of twelve qualities. The new major preferences heading the list are (1) concern with the sexual satisfaction of the woman, (2) the ability to be a good economic provider, and (3) having strong moral views about what is right and wrong.[26]

Similarly, the view of women's role has undergone change. In a four-year follow-up study of college students, a marked decline in the endorsement of a traditional role definition for women was found. At the time of entry into college in 1967, a national sample of freshmen were asked their opinions concerning the statement "The activities of married women are best confined to the home and family." At that time, 66 percent of the men and 44 percent of the women indicated agreement ("agree strongly" or "agree somewhat"). A resurvey of the same respondents in 1972 showed a sharp decline in endorsement of the traditional position, with only 30 percent of the men and 15 percent of the women agreeing with it.[27]

Statistics indicate that young women are also catching up with men in areas that are eminently destructive—signaling, possibly, that they are now exposed to the same tensions typical of the male role. Such tensions lurk particularly in urban centers. For instance, metropolitan areas across the country have experienced a phenomenal rise in the female suicide rate during the decade of the mid-1960s to the mid-1970s. Los Angeles County, for example, reported that the suicide rate for males under twenty years of age went from 3 to 10 per 100,000 population, a more than threefold increase. However, for females in the same age group the change was from .4 to 8, a twentyfold increase. Similarly, while the suicide rate for males between twenty and thirty years of age slightly more than doubled, the rate for females of the same age increased over fourfold.[28] Girls particularly vulnerable to suicide were "those whose fathers have been either uncaring or long absent from home, and first-born girls, particularly those with younger brothers."[29]

Increase in female suicides appears to be a typical postindustrial phenomenon and can also be illustrated by the German example. In the 1960s and 1970s the proportion of women among the nation's two to three percent

[26]Daniel Yankelovich, *The New Morality: A Profile of American Youth in the 1970s* (New York: McGraw-Hill, 1974), p. 39.

[27]Alan E. Bayer et al., "Four Years After College Entry," *ACE Research Report*, 8 (Washington, DC: American Council on Education, 1973).

[28]"Young Suicides," *Society*, 9 (June 1972): 12.

[29]Pamela Cantor's research at Boston University reported in *Time*, January 3, 1972, p. 57.

alcoholics was only 10 percent. Statistics from the early 1990s indicate that the proportion has increased to 30 percent.[30]

An "empathic ecological explanation" of the fluctuations of suicide rates was offered by psychiatrist Daniel Offer and his coworkers, who studied the suicide rate among adolescents over several decades. They hit upon a significant positive correlation between adolescent suicide rates and changes in the proportion of adolescents in the U.S. population. Apparently, density of youth population is significant insofar as "it may be more difficult for an adolescent to gain a sense of self-worth and to find friends in the large impersonal high schools of today than in the smaller schools of the past.[31] The researchers suspect that an isolated and depressed youth may interpret his or her efficiently bubbling environment as a sign that everybody is functioning fine while he or she is not. Observing seemingly well-functioning peers, and assuming they are such without knowing for certain, may further lower already low and vulnerable self-confidence and push him or her into withdrawal. A resulting sense of hopelessness may plunge the youth into attempted or completed suicide.

The ecological explanation may explain why suicides in urban centers are strikingly higher than elsewhere. It may specifically explain the extreme increases in suicides among women in urban settings. Persons with greater affiliative and relational needs—as women are found to have according to pertinent studies—may react more acutely to urban isolation.

In addition, the Offer team found that girls consistently feel worse about themselves on *all* self-image scales, particularly on the self-esteem scale.[32] As if that were not enough, the girls of the 1970s surveys felt worse than those in the 1960s surveys. It is possible that the generally worsening self-image of young women, for whatever reason, contributes to the "catching up" with the male suicide rate.

Another conspicuous symptom of changing life conditions of the American woman is reflected in the number of violent crimes performed by women, which has increased at rates six and seven times greater than that of crimes of violence committed by men. Rutgers University Professor of Criminal Justice Freda Adler did a study of the impact of political and social changes on the criminality of women and found that the "new woman" in crime—from the liberated prostitute to the revolutionary terrorist—is responsible for the striking ascent of the female crime rates especially in homicide, armed robbery, embezzlement, and aggravated assault.[33]

---

[30]H. W. Goedde and D. P. Agarwal, "Genetic Protection," *German Research*, Fall 1990, p. 10.

[31]Offer, Ostrov and Howard, *The Adolescent*, p. 124.

[32]Ibid., p. 95.

[33]Freda Adler, *Sisters in Crime: The Rise of the New Female Criminal* (New York: McGraw-Hill, 1975).

On the positive side of the women's liberation movement, an influx into formerly male-dominated training and professions, such as medicine, dentistry, law, engineering, and politics has been noted. For example, female enrollment in medical schools increased from 13 percent in 1972 to about 25 percent in the fall of 1974, and more male than female medical students are dropping out during the first crucial year. Similarly, female enrollment in law schools has progressively increased, from 3.6 percent in 1960 to 9.3 percent in 1971 to 20 percent in 1974. The American Bar Association reported that the proportion of practicing female attorneys is sharply increasing, rising from 2.8 percent in 1972 to 7 percent in 1975.[34]

While an upswing in female careerism was sharply noticeable during the 1970s, the 1980s have seen a slowing down of this trend. Taking the decade of the 1970s as a whole, nearly all careers experienced increases in the percentage of female participants. Here are a few examples:

Engineers, .8 to 2.9
Lawyers and judges, 3.6 to 12.4
Physicians, dentists, and related practitioners, 9.3 to 11.9
Social scientists, 21.3 to 34.5
Managers and administrators, 17.6 to 24.6
Construction laborers, .5 to 2.7
Truck drivers, .6 to 2.1[35]

Female influx into professional careers is significantly encouraged by educational achievement—as illustrated by the diminishing differential in male/female completion of higher education. For example, in 1950, 329,000 men and 103,000 women earned bachelor's degrees, the difference being 226,000. The difference has consistently decreased since then, and in 1978 it amounted to only 53,000, with 487,000 men and 434,000 women obtaining college degrees.[36]

The essence of the ongoing changes seems to be that many young women are no longer playing the traditional female role but are working out various types of role combinations and innovations. Teenage girls demand a great deal more than just marriage and motherhood. While they expect to experience some aspects of the old domestic role (spouse, children, home), they also want to complete their education and pursue a meaningful career. Hence the erstwhile dilemma of choosing between one or the other lifestyle is now replaced by the dilemma of trying to combine both. To come to grips

[34]"Women: Still Number Two but Trying Harder," *Time*, May 26, 1975, pp. 40–41.

[35]*Statistical Abstracts of the United States*, 101st ed. (Washington, DC: U.S. Department of the Census, 1980), pp. 418–20.

[36]*Statistical Abstract of the United States* (Washington, DC: Government Printing Office, 1980), p. 165.

with this expanded lifestyle, today's young women must be goal-directed, assertive, and highly adaptable. In order to make the combination of instrumental and expressive roles a creative and happy experience, young women must learn to cope with the tension and confusion that role experimentation usually produces and must be resourceful enough to resolve conflict.[37]

A suggestion was offered by educator Susanne M. Shafer on how to overcome difficulties of role combinations. She suggested a sequential model, whereby girls should plan their lives in phases, for example, school, work experience, career choice, college, marriage, motherhood, reeducation, and reentry into productive work.[38]

The 1980s have seen increasing numbers of women align themselves with this theoretical model. However, some significant deviations are emerging. After college, more and more women prefer to firmly establish themselves in a career, pursue it for an *extended* period, and finally, in their thirties or even forties decide on motherhood—with or without benefit of being married. The proportion of women aged 25 to 29 years who are still childless has jumped sharply. For example, among women born in 1950 (the cohort of 1950), 25 percent had had no children as of 1980 at age thirty, compared with just 14 percent for comparably aged women born ten years earlier. The rate for mothers in their thirties having a first child increased 66 percent, rising from 7.3 first births per 1000 women aged 30 to 34 in 1970 to 12.1 in 1980. The rate for women aged 35 to 39 rose by 33 percent during this period, from 1.8 to 2.4. The steady increase in first-birth rates for women in their thirties has occurred at a time when birth rates for women of other ages have generally fallen, including rates for the traditionally high first-birth categories of women in their teens and early twenties. The desire of many women to complete their education and become established in a career appears to be the important factor in accounting for the high levels of postponed childbearing. In 1979, nearly half of the first-time mothers aged thirty to thirty-four had completed four or more years of college, compared with just 28 percent in 1970.[39]

These postcareer mothers tend to treat motherhood as a sort of second career and attach the dimensions of careerism to the motherhood experience. As a consequence, the child is often metamorphized into a "project" that must prove "successful motherhood" just as the preceding career was meant to yield success and self-realization. It would be worthwhile to specu-

[37]See extensive treatment: David R. Matteson, *Adolescence Today: Sex Roles and the Search for Identity* (Homewood, IL: Dorsey, 1975).

[38]Susanne M. Shafer, "Adolescent Girls and Future Career Mobility," in Robert E. Grinder, ed., *Studies in Adolescence* (New York: Macmillan, 1975), pp. 114–25.

[39]U.S. Department of Health and Human Services, *Monthly Vital Statistics Report*, 31 (May 27, 1982).

late whether or not these postcareer mothers will swell the ranks of those mothers who have come to be defined as "momistic."[40]

While it is true, as we said initially, that the male role has hardly changed, the male nevertheless has had to make adjustments to the more liberated female role. While his options have not changed, those of women have, and the man must adjust to them. Women, on the other side, may evolve their options without needing to consider a changed male role. Their task is to expand their role, and men's task is to adjust. Both tasks require time and patience, and will inevitably produce their share of confusion, frustration, and even animosity.

Mirra Komarovsky introduced the findings of an important study on men's role perceptions by acknowledging that "gender roles today reflect massive institutional and cultural disorganization."[41] She found that although most college men idealistically espouse men's liberation, just as they support women's liberation, they suffer from a dilemma she calls a "double bind." While the young men seem to genuinely favor women's liberation and express a verbal and ideological commitment to it, they experience apparent difficulties in translating this idealism into reality—and, all the while, are unaware of the gap between ideal and real. The double bind arises when they desire a partner who is an equal but who, at the same time, never threatens them or has divergent or contradictory needs—an equal, in short, who is willing to be subordinate. However, by definition, once a woman subordinates herself she is no longer an equal. This contradiction manifests itself in such incongruous expectations as men wanting women to pursue a challenging and creative career, but simultaneously assuming that she will leave her career upon the birth of the first child and, from then on, be a full-time mother and homemaker. Komarovsky concludes that the path of men toward "liberation" is infinitely more complex than that of a mere "escape" from the traditional male role.

In view of the adjustments men have to make, the findings of a study scrutinizing what happens when young men and women meet are pertinent. Overriding the traditional assumption that achieving men and expressive women get along better with each other than men and women whose personalities are less complementary, the study found that it is the androgynous (combining masculine and feminine traits) man and the androgynous woman (measured on the sex-role scale by Stanford University psychologist Sandra Bem) who, when meeting a person for the first time, proved more flexible, communicative, and rewarding. Androgynous people among a sample of college students talked, gestured, smiled, and looked at each other

[40]Hans Sebald, *Momism—The Silent Disease of America* (Chicago: Nelson-Hall, 1976).
[41]Mirra Komarovsky, *Dilemmas of Masculinity: A Study of College Youth* (New York: Norton, 1976), p. 2.

more often than did the traditionally male and female people. The researchers concluded that androgyny makes for more comfortable interaction.[42] However, the study leaves open whether this initially more comfortable interaction will necessarily result in predictable interaction later on.

A skeptic posed the question: Do women really admire the "soft" man? The Alan Alda Syndrome looks splendid on the screen, Sam Allis warned, but women like Alda "not because he epitomizes the sensitive man but because he is a multimillionaire superstar success who also happened to be sensitive." Men are still defined by their performance in the workplace, Allis added. "If women don't like their jobs, they can, at least in theory, maintain legitimacy by going home and raising children. Men have no such alternative . . . If women have suffered from being sex objects, men have suffered as success objects."[43]

From the discussion of the various data presented in this section follows a number of implications for the new man–woman interaction: (1) A decrease in predictability of how one or the other party will act, (2) an increase in the necessity to establish a self-definition that is not merely grounded in gender identity, and (3) a demand to base decisions not on rigid role images but on genuine personal feelings and preferences.

In summary, the modern teenage girl will be exposed to a score of changes and will have to orient herself accordingly:

1. She will experience a decrease in the protection traditionally accorded to women and will be more "on her own" than her mother's generation. As a transitional temptation, she may attempt to juggle the old and the new roles to her advantage—often unfairly so.
2. She will be faced with a rapid increase of options and can expand her preferences nearly infinitely. This includes possibilities in professional careers, education, and lifestyles. Within the latter, she is able to choose among the single status, marriage, family, divorce, abortion, birth control, cohabitation, and so forth.
3. She will be faced with a vastly more complex life that is based less on predictable, rigid blueprints and more on uniquely personal encounters and feelings. The skill to make personal decisions will demand independent thinking.
4. She will become involved in an intense search for her true self, since a cultural matrix based on gender will no longer spell out her identity.
5. She will experience a definite increase in demands on her intellect and responsibility. Having to make independent decisions calls for knowledge, insight, and accountability for the consequences.
6. She will have to learn to cope with increasing frustration and anxiety. While frustrations due to inequality will decrease, frustrations due to life's complexity

[42]William Ickes and Richard Barnes, "Boys and Girls Together—and Alienated," *Journal of Personality and Social Psychology*, 36 (July 1978): pp. 669–83.

[43]Sam Allis, "What Do Men Really Want?" *Time*, Special Issue: Women—The Road Ahead, Fall 1990, p. 81.

and the loss of the security of the old role will more than replace the old frustrations.

THE UNPREDICTABILITY OF SOCIAL CHANGES AND REVERSALS

One of the vexing things about sociological observations is that as soon as they are made, published, and deemed trustworthy descriptions of social reality, new changes emerge over the social horizon, making the old observations obsolete. The seemingly firm ground gained by women's liberation is not necessarily an exception. Hence the adoration of androgyny, the acceptance of women as equals in the arena of career competition, and other achievements of emancipation may not be conquered ground that will never be lost again. Historians know that one cannot make such absolute assumptions. Sociologists, more narrowly focusing upon the here and now, sometimes forget this.

The point is that social-psychological dynamics sometimes shift certain processes into reverse gear and, instead of a constant forward motion, regression to earlier stages takes place. Traditional masculinity and femininity may be waiting in the wings of the social stage, ready to reappear and resume the old scripts.

While this is not the place to dwell on the specific ingredients in the social dynamics that may propel the reversal, it suffices to say that they will most likely prominently feature the frustrations young people experience from role uncertainty and role confusion. There is emotional comfort to be found in social certainty, in knowing one's role and place in the social fabric. This emotional need may well play a major role in eroding the emancipation process.

The late 1980s and early 1990s show signs of reassertion of traditional standards of femininity and masculinity, especially as they were and still are cultivated in the mainstream American middle class. A revealing content analysis of *Seventeen,* a slick teen magazine catering to middle- and upper-middle-class girls, shows the fluctuation of and the return to the old traditions. Professor Kate Peirce concluded from her content analysis, spanning nearly 25 years, that the image of the "in" girl presented by the magazine suggests that she concern herself with "appearance, household activities, and romance and dating. 60% of the editorial copy for each issue for the years 1961, 1972, and 1985 dealt with beauty, fashion, cooking, and decorating."[44] In 1972, a year still heavily influenced by the counterculture, the traditional

---

[44]Kate Peirce, "A Feminist Theoretical Perspective on the Socialization of Teenage Girls Through *Seventeen* Magazine," *Sex Roles,* 23 (October 1990): 491.

image was modified and matched by "self-development" concerns of a more feminist nature. However—and this is the important point—in 1985 the proportions of the two types of fare returned to their 1961 lopsidedness, indicating that the feminist influence was not permanent. In essence, the image of the girl was again affined to kids, kitchen, and housework and the man–woman relationship was again cast into the traditional feminine–masculine mold.

Whether the reversal to the traditional feminine role as reflected in *Seventeen* is an anomaly and a nongeneralizable editorial quirk of the magazine or whether it heralds a reversal that will increasingly become applicable to the general female population awaits further observation. In the meantime it might be a good idea to keep in mind that history is replete with examples of the most incredible reversals and regressions.

MOMISM: INFLICTING PERPETUAL ADOLESCENCE[45]

The Nature and Rise of Momism

Momism has arisen as a peculiar perversion of the personality function in the modern family and focuses on the type of mother who uses her child to gratify her neurotic needs. While the mother, to all outward appearance, does a fine job, her child-rearing practice is geared toward retaining the child and converting him or her into a perennial adolescent.

The rationale for treating this clinical issue here is that it deals with an adolescence-producing problem that is increasing in the United States and has assumed regular features in the structure of American society: with amazing frequency, Momism has become a feature of the American middle class. Statistics indicate that increasing numbers of middle-aged women (after having experienced extrafamilial careers), as well as increasing numbers of younger, unmarried women, aspire to enjoy the psychological gratifications expected from motherhood. (Chapter 8 presents related statistics.) In the process they approach motherhood with careerist principles in mind.

Early writers to call attention to Momism included Philip Wylie and Sidney C. Howard.[46] They felt that American motherhood was becoming a public danger, inflicting psychological harm on children. They stimulated investigation by social scientists, and the reference to a "Mom" gradually

---

[45]The treatment of Momism in this section focuses on a specific application of the concept—its effects on adolescence. A fuller discussion can be found in Hans Sebald, *Momism—The Silent Disease of America* (Chicago: Nelson-Hall, 1976).

[46]Philip Wylie, *Generation of Vipers* (New York: Rinehart and Co., 1942), and Sidney C. Howard, *The Silver Cord: A Satire in Three Acts* (New York: Scribner's, 1928).

became a concept describing the type of mother who retards her child's maturity.[47]

In previous generations, the wife-mother role was more or less the only life task available to women. Although this meant limited freedom, it also meant little anxiety, since women's lifestyle was free from ambiguity. With the advent of women's liberation, the traditional role became only *one* of a spectrum newly available. While this change added freedom to the lives of women, it also added a new worry. It brought restless soul-searching to clarify the question of how the new options could best be used. Liberation from the old-fashioned role introduced the same compulsion toward achievement as has been the psychological torment of the male.

And it is at this juncture that many a half-liberated woman takes an ironic turn: she opts for staying home and becoming an outstanding mother. Motherhood becomes her career, with the output of "perfect" children the tangible evidence of her success. It seems that the visions of liberation did not necessarily match the more slowly changing social structural arrangements that perpetuate the conditions that keep women at home. In other words, psychological emancipation is not fully implemented by structural emancipation. This structural-lag condition inflicts feelings of relative deprivation on the woman who wants but cannot step out into the professional world. Opportunity to compensate for deeply felt deprivation is visualized in a new type of motherhood that establishes evidence of competence. What is overlooked in the haste to preserve self-respect is the fact that the child is not accepted as an end in him- or herself, but only as a means—and a young personality used for the alleviation of a neurosis cannot help but acquire its own.

Focus: The Mother-Son Relationship

Momism usually involves the mother-*son* relationship, since a girl, even if dominated by her mother, can adopt her manners, imitate her, and take on her role. In fact, this is the way many Moms are created: a girl patterning her behavior after mother. She is free to do so since both imitator and imitated are of the same sex. This is reflected in the findings of researchers, who found that girls resemble their mothers in terms of personality much more

---

[47]Edward A. Strecker, *Their Mothers' Sons: The Psychiatrist Examines an American Problem* (New York: Lippincott, 1946); David M. Levy, *Maternal Overprotection* (New York: Columbia University Press, 1943); Erik H. Erikson, *Childhood and Society* (New York: W. W. Norton, Inc., 1963); Martha W. Lear, *The Child-Worshipers* (New York: Crown Publishers, 1963); Margaret Mead, "What Is Happening to the American Family?" *Journal of Social Casework*, 28 (November 1947): 323–30; Arnold W. Green, "The Middle-Class Male Child and Neurosis," *American Sociological Review*, 11 (February 1946): 31–41; and Patricia C. Sexton, *The Feminized Male: Classrooms, White Collars and the Decline of Manliness* (New York: Random House, 1969).

than boys.[48] (The boy's vulnerability to Momism justifies the masculine pronoun when referring to "child" in this discussion.)

Most American fathers are only peripherally involved in socializing their children. This explains why the boy is more vulnerable to Momism than the girl; he lacks a close and daily visible male model. In fact, Momism can occur only if the father fails to enact his part in child-rearing.[49]

The Core Technique

The typical Mom tries to achieve her "success" goal by manipulating the child's behavior by extending or withdrawing love, or by promising to do so. It is powerful "love"-oriented sanction that is responsible for impairing personality growth in the child and establishing a mother-dependency that does not go away when he reaches adolescence; it should be replaced with personal autonomy. Since love is experienced as something *conditional—* contingent on how he behaves and not as something he deserves on the basis of his innate worth—the slightest disapproval of mother (and later of any outside authority) will cause him anxiety. His feeling of acceptability depends on constant approval by others. A mind so conditioned has little reprieve from anxiety.

An important element of this conditioning process is the boy's belief that he *needs* that love. "Not the need for parent love, but the constant threat of its withdrawal *after the child has been conditioned to the need,* lies at the root of the most characteristic modern neurosis."[50] Empirical evidence suggests that maternal achievement pressures are more effective than paternal pressures because of mother's use of the "love"-oriented sanctions.[51]

A tentative profile of the Mom has emerged by now. She (1) is most likely middle class; (2) has a good education, has been steeped in "scientific child-rearing," and has been affected by the promises of the feminist movement; (3) has turned to mothering as a method of producing evidence of competence and "success"; (4) has no husband or one who is merely peripherally involved in the socialization of the child; (5) has a son, usually an only

---

[48]Ruth E. Hartley, "Children's Concepts of Male and Female Roles," *Merrill-Palmer Quarterly,* 6 (January 1960): 83–91; Lionel M. Lasowick, "On the Nature of Identification," *Journal of Abnormal and Social Psychology,* 51 (September 1955): 175–83; and David B. Lynn, "The Process of Learning Parental and Sex-Role Identification," *Journal of Marriage and the Family,* 28 (November 1966): 466–70; and *The Father: His Role in Child Development* (Belmont, CA: Wadsworth, 1976).

[49]Fitzhugh Dodson, *How to Father* (Bergenfield, NJ: New American Library, 1975); Michael E. Lamb, "Paternal Influences and the Father's Role," in John Keating, ed., *Social Psychology 82/83* (Guilford, CT: Dushkin, 1982): pp. 68–73.

[50]Green, "The Middle-class Male Child and Neurosis," p. 39 (Italics added.)

[51]R. R. Sears, E. E. Maccoby, and H. Levin, *Patterns of Child-Rearing* (Evanston, IL: Row & Peterson, 1957); and Garven Hudgins, "Cheating: Grave Pressures," *AP Education Service,* February 1969.

child, she uses for alleviating feelings of relative deprivation; and (6) uses the "love"-oriented conditioning.

No two Moms are exactly alike, and their styles of manipulation differ widely; they are notably colorful and could fill a museum of psychopathology. While some may meet the above profile only partly, they all seem to have one thing in common: They manipulate the child in such a way that he remains dependent. The "love"-oriented sanction system is patently suited to serve that goal.

Although essentially retaining this core technique, some Moms become specialists in the style in which they apply the leverage. Major types include the overindulgent, overprotective, permissive, domineering, child-worshipping, "star," absolute authority, and "martyr" Moms.[52]

Consequences: From "True Believer" to Suicide

Common elements can be observed among the affected males: (1) the inability to make decisions; (2) feelings of inferiority; (3) a particular brand of anxiety; (4) patterns of irresponsible behavior; and (5) emotional parasitism, that is, insufficiently controlled narcissism and egocentrism.

These consequences do not always become obvious. The Momistically impaired person tends to gravitate toward a "normal" situation, such as a marriage where he locks into complementary interaction. In most instances he marries a Mom type who substitutes for his erstwhile Mom. This constitutes the "silent majority" of which no one takes much notice.

There are also the sensational types: the sexual deviate, drug addict, psychopath, schizophrenic, and suicide. For example, a team of New York City social workers trying to discover why they were unsuccessful in helping young addicts found the latter's mothers employing various stealthy techniques to keep the sons addicted and thereby Mom-dependent. One mother was the "martyr" Mom; another bailed her boy out of jail while he waiting to be admitted to a hospital for addicts.[53] Some mothers encouraged the drug habit by giving their sons ten dollars every day "for a haircut," or fifteen dollars "for a shirt." Similarly, the Family Institute of Chicago, studying heroin and barbiturate addicts, discovered that the stars of the drama were the inefficient father, the domineering-but-protective Mom, and the helplessly dependent son.[54] Additional examples have been described by David

---

[52]These types are discussed in detail in Hans Sebald, *Momism: The Silent Disease of America.*

[53]"Mom Is the Villain," *Time*, May 21, 1965, p. 83.

[54]John Schwartzman, "The Addict, Abstinence, and the Family," *American Journal of Psychiatry*, 132 (February 1975): 154–57.

McCullaugh who sampled the list of famous personages whom he suspects of Momistic affliction.[55]

Other writers focused on extreme cases, such as a thirty-seven-year-old Wisconsin man whose mother took him everywhere in a wheel cart, allegedly because he suffered from polio. Welfare officials finally prevailed and had him examined—he was found capable of walking. It was his mother, not polio, who had disabled him. When the son had been temporarily removed from the mother at age fifteen to attend school, he curled up in a fetal position and remained in this position for twenty-two years, spoon-fed, diapered, and wheeled around by his mother who insisted that "I like him just the way he is."[56]

A common and yet often undetected outcome of Momism is the individual who has always relied on his mother for decision making and who later adheres to a substitute decision making figure. He may become a "true believer," who exhibits a total submission to some supposedly infallible and omnipotent ideology or charismatic leader.[57] It is from people of this temperament that totalitarian movements (be they religious or political) recruit some of their most fanatic followers.

A study in Scandinavian countries discovered correlations between the suicide rate and the style of child rearing.[58] Denmark, with one of the world's highest suicide rates, is characterized by a child-rearing style that creates highly guilt-conscious and dependent personalities. When forced to face an important situation demanding a major decision, a victim of Momism may withdraw from reality to escape pain, guilt, and insecurity—and the ultimate withdrawal can be achieved through self-inflicted death. Norway, with one of the lowest suicide rates, is much like Denmark in most variables, *except* in child-rearing procedures.

The consequences of Momism should be understood with the following points in mind:

1. The effects usually overlap and form combinations.
2. Mother influence can of course be detected in the lives of entirely healthy males, and a pathological connotation should not be attached to all symptoms.
3. Momism should therefore be defined as exceeding normal influence to the point of crippling the personality.
4. Duration of symptoms of Momistic impairment differs from victim to victim, in some cases lasting a lifetime and in other cases disappearing soon after the offspring leaves home.

[55]David McCullaugh, "Mama's Boys," *Psychology Today*, March 1983, pp. 32–38.

[56]"Rehabilitation: Return From the Womb," *Time*, May 17, 1963, p. 93.

[57]This concept was first coined by Eric Hoffer, *The True Believer* (New York: Mentor Books, 1951).

[58]Herbert Hendin, *Suicide and Scandinavia* (New York: Grune and Stratton, 1964).

5. Only a proportion of males suffering from such problems as drug addiction, homosexuality, and suicidal tendencies can be traced to a Momistic experience.
6. Momism can ensue only when the father defaults in helping with child rearing.
7. Diagnosis of a disturbance as an outcome of Momism is often difficult and should be attempted only after careful investigation.

DADISM: WHAT HAPPENS TO PAPA'S LITTLE GIRL

It would be misleading to imply that the stifling influence that a mother can bring to bear on a son is without equivalent in the father-daughter relationship. In that case it is usually the domineering and patronizing father-daughter relationship, a form of Dadism, that can truncate the girl's personality development. But there is a significant cultural difference. As mentioned in an earlier chapter, the boy's masculinity is still upheld, and serious deviation from it is negatively sanctioned in our civilization. Not so with the girl's femininity. The modern female has a vast range from which she can choose her role, ranging from old-fashioned femininity to the modern egalitarian stance. Dadism inculcates the former, that is, he raises, manipulates, and conditions Papa's little girl in the ways of feminine submissiveness. And by cultural dictum, there's not much wrong with that.

> To all appearances it is done in good taste and style: he is merely producing a feminine personality with society's stamp of "good housekeeping." The little girl will receive top grades from her father (later from her teacher, boy friend, and spouse) for growing up to be timid yet "sweet," indecisive yet "compatible," dependent yet "supportive," unsure of herself yet "loving"—in short, "very feminine." This is the way society has camouflaged the stifled personality of females. They cause no problems. They fit a system of male supremacy.[59]

Because these girls are acceptable to our cultural standards—at least to a time-honored set of them—they don't appear to be as pathological as the boys suffering from Momism. The father-dominated girl is cast into the complementary feminine role that does not cause adjustment problems—as long as the traditional role behavior is expected from them. (The traditional acceptability of submissive femininity is also the reason for the sparsity of research done in this interesting area.)

Dadism and its peculiar feminine product may not go unchallenged forever. The attack on the traditional feminine style by the women's liberation movement appears to have made some inroads on raising the subservient girl. With advanced emancipation, this age-old power play may eventually be perceived for what it really is: the interference with the process of a

---

[59]Hans Sebald, *Momism—The Silent Disease of America*, p. 115.

girl's unfolding her true potential and unique personality. It will be branded as hindering a young woman from developing her own personal identity.

SUMMARY

Behavioral orientation is not limited to membership groups, but can be a product of identification with abstract reference groups. Understanding of the behavior of modern adolescents has become difficult because of their exposure to multiple, shifting, conflicting, and sometimes unclear reference groups. This accounts for misunderstood and unexplained behavior patterns, including deviations from adult norms and confused and situationally compartmentalized behavior.

Significant others are models influencing personality development. Traditionally, parents served as such important figures, but modern conditions have diminished the effectiveness of personal models. Among these conditions are the abundance of available reference groups, the relative invisibility or absence of personal models, and exposure to characters portrayed in the mass media.

The traditional sex-specific expectations have become blurred. Nonspecificity has created new freedoms. However, the price for freedom of individuality is uncertainty and anxiety. Erosion of traditional sex-role definitions has come to greatly affect the boy–girl interaction and the personality of the teenage girl. Young women manifest their role change by altered behavior in many areas; for example, in sexual activities, intellectual expression, competition, and such negative phenomena as crime and suicide.

The tendency of many modern mothers to perceive motherhood as a form of career with the corollary of product-centeredness and success orientation has warranted a new concept: Momism. It seems that this new type of careerism affects particularly the mother-son relationship, with great detriment to the boy's personality. Dadism deals with the father-daughter relationship in a different way: the girl's personality is cast into the supplementary feminine role which in our culture is not necessarily perceived as pathological, though close examination may reveal a stifled and limited personality growth.

5

Conditions of Postindustrial Life

The structure of postindustrial society is eminently adolescence-inducing. Super-industrialization has accentuated the discontinuity and the isolation of social positions, converted education into a custodial institution, depersonalized the authority hierarchy, and altered cultural attitudes toward the meaning of work and material achievement. The impact of these conditions on young people is discussed in this chapter.

ISOLATION IN MODERN SOCIAL STRUCTURE

Probably the most striking feature of postindustrial society is its complex network of positions. The division of labor, the way society distributes the functions necessary for its maintenance, includes such fine subdivisions that most people would be unable to identify all of them. An example is the network that regulates automobile use: the operator-licensing office, the auto-licensing office, laws, courts, law-enforcement agencies, the highway department, driver's education classes, insurance companies, and so forth.

Since American working conditions rarely give the individual a chance to do a "whole" job, a sharp discontinuity arises between the life of the child and the life of the adult. The life of the child is more holistic, in that his or her early education and training usually take in the broadest range of different curricula and activities. In late adolescence, when a youth begins a job, this broad range abruptly narrows, and the individual must focus on one particular activity for which he or she probably was not specifically prepared and may require new training and education. The job may be so specialized that, as a child or teenager, he or she may not have had a model or role definition to aid in understanding the new situation. As a result, thousands of teenagers who enter the labor force immediately after, or even before, graduation from high school are unable to decide which vocation will provide personal fulfillment. Their reactions often take the form of discontent and frequent job changes.

To see the multispecific nature of modern social structure in the right perspective, it is necessary to elaborate on two interrelated phenomena. One is the nature of the general culture and the other is the process of achieving personal identity. As already mentioned in Chapter 2, there seems to be a gradual shift of identity-genesis from the culture to one's specific social position. This trend was brought about by diminishing persuasiveness of the culture and, at the same time, by an increasing social-structural specialization. The multispecific social system makes it increasingly difficult to interpret its variegated life experiences into generally understandable terms.

Sociologist Daniel Bell recognized this development and saw the general cultural plateau of postindustrial society undergoing a kind of atrophy because of the outgrowth of technical specialization.[1] He understood culture as a symbolic expression of the common social processes in which people are involved in everyday life. People need such symbolic expression to communicate and share their experiences with one another. But superindustrialization impedes such sharing, and the common ground for symbolic expression is eroding away under the growth of a highly specialized division of labor. Consequences have been felt in all sectors of life and have been symptomized as political alienation, work dissatisfaction, and the general feeling of ignorance and powerlessness vis-à-vis an unfathomable and amorphous industrial-scientific complex. In short, culture is failing in its function to serve as a forum through which people can find common expression. Our advanced technology, with its finely divided and isolated work patterns, inhibits the formulation of common symbolic expression and fosters isolation and alienation.

What modern society fails to provide in terms of ideational guidance it tries to make up in bureaucratic guidance. But this effort is of little help. Indeed, it worsens the situation because it adds to *anomie* an element of unfreedom that blocks the search for new principles and prohibits experi-

---

[1]Daniel Bell, "The Post-Industrial Society," in *Technology and Social Change*, ed. Eli Ginzberg (New York: Columbia University Press, 1964), and *The Cultural Contradictions of Capitalism* (New York: Basic Books, 1976).

mentation with new behavior patterns. Thus, as Peter Berger, Brigitte Berger, and Hansfried Kellner pointed out, alienation through bureaucratization turns modern humans into "homeless minds" in search of a meaningful culture.[2]

As a consequence, people depend on discrete social positions for personal identity and partially ignore a culture that is too general to represent the wide spectrum of life experiences. In fact, in this type of society, culture *cannot afford* to be specific, since it would contradict or discriminate against the life experiences of many members.

It is true, however, that the superficial and sensate ingredients of postindustrial culture are widely shared, creating the impression of a culture of substance and viability. But a close look reveals that most messages and images are geared toward sensate appeals or common anxieties and not toward an ideational union or commitment. The common cultural denominator intelligible to the masses of the postindustrial society is the sensate. (Echoes of Sorokin's philosophy of history!) Postindustrial people compensate for *anomie* and superficiality by clinging to social positions for directions and goals.

This situation creates identity problems for youth. While still generalists, dependent on vague and nonspecific cultural "blueprints," young people suffer from *anomic* conditions that create difficulty in answering "Who am I?" unless parental guidance and value indoctrination compensate for cultural nonspecificity. It is not until the young person enters and feels at home in a specific position that a sense of trustworthy identity develops. This, then, is the dilemma of modern adolescents.

The above generalizations, applicable as they may be to the majority of American youth, require several modifications. The first deals with the institution of apprenticeship, a process whereby the young are systematically introduced into the adult division of labor. An apprentice had a defined status, with rights and obligations specified in a contract, and spent from three to six years under the supervision of a master. After successful completion, he or she was initiated (by rite of passage) into the rank of journeyman and henceforth regarded as an adult.

The United States tried to encourage the tradition of apprenticeship through the National Apprenticeship Act of 1937, wherein the Secretary of Labor was "authorized to formulate and promote the labor standards necessary to safeguard the welfare of apprentices, to encourage the inclusion of such standards in contracts, to bring together employers and labor for the formulation of programs of apprenticeships."[3] About 420,000 Americans

[2]Peter Berger, Brigitte Berger, and Hansfried Kellner, *The Homeless Mind* (New York: Random House, 1973).

[3]*United States Congressional Record,* Chapter 663, Washington, DC, August 1937, p. 664.

benefited from this legislation in 1980 and were trained as carpenters, electricians, iron workers, barbers, butchers, painters, printers, roofers, and in many other skills. The number of such registered apprentices had substantially increased over the preceding ten years which was only 155,000 in 1962.[4] The Bureau of Apprenticeship and Training of the United States Department of Labor suggested a composite portrait of the "typical apprentice": he is a "married 25 year old male high school graduate with no physical handicap, presently in his third year of apprenticeship, and whose father does not work in the same trade. Prior to his apprenticeship he did have a full-time job, and his chances of being a veteran are about even."[5] While apprentices are still predominantly male, the 1981 Report shows that the proportion of women is steadily increasing; it was 4.3 percent in 1978 and 6.4 percent by 1980.

The second qualification deals with the widespread custom of teenagers working part-time during their school years. This practice sometimes prepares them for positions and hence reduces the "culture shock" when entering the adult position. The important functions of part-time work experience for a teenager include: (1) a feeling of economic independence; (2) a feeling of self-reliance; (3) a strengthening of self-respect; (4) acceptance of proper sex-role behavior; (5) rehearsing and practicing socially responsible behavior; and (6) facilitating the process of selecting and preparing for a final occupation.

Another modification must take into consideration the direction young people often obtain through their families. This is particularly true for youngsters growing up in families strongly bonded to religious belief and/or subcultural tradition. For example, a youngster growing up and taking active part in a Mormon community, or one following the Amish way of life, or one integrated in a fundamentalist Christian tradition may not have the problems of forming a personal identity as those growing up in a more liberal and secular family. (Though it must be added that such identity transmission may mean foreclosure of a more individualistic identity formation.)

PURSUIT OF INSTANTNESS

One of the most cherished goals of supertechnology is *instantness* of result and gratification. One may view the achievement of instantness as the acid test of a postindustrial society's capability of providing goods and services. The rationalization of processes of manufacture and service creates a soaring productivity, and postindustrial economy holds out at least two promises: the

---

[4]U.S. Department of Labor, *Employment and Training Report*, Government Printing Office, Washington, DC, 1981, pp. 45, 46.

[5]U.S. Department of Labor, Apprentice Survey, Code 321, Government Printing Office, Washington, DC, March 1975, p. 8.

promise of instantness of gratification and the promise of elimination of scarcity.

Given the American obsession with time and efficiency, it comes as no surprise that this society has become the prototype of *technological instantness* and has assumed virtual world leadership in this capacity. Promises of instant results abound and have become an ever present feature of consumerism. Numerous products and services are promoted with the adjective *instant*. Examples include drugs ("instant relief" through Dristan/Aspirin/Excedrin/Rolaids/and so on, "instant sleep" through Sominex), food ("instant" coffee/rice/breakfast/pudding/potatoes/and so on), transportation ("instant transportation" through Boeing 747), communication ("instant communication" through satellite relay), finance ("instant credit" by supermarkets), religion ("instant prayer" by dialing a number), cosmetics ("instant hairsetting" by Clairol), recreation ("instant dancing through dance studios), and so forth.[6] The range of modern instancies has created the impression that instancy is unlimited. This is an illusion. While in many sectors of modern life the expectation for immediacy is realistic, in some sectors it is unrealistic. Hence the vision of and the insistence on instantness in *all* aspects of life are delusory.

Modern adolescents are particularly receptive to this delusion. The inventions and miracles of modern science are no longer awesome to adolescents; they are taken for granted and expected to be available whenever desired. In short, youthful attitudes include the naive belief in and the unabashed demand for instantness in *all* areas of life. This includes the extrapolation of the principle of *instant results* from the feasible to the nonfeasible.

One area where instancy is not feasible is mental achievement and psychological maturity. There are no instant "knowledge pills."

Adolescents are involved in an intense process of mental development and must learn a culture, memorize a vast body of technical knowledge, and, at the core of all these mental tasks, form a personal identity. Our technocracy's ethos of instantness seduces them into believing that shortcuts and instant achievements can be had in these intricate processes. In the process, the American ethos of the right to the pursuit of happiness becomes corrupted into the assumption of the right to *instant happiness*, and deferment of gratification becomes unintelligible and repugnant to American youth.

The postindustrial promise of instantness and youth's natural hedonism coalesce into the tenacious inclination to eschew delay and tedious effort. Postindustrial adolescents grow up with a vastly diminished concept of the scarcity of goods and services. The pioneer era and the hardships of the Great

---

[6]See details in Hans Sebald, "The Pursuit of Instantness in Technocratic Society and Youth's Psychedelic Drug Use," *Adolescence*, 7 (Fall 1972): 343–50.

Depression are to them mere historical anecdotes, encountered only when an instructor insists that they read assignments or when a grandfather relates "stories." Emphasis in American life is no longer on producing, but on consuming—and on being able to do so instantaneously. These changes have had impact on the American mentality for already two to three decades, and the symptoms have become noticeable in many sectors of public life.

The educational institution is an example. College education has increasingly come to be viewed as just another "right," the ingredients of which a student should be able to enjoy instantly. Students intuitively try to make it palatable and add it to the list of American "fun and instantness." Americans, accustomed to instantness in life, experience difficulty in coping with exceptions. As Bruno Bettelheim observed: "The expectation is that education can hand over knowledge and skill, and this nearly instantly."[7]

DIVORCING THE HOME FROM THE WORKPLACE

In industrialized societies, the setting for raising children and the setting for employment have become separate realms. The practice of commuting from the home to the place of employment seems to be directly correlated with the degree of a country's industrial development. For example, in the 1950s West Germany had roughly 3 million people commuting to jobs in communities outside their own. In 1965, with progressing technology, industrialization, and affluence (but the same national population figure), the number of commuters was 6.3 million.[8]

Most urban families no longer practice the tradition whereby the son takes on the occupation of his father and the daughter that of her mother. (However, most girls still learn the wife-mother role through the mother.) James S. Coleman found that in the city and the suburbs less than one out of ten boys intended to pursue the occupation of his father.[9] In most cases, the children are not familiar with the specific type of work their fathers do, and when they assume their own vocational activities they are received into a completely new surrounding. The abrupt change from primary socialization in the nuclear family to secondary socialization in the job can create considerable confusion.

Conditions of modern society have gradually changed the family from a production unit to a consumption unit. Each member is *individually* engaged in the production process. This is strikingly different from the tribal or folk

---

[7]Bruno Bettelheim, "Student Revolt, The Hard Core," *Vital Speeches of the Day*, 35 (1968–69): 406.

[8]*The Bulletin*, Press and Information Office of the Federal Republic of Germany, Bonn, November 9, 1965, p. 6.

[9]James S. Coleman, *The Adolescent Society* (New York: Free Press, 1963), p. 7.

societies where the consanguine family is a production unit as well as a consumption unit and where only the most elementary division of labor exists. The network of positions may comprise merely a few simple status definitions, such as hunters, warriors, chiefs, housekeepers, and so on. This type of social structure prevents discontinuity between the position of the child and of the adult, since children experience early involvement in visible and imitable work. Primary and secondary socialization are merged into one process.

In contrast, in a rapidly changing and highly rationalized society education within the family has been replaced by formal institutions covering an ever longer span of time. Nonfamilial education and training has resulted in a by-product: the evolution of *social systems* that resemble subcultures with norms and values of their own. As a result, not only have education and job training been removed from parental supervision, but so has youth. They now belong to a society of peers, a society whose natural habitat is the campus of the high school or college.

The population of this youth habitat has risen sharply over the last decades. In 1900, only 11 percent of America's high school-aged youth were *in* high school; in 1930, the proportion was 51 percent;[10] today it is estimated at well over 90 percent. The emphasis on formal education is directly correlated with industrial development—a correlation observable the world over.

When it is the mother who works away from home, especially in a one-parent situation, a by-product sometimes is the so-called latchkey child who returns from school in the afternoon and spends unsupervised hours until mother comes home. (An alternative is the day-care center child, discussed below in the section on Home away from Home.) The number of latchkey children in the U.S. has been estimated to be roughly 10 million,[11] and for many years researchers have talked about the psychological pros and cons for this type of child. They have arrived at divergent conclusions. The negative view held that the child is prone to experience feelings of neglect, even rejection, and thus develops behavior problems. More recent findings seem to suggest that such concern is usually overdrawn. One study compared children who spent after-school hours unsupervised with a matched group of children who were cared for by adults. The researchers found no significant differences. Latchkey children were as high in self-esteem as were those under adult supervision.[12] Cornell University psychologist Urie Bronfenbrenner, a researcher of the latchkey situation for many years, basically agreed with this finding and concluded that what really matters is whether there are expectations about how children occupy themselves during unsupervised

---

[10]James S. Coleman, *Adolescents and the Schools* (New York: Basic Books, 1965), p. 7.
[11]Amitai Etzioni, "US Needs," *U.S. News and World Report*, January 9, 1984, p. 59.
[12]Jeff Meer, "Children—Alone but not Neglected," *Psychology Today*, August 1985, p. 11.

time. Moreover, each child is different, and structured self-care arrangements need to be individually adjusted.[13]

Nonetheless, the opportunities to get involved with peer groups and possibly with subcultural activities of course increase with the amount of time children are on their own.

EDUCATION IN POSTINDUSTRIAL PERSPECTIVE

The modern educational institution plays a salient role in the lives of the young and calls for a separate examination. Hence the major discussion is deferred to Chapter 9. A brief summary preview is offered at this time for the purpose of indicating that the topic has an important place in the array of postindustrial conditions.

Nonfamilial Education

Modern education has assumed a ghetto existence away from most adult institutions. This is particularly true of high school campuses, the Teenland America, where students pursue their own values, styles, and lingo. Never before have the institutions of the family and of education been such separate experiences. Many families do not see the values they cherish reflected in the schools. Such nonfamilial education has aroused opposition in ethnic groups, who fear their children might be unduly exposed to worldly and decadent influences. One example is the Amish, who have opposed "worldly" education persistently enough to persuade the authorities to grant them their own Amish-run schools. Obviously, the vast majority of American school-aged children do not have such a unitary experience. They continue to experience a parallel socialization process with family and school remaining separate, if not opposing, institutions.

Longer Education

There has been a steady increase in years added to the formal education of Americans. Roughly half of the American population now has finished high school *and* spent some time in college. Prolonging the sojourn in academia means prolonging adolescence by offering a moratorium on social responsibilities, allowing time for psychological growth, and delaying career decisions.

The extended segregation of the young from adult life unintentionally created a setting conducive to: (1) peer influence and subculture formation;

---

[13]Ibid.

(2) freedom of sexual experimentation; and (3) mate selection beyond the constraints of parental control.

Custodial Education

While longer education is in part a function of the necessary preparation for sophisticated careers, it is in part also a holding pen to keep the young from invading the labor market too soon and adding to unemployment pressure. The increasing concern voiced over the educational dropout is motivated less out of awe for the presumed knowledge disseminated through the educational process than out of worry of not knowing what else to do with the masses of America's young.

HIGH MOBILITY

Urban-industrial Americans are among the world's most mobile people. Precisely how this trait affects American youth and their adolescent experience is not yet fully understood. Probably the best that can be done is to suggest plausible hypotheses.

First, what is meant by mobility? The term has several meanings. One refers to movement within the social structure, either vertically or horizontally. Changing from the occupation of waiter to that of doctor would be an example of vertical mobility, while changing from factory worker to construction worker would be an example of horizontal mobility. Mobility can also refer to geographic movement—a kind of mobility that is remarkable among Americans.

Vertical Social Mobility

This type of mobility compares members of one generation with those of the next (generational mobility) or compares different stages in the life of one individual (career mobility). The focus here is on generational mobility and the resulting discontinuities. Part of the American heritage is the Protestant ethic, which includes a mobility ethic that encourages Americans to achieve "success" in life. Hence, the young are not necessarily encouraged to follow in parental footsteps, but to improve on the latter's lives.

In most industrial societies, the placement function of the family has declined. While it is true that children identify and are identified by status and prestige of their families, as teenagers and young adults they become detached from familial influence, and social standing depends increasingly on personal achievements. The status eventually achieved may be on a different level from that of the parents. In postindustrial society, family origin affects the status of the individual only indirectly, by influencing opportunities for educational and occupational achievements.

Research in American generational mobility has shown widespread discontinuity between the careers of the parents and the offspring. Sociologists Cecil C. North and Paul K. Hatt surveyed sons' deviations from fathers' occupations and revealed that, with the sole exception of farming, no occupational category achieved more than one-third generational continuity.[14] It should be noted that those who classified their occupation in the same general class as their fathers' did not necessarily occupy the *same specific* occupation, implying that a great deal of horizontal mobility existed *within* the broad occupational classes. Coleman found that few boys planned to follow in the occupational footsteps of their fathers. His survey showed 23 percent of boys in small towns and only 9.8 percent of boys in city and suburban schools planning to enter their fathers' occupation.[15]

The mobility ethic can have a devastating impact on those adolescents who fail, as some must, in the process of status striving. In a society that encourages all to strive and that promises success to those who are capable, failure is considered evidence of personal inadequacy. For those who achieve upward mobility, difficult adjustments are required. This problem is frequently evident in both the research literature and the popular "success" story, describing the situation of the rich and successful but unhappy and maladjusted man or woman.

Lack of family continuity and tradition may present teenagers with an obscure future for which they have no visible models. They are called upon to make one of the most vital decisions in life—choosing a career. The mobility ethic, expecting the teenager to go beyond the family's level of achievement and improve his or her level of social prestige, contributes additional pressures. By ruling out parents as occupational models, a familiar sociocultural orientation is rendered irrelevant. Most teenagers who choose an occupation or vocational training that differs significantly from their parents' undergo a shift in life orientation often comparable to "culture shock."

Horizontal Social Mobility

The 1980s reflected a typical postindustrial phenomenon: high mobility of American workers within the general confines of their vocational categories. Rapid economic and technological changes prompted over 11 million workers, roughly 10.5 percent of the work force, to change jobs during a

[14]Cecil C. North and Paul K. Hatt, "Jobs and Occupations: A Popular Evaluation," *Opinion News*, 9 (September 1947): 3–13.
[15]Coleman, *The Adolescent Society*.

year's time. This has been computed to mean that, on the average, the American worker changes jobs 11 times during his or her life.[16]

Geographic Mobility

Approximately 17 percent of the American population changes address each year,[17] compared with about 12 percent in Europe and 8 percent in Japan.[18] If we accept the theory that development of a stable personality depends on a consistent environment, disruption of life patterns through frequent moving should negatively influence the adolescent experience, prolong it, and aggravate confusion. Research has revealed that children and adolescents whose families move are dismayed about losing friends, worried about making new ones, and show a decline in scholastic achievement. Highly mobile youths (who have moved twice or more) exhibited notable maladjustments to peers and were less frequently chosen as playmates than youths with local roots.[19]

Military families are prototypes of this mobility, and their children have been found to be characterized by social and psychiatric troubles. Psychiatrist Don M. LaGrone found 12 percent of all children and adolescents on a base in need of psychiatric help and diagnosed 4 percent of them as psychotic. Causal to these conditions, he felt, were extensive father-absence, the families seeing themselves as transients with no roots, and children moving from school to school so frequently that they had to break into peer groups repeatedly as the "new kid" and were often the school's scapegoats.[20]

Other studies of youngsters of military families have found that lengthy separation from one parent, usually the father, caused interesting psychological upheavals. For example, navy personnel may ship out for six to ten months at a time. How children react to these separations, virtually creating temporary one-parent families, depends largely upon their age. Tom, a high-school junior, reports that his father was on the ship twice, each time for eight months. The first time, Tom was a toddler and can't remember when his father returned. The second time, Tom was a teenager and cast into the role of being "the man of the house" during father's absence. Upon father's return, father and son experienced a power battle, for now father resumed

---

[16]"Tomorrow," *U.S. News and World Report*, August 15, 1983, p. 12.

[17]"US Census," *U.S. News and World Report*, May 14, 1984, p. 24.

[18]U.S. Department of Labor, *Economic Forces in the United States* (Washington, DC: Government Printing Office, 1973); and AP report (Washington, October 20, 1975).

[19]Joseph Schaller, "The Relation Between Geographic Mobility and School Behavior," *Man–Environment Systems*, 5 (May 1975): 185–87.

[20]Don M. LaGrone, "The Military Family Syndrome," *American Journal of Psychiatry*, 135 (September 1978): 1040–43.

being "the man of the house." Certain privileges, such as staying up late with mom to watch television or escorting her to certain functions, were rescinded and Tom reacted with confusion and resentment. A daughter may similarly react upon the return of a uniformed parent.[21]

It seems that the worst stress resulting from moving or from the temporary one-parent situation occurs during the junior or senior year in high school, for this is the time of strongest involvement and identification with peers. It is feared that after having to leave close friends repeatedly, these teenagers learn to establish superficial friendships.[22] Studies have found that military adolescents spend more time with their parent or parents—whether completing homework, playing games, or doing chores—than with other adolescents. "Both groups showed the normal adolescent break from parents, but it came somewhat later for the military youth."[23]

Vance Packard takes this contention a step further and, in *A Nation of Strangers*, expresses concern that too many Americans move too often, become rootless, and contribute to the decline of a sense of community.[24]

While the effects of frequent moving can be interpreted as disruptions of identification processes, they can also be interpreted as providing the young with extra opportunities for learning and greater variety of reference persons. One could argue that adolescents subject to mobility acquire more information and better insight. This may make the process of identity growth more complex (compared with the process of the nonmobile youths who stay in one community), but not less valid or stable in its final outcome. In fact, one might argue that for the nonmobile, roots become ruts. At this time, the statistical question waiting to be researched is: How many people adapt easily to and grow emotionally and intellectually by moving, and how many suffer and how seriously?

HOME AWAY FROM HOME

Many American children are raised, partially or wholly, away from the parental home. Some children are entrusted to the care of a partial home while their mothers are employed full-time. Others are victims of disabled or delinquent parents and grow up in welfare institutions. Still others are delinquent youths who serve time in juvenile or rehabilitative institutions. This discussion deals with those children in day-care centers part-time and those in welfare institutions full-time.

---

[21]Patricia Long, "Growing Up Military," *Psychology Today*, December 1986, p. 34.
[22]Ibid., p. 35.
[23]Ibid., p. 36.
[24]Vance Packard, *A Nation of Strangers* (New York: David McKay, 1972).

The Day-Care Center

Day-care centers enable mothers to simultaneously pursue motherhood and an occupation outside of the home. Day care was available in 1987 for nearly 25 percent of the almost 10 million preschool children whose mothers worked. In 1970 only 13 percent of the 5 million preschool children of working mothers were in day-care centers. This means that within one decade the proportion of the children in day care nearly doubled.[25]

Effects of maternal employment on children's personalities have been studied by many investigators. Examination of the research literature by Edith H. Grotberg revealed a diversity of findings regarding the correlation between mother's employment and children's delinquency, school and personal adjustment, and academic achievement.[26] While some studies demonstrated the positive functions of day care, such as increased language skill and a sense of security within a group setting, others concluded negatively, pointing up reduced capacity for emotional attachment, diminished sense of autonomy, and stifled creativity.[27]

The findings fail to add up to a consistent picture, and suspicion is warranted that research has ignored important variables. There are many relatively unexamined conditions that play an intermediary role between a mother's work away from home and the personality formation of the child. For example, one study discovered that a mother's liking or disliking of her job is significantly associated with how she interacts with her children. Mothers liking their work had more positive relationships with their children, though their children exhibited nonassertive and dependent attitudes. Mothers who disliked their work had more negative relationships with their children, and their children exhibited assertive and hostile attitudes.[28]

Correlations of this nature remind us of the complexity of the matter and of the many variables that enter into the picture. Such variables must be explored before we can obtain a clearer view of maternal employment and its impact on children.

The Full-Time Institution

Full-time institutions are for youths who have no, or no adequately functioning, parents. Information derived from studying youths in such

---

[25]U.S. Bureau of the Census, *Current Population Reports,* "Child Care Arrangements," Series p-70, No. 20, U.S. Government Printing Office, Washington, DC, 1990, p. 5.

[26]Edith H. Grotberg, *Review of Research, 1965–69, of Project Head Start,* U.S. Department of Health, Education and Welfare, Office of Child Development, 1969.

[27]Bruno Bettelheim, *The Children of the Dream* (New York: Macmillan, 1969).

[28]Lois W. Hoffman, "Effects of Maternal Employment on the Child," *Child Development,* 32 (March 1961): 187–97.

settings is more conclusive than that concerning day-care-center children. Clinicians have long agreed that substituting the parental home with the anonymous crowd in an institution has detrimental effects on children.

The case has been stated by Dr. Lauretta Bender, who observed approximately 6,000 children in New York's Bellevue Hospital for more than a decade and noted that children parentally deprived for one or more years were rarely able to adjust in foster homes: they all appear retarded, untrained, and impulsive in their behavior. As they grow older and the demands of society increase, their behavior becomes progressively more asocial.[29]

Another study reported the transfer of thirteen orphaned children, less than three years old, from the state institution where they had been living to a home for retarded women.[30] Two years later, the children showed a surprising increase in intellectual proficiency, while children who had remained at the state orphanage retained marked impairment of mental abilities. A follow-up study showed that the transferred children grew up to be normal members of the community, while most of the children in the orphanage were retarded and spent the major part of their lives in institutions. The explanation for the different outcomes was ascribed to the love and attention that the thirteen children received from the retarded inmates. The two reports are typical of numerous observations of what can happen to children reared in institutions.

A crucial shortcoming of institutional homes is the number of youths per adult supervisor or nurse. The Child Welfare League of America recommended no more than approximately six children per adult. In most institutional settings, this suggestion remains utopian. Consequences of serious understaffing and parental deprivation include the following:

1. With understaffing, anonymity is unavoidable. The child with its needs, opinions, and dreams does not receive sufficient attention *to feel known*. In fact, it is usually necessary for the nurse or supervisor to avoid emotional involvement with individual children. To carry the emotional burden of each child would be beyond the staff member's endurance.

2. The child may be disturbed by the perfunctory atmosphere of the institution and wonder whether he or she is really wanted. The feeling of *full acceptance* is immensely significant to a child, and its absence can result in feelings of personal worthlessness.

3. The experience of *physical affection* is of utmost significance in the development of a healthy personality. The effect of the caressing touch has been demonstrated in laboratory animals. In experiments with two sets of

[29]Lauretta Bender, *Aggression, Hostility and Anxiety in Children* (Springfield, IL: Thomas, 1953), p. 153.

[30]Stephen A. Richardson, "Retarded Children," *Trans-Action*, 6 (September 1969): 6.

rats, all variables were kept constant, except that the experimental group received physical caresses daily. The fondled rats gained weight faster, matured earlier, appeared healthier, and generally expressed greater vitality than the rats in the control group.[31] The basic condition underlying this finding can be extrapolated to humans. Its significance applies to the institutional setting insofar as it rarely affords conditions where the child finds sufficient physical intimacy.

4. Children have an interminable need for *question-answer* interaction. Their constant "why," "how," and "what-is-this" can hardly draw adequate responses in an institutional environment and their curiosity must go unsatisfied. This may generate indifference, dullness, and, in extreme cases, even retardation.

5. Human qualities appear to be the product of the primary family group—a sense of loyalty, cooperation, affection, and consideration. As Charles H. Cooley pointed out, these qualities are universal because of the universal primary-group experience and they constitute essential elements of what is loosely called "human nature."[32] The question arising in conjunction with the substitution of institutional homes for the primary familial home is: what modifications, if any, does the institutional substitute have on the *human nature* of the child? Will the child's sense of kindness, sympathy, and affection be reduced? Will the child develop characteristics of the sociopathic personality, showing little regard and sympathy for the suffering of others? A vast amount of research findings, a few of them already mentioned above, point to example after example of sociopathic products of institutional child rearing.

6. Institutional upbringing may add complications to the process of transition from child to adult status. A common criticism of subjecting the child to constant adult supervision is that it *prolongs dependency*. The child is deprived of the opportunity to make independent decisions, lacks opportunity to roam about, cannot escape from constant adult supervision—conditions that are inimical to developing an independent personality. Under constant supervision, the child becomes passive and prefers to let others take the initiative. Such attitude patterns cause serious problems when the individual tries to assume adult responsibilities.

7. Institutional upbringing may fix the child's loyalty and value-orientation on the institutional *peer group*. They learn early to adhere to norms and values different from those of the home and the adult world.

---

[31]Victor H. Denenberg, "Animal Studies on Developmental Determinants of Behavioral Adaptability," in *Experience, Structure and Adaptability,* ed. O. J. Harvey (New York: Springer Publishing Co., 1966), pp. 123–47.

[32]Charles H. Cooley, *Social Organization* (New York: Scribner's, 1915), pp. 23–24.

ADOLESCENT AFFLUENCE

The boost that teenager affluence has on the youth subculture was recognized years ago. Sociologist Jessie Bernard went as far as seeing the relationship in terms of strict causation: "Our teenage culture is a product of affluence. It is possible because our society can afford a large leisure class of youngsters not in the labor force but yet consumers on a vast scale, or, if in the labor force, free to spend their earnings on themselves."[33]

The causative implication of this statement is overdrawn. Affluence does not cause the teenage subculture; it has its origin in adolescence. While the affluence of late twentieth-century America causes neither adolescence nor the subculture, it effectively promotes the spread and survival of the collective expression of adolescence—the teenage subculture. This is achieved through teenagers' buying patterns, the interests of the business world, and reinforcement of stereotypical teenage behavior.

Reinforcement of teenage behavior is primarily the result of rewards obtained through conforming to peer norms. These rewards are popularity and prestige in the peer group. Adherence to peer patterns often necessitates material implementation and may involve a car, "in" clothes, electronic gadgets, cosmetics, recreational paraphernalia, and other goods and services. In order to buy the latest fads and fashions of the subculture, a teenager must have financial means. Statistics indicate that such means are available and modern teenagers control a large share of society's affluence.

Estimates from national surveys show that spending by teenagers (thirteen to nineteen years old) grew from $29 billion in 1977 to about $39 billion in 1980.[34] "From cosmetics to pizzas and from electronic games to records, teenagers and young adults make up a huge market . . . that seems resistant to recession and inflation."[35] The majority of youngsters enjoy parental safeguarding of their basic needs (housing, food, insurances, clothing) and hence are free to spend their money on leisure and luxury. The University of Michigan's Institute for Social Research found that about 40 percent of college-bound high school graduates already owned cars and that 50 percent of those not going to college owned theirs. The presumedly financially struggling American college student has, on the average, $173 per month to spend on pleasure, after room and board are paid.

High school youngsters also have an impressive consumption record. While it is impossible to cover all the market habits of American teenagers,

---

[33]Jessie Bernard, "Teenage Culture: An Overview," *Annals of the American Academy of Political and Social Science,* 338 (November 1961): 3.

[34]"Youth on the Move," *U.S. News and World Report,* January 5, 1981, pp. 72–76.

[35]Ibid., p. 77.

studies have provided enough data to form a general picture. Some of these data are mentioned below. The *Media Book '79* lists the following items:

> About half of the teenagers own cameras (40 percent of the boys, 55 percent of the girls)
> 80 percent go to movies on a more or less regular basis (Gallup Report 1981 indicates that only 2 percent of American teenagers "never attend")
> 15 percent have traveled abroad within three years prior to the survey over 40 percent play tennis
> about 20 percent ski
> 86 percent of the boys and 77 percent of the girls have driver's licenses
> 39 percent of the boys and 53 percent of the girls buy records
> in comparison, a relatively low 29 percent of the boys and 43 percent of the girls buy books
> 52 percent of the boys and 62 percent of the girls have bicycles
> 42 percent eat at fast food restaurants once or more a week, with eight out of ten of them buying hamburgers[36]

Do teenagers spend their own money on such consumption? Not necessarily. The Sacramento Metropolitan Teenage Market Study disclosed that teenagers usually pay out of their own pockets for records, radios, and entertainment. This tendency increased during the 1970s, with 19 percent of the teenagers spending "parents' or others' money" in 1970, but only 10 percent did so by the mid-1970s. On the other hand, the proportion of parents or others buying jewelry, shoes and clothes for teenagers sharply increased during that period, going, for example, from 33 to 43 percent for jewelry, 37 to 52 percent for shoes, and 54 to 70 percent for clothes.[37]

To what extent do teenagers make their own buying decisions? Over 90 percent of the teenagers themselves—and not their parents—make buying decisions for almost all items.[38]

How do teenagers acquire their financial resources? One of the most common sources is the weekly allowance. The Sacramento surveys indicate that allowances have kept pace with inflation. During the 1960s, 95 percent of high school students received up to $15 a week; in 1970 and 1974, 92 and 80 percent, respectively, fell into this category. Conversely, the proportions receiving $15 or more increased from 5 percent in the 1960s to 8 percent in 1970 to 20 percent in 1974. There were no significant allowance differences between boys and girls.[39] Many students hold part-time jobs to boost their finances. Surveys in 1964, 1970, and 1974 found weekly earnings up to $15,

[36]*The Media Book '79* (New York: Barlow & Papazian, 1979), pp. 469, 471.

[37]H. Nicholas Windeshausen and Paul A. Williams, *Sacramento Metropolitan Teenage Market Study* (Sacramento: California State University Center for Research, 1974), p. 26.

[38]Ibid., p. 22.

[39]Ibid., p. 8.

respectively, for 67, 45, and 42 percent of those responding. Conversely, again reflecting inflation, the over-$15 group increased from 33 to 55 to 58 percent. There were significant gender differences in income: 77 percent of the boys earned above $15, but only 28 percent of the girls fell into this category.[40] Another estimate of teenagers' (fifteen to nineteen years old) income put it at $2,370 per year during the early 1980s—all of it discretionary income that could be spent on leisure and luxury.[41]

It is interesting that despite differential income girls outspend boys early in life, a lead they apparently never relinquish. In a Rand Youth Poll's charting of twenty years of fiscal habits of America's youth, girls have consistently held a spending lead over their male counterparts. In the late teens, the gap is widened further. This raises intriguing questions. Since they earn *less* but spend *more* than boys, where and how do they get their finances? A plausible answer may be that parents buy more of the necessities for girls than boys. In addition, their boyfriends pay certain luxury and social expenses for them. Thus they can more freely spend the money they have.

Traditional male chivalry in paying for date expenses is now frequently modified by a more egalitarian philosophy. But this cannot be generalized. As in so many other realms of male-female interaction, also the expectations concerning financial responsibilities have increasingly assumed a more individualistic character. Nonetheless, it is usually reserved for the female to indicate—subtly or bluntly as it may be—what the expectations are to be. The male usually has little choice but to adjust to them.

Aware of the teen buying potential, the American business world is trying to cater to youth's tastes. It would be misleading, however, to understand the teenage influence as a one-way causality. Merchants, ad writers, and market researchers grasp the enormous potential available for exploitation and are manipulating, if not actually creating, the tastes and styles of the young. Therefore the marketing system consists of a complex interrelationship between preferences of teenagers and manipulations of the marketeers. In exactly which proportions the etiology of styles evolves is not known at this time. In any case, the teen market is a volatile one. Sometimes, a few youngsters will suddenly wear something to school, and then everybody has to have it. Sometimes the fad is grubby work pants ("gas station" pants), and a year later it is printed turtlenecks.

Predictably, the American business establishment tries to profit from teenagers' buying power and their apparent need for their own styles and fads. What are the industry's means of exploring and exploiting? A premium is on sheer inventiveness. For example, in the 1980s a San Francisco firm

[40]Ibid., p. 7.
[41]"Youth on the Move," p. 78.

came out with rock concert souvenirs such as T-shirts selling for $8.00 a piece to the crowds worshiping their idols. Signifying that their necessities are somehow taken care of, teenagers provide an immensely profitable market for sports equipment. Some of the best-selling items during the early 1980s were skis and equipment for racquetball, jogging, and exercising. Of perennial profitability are soft drinks, and manufacturers—while addressing all ages—direct their appeal particularly at the young. The Coca-Cola Company developed Mello Yello, a low-carbonated drink, to sell to teenagers who are into sports. Marketing experts seem to agree on the principle that if you want to capture youth, you must lure them with a gimmick. Hence theaters and pizza parlors have pinball machines and arcade and video games; department stores use disco music, blinking lights, and space-age displays; fast food restaurants almost exclusively use children and teenagers in their advertisements; sports stores use champion skaters, skiers, and swimmers in their commercials; beer brewers display hardy, youthful outdoor people "slamming down" a Lite; ads in college papers read, "You didn't get the courses you wanted. But you got Friday off . . . Now comes Miller time."

This brings into play the power of the mass media. Many advertisement specialists believe the best way to reach teenagers is via the radio. Rock stations still draw the biggest audiences and hence are favorites for advertisers. Of course, there is also the advertising power of TV. In any case, an enticing mass-medium depiction of consumption patterns can establish and sustain the marketing plans of the industry.

The economic power of teenagers is not limited to their actual financial means; it includes their psychological power, manifesting itself through the peculiarly youth-oriented market in the United States. Teenagers stimulate most mass buying trends by functioning as persuasive agents in their families. Surveys have indicated that teenagers have weighty influence on their parents' purchases of automobiles in 69 percent of the cases, on 68 percent of vacation plans, 66 percent of the food buying, and 54 percent of television purchases.[42] A 1989 Roper Report found that children decide 74 percent of the time what leisure activities their families will pursue, and approximately $50 billion a year in household spending is influenced by children.[43]

In summary, adolescents' expenditures are not made randomly but are selectively invested in goods and services that enhance popularity among peers. The selections are usually in accord with short-lived fashions of the subculture and they create a feeling of belonging. Material implementation furthers identification with subcultural standards and in this way promotes the survival of the subculture. Also, material implementation facilitates com-

[42]"Millions of Young Adults, A New Wave of Buyers," *U.S. News & World Report*, 72 (January 17, 1972), 16.
[43]Richard Corliss, "Kid Power," *Time*, January 6, 1991, pp. 81–82.

munication within the subculture—communication that does not have to be verbal, but can speak through the visible common style and fashion. Faded jeans, therefore, are not just clothes but a symbol.

It is through this reinforcement that adolescence has obtained structure and internal statuses and become a way of life. This way of life is not wholly acceptable to the adult world and is viewed with ambivalence. In the final analysis, adolescent "status" is paradoxical in that it is relatively structured from the *inside* of the subculture, but is uncertain *within* the adult world.

SOCIOSOMATICS: SOCIETAL INFLUENCES ON BIOLOGICAL DEVELOPMENT

The sociological view of human beings is regrettably limited. It tends to regard them as interactional units or status entities but rarely as biological creatures. And, yet, we are both. Because of this neglect, the relationship between societal (social, cultural, and technological) factors and the human body is insufficiently studied. While psychologists and clinicians study the relationship between mental states and physiological responses (classified as *psychosomatic*), few social scientists have explored the impact of social and cultural conditions on the human body. One might call this influence *sociosomatic*, referring to sociocultural variables on one side and the human body on the other. Sociosomatic processes accelerate and become noticeable under conditions of rapid social change or cultural innovation.

Since young people are always in the chronological front line, they are the first to experience the impact of innovation—not only as social units but also as biological organisms. The following discussion attempts to recognize some of the important influences on the biological development of adolescents.

The most significant biological process during the period of adolescence is pubescence. (*Pubescence* is derived from Latin *pubertas*, "age of manhood," and *pubescere*, "to grow hairy.") While adolescence refers to the period of social maturation, pubescence refers to the physiological development during which the reproductive system matures. Pubescence normally corresponds with early adolescence and ends with the appearances of secondary sex characteristics and the achievement of reproductive ability. These changes usually take place over approximately two years. The exact age at which reproductive maturity is achieved varies widely and is influenced by many factors.[44]

Of these factors, gender difference plays a major role. Girls mature

---

[44]Phyllis B. Eveleth, "Timing of Menarche," in Jane B. Lancaster and Beatrix A. Hamburg, eds., *School-Age Pregnancy and Parenthood* (New York: Aldine, 1986).

about two years earlier than boys. Climate, however, seems to make little difference. It was once thought that girls who grew up in a hot climate developed earlier than those who grew up in a cold one. Actually, researchers found a tendency toward earlier maturation in the temperate zone rather than in either tropical or arctic regions.[45] In general, however, scientists reject assumptions of climatic determination. Race seems to have even less effect than climate. In two studies, age at menarche (first menstruation) for black girls did not vary significantly from that of white girls who lived in the same places and had similar socioeconomic backgrounds.[46]

The most influential factors seem to be nutritional and medical ones.[47] This is where sociosomatic processes enter the picture, where social and cultural conditions have marked influence on biological development and age of maturity. A social environment that uses recent scientific insights in these areas—as is typical of postindustrial society—usually lowers the age of pubescence. Among the various aspects of scientific progress, better nutrition is the most significant factor. Scientific standards of nutrition, hygiene, and medication are more common in urban-industrial societies than in tribal or agricultural societies and more common in the middle and upper socioeconomic classes than in lower classes. This is why a consistent difference of menarcheal age exists between higher and lower socioeconomic classes, a difference verified by international studies. Menarcheal difference between higher and lower classes was found to be two months in Copenhagen, Denmark; three months in Bristol, England; eight months among blacks in New York; six months among Hindus; ten months in Durham, South Africa; and five months among South African Bantu.[48]

A related study found Japanese girls born in Japan but reared in California to be one-and-a-half years ahead of Japanese girls born in California but reared in Japan. The racial factor was constant between the groups, and the groups were large enough to include comparable cross-sections of social

---

[45]David P. Ausubel, *The Theory and Problem of Adolescent Development* (New York: Grune and Stratton, 1954).

[46]Comradge L. Henton, "A Comparative Study of the Onset of Menarche among Negro and White Children," *Journal of Psychology*, 46 (July 1958): 65–73; and N. Michelson, "Studies in Physical Development of Negroes, Onset of Puberty," *American Journal of Physical Anthropology*, 2 (June 1944): 151–66.

[47]Ann C. Petersen, "Can Puberty Come any Earlier?" *Psychology Today*, February 1979, p. 45.

[48]K. W. Boylen, G. Rasch, and M. Weis-Bentzon, "The Age Incidence of Menarche in Copenhagen," *Acta Obstetrica et Gynecologia Scandinavica*, 33 (1954): 405–33; R. C. Wofenden and A. L. Smallwood, *Annual Report of the Principal Medical Officer* (Bristol, England: City and County of Bristol Education Committee, 1958); E. Kark, "Puberty of South African Girls, III, Social Class in Relation to the Menarche," *South African Journal of Laboratory and Clinical Medicine*, 2 (1956): 84–88; and A. G. Oettlé and J. Higginson, "Age at Menarche in South African Bantu Girls," *Human Biology*, 33 (May 1961): 181–90.

stratification. The researcher concluded that the difference was due to the better diet of the girls who grew up in California.[49]

Heredity contributes to the determination of the time a girl experiences menarche. Daughters of early-pubescent mothers tend to reach menarche earlier than those of late-pubescent mothers.[50]

Effects of various factors reinforce each other and at other times neutralize each other. For example, if a German girl whose mother matured at eleven was brought up during the war and experienced nutritional deficiencies, she may have started menstruation at a later age. But the daughter of a late-maturing mother of a poor family may reach menarche earlier if the family moves up the socioeconomic ladder and provides a better diet. A double effect is experienced by the daughter of a late-maturing mother deserted by the husband and living under depressed economic standards. The girl is prone to reach menarche at an even later age than her mother.

Intergenerational comparisons of menarche have revealed an ever-decreasing menarcheal age in most societies. This especially is true of societies with improved standards of nutrition and sanitation. Complete records are available in Norway, covering the period from 1840 to 1950. Average menarcheal age in 1840 was seventeen years, one month. This age decreased consistently, until in 1950 it arrived at thirteen years, three months—a decrease of almost four years.[51] Similar changes have been found in Sweden, Germany, Denmark, England, Finland, Japan, and the United States.

In the United States, a study comparing mothers and daughters found the average menarcheal age for the mothers to be 13.99 years and for the daughters 13.61 years.[52] Another study found that American college women born around 1920 reached menarche six months earlier than those born around 1900.[53]

The reason reference is made almost exclusively to the pubescent process of girls is that there is no clearly defined method for determining the onset of pubescence among boys. There is no equivalent sign as unmistakable as menstruation. Indications of male pubescence are appearance of pubic hair, voice change, and nocturnal emission. However, not all of these male pubescent characteristics appear at the same time; several may go unnoticed for some time.

[49]Paul D. Ito, "Comparative Biometrical Study of Physiques of Japanese Women Born and Reared under Different Environments," *Human Biology*, 14 (September 1942): 279–351.

[50]Harley N. Gould and Mary R. Gould, "Age of First Menstruation in Mothers and Daughters," *Journal of the American Medical Association*, 98 (April 1932): 1349–52.

[51]V. Kiil, "Menarche-alderen hos skolepeker i Oslo og sammenhengen mellom menarche-older og fysiskutwicklung statistiche," *Kvartalashelft*, 43 (1954): 84–88.

[52]Gould and Gould, "Age of First Menstruation."

[53]Clarence A. Mills, "Further Evidence on the Reversal Human-Growth Tide," *Human Biology*, 13 (September 1941), 365.

Conditions of urban-industrial society have influenced not only timing of maturation but also quality. In 1961, researchers compared measurements of thirteen-year-old white Iowa schoolgirls with those of girls of the same age taken in 1880, 1899, 1916 to 1919, and 1937 to 1939.[54] Comparison showed progressive increase in all physical aspects except head width. Comparison of measurements taken in 1880 and in 1960 showed that girls of 1960 were taller by four inches in mean stature, heavier by twenty-two pounds in mean weight, and not different in head width.

The average boy of mid-twentieth century is five inches taller and twenty-four pounds heavier than his counterpart of 1880.[55] The average soldier in the United States army during World War II was three-fifths of an inch taller, almost ten pounds heavier, and better nourished than the average World War I soldier.[56] College students today are taller and heavier than their counterparts of twenty-five years ago. Today's athletes outstrip yesterday's stars in nearly every discipline. In the eighteenth century, the king of Prussia, Frederick the Great, had to search all over Europe to find enough men six feet tall to serve as his special guards. Today, he could find that many in almost every large high school. Visitors to museums are frequently astounded by the size of armor and other garments worn by medieval knights; they give the impression that twelve-to-fourteen-year-old children went on the Crusades. Actually, armor was worn by adults who on the average were several inches shorter than today's adults. The measurements of recruits in countries that have had universal military draft show consistent increases in both height and weight over the past generations.[57]

The examples given show that these increases are due to greater availability of food, a more balanced diet even among the poor, more equitable distribution of the countries' wealth, improved medical care, the resulting decrease in illness and epidemics, and virtual elimination of child labor.

"Natural experiments" tested the role of nutrition in the maturation process and revealed a direct correlation between quality of nutrition and physical development. Adverse effects of inadequate nutrition were observed during three socio-economic upheavals: World War I, the Great Depression, and World War II. All three catastrophes had a direct impact on the growth of children and teenagers. During World War I, there was a slowing of growth among the children of nations that were intensely involved in the war.

Reliably documented correlations between nutrition and physical measurements come from Stuttgart, Germany, where children were measured

[54]Howard V. Meredith and Virginia B. Knott, "Descriptive and Comparative Study of Body Size on United States School Girls," *Growth*, 26 (December 1962): 283–95.

[55]Luella Cole and Irma N. Hall, *Psychology of Adolescence* (New York: Holt, Rinehart & Winston, 1965), p. 23.

[56]Ibid.

[57]Ibid.

every year since 1910, with records available for both the *Volksschule* (elementary school) and the *Oberschule* (secondary school).[58] The records show marked reductions in weight and height during times of national crisis. For example, around 1925, the average weight for all age levels declined sharply. These were years of severe inflation. Concomitantly with recovery from the national economic disaster, there was an upswing in physical measurements. During the first years of World War II there was an increase in weight, probably because Germany acquired food supplies through conquest. Over the subsequent four years, however, the average weight declined rapidly and remained low for two or three years after the end of the war.

An additional insight grew out of this study. There was a consistent difference between pupils in the two types of schools. Since the German system allows youths of the same age to attend either the *Volksschule* or the *Oberschule*, comparison between pupils of the same age was possible. The *Oberschule* draws enrollment primarily from upper socioeconomic classes. Regardless of national crises, the average measurements of the *Oberschule* pupils *always* remained above those of the *Volksschule* pupils.

The direct correlation between socioeconomic background and physical growth has been verified in Germany as recently as the 1980s. A survey showed that students from unskilled working-class families had the smallest measurements, while those from professional and business families had the largest. Students from the middle of the socioeconomic range—from skilled working-class and farm families—had in-between measurements.[59]

The influence of a national crisis on the growth pattern of children was observed in America during the Great Depression. The greatest impact was among the children of middle-class parents, who met the crisis by reducing the quality of food rather than relying on public relief. Interestingly, the children of the lowest income groups actually gained weight during those years, probably because the food given to them in public kitchens or through charities was better than the diet their parents had been able to provide.[60]

Rate and quality of growth correlate positively with socioeconomic status. The differences are small but consistent from one study to another. Children of professionals or business executives are on the average taller and heavier than those from middle-class homes, who, in turn, exceed in all aspects of growth the children from the lowest socioeconomic class.

American society is characterized by factors favoring earlier maturation and superior physiological development, with a concomitant intensifying

---

[58]Paul E. Howe and Maria Schiller, "Growth Responses of the School Child to Change in the Diet and Environmental Factors," *Journal of Applied Physiology*, 5 (August 1952): 51–61.

[59]"Karlsruhe: Studenten immer länger," *Mitteilungen*, Deutsche Akademischer Austauschdienst (DAAD), Bonn, November 1982, p. 17.

[60]C. E. Palmer, "Height and Weight of the Depression Poor," *United States Public Health Reports*, 50 (1935): 1106–13.

effect on adolescence. While earlier maturation creates a longer period of adolescence, and while superior maturation produces a youth with the capabilities and physical appearance of an adult, he or she is not allowed to act as an adult.

Although the age of pubescence has begun to level off in the United States, we can assume that the teenage subculture will soon include ten-to-nineteen-year-old youths rather than thirteen-to-nineteen-year-old youths.

Postindustrial society is delaying adulthood for educational, economic, and other reasons, and improved biological care shortens the period of childhood. In-between lies an expanding period in which a person's physical and sexual maturity is out of phase with his or her social position.

SUMMARY

Postindustrial life accentuates the adolescent experience. Most influential in this aggravation is the complex network of positions making continuity from child to adult status difficult. The division of labor in postindustrial society requires specialists to occupy a vast range of highly specific positions. Children are "generalists." When they enter adolescence, the generalist standing becomes dysfunctional and they must choose a specific but relatively unknown position. Most teenagers know little about their parents' occupational responsibilities, and only a small proportion follow the occupation of their parents. This situation calls for nonfamilial preparation for the adult position. High schools and other institutions have replaced traditional preparation within the family setting and assumed *in loco parentis* authority. Since technological progress is continuously eliminating the need for unskilled manual labor and creating new technical and managerial positions, training and education of adolescents have become more complex and time consuming. This adds more years of poorly defined status to the adolescent experience.

American schools have become holding pens trying to prevent the onrush of millions of sixteen-year-olds into the labor market. The holding-pen nature of modern education has been sensed by the students and has created among them a sense of meaninglessness. Students' resentful attitudes are compounded by many young Americans' expectation that postindustrial society's promise of "instantness" can be applied to mental tasks.

In addition to geographic mobility, extensive social mobility increases uncertainty by inducing the teenager to improve, strive, and enter a career with prestige.

Frequently, socialization of the young takes place in nonfamilial institutions. Clinicians have found that parental deprivation disables the young, inducing defects in achievement, identity, assumption of adult responsibilities, and acquisition of normal emotions.

Adolescents' affluence allows them to materially implement peer standards. They signify membership in the subculture by material implementation and thereby reinforce a collective identity.

Modern medicine, technology, and especially nutrition have lowered the age of puberty. Since the upper limit of adolescence is not lowered, increasing proportions of America's youth experience adolescence.

6

American Culture and Its Imprints

CULTURE: A SOCIOLOGICAL EMPHASIS

While the preceding chapter discussed the impact of major structural, technological, and biological conditions on the adolescent experience, this chapter explores the influence of a more abstract phenomenon: culture.

The concept of culture varies with the frame of reference. For example,
the colloquial connotation usually deals with the "finer things" in life, such as
art, music, theater, dance, literature, etc. Anthropologists refer to either
physical or nonphysical culture or to both, including all human creations.
Physical aspects of culture refer to the products of technology; nonphysical
aspects to ideas, knowledge, and common symbolic expressions.

The latter dimensions of culture are important to the sociological
discussion, since they emphasize *rules, expectations, and values of society,*
making up the "blueprint" for behavior that society imposes on its members.
This blueprint consists of cultural dicta and is enforced by social sanctions (by
punishment for deviation, reward for conformity). It is a powerful force,
capable of evoking compelling reactions, such as guilt and shame in cases of
violation, and pride and self-esteem in cases of adherence. The following
discussion uses the term culture primarily in the sense of a blueprint for
behavior maintained by formal as well as informal sanction systems.

THE NATURE-NURTURE CONTROVERSY

Although social scientists agree that modern teenagers are characterized by restless and confused behavior, they differ in explaining this behavior. While most sociologists and psychologists argue for an environmental, primarily cultural, explanation, a few opt for a biogenetic hypothesis. The question of whether *nature* (biological conditions) or *nurture* (social environment) is responsible for a given behavior pattern is an old one and has been asked in relation to various stages of life. The assumption that a causal relationship exists between the physiological, especially endocrinological, changes during pubescence and the adolescent's behavior has been largely discarded in favor of the cultural explanation.

It is for historical interest that we refer to G. Stanley Hall, frequently called the father of the psychology of adolescence. He promoted a biogenetic theory that became well known in the 1910s and 1920s and became the credo of many educators and psychologists.[1] In fact, the concept of adolescence was brought to the attention of the public through Hall's writing, starting during the last two decades of the nineteenth century.

Hall's psychology of adolescence assumed a causal relationship between pubertal changes and social-psychological adjustment problems. It translated Darwin's concept of evolution into a psychological theory of individual recapitulation, asserting that the experiential history of the human species had become part of the genetic structure of each individual. The law of recapitulation maintained that the individual organism, during its development, passes through phases that simulate the developmental stages of the human race from early animal-like primitivism through an era of savagery to the more recent, allegedly more civilized, ways of life that characterize maturity. "Ontogeny recapitulates phylogeny" is the famous adage derived from this theory.

Hall's first major developmental phase includes the first four years of life, when the child is still crawling. Presumably this corresponds to the animal stage of the human race, when the species was using four legs. The period of childhood, ranging from about four to eight, corresponds to the epoch when hunting and fishing were humans' main activities. This primitive way of living is reflected in children's play preferences, such as playing cowboys and Indians, using toy weapons, and building caves, camps, and other hiding places. The latter activities putatively parallel the cave-dwelling culture of early history. Youth, from eight to twelve, recapitulates the life of savagery of several thousand years ago. Hall considered children in this stage to be receptive to learning skills and discipline. Adolescence ranges from puberty to the attainment of full adult status, which occurs between twenty-

[1]G. Stanley Hall, *Adolescence*, 2 vols. (New York: Appleton-Century-Crofts, 1916).

two and twenty-five years of age. Hall ascribed the idiom *Sturm und Drang*[2] (storm and stress) to this stage and likened it to the time when the human race was in a turbulent, transitional stage. In late adolescence, the individual recapitulates the initial phase of modern civilization and enters the end phase of the process: maturity.

These developmental stages are presumably brought about by biologically innate forces that control growth and behavior. Human behavior was thought to manifest itself therefore in unchangeable patterns regardless of differences in the cultural environment.

Cultural anthropologists challenged this assertion in the light of cross-cultural observations.[3] They pointed to societies where adolescence did not exist, thereby invalidating Hall's claim that the adolescent's dispositions are universal expressions of innate drives.

However, Hall and his followers continued to insist that socially unacceptable behavior, the type held analogous to earlier historical phases, must be tolerated by parents and educators, since it is part of unavoidable stages in the social development of the individual. These psychologists reassured parents and teachers that objectionable behavior would vanish of its own accord in subsequent stages of development and that corrective measures were neither necessary nor advisable. Remnants of this theory still occupy a place in American educational philosophy embedded in such ideas as Gesell's concept of maturation.[4] In fact, Hall's theory played a role in the formation of the educational philosophy of permissiveness—a child-rearing style that has become widespread in America. Like Rousseau, whose educational philosophy is illustrated in *Émile*, Hall believed that the adult should not interfere with the natural course of development, which is determined by directional forces innate to humans.

Although G. Stanley Hall has almost been forgotten, if not rejected, he has left his mark on the theories of adolescence. His critics denied the validity of conceptualizing personal growth in terms of "stages," yet this is still done.

---

[2]Hall was strongly influenced by a movement in German literature that was led by Schiller and Goethe. The literary trend extolled idealism, search for goals, revolution against the old, expression of personal feelings, passion, and suffering. Hall drew an analogy between the objectives of this group of youthful writers at the beginning of the eighteenth century and the psychological characteristics of adolescence.

[3]One of the first and most incisive challengers was Margaret Mead, *Coming of Age in Samoa* (New York: William Morrow, 1983). However, recent reexamination of Mead's data revealed her "nurture" bias and her consequent misrepresentation—albeit unintentional—of growing up in Samoa. See Derek Freeman, *Margaret Mead and Samoa: The Making and Unmaking of an Anthropological Myth* (Cambridge, MA: Harvard University Press, 1983).

[4]Arnold Gesell maintained that maturation and growth is a process that should not be interfered with. He assumed that time alone will solve most of the normal problems of the child and that difficulties and deviations will be outgrown. Arnold Gesell and Frances L. Ilg, *Infant and Child in the Culture of Today* (New York: Harper & Row, 1943).

His critics charged him with exaggerating the "storm and stress" symptoms, yet this is the preoccupation of many psychologists of adolescence today.

A realistic assessment of the nature-nurture question will probably result in neither an extreme environmental nor an extreme biogenetic statement, but rather in a balanced view. Without doubt, the physiological upheavals during early adolescence are capable of profoundly influencing the psychological processes and the social behavior of the young individual. However, the vast majority of modern behavioral scientists ascribe greater influence to the cultural environment's interpretation of this physiological turbulence than to the physiological processes per se.

Cultural interpretations establish the meaning of an event, thing, or physiological process. Humans, as creatures who interpret symbols, do not react to things and happenings as such, but mainly to the meanings attached to them. From a cross-cultural point of view, it is possible to observe a nearly endless *differential interpretation of neural impulses*; that is, one and the same physiological process can be perceived in totally different ways.

PUBESCENCE AND CULTURAL VALUES

As mentioned in the preceding chapter, urban-industrial society tends to cause earlier onset of pubescence and extends the adolescent period into younger age groups. This implies that concomitant sexual needs occur at a progressively younger age.

The young adolescent's awareness of physiological changes—even if they were not accompanied by any particular cultural interpretation—would be enough to cause him or her alarm. Bodily changes take place too rapidly to give the child enough time to adjust. When a negative cultural interpretation of the sexual maturation process is added, it leaves a powerful and often lasting impression.

American culture turns pubescence into an adolescence-reinforcing event by making the young feel that they go through a stage that should not be mentioned. Both girl and boy develop ambiguous perceptions of their bodily changes that often result in nonacceptance of themselves.

In contrast, in many so-called primitive tribal societies, pubescence is celebrated. For example, the Apache Indian girl's menarche is celebrated by a priest who kneels before her to obtain her blessing.[5] Four ceremonial days honor the Navajo girl's puberty. She is bathed and decorated; relatives bake corn cake; songs and chants are offered; and young men run the dawn races.[6]

[5]Ruth Benedict, *Patterns of Culture* (New York: New American Library, 1950), p. 26.
[6]Charlotte J. Frisbie, *Kinaaldà: A Study of the Navajo Girl's Puberty Ceremony* (Middletown, CT: Wesleyan University Press, 1967).

DISPARITY BETWEEN BIOLOGICAL ADULTHOOD AND SOCIAL ADULTHOOD

American culture prescribes sexual neuterness at a time the young have just achieved sexual potency and are characterized by intense sexuality. Biologically, the vast majority of adolescents are as capable of the reproductive act and as much in need of erotic release as the adult. But, while teenagers are sexually adult, they are not yet socially adult; they are called "minors," and this cultural norm is legally edged: not one state in the union permits marriage under the age of eighteen without the consent of the parents.

The social immaturity ascribed to teenagers has serious implications for their sex lives. American mores discourage young adolescents from expressing their sexual interests; sexual expression, be it heterosexual, homosexual, or autoerotic, is disapproved. Yet the majority of adolescents have been both sufficiently informed and encouraged by mass media fare to choose actual sexual experimentation over passively limiting themselves—as utopian cultural standards would seek—to fantasies or nocturnal emission. Without exception, survey data have shown high rates of masturbation, petting, sex play, and intercourse.

Representative survey findings of 1979, collected by UCLA sex researcher Aaron Hass and based on samples across the nation, show that among fifteen-to-sixteen-year-olds 43 percent of the boys and 31 percent of the girls have had intercourse. Approximately 28 percent of the boys and 7 percent of the girls report ten or more sexual partners. In the same age group, 80 percent of the males and nearly 50 percent of the females report they masturbate at least once a week. Nearly 70 percent of the girls and 90 percent of the boys approve of oral sex, and, among seventeen-to-eighteen-year-olds, over half of each group has performed it.[7]

The Kantner-Zelnik surveys, corroborating many others, show that teenage sexual activities have increased over the past decades. National samples indicate that the proportion of fifteen-to-nineteen-year-old girls having premarital intercourse has grown from 30 to about 50 percent in 1979.[8] These figures confirm the findings of various surveys showing increases in premarital intercourse rates for all groups of young Americans, but particularly for women, who now roughly match the men's rate.

Since premarital sexual behavior deviates from cultural norms, most sexually active teenagers experience feelings of guilt and shame. Recognizing that they have violated standards imposed by adults, they develop a sense of alienation. Feelings of shame and guilt are easily converted into feelings of rejection and hatred against those causing the self-punishing emotions. Ulti-

---

[7]Aaron Hass, *Teenage Sexuality* (New York: Macmillan, 1979), pp. 53, 54, 67, 68, 86.
[8]"Contraception," *Psychology Today*, November 1980, p. 100.

mately, a reinforcing vicious cycle forms between the rejector and the rejectee. This holds especially true when the parties involved are collectivities, since feelings of rejection toward outsiders thrive most vigorously if an ingroup supports and rewards hostile attitudes. The rejection that teenagers perceive because of their sexual attitudes and activities is in this way transformed into feelings of belonging to the peer group, which accepts them as they are.

THE LACK OF RITE OF PASSAGE INTO ADULTHOOD

Life in society consists of a series of passages from one age group to another, from one occupation to another, from one institutional membership to the next — in other words, from one status to another. In parts of the world, the progression from one status to the next is accompanied by ceremonies publicly proclaiming entry into the new status. Sometimes the ceremonies are of a sacred nature, suggesting divine sanction of the new role and entrusting the individual with rights and obligations. In all cases, these rites are public rituals, manifesting the consensual quality of the transition.

Certain transitions are universal. Birth, puberty, assumption of adult responsibility, marriage, parenthood, and death are examples of universal experiences. These and other crises are usually accompanied by rites of passage designed to carry the individual from one phase of human experience to another. Although the celebrations may differ in detail and manner from one culture to another, wherever they are present they essentially serve the same three functions:

Informing. The initiate is informed of his or her new rights and obligations. Sometimes this may involve a special period of training and indoctrination supervised by qualified elders of the community.

Announcing. The community is alerted to the fact that a given person assumes a new status and that the actions and reactions of its members must now fall in line with new role interaction.

Emotionally anchoring. Humans respond to rituals profoundly. More persistent loyalty and commitment can be elicited through them than through almost any other means. Taking on a new role in the eyes of the public and witnessing its decisive approval presents the young with a validated reinforcement that gives him or her a feeling of belonging to the new status. The initiate does not *play* the new role; he or she *becomes* the role. (Points 1 and 3 are obviously not implemented in birth and death, where the rite is solely for the benefit of the community.)

The rite of passage in the context of adolescence concerns the transition from the status of child to the status of adult. It is popularly held that the transition is indicated, if at all, by puberty rite. However, it is necessary to distinguish between the rite of passage concerning physiological puberty and "social puberty"; they are different and only occasionally converging phenomena.

Many privileges, such as sexual expression, marriageability, and adult responsibilities do not depend on puberty but may be experienced earlier or later, depending on the individual and the social environment. Nonsynchronization of physiological puberty and social puberty can be illustrated by many examples, such as the fact that in Italy girls are legally marriageable at age twelve, when barely 10 percent of Italian girls have started menstruating. In France it is legal to marry at sixteen and one-half years of age, but the average age of puberty is around fourteen.[9] Thus, in Italy social puberty precedes physiological puberty, while in France it follows.

Among the Salish Indians of British Columbia, membership in an endogamous adult class begins with a name-giving ceremony, which always comes later than the ceremony of puberty. The father prepares an elaborate feast and invites the relatives. When all have gathered, the father leads his son, together with sponsors, onto the roof of the house and begins a prescribed dance and song. This is followed by distribution of gifts in the name of ancestors. Then the father asks forty nobles to act as witnesses, while two elder chiefs step forward with the young man between them and announce the name and the titles of that ancestor after whom the father wishes the son to be named. In most cases it is the grandfather. The crowd expresses consent through hand clapping. Once more, gifts are distributed, and a meal follows; afterward the young man is known by the name and title received at the ceremony.[10]

This custom is not as unique as it may appear. For example, in Japan and Europe during the Middle Ages, the coat of arms corresponded to the totem and sacred symbols and tatoos for age groups or secret societies. Bestowing of the coat of arms, like that of the totemic emblem, is a rite of passage into an adult group.[11] Among the Masai of Kenya, circumcision as a ritual of social puberty occurs as soon as boys are considered strong enough to undergo the elaborate rite, usually between twelve and sixteen. The date sometimes depends on the affluence of the boy's family. Circumcision may be performed earlier if the parents are rich; if the parents are poor, the ceremony is delayed until they can pay the cost. The ritual of circumcision

---

[9]Arnold van Gennep, *The Rites of Passage* (Chicago: University of Chicago Press, 1960), p. 66.

[10]Ibid., p. 101.

[11]Ibid., pp. 101–02.

takes place every four to six years; all boys who are circumcised at one time belong to an age group bearing a special name chosen by the chief. Simultaneously with or prior to the rite of passage for the boy, the father must undergo the rite of "passing the fence," signifying acceptance of the status of "old man," after which he is called "father of (name of his offspring)."[12]

Another example of the independence of initiation rite from puberty is the bar mitzvah. It takes place when the Jewish boy is thirteen and presumably enters the age of responsibility and religious duty, thereby acquiring adult status. The bar mitzvah has been reduced to mere religious ceremony with little or no bearing on the public and secular life of the boy. Obviously, a thirteen-year-old boy is not eligible for marriage and may not assume adult status in the larger American community.

Because of discrepancy between physiological maturation and ascription of adult status, it is incorrect to refer to *initiation rites* (entry into adult status) as puberty rites. In virtually all societies the age at which young men and women are allowed to marry does not coincide with physiological puberty, and if one day the two moments, one social and the other physiological, come to coincide, they will do so only as a result of deliberate planning.

American culture lacks *both* puberty and initiation rites. Puberty is a taboo issue and is not accompanied by a public ritual with status-clarifying effect. Likewise, there is no definitive rite of initiation into the adult world, although a legal age is set for marriageability and franchise. However, prior to these particular privileges, there is partial assumption of adult responsibilities and privileges through military service, employment, driving an automobile, and so on. One cannot speak, therefore, of a *certain age* at which the young of our society move from one status to the other.

Clarity of one's social position and integration into the system is a recognizable human need. To meet this need, a number of prerequisites must be completed, one being a clear introduction into one's status. Absence of a transition rite reduces awareness and clarity of one's status and can create maladjustment.

If society is to prevent this type of maladjustment, it must (1) clearly define roles, (2) cultivate consistent responses toward role incumbents, (3) respect the importance of each role, and (4) observe a transition procedure that clearly signals the change of role.

These principles are not available for the majority of American teenagers. There is role confusion, condescension toward their age group, inconsistent response patterns on the part of the larger society toward the young, and lack of transition procedure.

---

[12]M. Merker, *Die Massai, Ethnographische Monographie Eines Ostrafrikanischen Semiten-Volkes* (Berlin: Reimer, 1904), p. 55.

VALUE CONFLICT: THE ALL-AMERICAN DICHOTOMIES

Although dualism in value patterns can be observed in most modern societies, American society appears to subject its members to extreme contrasts. Some deserve special mention because they cause confusion and uncertainty for all Americans, whether young or old:

Competition versus cooperation.   American society maintains the value of fierce competition and glorifies a "winner"—whether it is a beauty queen or a farmer raising the finest cattle. The goal of economic success has been heavily stressed and has strained institutional regulations and the permissible means for its attainment. In extreme instances, only questions of technical effectiveness have entered into the choice of means for the goal, and "business is business" has been the apology of robber barons, organized crime, and racketeering.

However, the generosity of the American people is proverbial. There exists an enormous range of voluntary humanitarian activities in America such as the Community Chest, service clubs, public welfare agencies, religious charities, private philanthropies, and the Peace Corps.

The polarity of competition and cooperation is part of many situations involving young people. In school, boys and girls become aware very early that they are competing with one another. The typical American grading system, the "curve" method, automatically converts students into competitors. Yet students are expected to cooperate when it comes to other aspects of interaction, such as dating, courting, and marriage. Necessity of frequent, abrupt switches from one attitude to the other and unclearness of when and how to do so introduce confusion into the boy–girl, and later man–woman, relationship.

Work versus leisure.   Puritan tradition viewed successful work as a sign of divine grace. The metaphysical directive to work was the norm in the older rural culture of America and is still extant in rural areas and subcultures that have not yet assimilated postindustrial attitudes toward leisure and consumption.

Modern American youth's attitude toward work mirrors the economic conditions of the nation. During the early 1970s, propelled by idealistic counterculture philosophy, youth took material security for granted and looked for psychological rewards ("self-realization") when choosing a career. The attitude was reflected in Yankelovich's survey findings: 57 percent of college and 52 percent of noncollege youth felt confident that they would "make as much money as they want." Yet their confidence apparently was not based on the Protestant ethic, since their belief in "hard work always pays off" declined from 79 percent in the 1960s to 56 percent in the 1970s.[13]

With worsening economic conditions, the 1980s and early 1990s saw a return to basic material concerns by American youth. College students realized that they were facing hard times in which the work ethic again played a role. But a modification had also developed: Young people expected the work ethic to be supplemented, if not replaced, by social welfare programs.

At the same time, we have observed continuing conspicuous consumption. For example, despite gas prices, hotel fees, and import duties, America's lakes still teem with speed boats, hotels still show "no vacancy" signs, and young people are saturated with foreign-made goods. The last decade of the twentieth century still reveals the contrasting values of hard work and of consumption patterns anchored in post-industrial affluence.

Piety versus freethinking. Public opinion polls have shown that freedom is repeatedly mentioned as one of the most cherished advantages of American life. Most Americans are proud to remember such freethinkers as Walt Whitman, Ralph Waldo Emerson, and Henry Thoreau. When it comes to concrete instances, however, "free thought" rapidly loses its appeal. It is often said that America is a land of freedom of religion, but hardly *from* religion. For example, one who publicly admits being an atheist often meets with suspicion and rejection. This conflict between "free thought" and Christian piety has been visible in long, drawn-out battles and polemics concerning prayer in public schools.

Individualism versus conformity. The "individual" in American life is conceptualized as an independent and inventive agent, morally responsible only to him- or herself. While theoretically this idea is still maintained, considerable dependency and conformity has developed in American life. Regulations have been introduced, presumably guaranteeing economic well-being for all, including social security, Medicare, and obligatory retirement funds. Critics call these measures "welfare state practices" and claim that freedom is no longer tied to a system of private property and passive government.

American youth are introduced to many glorified, historical exposés of "rugged individualism" and encouraged to emulate this "truly American" trait. On the other hand, they are constantly challenged to conform to national and patriotic standards. Although conflicting values have been part

[13]Daniel Yankelovich, *The New Morality: A Profile of American Youth in the 70s* (New York: McGraw-Hill, 1974), pp. 84, 87, 103.

of any era, they were particularly visible during the 1960s and early 1970s when dissent against the Vietnam War ran high. A powerful faction of public opinion, the "silent majority," recognized dissent not as an expression of individualistic thinking but as subversive and un-American. It is interesting to note that factionalism also split the youth population, dividing them into "hawks" and "doves."[14]

New national and international issues will continue to challenge youth. They will have to decide whether to adhere to or dissent from governmental policies. Each generation of young Americans will have to learn anew that the cultural blueprint for individualism is ambiguous and situational—imposing on them the nongeneralizability that prevents simplicity and predictability in social life.

Sex versus chastity.   One of the most vexing clashes of values in American life deals with sexuality, and its corollary of sex appeal and youthful prowess, on one side, and the virtue of chastity, with its corollary of Christian asceticism generally, on the other side. Shifting emphasis on the continuum between these poles makes generalization difficult. The past several decades have seen interesting oscillations.

From the 1960s to the late 1980s young Americans have expressed what might have been the freest sexual standards in American history, possibly warranting the label of Sexual Revolution for a part of that period. But even during those years the battle between American values never abated, the virtue of chastity was propounded by concerned parents, educators, and, above all, clergymen. Strangely enough even voices from the New Left chimed in, joining conservative views by pointing out that American culture promotes commercialized "sex and love" and made it part of the all-American fun syndrome. In the process—says Herbert Marcuse, a leader of the socialist fraction of the counterculture—the liberalization of sexualization has been taken advantage of by the capitalist system and used as a repressive means, dulling the political sensitivities of the masses. In a sense, commercial sexuality has taken over the role of religion as the opium of the masses.[15]

At the same time, however, puritanical values refused to surrender and were still able to oppose sexual liberation and inflict those well-known control emotions of guilt and shame on young Americans.

Then an unexpected element entered the scene: the sexually transmittable condition of AIDS. This lethal condition suddenly rejuvenated Puritan attitudes. AIDS accomplished virtually overnight what years of preaching

[14]Hans Sebald, "Voices of War and Peace—What Do They Know? Attitudes and Knowledge about the War in Southeast Asia," *Pacific Sociological Review*, 14 (October 1971): 487–510.

[15]Herbert Marcuse, *An Essay on Liberation* (Boston: Beacon Press, 1969).

from the pulpit had failed to achieve: reconsideration of standards of chastity. One could, however, argue that embracing chastity during the last years of the twentieth century was less an endorsement of a value and more the heeding of medical warning. The official tolerance, even promotion, of the sale of condoms on campuses seems to indicate that reining in liberal sexual behavior is more an issue of health than of virtue.

Implications.   In summing up the meaning of such polarities in American culture, one could say that the American mentality is beset with contradictory values. These inconsistencies add vexation to the lives of adolescents, whose learning must proceed situationally instead of holistically. This means they must assess each situation as to which side of the polarity is to be implemented. Erving Goffman used the term "frame analysis" to describe the nature of charting one's journey through American life: each situation, like one picture in a film strip, must be analyzed individually and independently from the previous or following frame.[16] If the theory is accepted that a healthy personality at peace with itself requires an integrated *Gestalt* of views and attitudes, then contradictory cultural values will have confusing and possibly even pathological effects.

VALUE CONFLICT: THE CHILD-ADULT DICHOTOMIES

No culture ascribes the same blueprint to all participants. Humans at different chronological stages have different needs and capabilities; nowhere is a child required to act like an adult, and neither is a mature and healthy adult allowed to act like a child for any length of time. The differences that various cultures have with respect to time of role transition and to degree of role distinction vary greatly. In some societies, mostly the small and so-called primitive societies, children assume adult roles at an early age, while in the large and modern societies children grow into adulthood via a nondescript phase that separates adulthood from childhood by as much as ten years. With respect to degree of role differentiation, American culture goes to great lengths to emphasize contrasts between the roles of child and adult, prescribing for each distinct sets of expectations. This principle can be exemplified by a number of specific opposing role expectations.

Responsibility versus nonresponsibility.   In many tribal societies, child-rearing techniques achieve a continuity of activities that is not limited to daily nurturing patterns but is extended to include responsibilities that, in

---

[16]Erving Goffman, *Frame Analysis: An Essay on the Organization of Experience* (Cambridge: Harvard University Press, 1974).

our society, are reserved for adults. For example, in the United States a child is declared nonresponsible with respect to serious adult work. Americans consider it a rule that the child wants to play and that the adult has to work, forgetting that in many societies the mothers take their babies along to their daily work, carrying them in shawls or baskets close to the body. The child thus has an opportunity to observe adult work and, as soon as the child is old enough, he or she takes on tasks that are important and yet suited to his or her strength—thereby precluding formation of a dichotomy between work and play.

In American society, the law enforces the child/adult dichotomy. For example, a child cannot be accused of a crime but only of "delinquency." The legal and moral burden is the parents' because the child presumably has not yet reached the "age of legal responsibility." The question of *when* the social and legal reaction to a child's "delinquency," either in terms of penalty or correction, is commensurate with the child's understanding raises a difficult issue. There has been suspicion that permissive and "understanding" attitudes and counseling will only reinforce the delinquent pattern. What is needed, according to some psychiatric experts, is "reality therapy" that makes social reactions commensurate with the juvenile's understanding of his or her acts.[17] Readjustment of the legal machinery in this direction would assure that the juvenile would be held more responsible for his or her behavior.

The brutal killing of an infant by three boys, the oldest a ten-year-old, illustrates the nonresponsible status of a minor's action in American society. The boys were held in 1987 in the Milwaukee Child and Adolescent Treatment Center after they were found to have beaten to death a two-year old girl whom the oldest had been baby-sitting. When she dirtied her diapers, they were so irritated that they beat her with wooden slats pulled from a bunk bed, and also kicked her and jumped on her, causing fatal injuries. Legal consequences were limited to removing the boys for up to one year from their homes, but because of their ages they could not be sentenced to any form of detention. On the other hand, the girl's mother, a 26-year-old woman, was charged with child abuse for leaving the child in the care of a ten-year-old.[18]

Another example deals with Atlanta city officials' effort to stem the tide of juvenile gang activities, which had claimed the lives of scores of young people, including a four-year-old girl who was fatally hit while asleep in her bed when teenagers invaded a housing project in the middle of the night and sprayed it with bullets. Outraged by the killings, the authorities passed a new citywide curfew law, taking effect in November of 1990 and requiring teenagers under 17 to be off the streets by 11 p.m. weekdays and by midnight on Fridays and Saturdays. But it is not the perpetrator of the new law that is

---

[17]William Glasser, *Reality Therapy* (New York: Harper & Row, 1965).
[18]UPI Report, *The Arizona Republic*, March 15, 1987, p. A8.

being punished, rather it is the parents of the offenders who face up to sixty days in jail or a fine as high as $1000.[19]

Jerome S. Bruner, head of the center for cognitive studies at Harvard, thinks we grossly underestimate the perceptual and comprehensive capability of children. Bruner holds that children can learn any subject at any stage of their development and advocates that they be required to perform far more complicated tasks than they do. By not expecting much from children, we in fact condition them not to give much, thereby perpetuating the American myth that nonresponsibility for children is necessary.[20]

Sex versus sexless. Sexual attitudes and activities are the most complicated discontinuities in cultural learning. In virtually all societies the child must seriously modify his or her behavior at puberty or at marriage—these two occasions representing universal discontinuities in both sexual capability and sexual standards. At such times, the cultural prescriptions for sex may, for example, change preadolescent sexual license to marital fidelity or, as in a few societies, premarital virginity in either male or female to marital status with considerable sexual license.

Although some degree of discontinuity in sexual behavior is a universal condition, there can be continuity in one aspect: *continuity in sexual expression means that the child is taught nothing he or she must unlearn later.* Therefore, in spite of the universal conditions of puberty and marriage, one can classify some societies as facilitating continuity and others as imposing discontinuity.

For example, adults among the Dakota Indians observe great privacy in sex acts and in no way encourage children's sexual activities.[21] Yet one cannot speak of discontinuity, since the child is not indoctrinated in ways he or she must unlearn later. In a culture with this type of sex pattern, adults view children's sexual experimentation as in no way wicked but rather as innocuous play.

But the same *laissez-faire* attitude may be taken by adults in societies where such play is encouraged among young children. This is true of Melanesian cultures where adults exhibit sexual permissiveness and children feel free to indulge in sex play that is autoerotic, homosexual, or heterosexual. Although modified by marital regulation, the same open and hedonistic style is carried over into adult status, and no discontinuity is experienced.[22]

If society's emphasis is on reproduction, as for instance it is among Zuñi

---

[19]Chicago Tribune report, "Atlanta Hopes," *Arizona Republic*, November 25, 1990, p. B7.

[20]Jerome S. Bruner, *The Process of Education* (Cambridge, MA: Harvard University Press, 1963), pp. 33ff.

[21]Ruth Benedict, "Continuities and Discontinuities in Cultural Conditioning," *Psychiatry*, 1 (May 1938): 164–65.

[22]Ibid.

Indians, sexual expression among children is not encouraged. Although the Zuñi child is impressed with the prohibition of premature sex, the prohibition is not associated with sex itself but only with sex at a young age.[23] In Anglo-American culture the association is with sex as such and the adult often fails to unlearn the evil connotation of sex.

Dominance versus submission.   Americans tend to accept as universal the custom of viewing the adult–child relationship as dominant-submissive. This ethnocentric assumption has been exposed by anthropologists who studied cultures with different modes of intergenerational relations. In some cultures the terminology of address between father and son reflects a reciprocal relationship; the two are equal and the terms of their relationship will never change. When the son becomes a parent, he will establish the same relationship with his child. In societies with this type of equalitarian father–son relationship, the figure with a disciplining function usually is a close male relative, such as the mother's brother.[24] Such kinship conventions provide the individual with a behavior code he or she can follow from childhood through adulthood with minimal discontinuities.

In American society the child lives under parental authority by informal custom and formal law, reinforced by religious dictates of the Judeo-Christian heritage that threaten with damnation everyone who disobeys parents. This generational polarity raises questions for young people about when and how to shift from one mode of the relationship to the other.

Unrealism versus realism.   The culture of the American child, as well as probably of the entire Western Civilization, includes a fantasy world populated by fairies, ghosts, aliens, and other entities of doubtful empirical existence. While these figures are more or less straightforward figments of imagination and children have relatively little difficulty in recognizing them as such during their transition into the more empirically grounded older age, additional figures have been imposed on them through the mass media, especially television, that are far harder to identify as purely imaginary entities. There are two types of figures that are not so readily demystified. One deals with roles pretending superhuman abilities, stamina, and good luck. Our detective, adventure, and Wild West movies show an abundant load of these pretensions. The other deals with occult entities, the main fare of increasing numbers of thrillers and pseudoscience programs. Here is an exploitation of deep-seated human desires for external powers of whose good services we could possibly avail ourselves in times of need. They range from serious or semiserious claims of the existence of ghosts, apparitions, extrater-

---

[23]Ibid.

[24]Reference is to the Trobriand Islanders. Bronislaw Malinowski, *Magic, Science, and Religion, and Other Essays* (New York: Doubleday, 1954).

restrials, and the more abstract forces contactable through meditation or esoteric ritual.

The Youth Survey carried out by Gallup Organization, Inc. has provided data about young Americans' belief in supernatural phenomena, especially about the kind generally defined as occult. Questions were asked concerning belief in angels, astrology, ESP, witchcraft, Bigfoot, ghosts, clairvoyance, and the Loch Ness Monster. The samples represented two teenage categories, girls and boys separately, and the years of 1978, 1984, and 1988. When examining the latest available data of 1988 and comparing the proportions of believers between the age brackets, we notice that occult beliefs tend to increase with age; out of the eight categories, five showed increases, one stayed the same, and only two showed (relatively minor) decreases. When comparing the responses between the boys and the girls, we find that the boys reflect significantly higher proportions in six categories. Only when it comes to believing in astrology do the girls show a significantly higher proportion. (See Table 6–1.)

Teenagers' beliefs in the occult areas show mixed changes over the ten-years' span of the surveys. It appears that angels, ghosts, witches, and astrology gained, whereas ESP, clairvoyance, Bigfoot, and the Loch Ness Monster lost in credibility. (See Table 6–2.) Topping the list is the belief in angels, which interestingly enough should be classified more properly as a religious belief, showing a 74 percent belief record of the teenage population. Second on the list is now astrology with 58 percent, having moved up from third in the 1984 distribution. ESP comes in third; and witchcraft fourth.[25]

It is this kind of occult genre that stubbornly sticks in the minds of the young and is often difficult to dislodge when adult status begins to demand reorientation to more empirical and substantial approaches to life and life's

TABLE 6-1 Teens' Supernatural Beliefs—1988

	National %	Male %	Female %	Ages 13–15 %	Ages 16–17 %
Angels	74	73	74	74	73
Astrology	58	53	64	60	56
ESP	50	54	46	47	54
Witchcraft	29	30	28	26	34
Bigfoot	22	33	11	22	24
Ghosts	22	28	16	19	25
Clairvoyance	21	24	19	15	30
Loch Ness Monster	16	22	10	16	16

Source: The Gallup Youth Survey, Princeton, NJ. Reprinted by permission.

[25]Based on a report by Kendrick Frazier, "Gallup Poll of Beliefs: Astrology Up, ESP Down," *Skeptical Inquirer*, Vol. 13, Spring 1989, pp. 244–45.

TABLE 6–2   Trends in Beliefs

	1988 %	1984 %	1978 %
Angels	74	69	64
Astrology	58	55	40
ESP	50	59	67
Witchcraft	29	22	25
Bigfoot	22	24	40
Ghosts	22	20	20
Clairvoyance	21	28	25
Loch Ness Monster	16	18	31

Source: The Gallup Youth Survey, Princeton, NJ.
Reprinted by permission.

tasks. Exposure to and indoctrination with occult and supernatural phenomena at a tender age may hinder their unlearning at a later age and may partially explain why adults adhere to occult imaginations with perennial persistence. In other words, some persons never accomplish the transition from the child's unrealism to the adult's realism.

Hollywood has been playing a powerful role in cultivating the unreal in American life. The Hollywood connection is influential not only because this center of phantasmagoria produces unrealism, but also because many of its famous actors and actresses have made no secret of their occult convictions. Ghosts and poltergeists enliven not only the screen, but seem to populate many a celebrity's brain. These famous persons—bright, attractive, and lively as they are—present persuasive models to Americans, especially young Americans.

Implications. The above list of child–adult value dichotomies could probably be extended to include play vs. work, dependence vs. independence, and irrationality vs. rationality but the additions would largely overlap with the ones already discussed. In conclusion, American culture contains striking discontinuities between age groups to confuse the individual and strain interpersonal processes. The brunt of the impact of this situation is felt by adolescents who find themselves *between* two relatively well-defined roles. During their transitional existence they have to struggle with ambiguity, constantly trying to decide which set of values and which set of corresponding behavior they should endorse.

ANOMIE IN AMERICAN LIFE

Effects graver than those caused by conflicting values can result from a culture's failure to spell out *any* values or norms. Deviation from known norms or compromise between conflicting norms seems to be less destructive to personality and the social system than vagueness or lack of norms, since deviation or compromise at least starts with a stable point that potentially provides direction.

[Humans need structure,] a *Gestalt* that conveys a sense of direction, orientation, and stability. Such guides are intimately dependent on clear norms and expectations. A person not realizing any norms would be shiftless and unstable. Emile Durkheim recognized this principle in his classic study on suicide, and conceptualized one type of suicide as *anomic, the result of a person feeling meaningless in a normless environment*.[26] Anomie, derived from the Greek *anomia*, originally meant "lack of order" and was used by Durkheim to describe a social milieu in which control over the members has broken down. This breakdown liberates the individual from moral authority of the community, but at the same time results in personal disequilibrium manifested by a variety of antisocial behavior patterns that may include suicide, delinquency, and formation of subcultures.

Values, usually tied up with basic cultural goals suggesting *what* is to be valued, and norms, the rules of conduct spelling out *how* to go about achieving the values, can be considered two different phenomena. The relationship between them varies and can be classified in a number of ways. Robert Merton developed a typology and showed anomie to be a result of preoccupation with cultural goals in the absence of clear norms and means. In terms of American culture, values are suggested, but feasible ways of achieving them are not indicated. As a general example, American culture stresses monetary success, but fails to extend "a corresponding emphasis upon the legitimate avenues on which to march toward this goal."[27] This type of anomie can cause apathy, manifested by the rejection of goals and norms altogether. A prominent type of apathy results after a cultural goal is not attained in spite of intense striving. Reaction to failure may be anxiety expressed in moral fatigue and indifference. The individual may be left in a social vacuum, without direction or meaning.

The significance of anomie for adolescence is that it strikes hardest when social-structural security is not yet obtained, when the young individual is still a "generalist" trying to find orientation in the *general* culture. "General" is emphasized because youth lacks *specific* norms and directives, which come with adult positions. It is in the general culture that anomie operates, and the teenager is bound to suffer anxiety when attempting to derive direction from it.

Adults are faced with the same anomic condition when trying to orient

---

[26]Emile Durkheim, *Suicide: A Study in Sociology*, trans. J. A. Spaulding and G. Simpson (Paris: F. Alcan, 1897; reprint ed., Glencoe, IL: The Free Press, 1951).

[27]Robert K. Merton, "Social Structure and Anomie: Revisions and Extensions," in *Social Theory and Social Structure* (Glencoe, IL: The Free Press, 1949), p. 133.

themselves by abstract cultural features. However, adults have established clarity by means of concrete living patterns—patterns that are guided by positions in the social structure. Since the young are largely excluded from the division of labor of the adult world, they tend to group together and compensate for cultural vacuum by forming a culture of their own.

In conclusion, the psychological reaction to anomie is anxiety, the feeling of being lost in an amorphous surrounding. The reaction to conflict, on the other hand, is *frustration*, the feeling of anger against opposing points. American teenagers suffer from both. The attempt to escape from them leads to subculture formation, where teenagers find norms and values that fit together, thereby eliminating, at least temporarily, anomie and anxiety.

POINT OF ORDER: THE PROBLEM OF SELECTIVITY

This chapter attempted to identify causes of adolescence as they exist in American culture. To accomplish this, I focused on negative aspects of our culture to extract examples necessary to accomplish the analysis. The task can be compared to the job a medical doctor has to do when tracing the causes of a certain condition. The report may point to several physiological problems to explain the illness. For example, he or she may diagnose a malfunction of a certain organ, a deficiency in nutrition, and low resistance. The illness can be understood as the result of the constellation of these factors, and the diagnosis will fail to list all the healthy and normal aspects of the organism since they are of no importance to the diagnosis.

Similarly, in searching for the causes of the adolescent condition, a negative selectivity prevails and only those circumstances are reported that seem to explain it. We investigated the "organ" of culture and found certain characteristics that help us understand the development and persistence of the adolescent condition. Obviously, there are many cultural factors that do not contribute to this condition, but they are not our concern here since they contribute nothing to the diagnosis.

Hence, the picture that emerges from our examination is grimmer than the total reality. Not all aspects of culture work against the adolescent, and not all adolescents stand outside society's blueprint for behavior. Many American teenagers are sufficiently adjusted, and American culture is no more an ogre to the young than most other cultures. Before adolescents realize it, the vast majority of them have grown up and adjusted—and the erstwhile ogre has become a reasonably comfortable habitat.

America has many teenagers who have made a comfortable and even creative adjustment to their culture, enjoy its various institutions, and participate in its programs. A later discussion will touch on some of these aspects.

SUMMARY

American culture, as culture everywhere, is responsible for interpreting life's experiences and issuing blueprints for behavior. The blueprints of our culture contain a number of elements that add complexity to adolescence. The discussion dwelled on several major aspects.

Theories of tracing adolescent "storm and stress" to physiological maturation have largely been replaced by anthropological principles emphasizing the role of cultural relativity in perceiving such organic changes. In American society pubescent changes create adjustment problems because culture avoids giving adequate explanation for them. Youth is thus left unaided to cope with new growth patterns. Social adulthood is not synchronized with biological maturation. During the time teenagers are sexually mature but socially underprivileged, cultural interpretations cause them to feel guilty about sexual expressions.

American culture lacks a definitive rite of passage into adulthood. Transition unclarity creates maladjustments.

Americans are subject to such value dichotomies as competition and cooperation, piety and free thinking, sex and chastity, work and leisure, individuality and conformity. It is difficult for adults to decide which value applies in certain situations and even more difficult for teenagers still working on a basic orientation. Another schism of values breaks the continuity between child and adult roles. Children are kept from continuous involvement in responsibilities and decision making; they are also allowed to dwell in a fantasy world; later they are expected to relearn or unlearn many modes of thinking and behaving when entering adult positions.

Adolescents are particularly vulnerable to anomie in American life because they do not yet have access to specific positions in the productive sector that would help them derive identity and stability.

7

Social Change and Intergenerational Conflict

CONFLICT BETWEEN GENERATIONS

Conflict between older and younger generations is a perennial issue. The social dynamics of every society undergoing change promote tension between generations. Postindustrial society seems singularly afflicted, and a number of points show how this has come about.

Rapid Social Change

Part of the explanation of the generation gap lies in the pace of social change. In a rapidly changing society, established and respected norms of one generation become obsolete to the next. The older generation may greet innovations with mixed emotions ranging from caution to hostility. Nostalgia for the "good old days" is the universal reaction of elders to unfamiliar behavior patterns. The older generation's lack of familiarity with new styles frequently labels innovations as "weird," "immoral," or "subversive." These epithets, describing the younger generation, can be found in the diaries of virtually all eras. Exceptions to this rule are limited to a few simply-structured tribal societies in isolated localities in which the pace of social change is minimal.

The tempo of sociocultural change varies from society to society and can be measured on a continuum ranging from near-stagnancy to revolutionary reorganization. One way of classifying societies by their internal dynamics is in terms of the folk-urban continuum, with slow-changing societies at one end and dynamic urban-industrial societies at the other. Tempo of change is directly correlated with imbalance of perceptions and behavior patterns between the generations. This means that the faster a society changes, the wider the psychological distance between the older and the younger generations. In a nearly unchanging society, the young follow the norms and goals of the older generation so faithfully that the sociocultural fabric of society remains unchanged. Conversely, in dynamic society one would find the young clashing with the older generation, whose norms and goals have become obsolete.

Modern American society is a prime example of a rapidly changing social system. The turnover of technological and social innovations is rapid enough to create a milieu for each new generation notably different from that of the preceding generation, thus inviting adults to perceive youth as "rebellious" and youth to perceive adults as "old fashioned."

The explanation for the unusual amount of adult-youth conflict in modern society can be summed up by a few interrelated propositions, suggested by Kingsley Davis' classic paradigm:

1. Each generation learns culture early, and as its members get older, they have difficulty changing their views of right and wrong.
2. Cultural content in American society is changing rapidly.
3. Culture learned by the parental generation was different from that learned by the offspring, insofar as the adolescent learns from peers and from specific adults who are more current in their thinking.
4 Therefore there is a culture conflict experienced by parents and their offspring.[1]

Changing Status: Changing Perspective

An important social-psychological principle must be made clear at this time. An even greater source of intergenerational conflict than the sociocultural change on the societal level is the change of orientation on the individual level of the parents. It seems to be a truism that by entering into a new social status significant personality changes take place: the novice incumbent internalizes the expectations that go with the new status. This means that the role (rights, obligations, responsibilities, etc.) of the new social position becomes part of the personality system. It translates from the social

[1]Kingsley Davis, "The Sociology of Parent–Youth Conflict," *American Sociological Review*, 5 (August 1940): 523–36.

level to the personality level in the form of new motivations, aspirations, and feelings.

Many societies plant a rite of passage at the time of entering the position, helping the novice to drop an emotional anchor in the new position. Personal identification with position is a social-psychological process that all societies want to see accomplished. Societies could not survive if members would fail to identify with the proper roles and live up to the expectations that are embedded in the roles.

Parenthood is an important example of a position creating new feelings and a new outlook on life. Before people realize it, they abandon old ways when they assume the parental role, forget how they themselves felt and acted when they were the young generation, and their behavior reflects a new way of looking at things. This is a transformation that appears *deus ex machina* and actually should startle everyone involved. But usually it doesn't, because it is perceived as being absolutely normal. It would be considered abnormal if parents continued to frequent teen dancing places, date, and in general failed to discontinue behavior modes belonging to the teen subculture. In an astoundingly short time individuals who had gone through the typical teen years and adolescent conditions undergo major changes in attitude—and when they face their offspring, who exhibit pretty much exactly the same behavior styles as they did during their earlier years, they react from the vantage point of parents and no longer from that of a teenager. This explains, for example, why an erstwhile promiscuous teenager turns into a parent with puritanical attitudes toward the sexual behavior of his or her child; this explains why a previously rebellious youth becomes a conservative adult; this explains, in short, why parents the world over are conservative and tend to be disciplinarians, at least to some degree.

Seeing generational relations from this perspective explains why a certain amount of conflict seems to be inevitable and must be figured into the intergenerational equation.

Children from the perspective of parents are usually seen as having more freedom, less obedience, more resentment. Parents frequently and mostly subconsciously envy their children for their freedom, and would like to recapture it; and if retrieval fails—as it almost always must—they begin to regard that freedom with suspicion and even resentment.

In a specific historical frame, we see parents today who were the free and liberal youths of the counterculture and who are now conservative parents, not unlike the way their own parents had been. It is the power of the social role that works as the *perpetuum mobile* of parent-offspring differentiation and of accompanying conflicts. In sum, the generation gap is caused less by chronological difference and more by social-structural division. The division is between the role of parent and the role of offspring. And since this is a universal division, conflict between the generations is, to a large extent, a universal phenomenon.

Functionality of Conflict

Many observers of symptoms of strain between generations regard these dynamics as dysfunctional. This is a biased view that has to be balanced by pointing to functional aspects of youth unrest and agitation. Since young people are not committed to, and so are less likely to settle for, the status quo, they are able to function as a prime factor of innovation and societal improvement.[2] The young have not yet developed the vested interests that their parents are likely to have in either the ongoing economic system or the value structure, and thus are less likely to plead for the status quo. Being newcomers to the established order makes young people apt to sympathize with social movements that voice dissatisfaction with society. Being young in a modern society means, among other things, being marginal, not yet having vested interests in the existing social order and not yet being integrated in the economic and psychological fabric of society. The position of "outsider" explains youth's fascination with movements that are at the fringe of society.

Youth's lack of commitment to the existing order is not to be automatically viewed as a negative thing, but, can be interpreted as a potential resource. Static or slowly evolving traditional societies do not call on this resource and may even suppress it. However, dynamic societies often use it and even organize it for social progress.

Dangers of Conflict Resolution

One might conclude from this discussion that all youth movements are progressive or liberal, if not downright radical. But surely not all youth movements are progressive. The Nazi youth movement was certainly not politically liberal, at least not in the sense of opposing the regime in power.

Youth is in great need of security and stability, and its search for this type of emotional reward is so relentless that it can be exploited. Although young people often rebel against the reality in which they find themselves, they almost immediately want to replace it with another form of social reality. (Freedom from norms is unbearable!) Karl Mannheim noted that "dissociation from one's previous reality and the seeking of distance from the primary family environment are principal impulses. It is with a sense of liberation that the adolescent discovers alternative interpretations and new values. Self-assertion and defiance accompany this experience.[3]

If a suitable replacement of social reality is prepared for adolescents—as

---

[2]Karl Mannheim, *Diagnosis of Our Time* (New York: Oxford University Press, 1944).

[3]Karl Mannheim, *Essays on the Sociology of Culture* (New York: Oxford University Press, 1956), p. 165.

a clever nationalistic demagogue could easily provide—they may embrace it wholeheartedly and so, paradoxically, support the status quo by means of their rebelliousness.

It seems that the young find it difficult to endure multiple possibilities and loyalties since diffuseness confuses identities. If they arrive at an extra-familial loyalty, a schism may develop between them and their parents. As Mannheim saw it, youth's desire to attain distance from the family culture often leads them to embrace opposing values. Those who grow up in a rigorously traditional home may develop revolutionary leanings, while those with a liberal background may choose a conservative course. However, it must be noted that his theory was not supported by Richard Flacks' study of activist students, who generally came from liberal homes (see discussion below under Parental Reaction II). It is, then, with a great deal of caution that we accept the slogans and complaints that youth uses to legitimize rebelliousness against their social system. Is it invariably the true reason? Or is it an idealized excuse (a typical rationalization) to marshal legitimacy for one's alienation and disturbance? One could defend the notion that the criticism and outspokenness on the part of adolescents is not so much a function of the dismal state of society but rather a normal and almost universal expression of trying to strike roots in a bewildering world.

Socializing the Young: A Universal Confrontation

Aristotle commented over 2000 years ago, in a society far less subject to change than ours, that young people have exalted notions because they have not yet been humbled by life's trials and tribulations. All their mistakes are in the direction of doing things excessively. They would always rather do noble deeds than useful ones; their lives are regulated more by feeling than reasoning. They overdo everything—they love too much, they hate too much, and the same with everything else.

Aristotle noted that older people usually differ in such characteristics. After many years of struggles and mistakes, they have become more ponderous, see things in less than black and white, always "think" but never "know," and in their hesitation always add "perhaps" or "maybe," so that all their statements are of this kind: never unqualified.[4]

In other words, the changes through which society goes may not be the sole reason for conflict. Simply that the young are going through socialization contributes to the generation of friction between the old and the young.

[4]Aristotle, *The Art of Rhetoric*, trans. John H. Freese (Cambridge, MA: Harvard University Press, 1959), book 2, chs. 7–13.

Conflict and Subculture

Youth's dissent can be powerful and has been credited with achieving remarkable sociocultural changes. Many social scientists have interpreted youthful agitation as symptomatic of a subculture apart from the adult culture, and they have come to be known as "great gap" theorists.[5]

But others have taken issue with this interpretation, maintaining that youth has no real integration of its own. Thus there is no real subculture causing the generation gap, and guilt-ridden adults merely react *as if* there were a youth subculture and a generation gap.[6] A representative opinion was expressed by Joseph Adelson, who felt that his survey findings refuted the existence of such a gap.[7]

The trouble with these refutations lies in the violation of the social-psychological principle which says that a situation is real if the participants *perceive* or *define* it as real. Hence it becomes superfluous to question the existence of a youth subculture. If youth *behaves* as if it holds distinct values and has a subculture, then indeed it has one. And youth does in fact behave differently—whether on the basis of clearly understood values or not—and therefore has a subculture that bears its share of the responsibility for the existence of the generation gap.

Many dimensions must be taken into consideration in order to understand the generation gap. One deals with the "normal" condition of being young and, as already noted by Aristotle, having "exalted notions." Another deals with the pace of society's innovations, scientific progress, and "knowledge explosion." A third dimension consists of unique political events that cause a reaction on the part of young people, provoke their anger or fear. A fourth factor deals with cultural images, such as the American youth cult that invites feelings of inferiority among adults and fosters the tendency to accept

---

[5]Advocates of the "great gap" theory include Theodore Roszak, *The Making of a Counter Culture* (New York: Doubleday, 1969); Charles A. Reich, *The Greening of America* (New York: Random House, 1970); Margaret Mead, *Culture and Commitment: A Study of the Generation Gap* (New York: Basic Books, 1970); James S. Coleman, *The Adolescent Society* (New York: Free Press, 1963); and Edgar Z. Friedenberg, "The Generation Gap," *Annals of the Academy of Political and Social Science*, 382 (1969): 32–42.

[6]Researchers who refute the "generation gap" theory include Joseph Adelson, *Handbook of Adolescent Psychology* (New York: Wiley, 1980); Denise B. Kandel and Gerald S. Lesser, *Youth in Two Worlds* (San Francisco: Jossey-Bass, 1972); Vern L. Bengtson, "Generation and Family Effects in Value Socialization," *American Sociological Review*, 40 (June 1975): 358–71; Daniel Yankelovich, "The Generation Gap: A Misleading Half Truth," Paper presented at the meeting of the Eastern Sociological Society, 1970; Frederick Elkin and William A. Westley, "The Myth of Adolescent Culture," *American Sociological Review*, 20 (December 1955): 680–84; Daniel Offer et al., *The Adolescent: A Psychological Self-Portrait* (New York: Basic Books, 1981); and Majda Thurnher et al., "Value Confluence and Behavioral Conflict in Intergenerational Relations," *Journal of Marriage and the Family*, 36 (May 1974): 308–19.

[7]Joseph Adelson, "Adolescence and the Generalization Gap," *Psychology Today*, February 1979, p. 33.

youth's complaints as correct descriptions of societal malfunctions. We will examine some of these dimensions in the following section.

COMPETING AUTHORITIES: PARENTS VERSUS EXPERTS

In tribal or rural societies, social change is slow enough for a child to live the same kind of life his or her parents did. In more advanced societies that have more noticeable change, children often abandon their parents' ways and model their behavior on teachers, friends, and images in the mass media. However, changes fostered by postindustrialism have eroded even these models. Modern youth are like children of wilderness pioneers—the first natives in a new world. For the first time in history there are no elders who know all that the young know. In fact, parents who desire to keep up with current knowledge will have to reverse the traditional pattern and let their children teach them.

This creates an ironic situation. On the one hand, parents are charged with the obligation of introducing children to society, of proceeding with the necessary training, of exerting the necessary control to make the child conform to the demands of culture. On the other hand, parents suffer from cultural lag that leaves them a few paces behind in knowledge in many areas of modern life.

Knowledge Explosion and Expertise

Science and technology are constantly changing, modifying, and adding information in all branches of endeavor. Postindustrial life imposes a premium on the ability to constantly reorient and modify. In order to accomplish this with some degree of adequacy, an almost full-time dedication would have to be invested. Parents can rarely do this. Children, however, attend school, are exposed to the latest information, and *are* involved in this full-time pursuit. Students are at the frontier of knowledge—a frontier that is advanced by experts who are preparing the young for a future that comes faster for each generation.

As any professor knows, it has become exceedingly difficult to keep abreast of the publications and research reports in one's area of expertise. In addition, any particular area has shrunk to an amazingly narrow focus, and is continuing to shrink further. It is no longer possible, for example, to ask a sociologist about just any sociological problem and expect an answer. If the question involves religious behavior, the harried instructor might refer the student to a colleague who is a sociologist of religion; if the question concerns population shifts, the student is sent to a demographer; if it involves criminal behavior, a criminologist is suggested; and if it deals with adolescents, a sociologist of youth is consulted. But even within these narrow foci, publications and research reports pile up and drive even the bravest scholar to despair.

Parental Lag

The division of expertise has rendered parents helpless and increasingly poorly informed. It is normally impossible for parents to be specialists in more than one or two fields. Children and teenagers therefore obtain instruction and advice from specialists and experts. Through the schools, modern youth has access to the most recent discoveries in nearly all branches of science and knowledge, and can acquire insights and up-to-date information that ordinarily never reach the parents. Parents are preoccupied with making a living and providing their children with an education, and learn about the latest developments and discoveries—often inadequately—via secondary channels, such as popular magazines, newspapers, radio, and television. As a novelty in human history, parents are now instructed by their children.

"Halo" Effect

The socialization function carried out by parents was of course never limited to mere factual instruction and scientific information, but included ethical guidance, religious indoctrination, and practical advice. Yet the often conspicuous inability of parents to offer the latest piece of scientific knowledge has had a generalizing effect on the children, inducing them to disregard other aspects of parental competence. In line with this "halo effect," evidence of incompetence in one area tempts children to suspect incompetence in other areas and makes them doubt the ability of parents to introduce them to the adult world.

In Loco Parentis

Extrafamilial "experts" are now doing a substantial part of the rearing and instructing of children. The controversy of *in loco parentis* shows the increasing transfer of socialization function and accompanying authority to schools. Modern teachers with their expanded socialization function, including counseling and advising in matters of personal problems, such as sex and vocational plans, have unintentionally promoted parental obsolescence and reduced parental authority.

Irrational versus Rational Authority

Modern adolescents resent parents who wield authority over them when they feel that the latter are not qualified to do so; they insist on being independent decision makers in areas previously under parental sovereignty.

Authority based merely on position and power—such as the parents'—is increasingly branded by young people as "irrational," while authority based on knowledge (expertise) is defined as "rational." The tendency to engage in the "halo effect" increases the chances that the offspring will view his or her parents' decisions and advice as irrational and overbearing.

Youth finds it difficult to make the distinction between emotional maturity and intellectual acuity—a distinction that must often be drawn between parents and experts. By not drawing this distinction, the young often create confrontations. Parents who, in spite of cultural lag, insist on traditional authority, complete the ubiquitous drama (or comedy, as the case may be) of intergenerational friction and further alienate their offspring.

CLASH OF INFERIORITY COMPLEXES

American culture is responsible for the evolution of two mutually reinforcing complexes that have become elements in intergenerational conflict. They are the inferiority complex of teenagers and the inferiority complex of the parents. These emotional dispositions frequently lead to considerable tension and misunderstanding between the generations. Sociologist Clifford Kirkpatrick has conceptualized this interaction as "clash of inferiority complexes."[8]

The concept describes the subtle dynamics whereby offspring try to dethrone parents. Young people feel inferior because they are untried and lack experience. Feeling this deficiency keenly, they overcompensate by aggressiveness and pseudosophistication. Parents often feel a sense of inferiority because they believe they have passed their prime in life, are declining in youthful attractiveness and sexual prowess, and look back on a life of relatively minor achievements. When they look ahead, they perceive themselves as declining in importance.

When such opposite attitudes encounter each other, as they often do, they reinforce each other—sometimes to the point of exploding in animosity. It is a process of mutually reinforcing and cumulative social response. Youth's cockiness begets renewed insistence by parents that their authority must be upheld. As the final result, alienation between the generations emerges. This estrangement is often superficial and temporary, but occasionally it is tragic and of long duration.

It is important to understand that the collision of inferiority complexes reinforces the inferiority feelings of the two parties and consequently generates more tension. We have here another social-psychological *perpetuum*

---

[8]Clifford Kirkpatrick, *The Family as Process and Institution* (New York: The Ronald Press, 1955), pp. 266–67.

mobile that, at least theoretically, continues the parent-youth conflict as long as Americans cultivate the cult of youth.

THE YOUTH CULT

An element of the American ethos relating directly to the inferiority complex of parents is the cult of youth. American culture minimizes the role of the aged as a source of wisdom and a center of authority, and values the activism of youth, assuming that middle or old age hinders persons from being active and inventive. Old age connotes passive contemplativeness, the nemesis of youthful activism. Trial and error procedure is closer to the hearts of Americans than theory. The "doers" are thought of as young people who have physical vigor to experiment and create. For example, at forty or forty-five years of age, highly trained and experienced pilots are grounded because "they are too old for flying." The practice of "defunctioning" middle-aged and old citizens may result in "no-longer-needed" attitudes. The aged are "cared for" and kindly entertained—but safely away from the mainstream of life, in physical and mental isolation.

The youth cult focuses on the active young, allowing them to set the pace, themes, goals, and tastes of society. Older people can frequently be observed imitating the practices and the crazes of the young generation. It is an almost entirely new historical occurrence that dances and music are passed from teenagers to adults. This trend has evolved over the past few decades and was highlighted by such figures as the Beatles, who created music by the young for the young—creations that were avidly absorbed by adults.

Madison Avenue and American business in general have taken advantage of the American obsession with youthfulness. For example a huge, full-page ad in a daily paper demonstrates the value of paying top prices to sell a youthful appearance to adults. The magical elixir SilkSkin guarantees "younger-looking healthier skin," is endorsed by testimonials that declare that "I looked years younger and my face felt younger," and promises eligibility for "an all-expense paid trip to Hollywood to appear on California Cosmetic's national TV show *The Art of Looking Young and Beautiful.*[9]

It is virtually impossible to determine the causal direction between the youth cult and the parental inferiority complex. Has the youth cult created parent inferiority feelings, or are the parents compensating for bygone youthful attractiveness by adoring and imitating the ways of youth? The question of causal direction can probably never be answered. It is more important at

[9]"An Open Letter to All Women Who Want Younger-Looking Skins," *Arizona Republic,* March 4, 1988, p. D10.

this time to study the mutually reinforcing relationship between the two phenomena.

Manifestations of parents' obsession with youth are not well received by teenagers. They do not care to be imitated. In order to understand the negative reaction, it must be remembered that deep down teenagers feel inferior about themselves and about many of their activities. Persons who perceive themselves as inferior are likely to look down on others who show similar behavior patterns. A college freshman was quoted complaining that his parents were trying to behave like teenagers: "When you see yourself reflected in your folks, it's just awful." Adolescents, by definition uncertain, find their lives directionless in a social environment that decides to rely on their tastes. Adolescents need parents who are adult models and not buddies or imitators of their styles. The teenage peer group already provides companionship among like-minded trial-and-error oriented friends. Adults who try to join the ranks of the young are considered unwelcome renegades from the ranks of potentially helpful adult models.

PARENTAL REACTION I: PERMISSIVENESS

Many parents have become aware of their cultural-lag position and seek remedy. Willingness to communicate with their teenage children is evidenced by a wave of self-effacing literature that can be described as a "parents-are-problems" campaign. Personally and through the mass media, some parents have shown eagerness to learn from, adjust to, and listen to teenagers.

The status of parent is unabashedly labeled a social problem, and parents are often apologetic about being parents. Examples of educational literature, often aimed at teenagers to help in the "upbringing" and "understanding" of their parents, include such books as *Raising Children in a Difficult Time,*[10] *Parents in Contemporary America: A Sympathetic View,*[11] or articles such as "Children as Agents in Socializing Parents," "Parent-Teen Education—An Exercise in Communication," and "Expectations of Youth in Relating to the World of the Adult."[12]

The cultural-lag condition of the parents has also been appraised in popular teenage songs, advising more seriously than facetiously that teenagers should try to understand parents in spite of all the "foolish things they are doing," since they are at a difficult stage in life and need youth's understanding and forgiveness. Other indications that the socialization process has

[10]Benjamin Spock, *Raising Children in a Difficult Time* (New York: Norton, 1974).

[11]E. E. LeMasters and John DeFrain, *Parents in Contemporary America: A Sympathetic View* (Belmont, CA: Wadsworth, 1989).

[12]In *The Family Coordinator,* 19 (July 1970).

undergone considerable change come from interviewing teenagers. Their suggestions to remedy the communication gap typically demand of parents that they (1) must listen before teenagers can tell them anything; (2) must want to cooperate before there can be communication; (3) must update their views; (4) must think as teenagers think; (5) must make themselves available; and (6) must be more understanding.[13] Such expressions indicate that the direction of condescension and instruction has been reversed, proceeding now *from young to old.*

This modification of the age-old socialization process was stimulated by postindustrial conditions but was also helped by the American ethos, which emphasizes equality, usually in regard to sex, race, religious affiliation, and so on, but now also includes (young) *age*. In addition, American culture has little reverence for old age and hence has induced parents to be willing to learn from their children and even to adjust to their way of life. Innumerable articles, books, conferences, and PTA meetings vie with one another for the attention of parents, with the intention of educating them for their children and teenagers.

Other evidence of the parental (or general adult) effort to establish *rapprochement* with the teen world includes the adoption of teenage customs, fashions, and modes of behavior. In various social institutions, adults have promoted teen styles to retain adolescents' loyalty.

Innovations can even be observed in the religious institution, traditionally the most conservative bastion of culture. Services have been employing the type of music, prayer, and dance preferred by modern youth. Tunes of folk songs and the beat of jazz and rock 'n' roll have become acceptable in worship services. In 1967 the Roman Catholic Church relented in its nearly 2000-year-old adherence to sacred liturgy and Pope Paul VI issued a revolutionary document that allowed the use of secular tunes and rhythms in the Mass. The churches' adaptations to teenage styles include clothes, lingo, philosophy, and ritual. Churches have emphasized their adaptability by headlining newspaper ads with "Geared for Teenagers." Others invite the young to come and "wear anything you feel comfortable in."

Prayers are adjusted to teenage lingo, exemplified by *Treat Me Cool, Lord,* a collection of prayers by teenagers; and sermons refer to "hangups," "uptight," "let your hair down."[14] The Bible's bucolic imagery, with its reference to sheep, shepherds, fields, sowing, and harvesting, is thought to be largely meaningless to them. When a minister told a group of boys in Buffalo about the lilies of the field that neither toil nor spin, he encountered laughter—later he found out that in their argot a "lily" meant a homosexual.[15] The

[13]UPI report (New York, November 3, 1965).

[14]Carl F. Burke, *Treat Me Cool, Lord* (New York: Association Press, 1970).

[15]"The Bible," *Time*, March 5, 1965, p. 44.

minister subsequently encouraged the boys to rephrase biblical parables and adapt them to the conditions and the argot of their environment. In this way, the Good Samaritan became the "cool square" who helped a "mugged" victim after a "hood" and a "sneak" (not so "cool" as a "hood") had "passed by." The Christmas story was modified to show the setting in Buffalo during a convention when all hotel rooms were taken and the Savior's stable was a hot dog stand in some municipal park. The parable of the lost sheep was rephrased to be understood as a used-car lot owner who goes looking for the "heap" that someone "snitched."[16]

Leaders of various Christian churches have engaged "rap" jargon to attract teenagers and have introduced rap praying, rap preaching, rap music, rap songs and hits, and gospel rap. Stephen Wiley, an avid promoter of Christian rap and a leader of Teens for Christ, composed such songs as *Bible Break* and *Rappin' for Jesus*.[17] While abandoning age-old liturgical phraseology, rap uses slang to conjure up images with which modern teenagers can identify. No longer is their imaginability charged with the task to step into another world, the world of the sacred; rather religious imagery steps into their secular, everyday world.

The Reverend Clarence J. Rivers of the Catholic Archdiocese of Cincinnati defended the use of teen vernacular in church by saying that there is nothing wrong with entertaining churchgoers, that liturgy's main function is to entertain, and that the reason for a visible church is "to show something: it must be a show."[18] Religion's adaptation includes the musical *Godspell*, which uses clowns, jokes, and soft-shoe dancing to portray the life of Christ in American vaudeville style: "an 18-year-old youth, portraying Jesus Christ, ran down the aisle and leaped on the stage. He wore a Superman shirt and had clown make-up on his face."[19]

A United Methodist minister in Pennsylvania organized a ministry of clowns, mimes, dancers, and puppeteers, and arranged a workshop attended by over 700 clergy and lay leaders who wanted to learn skills to bring the gospel to the young in a lighthearted fashion.[20]

Many of those in the literary establishment adulated youth's style and presumed values, and referred to them as precursors of a new humanism: "Can anyone doubt that if everyone over thirty vanished tomorrow, there

[16]Ibid.

[17]Lawn Griffiths, "Fed Up with Teens' Behavior, Preacher Raps for His Savior," *Mesa Tribune*, March 17, 1990, p. 1D.

[18]"Father River's Songfest Hikes Beat," *Arizona Republic*, February 20, 1971, p. 8

[19]"Youth Group Presents Modern Version of the Life of Christ," *Arizona Republic*, December 9, 1972, p. 48.

[20]James Mann, " 'Soft Sell' is New Password for Churches," *U.S. News and World Report*, August 22, 1983, p. 32.

would be racial peace in this country in a year and a way found to end . . . war?"[21]

Persons in various professions have similarly endorsed, or at least acquiesced to, youth's way of life. A federal judge, for example, sides with youth's criticism of "adult hypocrisy";[22] a professor advocates the "open family" with children as "voluntary" members;[23] and some sociologists call on adults to fulfill youth's expectations: "Continuity of social support is most needed during the transitional stage of adolescence. But if support in the form of guidance is to come from adults (as it should), it must be they who fulfill youth's expectations and not the reverse."[24] The sociologists' suggestion means that youth may set standards and expectations and that adults are obliged not only to tolerate them but to actively assist in carrying them out. Maybe this is what the Hechingers warned of in their ominous book, *Teenage Tyranny*.[25]

In the historical perspective we can see that the combined forces of lowering the legal adult age to eighteen and the inroads forged into institutional rigidity by the counterculture of the early 1970s have caused *in loco parentis* authority to decline on college campuses. Students not only wanted more personal autonomy (as achieved through abolition of curfew rules, for example), but also codetermination of institutional policy, including academic expectations. In the wake of the counterculture, students' demands included having "relevant" courses and representation on faculty and administration committees. Their demands met largely with compliance by faculty and administrators. But, as discussed below, a trend to return to more restrictive standards became noticeable during the early 1990s.

Two interpretations of increased student freedom can be observed throughout the country: (1) as a welcome opportunity for youth to accept responsibility and to grow; (2) as a spilling over of adolescence into formerly adult-run institutions, resulting in lowering the value and maturity of institutional functions. The latter view is aligned with the goal of reasserting traditional authority and curbing social-structural implementation of adolescent thinking and behavior.

Similar permissiveness developed in high schools. Since the 1970s,

[21]Arthur Miller, "The War between Young and Old," *McCall's*, July 1970, p. 32.

[22]Charles E. Wyzanski, Jr., "It is Quite Right that the Young Should Talk About Us as Hypocrites. We Are," *Saturday Review*, July 20, 1968, p. 14.

[23]Larry L. Constantine, "Open Family: A Lifestyle for Kids and Other People," *Family Coordinator*, 26 (April 1977): 113–21.

[24]George Won and Douglas Yamamura, "Expectations of Youth in Relating to the World of Adults," *The Family Coordinator*, 19 (July 1970): 219.

[25]Grace Hechinger and Fred M. Hechinger, *Teenage Tyranny* (New York: William Morrow, 1963).

many rules have been swept away. Today, in almost all schools, students dress as they please, in class and out. Various fads in clothes and grooming are tolerated, including boys' shoulder-length hair, which used to be the most disputed and most severely persecuted item of teen styles. Many boys were prohibited from attending class or were even expelled from school because of long hair, while a drug conviction or other delinquency had much less consequence on continuing with school life.

In summary, many adults as well as institutions have attempted rapprochement with reproachful and alienated youth. The strategies employed seem to add up to a three-pronged thrust: *democracy, communication,* and *information.* Most adult-initiated programs purporting to bring about understanding between the generations were based, explicitly or implicitly, on these three concepts. The concept of democracy was applied to remind parents to consider teenagers as equals. The emphasis on communication was meant to encourage parents to keep in touch with teenagers and diligently work out misunderstandings. The emphasis on information stimulated parents to remedy the knowledge gap and acquire up-to-date information.

PARENTAL REACTION II: AUTHORITARIANISM

The permissive response of parents, and adults in general, to teenagers' invasion of public life has not met with unanimous approval. The American population is too heterogeneous to react uniformly to anything.

There are forceful voices challenging youth's inroads on adult authority. It is helpful to discuss three "reactionary" responses. One is the *turnabout reaction* of frustrated parents who have tried the approach of bridging the generation gap by pursuing the ideals of democracy, communication, and information. Another is the relatively unwavering philosophical conviction of many Americans that *adults should naturally wield authority and impose limitations* on the young. A third discussion deals with historical *fluctuations between permissiveness and authoritarianism* that appear almost cyclically in American society.

Many parents have suffered spectacular defeat in idealistic endeavors toward rapprochement. Their offer of equality, willingness to communicate, and eagerness to acquire information did not succeed in narrowing the gap, and many of them suffered disappointment. As a result, they are reconsidering their strategy, recalling "traditional rights," and demanding a new respect from adolescents.

Many have conceded that the notion of equality between parents and offspring is utopian. Their suspicion was borne out by such studies as Richard Flacks', which explored family backgrounds of rebellious students. He found that almost all of them had grown up in liberally oriented (equalitarian) homes but were among the least adjusted and satisfied youths.[26] In other words, the expectation that equalitarian treatment and child rearing would prevent generational strife was not supported. However, extremely alienated youth did not share this type of family background and were even more estranged from both family and society.

Parental attempts at communication fared no better. Some observers, such as Paul Goodman, felt that the attempts failed not because the message did not get through (indeed, it was understood loud and clear) but because it was unacceptable to the young.[27] However, John W. Aldridge regarded the typical intergenerational communication as an exercise in futility because youth used it to rationalize hedonism and immaturity.[28] It became a substitute for the hard look at oneself and for the search for solutions in one's own mental repertoire. Communication also served as reinforcement of in-group ideas by repetitively voicing slogans and criticisms and hearing peers do the same.

Other obstacles to fruitful communication include parents' limitation in finding time needed for resolving basic differences between generations. Moreover, it is doubtful whether intellectual communication can resolve basic emotional differences. It may be possible to establish an intellectual understanding of certain differences in tastes or convictions and still not arrive at rapprochement between the parties.

Finally, the vast majority of parents found it impossible to keep abreast of children's advanced scientific knowledge. To keep up with well-informed students would require parents to literally go to school with their offspring, listen to the same lectures, study the same lessons, and read the same up-to-date books and research reports. Few parents can afford such efforts. In general, then, many parents, frustrated in their campaign to promote "equality, communication, and information," began to reverse their attitudes and became more authoritarian.

Many vociferous Americans have assumed an authoritarian stance from the very beginning and insist that the traditional pattern of adults being the socializers and the young the socializees not be changed. They feel that this universal practice is necessitated by the fact that children are born culturally "unprogrammed," thus requiring socialization. It would be unrealistic to believe that the young always submit willingly to the manifold enculturation pressures exerted by their elders. Adult society determines standards of "right" and "wrong," and it is virtually impossible to discuss and explain the

[26]Richard Flacks, "The Liberated Generation: An Exploration of the Roots of Student Protest," *Journal of Social Issues*, 23 (July 1967): 52–75.

[27]Paul Goodman, *Growing Up Absurd* (New York: Random House, 1960).

[28]John W. Aldridge, *In the Country of the Young* (New York: Harper's Magazine Press, 1970), p. 101.

societal codes to the young in every situation of intergenerational contro-versy. Rather, it is frequently necessary to overrule the offspring without giving them equal opportunity. For example, children are not given a choice when a decision is made about going to school or not, or about playing with fire. If necessary, adults will coerce children to comply with standards and regulations. Thus, by definition, the socialization process implies inequality.

But American civilization tends to respect teenagers because of a deep-seated adoration of youth. A number of critics fear that, as a result, teenage influence has permeated public life and imposed teen standards. It is this adolescence-expanding process that has caused concern among critical ob-servers and has led them to call "corruption of adulthood" a "creeping dis-ease." The symptoms of this disease presumably are immature goals in music, art, and literature, replacement of adult English with limited vocabulary of the teen culture, and teen invasion of newspapers, television, and movies.

These voices deplore that too many concessions have already been made to youth's barbarism and warn that it is time to reverse the trend. An early alarm was sounded by the Hechingers in *Teenage Tyranny*, charging American society with surrender of adult standards to superficial teenage tastes and urging adults to reassert themselves. They do not believe that adolescents should be left in charge of their own lives, much less in control of the lives of any adults they can persuade or intimidate.

A sharp criticism of youth's barbarism was made by John W. Aldridge, who feels that adults are bluffed into self-accusation about being hypocrites, while it is the young who are the hypocrites. The young are remarkable for a number of inconsistencies, usually overlooked by guilt-preoccupied adults. The young profess an interest in improving society, but are actually only showing a parasitic interest; they are preoccupied with style, but show an endless appetite for banality; they are quick with moral severity when it comes to adults, but exhibit irresponsibility in their personal lives; they talk obsessively about the quality of university instruction, but are disinterested in ideas, imaginative literature, and the values of the Humanistic tradition; they are collectively vociferous and militant, but individually inarticulate and limp in manners; they proclaim a passion for individuality, but hew close to subcultural fashion; they flaunt their desire to "communicate" and to "relate," but suffer from lack of communicative substance; they sound a mystical belief in the primacy of intense feelings and profound intuition, but have neither the know-how nor the courage to implement their impulses in a creative lifestyle; and although they have more freedom of action and experimentation than previous generations, they are quick to complain of restrictions.[29]

Among the prominent personalities who have supported the reassertion

[29]John W. Aldridge, *In the Country of the Young.*

movement is psychoanalyst Peter Blos, who advises against permissiveness toward the sexual expression of teenagers, in spite of the fact that they mature earlier than previous generations.[30] To Blos, the young adolescent is psychologically still a child, regardless of his or her biological maturation. Allowing hasty sexual-emotional involvement may preclude emotional growth and stability. Blos even favors sex-segregated schooling for a while after puberty and disagrees with the argument that thwarting the young's evolving sex drive will be harmful. On the contrary, the young adolescent's personality will not only tolerate it but even profit from delay and repression, since it will channel youthful bravado into creative sublimations. Adults must set limits, deny youth's clamor for adult privileges, and refuse to be intimidated by charges of authoritarianism. While such steadfastness will cause tension and antagonism between parent and adolescent, it is the only way for healthy growth. The young need resistance and confrontation to acquire a realistic view of life and to work out a durable identity.

Psychologist Bruno Bettelheim warns that permissive parents create in offspring senseless uncertainty about identities and that resultant confusion and frustration will generate enough resentment to deepen the generation gap. Radical attacks on real evils have misled many well-meaning adults into overlooking the underlying motive: it is hate, not desire for a better world.[31] Bettelheim encourages the universities to act like firm but understanding parents and adhere to guidelines that will help students cope with inner conflicts.

MIT Professor Thomas J. Cottle zeroes in on the common misconception that taking it easy with adolescents is doing them a favor. He feels that tremendous harm can result when superordinates—the parents, teachers, and elders—try to equalize what must remain an asymmetrical relationship. Asymmetry refers to relationships wherein the services exchanged are of unequal and therefore noncomparable content, and the behavior of one party is not the cue for identical behavior in the other. It applies to situations where authority must be maintained in order to preserve clarity of interaction and promote success in the pursuit of common goals. Such situations include the parent-child, teacher-student, and doctor-patient relationships. In order to achieve goals, the participants must often carry out different functions. If they do not, and mistakenly assume that identical behavior will get them to the finish line, they will fail in the common project, become confused, and often face each other with mutual disgust. Young people's attack on authority, as healthy as it may be most of the time, should not obscure the service that authority renders. Authority is not to be toned down to the level

---

[30]Peter Blos, "The Child Analyst Looks at the Young Adolescent," *Daedalus*, 100 (Fall 1971): 961; and *The Young Adolescent: Clinical Studies* (New York: Free Press, 1970).

[31]"Youth: Confused Parents, Confused Kids," *Time*, September 5, 1969, p. 58.

of the young, "it is to remain firm in its commitment to preserve the essential asymmetry and the indelible generational separation, even if this means being seen as a 'square' "[32] Relinquishing authority would deprive the young of the necessary resistance against which they test themselves and of the guidance they desire.

Sociologist Robert A. Nisbet calls for the reassertion of faculty and administration authority and wants to restore the old identity of the university.[33] Students must relearn to accept their proper places and to recognize the function of school not as a political forum or sounding board for criticisms but as a place where scholarly disciplines are taught.

Some clergymen have joined the criticism of youth's lifestyle. Reverend Paul D. Urbano barely tolerates teen music and dancing, but condemns their "tribal language" as intolerably "dull," saying it conceals youth's refusal to learn subtleties and nuances because it requires effort and concentration.[34] Teen jargon is a coverup for laziness in learning English and cultivates nondiscrimination of differences in experience, feelings, and nature. As a consequence, teen jargon has an impoverishing effect, keeping imagination and descriptive ability of the young at a minimum.

The massive, critical, and often caustic reaction against youth's assertive and rebellious attitudes by the representatives of various institutions— including academe, church, literature, and politics—did not stop with mere rhetoric, but took on concrete forms during the late 1980s and early 1990s. Legislators in many states targeted teenagers for stricter rules. In Arizona, for example, serious discussion took place to consider withholding or rescinding driver's licenses of young people who drop out of high school. Additional consideration was given to passing stricter laws against teenage drinking and loud music. Lawmakers pursued policies to curb what they viewed as "juvenile excess." One bill before the Arizona legislators was to "give teens under 18 a one-year driver's license, renewable only if they stayed in school or graduated."[35] The bill also proposed to require teenagers to stay in school until age 18, rather than 16. The bill was indeed passed by the House of Representatives, but experienced delays in the Senate. Another bill sought to deter teenage drinking by establishing "zero tolerance" norm for the blood alcohol level; the bill passed the House slightly modified to a tolerated level of .03 percent. Similarly, strict regulations were passed concerning "boom-box" nuisance and petting between minors.[36]

---

[32]Thomas J. Cottle, "Parents and Child—The Hazards of Equality," in *Children's Liberation*, ed. David Ramsey (Englewood Cliffs, NJ: Prentice-Hall, 1973), p. 90.

[33]Robert A. Nisbet, "The University Had Better Mind Its Own Business," *Psychology Today*, 4 (March 1971): 22–37.

[34]Paul D. Urbano, "Tribal Language," *Arizona Republic*, June 20, 1970, p. 37.

[35]Ed Foster, "Teens Target of '90s Bills," *Arizona Republic*, April 17, 1990, p. 1.

[36]Ibid.

College students didn't fare much better. The early 1990s saw a move toward rethinking the legacy of the counterculture, of the various student protests, and of the abandonment of the university's *in loco parentis* authority, by which the administration could act "in the place of the parent." Many of the liberal academic reforms made during the 1970s and 1980s, such as abolition of core requirements and the introduction of "relevant" courses, have been gradually reversed. Even the sensitive issue of controlling the private lives of students has been reconsidered. No longer are mixed dorms and unlimited hours taken for granted. For example, starting with 1990, Boston University limited visiting hours and ruled that overnight guests could include only relatives and members of the same gender; and some campuses have reinstituted restrictions on alcohol at parties and in dorms.[37]

We have been discussing parental, or general, adult reactions as if all reactions fit into either one or the other category. This is, of course, not the entire picture: besides the nuances and shades of attitudes in between those categories, at least one additional category is worth mentioning. The *authoritative* adult reacts neither permissively nor authoritarianly, but acts out of self-confidence and understanding, hence with little need for defensive counteraction. Somehow they have achieved understanding of the motives that stir youth, and perhaps show more compassion than passion. Unfortunately, such adults probably are in the minority.

The majority reaction is understandable, however. Youth's extreme criticisms bring out extreme responses and seldom promote a balanced view. This is why the authoritative response is rare—it is an attitude unswayed by attack; it feels neither the need to fight back nor surrender—whereas the majority of people are less self-confident and attacks on them elicit defensive reactions, such as authoritarianism.

Some social scientists believe that the rising and ebbing of authoritarianism does not depend on specific national events but is an almost rhythmic or cyclic recurrence. While the etiology of this societal pendulum is not clear, we know something about the duration of the stages. Sociologist Seymour Lipset has calculated that each American social obsession or preoccupation— be it McCarthyism, student apathy, or the counterculture—has a lifetime of about five years.[38] After that it quickly fades.

Public moods concerning child-rearing philosophy seem to fluctuate in the same manner. The years of the counterculture were associated with a lessening of control and an increase in permissiveness. The late 1970s showed signs of tightening of control and movement back to authoritarianism. The 1980s were a period of reemerging harmony, when the young were less

[37]Jill Rachlin, "Rewriting the Code of Conduct on Campus," *U.S. News and World Report,* January 9, 1989, p. 56.

[38]Quoted in "The Graying of America," *Time,* September 17, 1973, pp. 76–77; also see Seymour M. Lipset, *Rebellion in the University* (Boston: Little, Brown, 1972).

critical of the old and the old were relatively reassured of their position. And the 1990s started out showing signs of society's more conservative and stringent attitudes toward the young.

Socialization attitudes seem to be in constant flux, and it is difficult to make accurate forecasts. There is constant polarization of pedagogic philosophies, with the permissive and the authoritarian vying with each other. What would probably help to calm the rough waters of intergenerational relations is greater self-acceptance on the part of America's middle-aged and older population, finding greater meaning in their life stages, and *acting* on the basis of their true identities and preferences rather than *reacting* to youth's styles — either positively (to the point of imitation) or negatively. This would earn them the respect of the young, prepare them as models, and reduce the conflict between young and old.

SUMMARY

A number of concepts and theories were discussed to help us understand the dynamics of intergenerational relations:

1. In a *rapidly changing society*, in which each generation experiences a different social climate, intergenerational tensions are bound to open a schism.
2. *The young do not yet have vested interest* in the existing social and economic order and are prone to challenge customs and values.
3. Even in a relatively even-tempered social setting not disturbed by rapid social change, the *common socialization process* would be enough to stir up conflict between generations.
4. A powerful psychological transformation comes with entering a social position as important as *parenthood*. Internalization of the role is enough to create confrontation between socializer and socializee. This is a manifestation of the power that social-structural arrangements have over individual personalities.
5. Parents suffer from *cultural lag* — from being continuously one step behind the offspring's information exposure — and are pitted against experts who manage the information flow.
6. The young cultivate a *halo effect*, generalizing from parental ignorance in scientific and technological details to parental incompetence in general.
7. Parental insistence on authority is frequently interpreted by the young as *irrational authority* they are entitled to oppose.
8. The American way of life embraces a *youth cult* that exaggerates youth's manipulation of the older generation.
9. The youth cult inflicts an *inferiority complex* on adults; inexperience and prolonged adolescent conditions impose an inferiority complex on the young. The two complexes reinforce each other and have cumulative effects.
10. Parental and general adult reactions to the dilemma of the generations vary. One reaction consists of *permissiveness*, whereby adults either passively tolerate the invasion of teen styles or actively seek rapprochement by trying to implement equality, communication, and information. A second type of reaction

opposes youth's inroads on public life and marshals the forces of traditional *authoritarianism*.

11. An additional category of adult response is the *authoritative* person who is more acting than reacting to youth, understanding their concerns and motives.

8

The Modern Family

Of the various groups to which we belong, the family has the most far-reaching impact on personality development. Quality of family interaction, and its bearing on the way the young grow into adulthood, is significantly affected by the structure of the family. A discussion of the modern family should therefore begin with a look at structural conditions.

Since the discussion focuses on aspects of the family that contribute to the formation of adolescence in American life, it must be selective and may at times appear one-sided or negative. But obviously, not all aspects of the modern family promote adolescence and not all families are the same in degree and manner of reinforcing adolescent symptoms.

As mentioned earlier, such communities as the Amish or Hutterites have succeeded in immunizing their young against adolescence by religious dogma, simple farm life, and isolation from public schools. Other minorities have curbed adolescence sufficiently so that it is different from the typical urban middle-class experience. Hence, the adolescent experience varies according to such background features as ethnicity, race, socioeconomic status, religion, and so forth.

This discussion dwells primarily on historical trends that have intensified the adolescent experience and affected most American families, especially the middle class. We have two concerns: (1) To show similarity rather than diversity among American families, and (2) to identify the new structural conditions that facilitated the rise of modern adolescence.

CHANGING STRUCTURE

Toward the Isolated Nuclear Family

In 1800, more than 90 percent of the population of the United States were farm families. This proportion consistently declined, amounting to 60 percent in 1900, 30 percent in 1930, 23 percent in 1940, 15 percent in 1950, 9 percent in 1960, 3 percent in 1980, and 2 percent in 1988.[1]

The traditional rural family often included such close relatives as grandparents, uncles, aunts, and cousins, and the child grew up in close association with them. In addition, occasionally such nonrelatives as maids and farm hands became permanent members of the household. While in 1910 almost every fourth American family included nonrelatives, in 1961 only every twentieth family included such a person.

In the traditional setting, many married children shared the household of their parents. In 1910, for example, 7.7 percent of married couples did not live in an independent household; by the 1960s this proportion had decreased to 2.1 percent. Statistics show that the average number of persons per household has decreased from about six in 1800 to 2.9 in the mid-1970s, making it the first time in American history that the average size of households has dropped below three, and to 2.7 in the mid-1980s.[2]

Factors that have reduced household size include the divorce rate, which in densely populated West Coast regions has run as high as 70 percent. About 50 percent of first marriages occurring in the 1990s end in divorce. For second marriages, the projected level is about 60 percent.[3] Estimates for the 1990s have put the proportion of American children living in one-parent households at 26 percent, amounting to a 23 percent increase over the previous decade. The estimate for black children is 57 percent, amounting to an 18 percent increase over the previous decade.[4] Living in one-parent families usually turns out to be a permanent arrangement for the children, since the remarriage rate, especially for women, is substantially lower than the rate of divorce for families involving children.

[1]U.S. Bureau of the Census, *Current Population Reports*, Series P–20, No. 439, Government Printing Office, Washington, DC, 1989, p. 3.

[2]U.S. Bureau of the Census, *Current Population Reports*, Series P–20, No. 398, Government Printing Office, Washington, DC, 1985, p. 8.

[3]Derived from U.S. Bureau of the Census data and compiled by Paul C. Glick, "Marriage, Divorce, and Living Arrangements. Prospective Changes," *Journal of Family Issues*, Vol. 5, March 1984, p. 23.

[4]Ibid.

An interesting component in the growth of one-parent families is the rise in the number of unwed mothers. The proportion of American children living with a mother who has never been married rose to 4.5 percent in the 1990s, up from 2.9 percent in the 1980s.[5] The mid-1980s Census Bureau figures show that over 20 percent of white births and 75 percent of black births were out of wedlock.[6] As would be expected, the overwhelming majority of single-parent families are headed by women. Because it is no longer such a stigma to be an out-of-wedlock mother, and because economic conditions make single parenthood feasible, young women are no longer rushing into wedlock once they become pregnant.

Another interesting change deals with childlessness. The women of age groups who traditionally have had children, but are childless today, roughly fall into two major categories: those who have decided to lead a childless lifestyle, and those who are postponing parenthood until they have accomplished certain other things in life, mainly an education and a career. The former, research has found, include a disproportionate number of only-children or first-borns who had to care for younger siblings and apparently were influenced by knowing the realism of child rearing.[7]

This change seems to affect college women in particular. Whereas in the 1950s only 9 percent of women of child-bearing age had no children, now 25 percent of college-educated women between 35 and 45 are childless. Apparently these changes are due to heightened individualistic expectations on the part of modern women, including education and careers, plus more stringent economic conditions. As public opinion expert Daniel Yankelovich opined: "In the 1950s a single breadwinner could support a family of five. Now it takes two breadwinners to support a family of four."[8]

More young Americans are postponing marriage to an older age. There has been a steady increase in the median age at first marriage. The average marriage age for men was 22.6 years in 1960, 23.2 in 1970, 24.7 in 1980, and 25.9 in 1988. The average age for women was 20.3 in 1950, 20.8 in 1970, 22 in 1980, and 23.6 in 1988.[9]

In addition, more Americans than ever before stay single. Based on the Census Bureau figures it has been concluded that during the 1990s "this country would be changing from one of the developed countries with the smallest proportion never marrying to a country with one of the largest proportions never marrying."[10] The percentage of Americans in their early

---

[5]Ibid.

[6]"Single Parent Heads US Families," *Arizona Republic*, November 5, 1986, p. C1.

[7]Martha Smilgis, "The Dilemmas of Childlessness," *Time*, May 2, 1988, p. 88.

[8]Quoted by Martha Smilgis, ibid.

[9]U.S. Bureau of the Census, *Current Population Reports*, Series P–20, No. 432, Government Printing Office, Washington, DC, March 1988.

[10]Glick, "Marriage," p. 13.

30s who have never married has more than doubled since 1970, increasing the probability that an increasing segment of the American population will stay single all their lives. Unmarried men 20 to 24 years old amounted to 78 percent of this age group in 1988, an increase of 23 percent over 1970. Unmarried women 20 to 24 years old amounted to 61 percent, an increase of 25 percent over 1970.[11]

These various changes have sometimes been equated with the change from an extended family, where the household included members of several generations plus other relatives and possibly also service personnel, to the nuclear family, including just parents and their offspring. This is, however, an overdrawn assumption. Excepting a few ethnic subcultures, the American family experience has had a tendency to be nuclear from the very beginning.[12]

The opportunities of this continent have always incited Americans to move on, to acquire, to seek their own "hearth," and to stake out their own physical and psychological parameters. Youthful activism, material acquisition, and individualism have never fully promoted the spirit of the classic extended family. Thus, the change in American family structure is more properly described as change from the larger nuclear family to a smaller nuclear family.

There have also been changes in the relationship between the family and the community — changes that are of equal importance in understanding the nature of the modern family. Due to growth in size of communities, resultant anonymity, increase in mobility, and retreat to individualism, the modern family has lost much of its integration into the community and has become isolated to a notable degree.

Looser integration into the community is matched by looser internal integration within the family. With today's emphasis on individualism, the family is no longer a coherent and enduring unit. A person's family used to be his or her unalterable fate, but late-twentieth-century Americans view marriage and the family as something arrangeable — just as occupations or homes are. If spouses feel disappointed, they leave; if teenagers are dissatisfied and feel shackled, they may leave, too. The reason is less often related to personal disillusionment with other family members than the simple desire to pursue one's own interests. Theologian Sam Keen encourages modern Americans to face the problem pragmatically, make mobility part of the family, and, through increased flexibility, save it. He likened the family to a gypsy caravan, which serves as a point of stability and yet, simultaneously, keeps on

---

[11]U.S. Bureau of the Census, 1988.

[12]Bernard Farber, *Family and Kinship in Modern Society* (Glenview, IL: Scott, Foresman and Co., 1973); Peter Laslett, *Household and Family in Past Time* (New York: Cambridge University Press, 1972), p. 575.

moving. Family members may leave the caravan occasionally and then again catch up with it.[13]

It is doubtful whether this vision will replace that of the family as being supposedly permanent, since the latter belief is a cherished American dream. Nonetheless, the vision may be closer to American reality than the dream, but that is usually neither recognized nor admitted.

CHANGING FUNCTIONS

The smaller and less stable family has signaled basic changes in how Americans relate to each other. The consequences of the changed structure and various other components of the new family lifestyle are discussed below.

Exit Role, Enter Individual

The traditional family can also be called the "institutional" family because institutional norms and procedures were preferred over personal attitudes and desires. Integrity of the family as a unit used to be safeguarded by the various members playing roles. Deviations were frowned on, punished by informal or formal sanctions, and made difficult by economic dependence on the family unit. Also, the role of spouse or offspring had metaphysical overtones and was commonly considered as a sacred "blueprint" not to be taken lightly. This was familism, the philosophy that the family's goals and purposes have priority over those of the individual.

The modern family, however, places a premium on interpersonal competence rather than on skill in role functioning. The traditional family with its legal rigidity and hierarchical structure has become outdated, and modern Americans seek "self-actualization." Emphasis is now on flexibility, looser integration, and greater individualism. The high divorce rate is a manifestation of these changes, indicating that we are now highly divorce-prone because of the lack of institutional coercion, the easing of economic limitations, and the acceptance of individual volition that is monitored by little other than the rewards of companionship.

This, however, should not be mistaken for abandonment of marriage and the family. On the contrary, Americans adhere to the family as an institution within which they expect fulfillment of emotional needs, which now emphasize individualism and personality functions. These functional changes call for competence in interpersonal relations. Safe but rigid role

[13]Reported in "American Family: Future Uncertain," *Time*, December 28, 1970, p. 39.

blueprints are replaced by a highly individualistic style of relating that requires sensitivity, increased communication, and constantly new interpretations of interactional situations.

Demands for interpersonal competence include new emphasis on sexual knowledge and sexual equality, problem-solving skill, sublimating proficiency when frustrated, willingness to resort to professional therapy, and skill in family and couple communication. Interpersonal harmony depends so heavily on improved communication that family sociologists have recommended communication theory be applied to the marital dyad.[14]

Adolescents must learn to replace old, rigid role matrixes with sensitive personal communication. This means giving up the age-old security of knowing *a priori* how to act or react in interpersonal situations, especially in the relationship between the sexes, and accepting the new freedom of being able to style uniquely and creatively every human encounter. Learning to act individualistically takes both courage and experience. While the young may have the former, they may lack the latter. Learning adequate responses to the liberalized style of human interaction constitutes an immensely difficult task—a task requiring the treatment of each social scene as a situation that presents unique problems and requires unique solutions.

Probably the change most vexing to the young is the altered female role. Increasingly, mothers fail to convey an easily predictable role model. Until recently, wives were supplementary to husbands and not expected to express a full range of capabilities. Today, women have much greater expectations— and also frustrations. Nearly 60 percent of American women are now employed, and when a woman is working, she has a new perception of herself, behaves more independently, and refuses to be cast in a cultural matrix. There are difficulties of adjustment to this derigidification process for everyone involved. Girls are thrown back on their personal identities and must become fully conscious of them. Boys, while witnessing the expanding role of the female, are still largely trapped in the rigid role of masculinity and must make concessions. Skillful communication seems to be the basic key for successfully coping with encounters between the sexes, and a family sociologist calls attention to a Family Communication Game that can be used for education and fun by high school students.[15]

Difficulties arising from the modern family situation are not to be necessarily construed as having a negative value. New equity and flexibility promise greater opportunity for creativity and identity formation and can lead to deeply rewarding relationships.

[14]Sherod Miller et al., "Recent Progress in Understanding and Facilitating Marital Communication," *The Family Coordinator*, 24 (April 1975): 143–52.

[15]William Saur, "Family Communication Game," *The Family Coordinator*, 24 (April 1975): 227–29.

From Status Ascription to Status Achievement

An individual growing up in the traditional family rarely had to be concerned with the question of social mobility, since he or she "inherited" the status of the family. A teenager at the turn of the century was exposed to considerably less intergenerational mobility than his or her counterpart of the mid-twentieth century. Familistic norms and values mitigated the problem of adolescent discontinuity, and a teenager knew his or her "place" in the family as well as in the larger society. Anxieties accompanying contemporary youth's task of determining their place and prestige in the social structure were thereby avoided.

Today, finding one's place is more individualistic. Although family background, especially if the family belongs to either extreme of the socio-economic spectrum, is still an important influence on status achievement, its influence has diminished and status differences between parents and offspring are common. Many modern families consist of members who differ in social prestige, primarily because they pursue different careers. In short, the criterion for social status in modern society is based more on occupational achievement than on family reputation. Some family sociologists go so far as to conclude that family obligations in modern urban-industrial society tend to detract from single-minded pursuit of highly prized personal success, be the goal scholarly, commercial, or professional.[16]

The shift toward individualism is reflected in such catch phrases as "proliferation of associations," "personality market," "individuation," and "self-actualization." More and more relationships are achieved and are relatively role-free, including those cultivated at school, at work, in numerous voluntary associations, and now also in the marital dyad. Achieved relationships are essentially idiosyncratic and potentially boundless. A pessimistic interpretation is that "herein lies their threat to the family, for they, like many other aspects of contemporary life, may readily infringe upon family claims, may alienate members from the family."[17]

The modern family's loss of the placement function, and thus its loss of the status-ascription function, has direct bearing on the problem of adolescence. Teenagers cannot expect much help from home during the process of working out a status by and for themselves. Their parents' statuses do not necessarily have finality in determining their own statuses. While family background is of minimal ascriptive effect, the achievement syndrome is of maximum importance. Absence of status certainty and prospects of an uncharted journey toward some yet undefined and obscure adult status may

---

[16]Charles W. Hobart, "Commitment, Value Conflict and the Future of the American Family," *Journal of Marriage and the Family*, 25 (November 1963): 405–06.

[17]Ibid., p. 406.

create feelings that are aptly described by contemporary teenagers when they say that they feel "lost" and are "going nowhere."

Again, it must be pointed out that negative aspects can be balanced by a positive gain: Modern teenagers have an unprecedented freedom to choose among different lifestyles. There may be something to be said for "being lost" and "going nowhere" for a while, instead of knowing from the beginning where one is going, but possibly neither liking the direction nor having the chance to change the course. Factual as well as fictional accounts of a past era are replete with the tragic stories of young individuals who had to pursue a course in life they had not chosen.

Limited Adult Models

The traditional family was able to provide a number of adults who could serve as significant models. This was possible not only because there were more individuals in the family but also because their work performance was more visible. In addition, the family was integrated into the community and could bring the young in contact with neighbors and relatives whose behavior and occupational pursuits could be observed. This helped the young to learn patterns of problem solving and derive value orientation.

In the isolated nuclear family, learning from available persons is extremely limited. Normally, there is only one adult of each gender present, and if this parent is not readily observable, the young lose models. A special concern of many social scientists is the middle-class boy who frequently suffers identity problems because of father absence.[18]

Even if the male child has the opportunity to associate with his father and observe his actions, one must allow for the possibility that this model, for whatever idiosyncratic reason, may not be acceptable to the child. Rejection of a father can lead to a situation in which the father changes from a model to an object of scorn. A frequent theme underlying cases of father rejection is modern youth's refusal to accept a person as a model whose only qualification is the *position* of father. Regard for institutions and formal positions has changed from the "sacred" to the "secular." Trying to uphold reverence and obedience for a position when it is occupied by a person considered unqualified can result in serious interpersonal disharmony.

Barrington Moore expressed one of the most poignant opinions on this matter. He accused the modern nuclear family of being "obsolete and barbaric" because of the young's "obligation to give affection as a duty to a particular set of persons because of the accident of birth." Moore called

[18]Michael E. Lamb, "Paternal Influences and the Father's Role," in John Keating, ed., *Social Psychology*, Annual Editions (Guilford, CT: Duskhin, 1982), pp. 68–73.

attention to "the exploitation of socially sanctioned demands for gratitude when the existing social situation no longer generates any genuine feeling of warmth."[19] Most important, he considered adolescence to be the outgrowth of the modern family's incapability of stabilizing the personalities of its offspring.

While Moore's ideas may have some validity, they are only partial explanations of the variables causing adolescence. Nevertheless, it is true that deprivation of role models may develop in situations where the offspring refuse to acknowledge parental authority. When father-absenteeism is combined with rebellious attitudes, sex-role identification indeed suffers. While such dysfunctional conditions were avoided in the larger traditional family, the nuclear family fails to offer children flexibility in choosing models, thereby complicating the transition from childhood to adulthood.

Moore's contention could be expanded to include mother-absenteeism from the home. Nearly 60 percent of all women now work, including a growing percentage of women with children. While it is true that this may entail a reduction of the time and the opportunities children have to use mother as a model, there is little support for the claim that this is detrimental to the child's personality. As already indicted in Chapter 5, psychologist Bronfenbrenner found that the decisive variable regarding the fate of latchkey children is the type of activities planned for the child by the working parent.[20]

It has been found, however, that outside work by mothers may be detrimental to the marriage. Mothers who work outside the home have a notably higher divorce rate. Scott South's findings were interpreted to mean that if a woman is in a better economic position to make it on her own, she may terminate an unsatisfactory marriage.[21]

Nonfamilial Peers

In the large, traditional family the child usually grew up with peers who were of his or her family group. They were playmates with whom they shared the same sentiments. Charles H. Cooley's concept of primary group found near perfection in this arrangement. Interaction was intimate, face-to-face, and self-perception was in terms of "we" instead of in terms of "I and they."[22]

[19]Barrington Moore, "Thoughts on the Future of the Family," in *Identity and Anxiety*, eds. Maurice R. Stein, Arthur J. Vidich, and Daniel M. White (Glencoe, IL: The Free Press, 1960), pp. 393–94.

[20]Discussed by Jeff Meer, "Children—Alone but not Neglected," *Psychology Today*, August 1985, p. 11.

[21]Quoted by Vincent Bozzi, "Till Death or Economic Hardship Do Us Part," *Psychology Today*, May 1986, p. 6.

[22]Charles H. Cooley, *Social Organization* (New York: Scribner's, 1909), p. 23.

This type of family blended primary and secondary socialization into one process and prevented marginality because integration into the consanguine family group was a lifelong proposition. When the young married, they would often remain in the household of the family of orientation, or at least in the same community.

In contrast, most modern nuclear families are isolated from kin and cannot provide playmates who are relatives. Modern youth grow up seeing few, if any, of their relatives; many of them live and grow up with only one parent. Hence, children of nuclear families find their playmates outside of the kin group and commonly transform the school environment into a primary source of friends.

Recreation and leisure have been transferred from the family to commercial agencies. Commercialization aims at individuals, or individuals in certain age groups, but rarely at families as units. This is reflected in movie ratings, music festivals, concerts, and pop musicals—all being events that have become age-specific.

Parents' prime competitors seem to be their children's nonfamilial peers, who, unlike siblings and cousins growing up in the same family system, frequently have divergent attitudes and fail to share common loyalty to one family. They are a peer group independent of family life. Thus, teenagers enter a marginal status with respect to both the family of orientation and the family of procreation. They are no longer an intrinsic part of the parental home and have not yet formed their own families. They are suspended between two membership groups and compensate by temporarily joining a subculture. James S. Coleman, in his classic *The Adolescent Society*, reported large, complex "teenage societies" among high school youth, organized along lines diametrically opposed to the standards of parents.[23]

Equally powerful is the influence of the mass media, particularly television. Prime targets of the television industry are preadolescents and adolescents. By the time children reach eighteen years of age, they will have watched twice as many hours of television as they spent in the classroom. Although some of the fare is realistic and educational, most of it is violent, unrealistic, and divergent from parental values.

Responsibility for youth's peer-family conflict lies partly with parents and partly with the changing structure of the modern community, according to psychologist Urie Bronfenbrenner.[24] Through evaluation of various statistics and their integration into a trend indicator, he predicts increasing isolation of American teenagers from parents and adults. Many factors conspire to

---

[23]James S. Coleman, *The Adolescent Society* (Glencoe, IL: The Free Press, 1961).

[24]Urie Bronfenbrenner, "Children and Families: 1984?" *Society*, 18 (January/February 1981): 38–41; *The Ecology of Human Development: Experiments by Nature and Design* (Cambridge, MA: Harvard University Press, 1979); and "Ecology of the Family as a Context of Human Development," *Developmental Psychology* 22 (1986): 723–742.

isolate the young from the rest of society: (1) decline of the large or even extended family, (2) separation of residential and work areas, (3) impersonal neighborhoods, (4) zoning ordinances, (5) occupational mobility, (6) child labor laws, (7) consolidated schools, (8) television, (9) age-segregated patterns of social and recreational life, (10) working mothers, and (11) delegation of child care, education, and therapy to experts. Bronfenbrenner regards the trend as a manifestation of decreasing opportunity for meaningful contact between generations.

Erosion of cohesiveness of the social network has isolating effects not only on the young but also on the family as a unit. Centrifugal forces generated within the family by its increasingly isolated position have propelled its members into different directions. As parents, especially mothers, dedicate more time to outside careers, children gravitate toward nonfamilial settings, some organized and others informal. For example, the number of children enrolled in day-care centers has more than doubled in recent years, and demand far exceeds supply. The young spend increasing amounts of time in the company of agemates to fill the vacuum created by withdrawal of parents and other adults.

Bronfenbrenner refers to sources showing that today's reliance on the informal peer group, at every age and grade level, has enormously increased, and that this is particularly noticeable among children from homes in which one or both parents are frequently absent. These peer-dependent youth describe parents as less affectionate and less firm in discipline. They also display greater pessimism about the future, rate lower in responsibility and leadership, and are more likely to engage in antisocial behavior.

Social scientists have interpreted these conditions as roots of alienation. Over time, they believe, these conditions will become more prevalent, and greater peer dependency as well as more serious manifestations of alienation will evolve. This, presumably, is the major explanation for rising rates of juvenile homicide, suicide, drug abuse, and other forms of delinquency.

Parents, Peers, and Autonomy

The contrapuntal peer association vis-à-vis the family should not be dismissed as entirely dysfunctional. Excepting certain destructive by-products, the peer culture can serve a valuable function. Mannheim reminded us that affiliation with peer culture is instrumental in loosening dependence on the family and should not be sweepingly defined as a "social problem."[25] Adolescents' desire to establish distance from their family groups finds implementation through affiliation with nonfamilial peers who, in concerted rebel-

---

[25]Karl Mannheim, *Essays on the Sociology of Culture* (New York: Oxford University Press, 1956).

liousness, try out new norms and values and in the process obtain skill in problem solving and develop unique identities. A major function of modern adolescence is renunciation of dependence on the family and substitution of peer groups for the family group. This substitution includes fulfillment of emotional needs essential for individual growth, such as stimulation, empathy, loyalty, the opportunity for role playing, identification, and sharing of guilt and anxiety.

It can be said, then, that the peer group facilitates the young individual's autonomy process and emancipation from the family. The end result is an individual who is relatively autonomous in three respects. First, there is *emotional* autonomy as the person relaxes ties to the family and emotionally unfolds to establish bonds of love, support, and confidence elsewhere. Second, there is *behavioral* autonomy as the person acquires skill and courage to do what he or she wants to do. Third, there is *ideational* autonomy as the person thinks and struggles through basic ideas and established personal convictions.

Some researchers disagree with the conflict theory and point out that if a contrapuntal subculture does in fact exist, it has been exaggerated and that in ordinary middle-class families cooperative and mutually rewarding relationships between parents and teenagers are more in evidence than conflict.[26] Moreover, by the time children become adolescents, they have more or less achieved independence from parents. Psychologist Albert Bandura argues that establishment of autonomy of the adolescent poses more of a problem for parents than for young individuals, since parents have to adjust to the loss of a family member. Having enjoyed a relatively harmonious family relationship, teenagers tend to be discriminative in their choice of reference groups and generally establish peer associations that allow implementation of norms and values they learned in their homes. Hence, peer-group membership is usually not in opposition to family values and generates little intergenerational conflict.

Bandura tries to explain the discrepancy between his research findings and the traditional theory by pointing out the distortions present in mass-media sensationalism; questioning the validity of generalizations from biased samples (such as data based on deviant adolescents); showing the rigidity of the theoretical approach, which glosses over individual variation; and stating the self-fulfilling prophecy that if adults label adolescents as rebellious, then rebellious they will become.

Eugene Thomas' study of political attitudes between generations supports Bandura's hypothesis,[27] revealing that children of highly politicized

[26]Albert Bandura, "The Stormy Decade: Fact or Fiction," in *Issues in Adolescent Psychology*, ed. D. Rogers (New York: Prentice-Hall, 1972).

[27]Eugene Thomas, "Family Correlates of Student Political Activism," *Developmental Psychology*, 4 (March 1971): 206–14.

parents tend to be like their parents both in political attitudes and political behavior. This supports the conclusion that stratification theory explains political activism much better than generational theory. While the latter presupposes that the young rebel against their parents and therefore resent symbolic authority figures, the former suggests that these attitudes cut across generational lines. Reuben Hill and J. Aldous, Jr. explored attitudes and beliefs of three generations and found that while behavior concerning practical issues (for example, the division of labor in the household) has changed, fundamental values such as religious beliefs have hardly shifted at all.[28]

Additional researchers questioning the validity of the assumption that youth-parent conflict is a primary feature of adolescence are Elizabeth Douvan and her associates, whose data consistently showed a more harmonious youth-parent relationship.[29] Their findings suggest a more peaceful scene than much theory and most social comments would lead us to expect: " 'Rebellious youth' and 'the conflict between generations' are phrases that ring; but, so far as we can tell, it is not the ring of truth they carry so much as the beguiling but misleading tone of drama."[30]

However, some of these researchers' data are based on narrow samples. Just as theorists may project generalizations from too broad a base, interviewers may project generalizations from too narrow a base. For example, most of the evidence that led Douvan to make the condemning statement cited above grew out of work dealing mainly with girls. In addition, little elucidation of data was provided to give a fuller picture of developmental changes. It seems, for instance, that seriousness of conflict is progressive; that is, it increases with age within the adolescent span. In one of the few instances where inquiry was directed at age-differentiated conflict and where girls were asked what they most disagreed about with their parents, the results showed three quite distinct peaks: the younger adolescents reported narrow narcissistic issues; the middle group had interpersonal problems; and the older girls were concerned with broader social issues. Thus, in the under-fourteen group, clothing and make-up were the types of issues over which there was most disagreement; in the fourteen-to-sixteen group, whom, when, and how to date appeared major issues; in the oldest group, most disagreements dealt with basic ideas. Not only do researchers like Douvan and Gold fail to commit themselves to a certain age category when they make generalizations (usually about a harmonious youth-parent relationship), but even

[28]Reuben Hill and J. Aldous, Jr., "Socialization for Marriage and Parenthood," in *Handbook of Socialization Theory and Research*, ed. D. Goslin (Chicago: Rand McNally, 1969).

[29]Elizabeth Douvan and Joseph Adelson, *The Adolescent Experience* (New York: John Wiley, 1966), and Elizabeth Douvan and H. Gold, "Modal Patterns in American Adolescence," in *Review of Child Development Research*, vol. 2, ed. L. Hoffman and M. Hoffman (New York: Russell Sage Foundation, 1966).

[30]Douvan and Gold, "Modal Patterns in American Adolescence," p. 485.

more important, they neglect to sufficiently clarify whether boys are equally restrained in their attitudes toward parental rule as girls appear to be. The Douvan studies suffer from the major weakness of comparing a small number of boys at one stage during their adolescent development with a large number of girls throughout the age range.

In any event, the reader is advised to accept either interpretation—the "conflict" as well as the "harmonious" theory—with caution and remain open to further insight that, hopefully, will eventually accrue.

The Law and the Young: Independence, Individualism, and Isolation

American society appears to look at marital and family affiliations as essentially private relationships outside of the purview of the public's meddling, be this informal interference or legal encroachment. This is not to say that the law is indifferent to what is going on in the family, but rather that serious dysfunctions within the family system are approached as *individual* matters and not as family issues.

If the adolescent exhibits disturbed or delinquent behavior, he or she is approached as an isolated individual and not as a representative of a primary group the disturbances of which he or she is manifesting. The law's pursuit is the individual, and jurisdictional interests proceed regardless of family context. The "hands-off" policy is particularly emphatic in the case of marital dissolution. In a sense, the law concerns itself only with keeping records of who enters and who leaves marriage.

This, then, is the individual-centered legal context within which rights and obligations of American children and teenagers must be understood.

A legal landmark in clarifying the young Americans' status was the Twenty-sixth Amendment to the Constitution in 1971 which gave eighteen-year-olds the right to vote and helped them to obtain many other legal privileges. The rights that eighteen-, nineteen-, and twenty-year-olds have gained include the right to own property, make wills, sign binding contracts, sue and be sued, marry without the consent of parents, and undergo medical treatment (including treatment for venereal disease) without parental approval.[31] The majority of states have granted eighteen-year-olds the privileges they formerly had to wait until twenty-one to receive.

In fact, the states are now extending "without consent" medical rights (including pregnancy care, birth-control prescriptions, abortion, treatment for venereal disease, drug addiction, and psychiatric problems) to youths

---

[31]"Kids, Sex, and Doctors," *Time*, November 25, 1974, pp. 91–93, and Lavelle E. Saunders, "Ignorance of the Law Among Teenagers: A Barrier to the Exertion of Their Rights as Citizens?" Paper presented at the Annual Meeting of the Pacific Sociological Association, Victoria, British Columbia, April 1975.

under eighteen. In all states (except Wisconsin) younger teenagers have the right to get treatment for venereal disease without consulting their parents. California's emancipated youth laws extend this right to anyone over twelve years old. New Jersey allows minors of any age to obtain pregnancy care and abortion without parental consent but, ironically, requires parental consent for contraceptive prescriptions up to age eighteen. Oregon has dropped the age of medical consent to fifteen, and Alabama to fourteen.

The age group most conspicuously affected by the new laws are college students, who have been freed from *in loco parentis* authority. Colleges may no longer require students to live in campus dormitories; out-of-state students may find it easier to establish legal residence within a state and thus pay lower tuition fees for state-supported institutions; parents may no longer get a chance to see the grades of their adult children or be informed of any trouble they have gotten into, unless their son or daughter specifically gives the college permission; students from higher-income families, previously barred from most financial aid in college, may now claim they are independent of parents, account for only their own income, and receive financial aid; and students can sue and be sued, which enables colleges to take students to court in cases of vandalism, disruption, or cheating without involving the parents, and, likewise, students can file legal complaints.

Many parents, educators, and administrators feel that their authority is being undermined. They perceive an exaggerated emphasis on individualism that results in too much independence for the young and that alienates them from their families. This alienation is deepened by moving individual-centered legislation to the forefront of human interaction. As legalistic consciousness grows, the informal cooperation and personal trust that used to be a natural part of family life is being diminished.

The Rise of the Personality Function

Industrialization has prompted the transferral of one traditional family function after another to specialized institutional settings. The economic and production function has been relegated to the factory and office; the educational function has been entirely absorbed by schools; the religious function has been formalized and is now the exclusive domain of the church or synagogue; the recreational function has been commercialized and is dominated by profit-seeking institutions like movie theaters and sports stadiums; the medical function has been transferred to the doctor's office and the hospital. Family members usually go to these places individually, not as a family unit.

The family is left to provide psychological security for its members, but little else. In short, the trend of increasing specialization in American society has affected the family and made it a specialist. It now specializes in gratifying psychological needs. The question of whether the modern family can meet basic personality needs, in particular such needs as the feeling of belonging and security, is important for youth's physical as well as mental health. Experience of structural discontinuity between statuses of child and adult is difficult and confusing under normal and secure circumstances. If, in addition, there is lack of psychological security, youth faces an extremely difficult time.

Many sociologists have attempted to answer the question of whether the modern family is able to offer this vital security, and two main theories have emerged. Interpretations of the changes in family life have led one group to answer "no" and the other "yes" to the question of the family's psychological functionality. Besides Barrington Moore, a well-known spokesperson for the "no" group, there is Carl C. Zimmerman, whose work offers an extensive historical study of the family, draws conclusions from previous societies, applies them to the contemporary scene, and predicts the doom of the modern family.[32] The hypothesis is supported by historical data suggesting that the modern family has lost too many functions to be of further importance. Since, according to Zimmerman, the disintegration of the family heralds the disintegration of the society at large, his theory has been called the *doomsday theory.*

Opposing interpretation is offered by Talcott Parsons, who presents a more optimistic point of view.[33] Changes are interpreted as processes reforming the family into an agency specializing in the *personality function.* This specialization is the American response to the need to derive from the family psychological security to a degree heretofore unknown.

These acute psychological demands appear to be symptomatic of the problem of identity, which can be considered the prominent mental problem of the modern era. It is within the confines of the family that Americans hope to find the answer to the basic question, Who am I? This burdens the family with an immense responsibility. If people fail to find the coveted identity and feeling of security in a particular marriage or family, they are apt to terminate membership and try anew with different partners. According to Parsons, this insistence on "self-fulfillment" explains the high divorce rate in modern America. The rate, as alarming as it may seem, does not necessarily indicate the doom of the family institution but rather the need of contemporaries to succeed in gratifying psychological needs. If the need is not met with one particular partner, the partner is changed; but the same conventional institution, marriage and the family, is used, reused, and upheld.[34]

[32]Carl C. Zimmerman, *Family and Civilization* (New York: Harper and Row, 1947).

[33]Talcott Parsons and Robert F. Bales, *Family, Socialization and Interaction Process* (Chicago: The Free Press of Glencoe, 1955).

[34]There is a significant difference between a particular *family group* and the *institution of the family.* The two should never be confused. The former refers to a specific group of people, in this case a primary group within which the members engage in an intimate face-to-face interaction. The concept of institution is more abstract, referring to norms, values, and customs with which society regulates family life.

Without necessarily endorsing Zimmerman's negative outlook, we nonetheless must acknowledge that the nuclear family is beset with difficulties that limit the success of the personality function. The detracting conditions include (1) high divorce rate, (2) insufficient family communication, (3) increasing numbers of mothers directing their attention to outside careers, (4) continuing remoteness of fathers from the socialization process, and (5) high mobility. These conditions cause many adolescents to be inadequately involved in family communication—without a definite sense of being accepted and understood, and without a basic trust in the stability of the family group.

Some of these detracting conditions must be singled out as particularly important. For example, communication is a skill not automatically earned by merit of being a parent but must be acquired by practice. How many children grow up doubting whether they are loved and accepted by their parents, consequently suffer under these doubts, and later in life reproach a reticent parent for not having communicated love and care? As mentioned earlier, proficiency in communication is imperative for success in the modern family, where role playing is no longer the predictable form of communication. To implement the modern personality function, the communication process must be improved by greater sensitivity and by spending more time on it.

But modern parents' time schedule has not always taken the need for more communication into account. Modern fathers are known as notorious shirkers of the responsibility to equitably share in socializing the young, and excuse themselves as being absorbed by their jobs. Admittedly, this aspect of modern family life seems to be undergoing modification thanks to the protests of the women's liberation movement. But the progress made in this direction tends to be neutralized by the mothers' newly acquired taste for career pursuits. While this may connote progress to many creative mothers who heretofore were cloistered in the kitchen and nursery, it may be an obstacle to the increased communication needed by the child in order to feel secure and understood.

Communication does not merely mean "talking to each other," it means *doing things together*, using the media of common projects, work, and recreational activities. These media can be used to express thoughts and feelings to each other, to get to know each other, and to feel a belonging to each other that can rarely be established by way of abstract verbalizations. Actions speak more convincingly than words, and the young can benefit immensely by shared feeling, touch, and motion—ingredients that will generate common emotions, which form the foundation for conveying the sense of belonging and security.

Another obstacle to the personality function is mobility. Spatial mobility of Americans is truly remarkable: every five years about one-half the U.S. population moves. In the process, they increase the variety of readjustments they must make, lose the immediate support of neighborhood and friendships they had enjoyed, and decrease informal discouragement against separation or divorce they had (or could have) derived from integration into the community.

Mobility plays a prominent role in the lives of businessmen, white-collar workers, and young executives who are constantly on relocation call for the corporation and have been called "corporate nomads." The price of promotion includes a willingness to be geographically mobile. A typical example is the mobility record of a newly promoted assistant secretary at Humble Oil and Refining Co., who at the age of thirty-three had moved six times in eleven years. His nine-year-old son had never finished more than one grade in the same school. Within ten months, a young aspiring executive of Johnson Wax was moved from Wisconsin to New York and then to Chicago to become regional office manager, with his son going through kindergarten in three different schools.[35]

Young people need consistency in life patterns, including physical and social arrangements, to achieve stable reference points. Informal associations like the peer group, neighborhood, and friendships, and formal associations like school, church, and clubs, constitute social-control mechanisms, and youth's integration into them has a stabilizing influence—provided that it is consistent and continuous.

Although one could say a few things in defense of the functionality of high mobility, for example that exposure to a wide variety of stimuli can contribute to a more sophisticated outlook on life and that job contingencies require knowledge of a variety of human interactions, they seem to be neutralized by such dysfunctions as exposing the young to too many stimuli (and possibly inconsistent ones) and to more people than can be meaningfully integrated in the understanding of the young—a typical consequence of overstimulation and overexposure. Although the relationships may turn out to be expedient and efficient, they tend to remain shallow. In other words, quality of human interaction is replaced by quantity. Relationships of deep understanding and genuine loyalty require time to grow—time many mobile parents fail to provide for their children. The sense of impermanence of these relationships intensifies the need for *some* relationship that is durable. And it is, given the impersonality of the larger social system, almost invariably the family that is sought out for this important function.

Now we have arrived at a circular irony. The family seems to promise personality security, commonly fails to live up to its promise, and Americans nevertheless keep trying to make marriage and the family work. It is like Sisyphus attempting to roll a boulder uphill, and the whole situation smacks of overdependence on a limited structural arrangement.

Whether these changes will eventually bring about the downfall of the

---

[35]"The Job: Corporate Nomads," *Time*, September 29, 1967, p. 56.

family system as we know it today are speculations that cannot be put to an empirical test at this time. In any case, the functional changes of the modern family can be summed up in three points: (1) a number of traditional family functions have been transferred to other institutions, (2) the modern family has become a specialized agency, (3) people turn to the family to derive a sense of total psychological security.

The Question of Primary Group Quality

The socialization experience in the family is so profound that what we conceptualize as "human nature" can be traced back to this primary group. The human organism responds to the slightest variation in style of socialization, and some modes complicate the adolescent process. It appears that a child growing up in a family that fulfills the criteria of a healthy primary group will be better equipped to cope with the contingencies of adolescence than a child whose association was either in a disturbed primary group or mostly in secondary groups.

Before pursuing this argument further, the question of what a primary group is must be clarified.[36] A primary group is characterized by intimate face-to-face interaction and spontaneous cooperation. It is primary in the sense that it is instrumental in generating the social nature of the individual. The psychological result of the intimate association is a blending of several individuals into a social entity in which one's self becomes an integral part of the common life and goals of the group. The emergent sentiments involve the sort of mutual identification for which "we" is the most natural expression. The members' identities become anchored in the feeling of belonging to the whole.

This does not necessarily mean that the atmosphere of the group is always one of harmony. There is often self-assertion and passion. But these sentiments are tempered by sympathy and a sense of common fate. While an individual member may show ambition, its chief motivation is the self-esteem he or she derives from the others, and interaction will be governed by allegiance to common standards of loyalty. This is the social-psychological background that explains why a child may come to dispute with teammates his or her place on the team, but will strive toward common glory for the team.

The most compelling examples of such primary associations are the family, peer group, and, decreasingly, the neighborhood or community. Primary involvements are virtually universal and are the basis of what is universal in human nature and fundamental in human sentiments.

The definition of secondary groups consists of elements that contrast

---

[36]The statement on the primary group, paraphrased in the following passages, comes from Cooley, *Social Organization*, pp. 23–24.

with the primary group—impermanence, casualness of contact, fewer ties of deep sentiment among the members, and a lesser degree of derivation of basic values from the group's norms and goals. In reality, groups do not come neatly divided into either primary or secondary types; rather, social reality presents us with a continuum, the poles of which we define as primariness and secondariness of group quality. Groups differ from one another not categorically, but in the *degree* to which the interacting behavior of the participants reflects primariness.[37]

Has the American family shifted along the continuum of primary-secondary group relations? In other words, is the nuclear family less primary than the traditional family? To answer this question, it is helpful to examine specific elements of the criteria of primariness.

An important element of the primary group consists of *common value orientation*. Family sociologists fear that consensus within the family, especially between the generations, has been eroded by modern socialization practices that promote more nonfamilial exposure of the young to nurseries, day-care centers, peers, schools, and youth subculture than to parents and relatives. Bias for the traditional growth process in the primary group family is reflected by a number of sociologists' negative views of the changes in family functions. They regret, as Hobart put it, that "the shaping of a human life, a human personality, a future of happiness or hell, which is best accomplished in the primary group, is turned over ever earlier and for longer periods to secondary, impersonal, social agencies."[38] These agencies tend to merely "handle" children in groups, rather than care for them as individuals.

Bronfenbrenner is even more outspoken about parental failure to enforce a value orientation in the children. Reporting about his cross-cultural study of child-rearing practices in America and West Germany, he admitted that he expected German parents to be stricter than American parents. Although the hypothesis was borne out by the findings, it was also found that the German parents were more affectionate and spent more time with the children. This calls into question what exactly is meant by *permissive*; perhaps it means that parents are not paying much attention to their young. American parents have been told by experts to "let children be themselves"; that counsel has been taken to mean "let them grow up by themselves." Bronfenbrenner rejects *laissez-faire* philosophy and believes that the young "should not grow up associating only with other children because they haven't much to give to each other."[39]

Teenagers themselves have complained that parents fail to give them

---

[37]Definitions like "primary" or "secondary" are ideal-type definitions; that is, they are useful—yet arbitrary—typologies. They are useful for tracing trends, comparing different systems, and facilitating communication. Ideal-type concepts are instrumental in many social analyses and can be called *heuristic* in nature.

[38]Hobart, "Commitment, Value Conflict and the Future of the American Family," p. 408.

[39]"The American Family: Future Uncertain," *Time*, December 28, 1970, p. 37.

guidance and are too permissive. It seems that they sense a need for more authoritative counsel. A national sample found that teenagers ascribe primary responsibility for excessive teenage drinking and use of "dope" to their parents' failure to wield enough authority.[40] This attitude illustrates teenagers' dissatisfaction with modern home anomie, which allows them a high degree of individual freedom but also creates uncertainty. Anomie is not characteristic of a primary-group setting; rather it offers rules and values of insuperable aid in stabilizing personality.

Common activities, another mark of the primary group, have drastically declined in the modern family. As discussed in previous chapters, the place of work is somewhere else, and children, unless they live on the farm, are not drawn into adult activities. Similarly, leisure activities are usually age-segregated because of different interest. If time is spent together, it is usually a passive gathering—watching television, traveling someplace, or being entertained—instead of doing things together.

A core trait of the primary group is that it forms the social nature of the individual. To what extent is the modern family still instrumental in carrying out this function? Is it imbuing the young with the same loyalty and empathy as the traditional family? Bronfenbrenner has found that all factors indicating growth, happiness, and effectiveness of the young are declining. Conversely, he discovered increasing isolation and evidence to anticipate impairment rather than improvement in competence and character of the next generation. His pessimistic conclusion was that the system for making human beings human in this society is breaking down and that "the destructive effects of these changes derive from the progressive segregation by age in American society, resulting in isolation of children and those responsible for their care."[41]

As a rule, parents gladly let other agencies take over socializing. Nurseries, kindergartens, schools, churches, and the various media of entertainment encounter little resistance from parents, who willingly surrender a territory that means fatiguing work, time, and often frustration. Television in particular has become a convenient baby-sitting device, changing the family circle to a semicircle.

Finally, the characteristics of the primary group include the blending of several individuals into a social entity. But in our age, the young do not defer individual goals to common goals; rather they look at the family as a pragmatic arrangement that can be useful but as only one alternative in learning values. In short, the family has changed from an end in itself to a means for individual purposes.

[40]Leonard Gross, "America's Mood Today," *Look*, June 29, 1965, p. 21.

[41]Urie Bronfenbrenner, "The Challenge of Social Change to Public Policy and Developmental Research." Paper presented at the President's Symposium, *Child Development and Public Policy*, Denver, CO, April 12, 1975, abstract.

This does not mean that the average family of today is of secondary-group quality. Rather, there has been a shift on the continuum toward more secondariness of group qualities, with the family playing a modified role in the process of extending identity. The proliferation of secondary-group affiliations and the impact of the mass media are to some extent replacing the socialization function of the family. It seems that both the family and the secondary influences are not meeting the needs of the young. The paradoxical result is that the young turn to the family for identity and warmth, but are confronted with its ineffectiveness in stabilizing personality and are thus driven back to the conflicting and piecemeal socialization of secondary groups.

PARENTHOOD: THE LAST STAND OF THE AMATEUR

The distress of the modern family has invited critics to blame parents for all the trouble, branding them amateurs in a world of experts. While unqualified accusations merely add insult to injury and overlook the fact that parents themselves are victims of changing times, some critical comments are well taken and should be discussed.

The need to control parenthood expresses itself most distressingly at the time of adolescence, when many of the young show evidence of inadequate parental help. Many parents did not know what the socialization process would demand of them and gullibly followed the all-American bandwagon of "parenthood as a natural and beautiful state of existence."

Regulation of, or even mere advice about, the individual's reproductive behavior is considered by most Americans as an encroachment on their "natural right" and flatly rejected. The noncooperative stance has prompted some social scientists to suggest radical measures for curbing unqualified parenthood; they believe that society must restrict the reproductive privilege. Sociologist Kingsley Davis suggested charging high fees for marriage licenses, levying a "child tax," reversing the traditional taxation of singles over persons having children, and legalizing sterilization and abortion.[42]

Anthropologist Margaret Mead recommended that Americans accept what seems to be a naturally evolving dual marriage system. One is the "individual marriage" for young couples not intending to have children; and the other is the "parental marriage" for couples planning to have children.[43]

[42]Kingsley Davis, "Population Policy: Will Current Programs Succeed?" *Science*, 158 (November 10, 1967): 738. A number of other sociologists have made statements basically in agreement with Davis' concern: Michael Young, Ronald Freeman, Bernard Berelson, Philip Hauser, Orville Brim, Jr., Brewster Smith, Reuben Hill, George M. Foster, Everett Rogers, Nicholas Demerath, and others, in "Meetings: Behavioral Science and Family Planning," *Science*, 158 (November 3, 1967): 677–82.

[43]"Margaret Mead Today," *Time*, March 21, 1969, p. 77.

Biologist H. Bentley Glass thinks that parenthood should be permitted only after a couple obtains a "child license."[44] The question of enforcement of such an ordinance is understandably pertinent. Glass suggests court-ordered sterilization of parents who violate the license law more than once.

Politicians also recognize the need for laws against irresponsible parenthood. For example, an Illinois state representative sponsored a bill in 1971 that would force Illinois welfare parents who had three children to be sterilized to preclude burdening the public with additional expenses.

These arguments warn that unchecked parenthood and population growth will reduce living standards and life chances for everyone and that the conventional view of parenthood as an asset to society needs drastic revision. Parenthood has become a liability, not only because of all-too-frequently poor parenting, but also because we are endangering our resources through overpopulation.

THE QUEST FOR ALTERNATIVE STRUCTURES

Disillusionment with the modern family has led to experimentation with alternative primary groups. The vast majority of experimenters are young individuals who try new arrangements that they hope will both give them the gratifications of the ideal family and spare them what they see as stifling elements of the nuclear family system.

Many of them fail to recognize, however, that frustration and sacrifice are essentially unavoidable ingredients of the universal experience of growing up and cannot always be explained by structural contingencies. Not understanding the near universality of emotional distress, they tend to blame the structure in which they find themselves at the time of self-search and during the process of growing up. Frustrating curtailment of desires and painful adjustments are hardly novel aspects of the human condition and cannot justly be blamed on the nuclear family.

This is not to say that the modern family system is faultless and could not be improved. Rather, it should remind us that there is no structural alternative that will do the soul searching, self-integrating, and growing up *for* the young. Hence, many a search for an alternative family system is really an attempt to run away from basic developmental tasks, an excuse to avoid responsibilities, and a confusion between reality and utopia. At the core of this confusion is a basic misunderstanding of what human nature is. The fact that youthful communes have an extremely short life span and an exas-

[44]Los Angeles Times Service (June 24, 1964); AP Report (Atlantic City, NJ, February 13, 1967).

peratingly high turnover of members bespeaks the pseudosolution that these alternatives represent. There is no support for the contention that the alternatives work better than the nuclear family.

Complaints about the modern nuclear family are legion. It has been accused of suffering from isolated structure and from atrophy of vital functions. Bronfenbrenner believes that the modern family is experiencing an unprecedented atrophy and that the all-too-frequent one-parent situation constitutes a highly unreliable structure.[45] Because of its maimed condition, the family no longer provides communion of religious belief, shared work experience, a medium through which to contact others in the community, and a source of convincing norms and values.

Additional complaints aim at the larger social system: the emptiness of organized religion, the meaninglessness of the Protestant ethic, the rigidity of Puritanical sexual mores, the anonymity of urban-industrial life, and the agonizing anomie of American culture.

These ills, many of the young feel, are not alleviated by the current family form, and they are seeking a structure that would correct its failures. Many college students admire the type of integrated environment of such groups as the Amish and Hutterites, the Israeli kibbutz system, and the type of tribal or village life of which they have learned through Margaret Mead's, Oscar Lewis', and Bronislaw Malinowski's anthropological reports. They believe that the Samoan way of growing up would be ideal since the organization of the household eliminates most of the seeds that germinate into the dysfunctional emotions and conflicts with which our nuclear-family-raised children seem to be afflicted. The Samoan child's world is composed of male and female adults, all of whom can be depended on and must be deferred to. In cases of disagreement between parent and child, or in cases where it would be useful for a child's learning of a certain skill, the child is free to move into the home of a relative. The child is not falsely protected from the realities of life: sex, pregnancy, childbirth, and death are all familiar occurrences. "Among the factors in the Samoan scheme of life which are influential in producing stable, well-adjusted, robust individuals, the organization of the family and the attitude toward sex are undoubtedly the most important."[46]

Life in the modern American family contrasts sharply with the Samoan vision. The differential fuels the dissatisfaction of modern youth who would like to revert to a type of extended family system that promises fellowship, integration, security, and all the other things they fail to find in the nuclear family.

The closest they have come to that ideal in their experimentation is the

---

[45]"A Look at the Disintegrating World of Childhood," *Psychology Today*, 9 (June 1975), 34.
[46]Margaret Mead, *Coming of Age in Samoa* (New York: Morrow, 1928), p. 228.

commune. Communes range from religious economy with sexual exclusiveness to group marriage.[47] Most communes hold property in common, but leave responsibility for other aspects of life to the nuclear units, including the care of children. Other communes have utopian or revolutionary orientations. Still others are non-ideological, the communards' chief concern being "experience"—perhaps with drugs, sex, the occult, or simply "relationships" through which they try to find intimacy and sharing.

While each commune is unique, some common traits can be discerned. To some degree they all share property, minimize competitiveness, and emphasize social concerns over utilitarian and financial gains. Commune dwellers search for meaning in life and strive toward personal growth, share the work necessary for maintaining property, dwelling, and livelihood, and share a common distaste for the Establishment.

Most experimental communes last only a short time, having an average life of two years. Individual membership lasts about eight months. Joyce Gardener, one of the founders of Cold Mountain Farm, illustrates the condition of rural and urban communes alike: "... empty people who had come to fill themselves, sapping our energies, needing to be taken care of and giving nothing at all—and now there were only between four and six couples and a few single people left. . . . We didn't find a way of sharing our vision . . . and we didn't have a shared vision to hold us together."[48]

Healing Waters, a commune in the desert of Arizona, demonstrated relative longevity. The commune, set around idyllic natural hot springs, attracted nomadic New Agers for nearly 10 years, and was held together by a core of, initially, idealistic leaders. Healing Waters grew food and maintained a number of New Age health practices, including vegetarianism and transcendental meditation. These activities evolved as specialties or instructional responsibilities of individual members. Presumably all property was held in common, the children brought along by some communards or born into the commune were considered the children of all, and the place welcomed people with "higher consciousness" from all over the country. Alas, in the early 1980s, disharmony erupted in the leadership clique and the New Age Mecca closed its doors to the New Age and turned into a commercial

[47]Saul V. Levine et al., "The Urban Commune: Fact or Fad, Promise or Pipedream?" *American Journal of Orthopsychiatry*, 43 (January 1973): 149–63; Bennett Berger et al., "The Communal Family," *The Family Coordinator*, 21 (October 1972): 419–27; Sallie Teselle, ed., *The Family, Communes, and Utopian Societies* (New York: Harper & Row, 1972); James W. Ramey, "Communes, Group Marriage, and the Upper-Middle Class," *Journal of Marriage and the Family*, 34 (November 1972): 647–55; Laurence Veysey, *The Communal Experience* (New York: Harper & Row, 1973).

[48]Joyce Gardener, "Communal Living: Economic Survival and Family Life," in *Changing Family: Adaptation and Diversity*, ed. Gordon F. Streib (Reading, MA: Addison-Wesley, 1973), pp. 117–18.

enterprise—with the decisive word spoken by the person holding legal deed to the land.[49]

Some communes make compromises with the nuclear family arrangement. An example was Lama, a commune north of Taos in New Mexico, where the members worked together growing and distributing crops, but withdrew to individual nests at nights: a tepee, an A-frame, or a tent, which they shared only with a spouse (or semipermanent companion) and the children. Most couples were married, had children, owned their own homes, maintained middle-class respect for property and work. Although the philosophy of sexual freedom was retained abstractly, it played a minor role in the actual behavior of the communards.[50]

Other communes deviated farther from the lifestyle of the American family and included such groups as the Sandstone Commune in Los Angeles, which kept varying in size between three and twelve members and usually included uneven proportions of men and women. They considered themselves an "intentional family" with sexual freedom, and as one member let it be known: "It's a smorgasbord. It's so much more exciting to have nine different dishes than just one."[51] The group hesitated to have children because it wanted to stabilize its "marriage" first.

The commune movement, then, is a quest for many dreams. It may be a quest for revolutionary restructuring of society, for economic security, for more meaningful relationships than the participants had in their parental homes, or for expanded experiences in respect to sex, drugs, and other interests.

For most, a communard role is short-lived and they fail to find the answers to their questions and the gratification of their needs. In most cases, the communal experiment fails because the members have compounded their problems through interaction with others who suffer from similar troubles of personal anomie. It resembles a situation where one blind person asks another blind person for direction. Sometimes the economic basis of the group is too weak to sustain membership. Sometimes the attempt at a common work project is sincere, but it fails because members lack experience, knowledge, and the actual physical stamina to do the work. Sometimes the animosity of neighbors causes a commune to break up. And in other cases, the commune gradually fades away because of inadequate leadership or because the participants lack the vision to formulate a common goal in the first place.

---

[49]Hans Sebald, "The Waxing and Waning of a New Age Commune—From Nudity to Business Suit," *Humboldt Journal of Social Relations*, Vol. 15, Winter 1988, pp. 1–27.

[50]"The American Family: Future Uncertain," p. 38.

[51]Ibid., p. 36.

Hence, the commune movement of the 1970s and 1980s has subsided. But it has not died. While most communes disintegrated, a few proved to have longevity. The idea of the commune is still alive and still attracts numbers of young Americans who hope to find it more rewarding than their nuclear families.

In contrast to the pessimism of Bronfenbrenner, many family sociologists believe that the companionship-type of nuclear family holds out greater promise than any other experimental arrangement, and that in spite of difficulties, it will survive as the preferred lifestyle. David and Vera Mace express this sentiment:

> The companionship marriage, based on intimacy, equity, and flexible interaction, offers a promising new lifestyle which in fact is the preferred choice of the great majority of men and women in our culture today. The other new lifestyles which have been given such prominence are by comparison of minor significance, and are best viewed as pioneering social experiments which as yet have come up with nothing that could remotely offer a viable substitute for traditional marriage.[52]

SUMMARY

Family dynamics penetrate into the individual's personality and have a decisive influence on how he or she weathers the crisis of adolescence. Family processes are complicated today because of rapid changes. The following points sum up major changes affecting the modern family and, in turn, the lives of adolescents:

1. Family structure has changed to the small nuclear family, which has relinquished integration into the larger social network and become isolated. The young have become deprived of concrete adult models, visible adult work, and familial peers. This increases the potential of associating with peers opposed to the family and stimulates the development of youth subcultures.
2. The modern family has abandoned numerous functions, now taken care of by outside specialization, and has itself become a specialized agency trying to fulfill the "personality function." With increasing isolation and anomie in the industrial environment, the individual has turned to the family to find direction. The identity quest leveled at so fragile a structure appears to be too much of a burden.
3. The family has changed from institutional to companionship interaction, minimizing role behavior and maximizing personal uniqueness. The new style calls for communicative skill.
4. Young people can no longer rely on the family's placement function, which

---

[52]David R. Mace and Vera C. Mace, "Marriage Enrichment—Wave of the Future?" *The Family Coordinator*, 24 (April 1975): 133.

used to define their standing in the community. Now they must rely on their individualism and personal decision making.

5. Modern legislation has given young people more freedom than any previous generation in America, but has done so without regard to family context. Independence from the family has increased the isolation of the individual.

6. The primary-group quality of the family has decreased. Secondary institutions have come to compete with the family. This raises questions about modern socialization's impact on "human nature."

7. Adolescence is often complicated by parents who lack insight and skill. Restricting such unqualified parenthood has become the preoccupation of a number of educators and scientists.

8. Youthful search for what may well be utopian has led to a quest for alternative structures to ameliorate certain limitations of family life. The commune, with a questionable success record, has been a limited experiment that was more common during and right after the counterculture years.

A final word. While it is true that throughout our discussion certain aspects were selected that promote adolescence and prove to be dysfunctional for literally everyone involved, these adolescence-generating effects do not exhaust all the consequences of family changes. Liberating effects have also been brought about by these changes. These include liberating captive creativity from the bondage of familistic servitude and enriching the personality market with talent, aptitude, and individualism. However, we must not forget that the human condition includes the eternal dilemma of not being able to combine two dreams of humanity: freedom and security. Normally we can enjoy only one at a time, and it seems that modern adolescents, whether they like it or not, are satiated with the former and hunger for the latter.

9

The Modern Educational Experience

TRENDS IN AMERICAN EDUCATION

The American ethos considers the right of every citizen to an education—elementary, secondary, and higher—to be as basic and undisputable as the "pursuit of happiness." But education for all was not always the conviction of the American public. Until late in the last century, education was primarily an elementary-school affair. Preparation for higher education was accomplished in private secondary schools and a few public schools. In 1870, for example, teenagers could choose from among only 800 public high schools. Those who attended institutions of secondary education usually had college in mind. Although in 1900 only 11 percent of the high-school-aged youth were in school, two-thirds of the graduates did go on to college—a proportion that has since never been equalled.

The appraisal of high school education in the United States used to be influenced by the European tradition that considered secondary education in the French *lycée*, the English grammar school, or the German *Gymnasium* as the proper experience for the "educated class." The children of farmers were usually not thought of as members of this class, and before or directly after the eighth grade they generally left school to work with the agricultural family unit. Similarly, workers' sons left school to become apprenticed for a trade.

The adulation of secondary and higher education is thus relatively new. Pragmatic reasons underlie this valuation. One involves the fruits of education and vocational training, which have increased the amenities of life. Another reason is the need to keep teenagers out of the labor force. This necessity has developed with industrialization, automation, and the rural-urban migration.

Automation has arrested the increase of blue-collar jobs while expanding the number of white-collar positions that require high school training— clerks, accountants, salespeople, and office workers. In effect, the division of labor no longer needs—or even allows—the labor of the young. Barred from the labor force as well as from free-roaming idleness, America's teenagers were "institutionalized" and delivered into the care of high schools. The institution of secondary education not only kept them out of the way, but even succeeded in preparing some of them for the new white-collar jobs. High school education ceased to be a voluntary matter chosen by the few who prepared for higher education and became an involuntary mandate for all. Statistics illustrate the trend: in 1900, 11 percent of the high-school-aged youngsters attended school; in 1920, 32 percent; in 1930, 51 percent; in 1940, 73 percent; and in the 1960s the percentage achieved a level of over 90 percent, at which it has remained ever since.

The expanding role of high school in the lives of the young is also illustrated by the percentage of young adults (twenty-five to thirty-four years old) who completed four years of high school. The proportion of white males was 36 percent in 1940, 51 percent in 1950, 59 percent in 1966, 77 percent in 1970, and over 80 percent since then. For white females, the proportion was 41 percent in 1940, 55 percent in 1950, 63 percent in 1960, 75 percent in 1970, and also over 80 percent since then. For black males, the proportion was 10 percent in 1940, 18 percent in 1950, 30 percent in 1960, 49 percent in 1970, and just under 70 percent since then. For black females, the proportion was 12 percent in 1940, 22 percent in 1950, 36 percent in 1960, 57 percent in 1970, and approximately 65 percent since then.

These figures show that over approximately the past thirty-five years the white males' and white females' high school graduation rates have nearly doubled; the black males' and the black females' more than doubled.

This upswing in educational participation by America's young modified the functions of secondary education. No longer were high school graduates destined only for college, but instead primarily for business and industry. Concomitant with the growth of the proportion of teenagers attending high school was a decline in the proportion of graduates enrolling in college. The college-entering proportion dropped from two-thirds in 1900 to about half in 1920 and finally to about one-third in 1940, indicating that the majority of teenagers preferred to go directly into jobs after graduation. This preference stimulated significant changes in secondary school curricula. Preparation became centered on immediate vocational fields rather than on extended higher education. This new emphasis gave rise, indeed often priority, to such short-range and practical goals as typing, bookkeeping, industrial arts, shop, and mechanics.

The change in the function of the high school, coupled with the coercive nature of attendance, has produced an essentially new atmosphere in the secondary school system. Academic preparation is no longer the prime objective; rather, general "life preparation" has moved to the forefront. Emphasis on seven basic principles of secondary education evolved: health, command of fundamental mental processes, mature home-membership, vocational preparation, civic education, constructive use of leisure time, and ethical character. More than academic endeavor, the pursuit of these principles constitutes a general program for "life adjustment." The responsibilities of high school teachers now include not only transmission of knowledge, but also character formation, the instillment of motivation, and the counseling of personal problems. In essence, by taking over character-forming functions from the family, secondary education became more a place of general socialization than of information service. Furthermore, this socialization experience was not optional; teenagers had to submit to it, and teachers were burdened with the extra task of convincing them that school was worthwhile.

This is not the end of the story of modern education in the United States. Industrialization and automation have progressed to the point where there is little demand for youth's labor after high school. College education has developed into another means of preventing youth from swamping the labor market, while at the same time trying to prepare them for the ever-increasing number of white-collar and other sophisticated positions. As a consequence, the steady decline of the proportion of high school graduates enrolling in college during the first half of the twentieth century has been reversed.

Since 1950, there has been a 10 percent average annual increase in the number of students entering college for the first time to work toward a degree. However, during the 1980s there has been a slowdown, with the number of those entering college increasing by only 2 percent annually. The decline is due to decreasing numbers of eighteen-to-twenty-four-year-olds in the population, not to a decreasing proportion of youth enrolling in college.

In any case, the American public is now almost as concerned about the college dropout as it is about the high school dropout. Postindustrial conditions do not require young adults in the division of labor, and their entry is delayed as long as possible after high school graduation. This expands adolescence and tends to create a population of restless youth.

EDUCATION—LARGELY A NONFAMILIAL EXPERIENCE

Although in modern societies the institutions of education and of the family have always been separate, they have never before been as unrelated as today. Values preached in school and values upheld at home are often unrelated or even contradictory; the information the child brings home from school is usually irrelevant to actual family life. In short, values and information gleaned from formal education constitute a theoretical manifesto that is more applicable to the outside world than to the family circle.

Some ethnic and religious minorities perceive this duality as a threat to their way of life. An example are the Amish, a Protestant sect living a simple rural life and attempting to survive as a religious enclave within a secular society. They often are at odds with the law, since their views on education differ from legal requirements.[1] Amish elders maintain that "worldly wisdom" taught in public schools undermines their way of life, rural simplicity, and religious values. Confrontations between the law and religious principles have repeatedly occurred in Iowa, Kansas, Ohio, Pennsylvania, and Wisconsin. When Amish farmers were fined for violating Wisconsin's compulsory school-attendance law, the issue snowballed and reached the United States Supreme Court in 1972. The court's decision upheld the Amish's right to religious freedom and restricted the state's compulsory attendance law. This minority was granted the right to maintain its own elementary schools staffed with Amish teachers and was declared exempt from having to send its youth to secular high schools.

State authorities had worried that Amish children who left school before the statutory age of sixteen might become burdens to the public. The record showed such concern to be unfounded: No Amish teenager in Wisconsin had ever been arrested for any crime, no Amish had ever had an illegitimate birth, and none had ever requested public assistance. Additional states complied with the Supreme Court's decision. For example, Iowa exempted Amish children from state education standards and allowed Amish teachers—who usually had only an eighth-grade education—to run their own schools. The Amish are reluctant to employ college-educated and certified teachers who, they fear, might steer their children away from the plain, soil-and-toil-oriented Amish faith. By adhering to this educational policy, the Amish accomplish two main objectives: to retain purity of religious faith and to preserve their young's time and interest for farm work.

By contrast, the dynamics of the urban-industrial society create com-

[1] Albert N. Keim, *Compulsory Education and the Amish* (Boston: Beacon Press, 1975). "In Pennsylvania: The Amish and the Law," *Time*, April 19, 1982, p. 12.

plex educational needs, which are due to at least three major conditions. First, there is rapid social change. American parents cannot mold their children in their own images, since they suffer from chronic cultural lag that may render a portion of their skills, knowledge, and attitudes obsolete. Second, the strong emphasis on individualism prevents parents from determining the occupation of the young by family rule. Rather than relying on familial norms and models for deciding on their future occupation, the young may prefer nonfamilial, formal education. This preference is related to the third condition, the high degree of specialization of modern occupational careers, which calls for vocational preparation outside of the family unit.

The effect of these three conditions has been to shift the responsibility of preparing offspring for their future "specialties" from the family to specialized institutions and to ensconce the young more and more in nonfamilial education.

The satirist Erma Bombeck, by making fun of the transfer of functions from the family to the school, may approximate reality to a valid degree when she quipped: "Barry's a discipline problem at home. What's the school doing about it?" Or: "Stan is depressed and doesn't want to go on living. Didn't the school see this coming?"[2]

An exception to this trend is, of course, found in home schooling, where parents obtain permission from the authorities to educate their child/children at home. The standards of many states are relatively lax and parents with minimum proficiency can usually qualify. In the state of Arizona the qualification requirements consist of passing the reading, grammar, and math proficiency examination for certification to teach in public schools.

IMPACT OF TECHNOLOGICAL INNOVATIONS

There has been a surprising modification of the generally nonfamilial nature of American education. It has been brought on by one of technology's most recent innovations — one that is increasingly finding its way into family life: the personal computer, commonly referred to as the PC. It is a tool for learning or entertainment — or, actually, an activity that combines both — and, for many American teenagers, it makes learning fun. How this revolutionary technological innovation would affect the young and their family integration used to be a question with an uncertain answer. The first in-depth study was completed by a New York University team in 1984 and revealed that the computer had far less impact on American family life than, for example, the

[2]Erma Bombeck, "Stoke the Home Hearth," *Arizona Republic*, October 4, 1988, p. 13.

automobile or TV had in previous decades.[3] And what impact it is having seems to be of a more positive nature. It appears that youngsters who work/play with their computers at home become more integrated in existing family patterns. Reasons for this seems to be that the teenager spends more time at home, using a stimulating device that is as much a toy as a learning tool. Furthermore, the quality of their school work seems to benefit from using it and earns them the praise of the parents. In addition, the home PC can be shared by parents and offspring in joint fun and learning.

However, there was also found the peril of addiction to the new tube. Some parents, the study showed, found it necessary to limit the hours the offspring were allowed to dedicate to their new obsession. One mother complained that her teenager's complexion turned the "color of cream cheese" as a result of spending marathon hours in front of the new screen.

The impact of TV viewing on the young seems to differ significantly from the impact of the computer. First of all, TV viewing occupies an enormous portion of youth's time, a portion only second to the amount spent sleeping, and on the average accumulates by age 18 to 22,000 hours, that is two-and-a-half years, which is exactly twice as long as the 11,000 hours they have spent in the classroom. In light of this impressive investment, it is important to note that virtually all pertinent studies agree that TV viewing, even programs we usually label "educational," decreases creative thought processes. Creative thought primarily refers to coming up with unique and effective approaches to solve problems. Apparently the technological properties of TV releases the human brain from having to translate TV's visual and auditory stimuli into imaginary pictures and sounds. The screen is doing all that for the viewer; there is no need for the brain to set into action circuitries to conjure up ideas as to how things look or sound—quite unlike in the reading experience where our brain is charged with the task to translate the printed or written word into visual, auditory, and other sensory perceptions. Largely unbeknownst to the reader, the brain is stimulated to creatively imagine the setting that the reading material suggests. TV fails to stimulate; it merely saturates.

Nationwide data published by the U.S. Department of Education in 1990 focuses on American eighth-graders.[4] The findings reveal that the youngsters spend an average of 21.7 hours a week watching TV, 5.6 hours doing homework, and 1.8 hours on outside reading. Girls read more than boys—2.1 hours vs. 1.5 hours a week. Children from Asian-American homes

[3]See discussion in "Family Living," *Time,* October 15, 1984, p. 109.
[4]*The American Eighth-Grader,* Superintendent of Documents, U.S. Government Printing Office, Washington, DC, 1990.

top the list in doing homework with 6.77 hours a week. Topping the list in TV viewing are black youngsters with 27.6 hours a week.

There is, according to the study, one advantage that young children exposed to a lot of TV watching have over children with little exposure. Highly exposed first-graders manifest a larger and better vocabulary upon entering school than their low-exposure classmates. This advantage, however, is short-lived and after the second to third grade the difference between the two groups gradually disappears.

The side effects of so much time spent in front of the screen—whether TV or computer—may be seen in American children's inferior proficiency in basic reading and writing skills. U.S. Education Secretary Lauro Cavazos revealed studies in 1990 that showed that the already dismal state of these skills in 1970 had not improved by the late 1980s. Other intellectual skills, such as analyzing information and expressing ideas, had actually declined. "Nearly 60% of 17-year-olds cannot read at the adept level, which is defined as the ability to find, understand, summarize and explain relatively complicated material."[5] The Secretary summed up his concern: "As a nation we should be appalled that we have placed our children in such jeopardy."[6]

Among the few bright spots in the report were indications that between 1970 and 1988 some gains were accomplished by Hispanic and black children. Though, on the average, they still fall below the white children's proficiency in reading and writing, the gap has narrowed.

EDUCATION—EVER LONGER YEARS

The most conspicuous feature of American education has been its ever-lengthening duration in the lives of the young. Census Bureau data show that the average American achieved over five more years of education in the 1980s than in the 1940s.[7] The education gains applied to all regions, men and women, blacks and whites, cities and suburbs. The proportion of Americans who have had four or more years of college has tripled since 1940, going from 4.6 percent to 14 percent today. As a result of these increases, the median educational level reached twelve-and-one-half years by 1980. This means that approximately one-half of all Americans now have finished high school and have spent some time in college. How much longer today's youth spend in

[5]"Basic Skills Eluding Pupils," *Arizona Republic*, January 10, 1990, p. 2.
[6]Ibid.
[7]U.S. Department of Health, Education, and Welfare, *Statistical Abstract of the United States* (Washington, DC: Government Printing Office, 1980), pp. 148, 149.

educational institutions is illustrated by comparison of the median education level of twenty-to-twenty-six-year olds and the over–sixty-five age group. The former group achieved an average of 12.8 years, the latter only 9.1 years — just over a year of high school.

The typically postindustrial shift of the teenage population from work bench to school desk can be illustrated by statistics from such countries as Germany. During the 1960s about 20 percent of the thirteen- to fifteen-year-old Germans were in the labor force (usually as apprentices); by the 1970s practically no members of this age group were working. For the boys of the fifteen-to-twenty category the decline was from 81 to 59 percent; for the girls from 78 to 57 percent.[8] This shift is even more clearly demonstrated by German census data showing the proportion of the teenage population in school increasing from 17 to 35 percent between 1960 and 1970, while, conversely, the proportion of apprentices dropped from 19 to 9 percent and the proportion of unskilled teen labor from 13 to 4 percent.[9] These statistics reveal the typical correlation between increasing postindustrialism and increasing years of formal education.

Ever longer years of higher education is a phenomenon found in all modern industrialized societies. An international survey carried out by the Ministry of Education of Germany in 1989 shows that between the 1970s and the 1980s an average of half a year has been added to the educational process, so that, for example, German university students now finish on the average at age 28. At the same time, their age at the beginning of their university studies increased from 20.9 to 21.6 years. Similar trends were found in other industrialized European nations.[10]

The United States has been prototypical in setting this trend — a trend continuing unabatedly into the last decade of the twentieth century when school enrollments leveled off or even dropped. Dropping enrollment is not indicative of shortening the educational experience but rather of declining *numbers* in age groups; the *proportions* of age groups enrolled have increased. Census figures concerning eighteen-year-old Americans show that in 1950 56 percent, in 1960 72 percent, in 1970 75 percent, in 1980 77 percent, and in 1990 close to 80 percent graduated from high school. In conclusion, most American youths are involved in long years of education during which they are suspended between childhood and adulthood.

[8]"New Work Habits and Life-Styles," *Bulletin*, Press and Information Office of the Federal Republic of Germany, Bonn, December 20, 1971, p. 350.

[9]"Jugend," *Kulturbrief*, Internationes, Bonn, Vol. 5, December 1975, p. 26.

[10]"Studienzeit," *Mitteilungen*, Deutscher Akademischer Austauschdienst (DAAD), Bonn, October 1989, pp. 14–15.

CRITICS OF TWO SORTS

The Liberal Point of View

The assumption that the protracted sojourn in the educational institution is primarily motivated by desire to absorb knowledge and learn skills has long since been revealed as illusory. School has assumed a custodial function and tries to stem the potential flood of over-sixteen-year-olds that could inundate the labor market. Such inundation would create job scarcity and bring about a disastrous swelling of the ranks of the unemployed. Postindustrial automation simply has no use for this excess of young workers. So they end up completing high school, entering college, and establishing their ghettos and subcultures.

Since youth's stay in high school is not always motivated by free will and enthusiasm about education per se, disharmony with authorities can evolve. In its overt manifestation the discord can degenerate into vandalism and other school-related delinquency. In its more covert manifestation the problem consists of a type of psychological warfare in which the administration tries to impose "colonial treatment" on the young, and where the young counter by rejecting the moral and intellectual expectations of the authorities.

A number of writers have attempted to illuminate this side of our educational system. Many have condemned the custodial function of schools and the isolation of youth from mainstream America. John Holt, for example, suggested that schools relinquish the "jail business" and stop numbing children by overdoses of superfluous authority.[11] He assessed malfunctions of American education in five points:

1. Schools fail to promote the growth of children and substitute the custodial function for the learning function. The young are in school because they are not wanted anywhere else.
2. Schools grade and label the young. This, presumably, is contrary to the true process of education. We cannot expect young people to trust us if they know, as before long almost all of them do, that a major part of modern educators' job is compiling records that will be used to judge them for the rest of their lives.
3. Schools have adopted a missionary zeal to explicitly indoctrinate patriotism, morality (especially sexual morality), competition, and the value of the profit system. More subtle indoctrination encompasses the vast field of modern consumerism—implanting the proper consumer attitudes toward grooming norms, dress, cleaning and bath products, cosmetics, and so forth.
4. Schools divide the young into winners and losers and then train them to accept

---

[11]John Holt, *Freedom and Beyond* (New York: Dell, 1972) and *Escape from Childhood* (New York: Dutton, 1974).

their roles. By this process, the Establishment is assured that the winners will defend the system without guilt and the losers without rancor.

5. The most offensive aspect of modern schooling, which is closely related to the previous point, is its unrelenting attack on the dignity and self-respect of the students, who are cast into simplistic hierarchical roles of winners and losers regardless of personal uniqueness.

Another critic was Paul Goodman, who considered it absurd to grow up in a society that compelled its young to go to school when they cannot profit by it.[12] He accused American schools of ignoring the most important problems of young people, such as job prospects, sexuality, and community processes. Although failure of schools to captivate student interest is usually rationalized by authorities as "failure to communicate," the truth probably is that the message has been communicated clearly but is unacceptable to the young.

Problems of school are symptomatic of the pathologies of society. Goodman felt that youth resents what American society fails to provide:

1. Opportunities and worthwhile goals.
2. Enough and visible work positions.
3. Honest public speech.
4. People who are to be taken seriously and can serve as models to youth.
5. Opportunities for imaginative minds.[13]

Another critic of American education is Edgar Z. Friedenberg, who disapproves of compulsory school attendance, believing that such compulsion strips victims of personal autonomy and civil rights. He thinks that coercion does not serve a truly intellectual function but bows to economic pressures of a society wanting to delay youth's entry into the labor market. "A people have no right to cling to economic arrangements that can be made halfway workable only by imposing an infantile and unproductive status on adolescents and indoctrinating them with a need for trashy goods and shallow meretricious relationships that they know to be degrading."[14]

The list of this type of critic could be extended. Although some of their criticisms are well taken, many are less than pragmatic; they are romantic, if not utopian. For example, George B. Leonard believes education could be ecstasy—pure joy, involvement, and growth for both student and teacher—but that competition and bureaucratic regimens turn off the student's

[12]Paul Goodman, *Growing Up Absurd* (New York: Random House, 1960).

[13]Ibid., p. 12.

[14]Edgar Z. Friedenberg, *Coming of Age in America* (New York: Random House, 1965), p. 249.

mind.[15] To overcome such obstacles in school, Leonard recommends that we "learn delight, not aggression; sharing, not eager acquisition; uniqueness, not narrow competition."[16] In the absence of an effective plan for restructuring our educational framework and changing our cultural premises, such suggestions fall more in the category of poetry than science.

The Conservative Point of View

A new type of educational critic began to speak up during the late 1980s. This one—unlike Holt, Friedenberg, and Goodman—was critical not because our system burdens the young with too much formal education and too many prescriptions, but for exactly the opposite reasons: we are not demanding enough; we are not using our educational setup to the fullest.

Chicago University Professor Allan Bloom caused a stir in 1987 with his book, *The Closing of the American Mind,* in which he attacked the way our nation educates its young people. He felt that the intellectual standard has drastically declined because of increasingly pragmatic school curricula and the decreasing emphasis on the classics, languages, and the humanities generally. He blames the decline on the consideration accorded to various clamorous groups demanding an adjustment of educational curricula to real-life conditions in America. He identified among these groups especially the feminists, the blacks, and other minority groups. He envisioned a sort of elitist education that would restore the mastery of certain basic civilizational knowledge.

Critical reviewers were quick to brand his vision as anti-democratic, unsuited to a society as heterogeneous as America's, and neglecting the pragmatic quest of the American character.

In a similarly provocative manner, University of California scholar Russell Jacoby (*The Last Intellectuals,* 1987), University of Virginia Professor E. D. Hirsch, Jr. (*Cultural Literacy,* 1987), and Boston University President John Silber ("Free Speech and the Academy," 1990)[17] have assaulted what they feel is an inferior educational process in late-twentieth century America. They turn against the neglect of teaching our Western cultural heritage, again emphasizing the role of classic literature in this connection, and against the mind-stifling atmosphere created by bureaucracy in the academic environment. Where are, Jacoby wonders, the young intellectual heirs to carry on the bold thinking of such splendid American scholars as David Riesman, John Kenneth Galbraith, and Daniel Bell? Jacoby blames the deterioration of academe's integrity and greatness on the double-effect of young academics

---

[15]George B. Leonard, "How School Stunts your Child," in *Children's Liberation,* ed. David Gottlieb (Englewood Cliffs, NJ: Prentice-Hall, 1973), pp. 145–66.

[16]Ibid., p. 162.

[17]*The Intercollegiate Review,* 26 (Fall 1990): 33–41.

seeking security and specialization. Instead of standing up to be counted as a critic, the new university intellectual prefers the feather-bedding offered by academe and its warm but stifling tenure.

Silber thinks that the price we are paying for the barbarism that came during the 1960s and 1970s—camouflaged as "relevant" courses in university and college curricula—is the loss of a universal vision and the encapsulation of the student in anti-intellectual splinter groups. He calls for a revitalization of the study of Western culture and its plethora of classic works, pointing to the universal and timeless value of such works as the *Odyssey* and the *Iliad*. In them, he believes, we find reported the rich range of human modalities, which give us insight into our common humanity and instill a vision of human nobility.

Once More: In Loco Parentis

While most of Bloom's, Jacoby's, and Hirsch's commentaries were directed at the college and university level, the late 1980s also showed a trend toward reassertion of institutional authority on the high school level. This once more brings into focus the concept of *in loco parentis* authority. After a lapse of this type of authority during the 1960s and 1970s, where a more liberal and permissive stance prevailed, the late 1980s and early 1990s saw teachers and administrators reasserting their right to be in control in the classroom and on the campus in general.

Examples include the case where a Missouri high school principal ordered the removal of two controversial articles from the school's newspaper. The student editor and her staff thereupon filed suit in court against the ruling, claiming their First Amendment rights as student journalists had been violated. The court battles climbed all the way to the U.S. Supreme Court, which in 1988 took the side of the school principal, upholding his *in loco parentis* authority.[18]

Another case dealt with the action of a New Jersey high school principal, who insisted on opening and searching a fourteen-year-old girl's purse. The girl had been caught breaking school rules by smoking in the lavatory. She denied the accusation and claimed she never smoked. Her purse, however, contained not only cigarettes, but marijuana as well—and several notes indicating that she was selling pot to other students. The principal then turned the matter over to the police. After several years of legal battles, including three lower court proceedings, the case reached the U.S. Supreme Court, which supported the school principal's action by pronouncing that "public school is a special place wherein the usual guarantees and restrictions

[18]"Censorship," *State Press*, February 4, 1988, p. 5.

of the Fourth Amendment regarding search and seizure of an individual or his property do not necessarily apply."[19]

Still another teenage issue made it to West Virginia's highest court. It upheld a rule in 1990 that allows young school dropouts to be denied or stripped of the driver's license. This was the first state to aim a law at the sixteen- and seventeen-year-old dropouts.[20]

THE CASE AGAINST COLLEGE

Some critics of American education have taken a radical view and actually suggest that a noncollege education might be preferable for large numbers of American youth. Sociologist James S. Coleman argued that the focus of American schools is too limited, too competitive, and fails to develop in students the ability to manage their own lives in a responsible fashion.[21] Schools not only fail to promote these qualities, they so monopolize young people's time and energy to prevent them from acquiring these skills elsewhere. Until a few generations ago, children learned adult qualities from family models. However, segregated by age, modern youth is saturated with information but deprived of experience. Coleman suggested an alternation between study and work to introduce students to the careers they choose. Prolonged education often renders a distorted view of adult life. Many colleges have tried to correct this by bringing the outside world into the classroom and introducing careers without harnessing students to them too soon.

The best solution, according to Coleman, would be to graduate the young earlier, at about sixteen, and place them in organizations like businesses, hospitals, factories, and symphony orchestras. These establishments could make use of the youths' contribution, while training them and supervising further part-time schooling. This would be a fundamental shift from the customary American view of education as a means of secular salvation to the old way of socializing through apprenticeship. Coleman's design would provide all sixteen-year-olds with vouchers worth four years of college tuition; the vouchers could, however, also be used to join an apprenticeship program or for enrolling in a vocational school.

Implementation of Coleman's plan might diminish adolescence and its collective expression. Young people would usefully integrate themselves into society, build self-respect through meaningful work, and avoid being segre-

[19]"Search Rules," *Time*, January 28, 1985, p. 77.

[20]"'No School, No Drive' Law Is Upheld," *Arizona Republic*, December 1, 1990, p. A4.

[21]James S. Coleman et al. *Youth: Transition to Adulthood*, Report of the Panel on Youth of the President's Advisory Committee (Chicago: University of Chicago Press, 1974).

gated. Integration would reduce unrealistic segregation from adult responsibilities and limit the breeding of subcultural lifestyles.

Another argument against the pressure to attend college was raised by Caroline Bird, who believed that the majority of college students are not in college because they like it or because they want to learn. She estimated that hardly one-fourth of the students enjoy academic work and that the rest, at best, experience college as a social center and at worst as a detention center preventing them from entering adult life for several more years.[22] During these years students feel unwanted and useless. Postindustrial efficiency, with its labor-saving automation, renders them superfluous. To get them temporarily out of the way, we send them to college—where only a fraction of them are intellectually motivated and prepared to enjoy studying. According to Bird, many college students describe their time in college as if it were a sentence to be served—and yet, as unpleasant as it is, preferable to the drudgery of a boring job or to the possibility of being unemployed.[23]

AMERICAN EDUCATION IN PERSPECTIVE

The attacks on American education are legion. And they usually come from within and not from without the nation, being part of the syndrome of American self-consciousness. Hardly any other nation indulges in such merciless self-criticism.

One cannot help but wonder how much of the criticism is based on romantic expectations and utopian fancy instead of on realistic assessment. For example, such critics of the American school system as Edgar Z. Friedenberg, Paul Goodman, John Holt, George Leonard, and David Gottlieb have complained that schools require adolescents to surrender and/or suppress their creativity, individuality, and identity to the demands of the skill- and information-oriented curriculum in order to qualify for "success." Schools have been accused of causing foreclosure of creative and individualistic potential for the sake of making children acceptable to postindustrial society in general and the school authorities in specific. The price is too high, these critics claim, and the diminishing of unique individuality and the obscuring of personal identity is a defeat not justified by the educational accomplishments gleaned from American schools. Most of all, these critics feel that the true happiness of the young is foreclosed.

Part of the argument, as in most issues in life, is correct. It is undoubtedly true that the socialization process, be it couched in formal educational

[22]Caroline Bird, "College Is a Waste of Time and Money," *Psychology Today*, 8 (May 1975): 28.
[23]Ibid., p. 32.

terms or in informal familial terms, necessitates some degree of abrogation of individuality and establishes some degree of conformity. How could it be otherwise? The young everywhere must be socialized, and individuality can be tolerated only within certain limits.

Perusal of the writings of these romanticist critics creates the impression of a Rousseuan presupposition: the myth of the innocent child of nature, the innate goodness and fairmindedness of the young, and the destruction of these natural impulses by our corrupt urban-industrial society. From a sociological perspective, there is no evidence to support such wishful thinking. In fact, one could cite research showing that those young individuals who have made adjustments to school and society, thus falling in the category of the supposedly foreclosed subjects, were more comfortable than those fighting foreclosure. They were more comfortable in school and held more positive attitudes toward their educational experience, whereas the uncommitted and searching (those taking unbridled advantage of the adolescent moratorium) evaluated their educational experiences negatively.[24]

Of course, this finding could be turned around and used in favor of the romanticist critics, presumably showing the placidness of the suppressed individuals. But any style of socialization, including the formal educational process, will create problems and leave many wishes unfulfilled because of the very definition of socialization, which implies involuntary submission to the indoctrination of a culture. The American system must be viewed with these universal limitations in mind.

From a cross-cultural perspective, the American educational structure is a far greater success than many guilt-racked Americans would allow. In spite of certain limitations, it does function as an equalizer between racial, ethnic, and socioeconomic groups. If it has not shone with particular brilliance in this respect, the fault does not lie with the structure of the American school system, which probably has the soundest potential of any school system in the world. Many European systems do not offer this potential. Their educational structure is a *parallel* system whereby most children go through nine (it used to be eight) years of elementary education plus two years of part-time school and are then irrevocably finished, while a minority—usually of upper socioeconomic background—switches in the fourth grade to a radically different system that eventually allows them entry into the university. These parallel structures divide the young into elite and proletariat, into intelligentsia and passive masses. Quite differently, the American system pursues a *sequential* structure that allows the individual to continue in educational endeavor, to continue where he or she left off. It is a democratic system and the structure bears it out, permitting everyone to

[24]A. S. Waterman and C. K. Waterman, "The Relationship between Ego Identity, Status and Satisfaction with College," *Journal of Educational Research*, 64 (1970): 165–68.

progress, drop out, and reenter without having experienced a prohibitory bypassing of certain mandatory and absolute switching points.

Another oversight of the critics deals with the assumption that the school is not only the central instrument of education (which it certainly is), but also nearly the only one, which it certainly is not. When it is argued that the home and the mass media have more to do with the success or failure of education than do the schools themselves, such observations are received as a sort of treason against the august function of education.

But the facts indicate that the educational structure is paralleled by so many other socialization influences that shape the attitudes of the young that their success or nonsuccess in the educational structure can no longer be blamed on this structure alone. Take alone the fact that the average American child spends more hours in front of the television screen than in the classroom, and that his or her affiliations with formal and informal organizations, clubs, and groups have proliferated to the extent that school is just one of them.

Perhaps we ask too much of school. In the past we expected our schools to accomplish what in the Old World the family, the church, apprenticeship, and the guilds accomplished in concert. Today we ask that the school render the services of what their modern equivalents, plus a hundred voluntary organizations, fail or refuse to do. In short, modern American schools have become the scapegoat for the failures and shortcomings of a multiphasic and anomic society.

What parents, particularly middle-class parents, expect school to give to their offspring amounts to virtually *everything:* loving attention, advanced babysitting, academic brilliance, effective preparation for a profession, character building, skill in getting along with others, a sense of creativity as well as a sense of conformity, athletic excellence, and, most pronouncedly, psychological health (whatever that may mean). The dropout is seen as the patent failure of the school in conferring these qualities to children. With a peculiar zest for guilt feelings, many Americans, including what appear to be masochistic educators, actually believe in a simple cause-effect relationship—the cause for dropping out is the failure of the school.

Notwithstanding the enormous difficulties and the staggering demands leveled at the American educational structure, American education renders an amazingly successful service.

This is not to say that the American institution of education is free from serious problems and awful deficiencies. (Discussion will once more touch on this topic in Part V, Challenges and Outlook.)

Probably the greatest dilemma of the American high school lies in trying to do justice to a divergent population of students: to those preparing for entry into the labor market and those preparing for college. The American democratic ethos tries to safeguard the privileges of both groups, and in the process perpetuates the dilemma and makes it practically unsolvable.

This makes high school the weak link in the American educational system. But what are the alternatives? A European system that favors some sort of elite and sorts out, at a preposterously young age, the "lower" from the "higher" educational material? Most likely this would result in unspeakable, even though unintentional, hardship for masses of young people who recognize their interests and their educational potential at a later age—an age when they find themselves excluded from the trajectory of higher education.

The Europeans, incidentally, have learned from the tragedies of this arbitrary and parallel system and are trying to correct it. In the process of modifying their archaic structure, they are working out a "middle way" that presumably gives young people a second chance at higher education once they have bypassed the significant switching point at age ten. But the overall structure has become only more cumbersome and complex. Worst of all, it has failed to eliminate the socio-economic bias of the old system: West German official reports in 1982 admitted that the elite/proletariat pattern is still recognizable, with only 14 percent of all university students coming from working-class families. This statistic becomes more glaring when one considers that working-class youngsters are the largest group in the student-age population of West Germany.[25] Many European educators wish they had inherited a sequential system like the American one with its democratic simplicity rather than a structure that divides the young into categories alienated from each other by different unbridgeable educational careers.

SUMMARY

Education in postindustrial society is nonfamilial, longer, custodial, and *in loco parentis*. In addition, it has assumed a ghetto atmosphere that age-segregates the population and promotes the formation of a subculture. It is typical of modern society to shift the teen population from work bench to school desk. High school education has become not only a "basic right," but also a coercion. This reflects not merely an abstract value of the American society, but also the necessity of keeping the nation's youth from entering the labor force at an age when they are unprepared for the labor market, and when the labor market is unprepared for them.

Some critics suggest a case against the pressure to continue education on the college level. Unmotivated and unqualified youth might do better and be happier with alternative careers and vocations.

Technical innovations have left their marks on the educational process, as well as on family life. TV has been found to suppress creative thought and probably detracts from the learning process, whereas the computer seems to

---

[25]"Bildungspolitik," *Mitteilungen*, DAAD, 5, May 1982, p. 7.

supplement and even encourage learning, as well as integrates into family life.

Two types of critics should be noted. One accuses the American school system of squelching the development of individuality and creativity and goes as far as hinting that the dropout is one who tries to preserve these qualities. Much of such criticism is based on romantic visions of what some kind of hypothetical human being might be—"if the school would only give him or her a chance." The myopia of the criticism overlooks that (1) postindustrial society has spawned so many other influential media and affiliations that the blame for failing to successfully socialize the young can no longer be justifiedly laid at the doorsteps of the school; (2) socialization is not a liberating process but by definition has to some degree a suppressive function; and (3) the sequential nature of the American school system is of greater democratic value than the European system, which is based on an elite/proletariat dichotomy.

The other type aims criticism at the college and university level and largely is critical for such reasons as the neglect by the American educational system to insist on teaching the cultural heritage of Western Civilization—its history, literature, and philosophies.

10

The Role of Television and Other Mass Media

Human beings have the capacity to think in symbolic terms and need not rely on the actual presence of persons or objects to form views of themselves and the world. Humans are also inventive and have created mass media to expose vast audiences to a constant barrage of stimuli that bear significantly on personality development.

SCOPE OF EXPOSURE

Of the various media, television reaches nearly all people in this country; it is notoriously popular, easily accessible, and commands the largest share of time Americans spend on any of the mass media. Television has absorbed some of the functions of the press, radio, and movie industry. Movies, for example, have become almost synonymous with television, and it is only a matter of time before the latest productions can be seen at home. Television is probably the most influential source of common experience in the lives of American children, and, along with home and school, has come to function as a major socializing agent. Through mass media, the actual live person or group can be bypassed, and personal interaction can be replaced by the spectator–mass-media relationship, allowing an almost unlimited range of vicarious identifications.

One should not conclude that the significant other person and the concrete group have been replaced entirely. The feeling of security that a child derives from association with caring parents is still of paramount importance for personality development. But needing parents and wanting to be like them are two different processes. The first deals with the need for security and the second with the absorption of ideas, impressions, and behavior styles. Parental care is a universal imperative for survival that has rarely been successfully replaced, while identification is a process allowing alternative objects of identification. Mass media offer a vast number of such alternatives. Modern children, although depending on their parents physically, can select ego images from the characters presented by ubiquitous mass media. Through screen, radio, and print, characters of many different types are presented to youth, who cannot escape from the incessant flow of stimuli and cannot avoid incorporating some aspects of these "types" into their behavior patterns and identities.

The effects that the mass media have on the personality of the young are not yet well known. It may safely be assumed, however, that the effects are not superficial, when one considers that over 99 percent of American homes have a minimum of one television set and that among American children time spent viewing television ranks second only to sleeping.[1] By the time the American teenager reaches eighteen years of age, he or she will have watched an average of about 22,000 hours (that is approximately 2½ years) of television compared with 11,000 hours spent in the class room. The average American, both child and adult, views over six hours of television daily. By the age of fourteen, the typical viewer will have witnessed 11,000 TV murders; by the age of eighteen he or she will have been exposed to 350,000 commercials.[2]

Television viewing starts early in America, and it soon starts to reflect the symptoms of addiction. A study at Michigan State University discovered that when four- and five-year-olds are offered a hypothetical choice between giving up television or their father, one-third would rather part with father.[3] Children get up early in the morning to watch television before leaving for school, and millions of children under the age of twelve watch television as late as 10 P.M. on week nights. The peak of television viewing is reached somewhere between the sixth and the eighth grades, just before entering the

[1]Robert M. Liebert et al., *The Early Window. Effects of Television on Children and Youth* (Elmsford, NY: Pergamon, 1982), p. xv.

[2]Joan A. Wilkins, *Breaking the TV Habit* (New York: Scribners, 1982), pp. 10, 13, 32.

[3]"Getting Unplugged," *Time*, October 11, 1982, p. 99.

adolescent years, and then decreases slowly until around the twelfth grade, when the adolescent is reaching a plateau of about two and one-half hours of television viewing a day.[4]

The main reason for the heaviest period of viewing occurring between the sixth and eighth grades and then dropping off can be found in the new freedom that this age group experiences in staying up later in the evening. The gradual decrease after this age is no doubt largely due to the social involvements of the adolescent. The television set is at home, and home is not where most adolescents want to spend their time. Their process of autonomy and their increasing interest in the peer group and in dating mean less time for television.

Americans most likely hold the world record in television viewing, but other countries are not far behind. Statistics show that West German children rate television their favorite pastime, spending approximately one and one-half hours daily watching it, and list as their favorite shows (1) comics, (2) wildlife shows, (3) children's programs, and (4) Wild West movies.[5] Concern about TV's family-destructive potential has been expressed on the highest government level. For example, in 1982 West German Chancellor Helmut Schmidt called on his nation to observe a family night at least once a week—*with TV off.*

Nonetheless, television as an internationally ubiquitous medium is on the rise. Its growing magnitude in technologically advanced societies illustrates the emphasis that postindustrial systems place on the service function, including entertainment, communication, and advertisement.

PROMINENT INGREDIENTS: UNREALITY AND VIOLENCE

Television portrays a variety of values that cannot fail to have impact on the young. A number of the dominant values conflict with those that most parents would like to instill in their children:[6]

1. Violence. It is virtually impossible to watch television without seeing humans killed, tortured, or maimed, and it has been estimated that by fourteen, the average child has seen 18,000 humans killed on television.
2. Unreality. Television exposes the young to a world of unreality that not only invites escapism from real life—a function of fantasy that is often useful—but

---

[4]Wilbur Schramm, Jack Lyle, and Edwin B. Parker, *Television in the Lives of Our Children* (Stanford, CA: Stanford University Press, 1961). Also see "A Profile of the American Eighth-Grader," Superintendent of Documents, U.S. Printing Office, Washington, DC, 1990.

[5]"Fernsehen," *Kulturbrief Inter-Nations,* 2 (August 1972): 22.

[6]Most points are based on a discussion by E. E. Le Masters, *Parents in Modern America* (Homewood, IL: Dorsey Press, 1974), pp. 159–61.

seriously distorts reality. Fantasy is more honest: it openly admits that it is not reality but simply a flight of fancy.

3. Sex. Sexuality is usually presented in movies and television on a physical level, both visually and verbally, but disguised as "love."

4. Idealization of immaturity. Idols and heroes are often immature and teenage-like and seem to have achieved wealth and fame with minimal talent.

5. Materialism. Many programs imply that happiness comes with success, and success means houses, cars, vacations, and so forth.

6. Instant achievement and solution. This theme glorifies the power of technology and promises instant solutions to life's problems. Many commercials peddle chemicals assuring immediate success in problems that range from romance to insomnia. During a two-hour television period, forty-two such claims were presented in the form of commercials.[7]

In addition to these themes, there are, of course, more positive values presented, and they will be discussed later in the chapter. For the moment, we are concerned with two dimensions: unreality and violence.

Unreality

Unreality is a generic concept that can be divided into fantasy and deception. *Fantasy* identifies itself as such and is youth's favorite in the form of cartoons, fairy tales, ghost stories, comedies, and science fiction. Although the interest in the fantastic is not new in history, the recent preoccupation with it is of more than literary significance. For the first time in history, it is now possible to intensively expose children to such themes every day. Interpretations of this preoccupation have described it as symptomatic of the present anomic age—as wishful thinking, as searching for solutions, as another version of longing for magic that can solve problems, and, finally, as escape from a world that looms confusing and perilous.

Rarely, however, does fantasy lead to confusion between real and unreal, and there is speculation that television fantasy, and the vicariousness with which the young experience it, has therapeutic effects by providing an outlet for frustration and a reprieve from anxieties.[8] Fantasy may even stimulate creative thought and the ability to solve problems.[9]

However, researchers have found that exposure to television—a prolific source of fantasy—does not significantly improve the child's school performance. Studies of two samples of children, one group with and the other without a television set at home, revealed that the group exposed to televi-

---

[7]Henry L. Lennard et al., *Mystification and Drug Misuse* (San Francisco: Jossey-Bass, 1971), and Hans Sebald, "The Pursuit of Instantness in Technocratic Society and Youth's Psychedelic Drug Use," *Adolescence,* 7 (Fall 1972): 343–50.

[8]For details on the function of fantasy, see Eleanor E. Maccoby, "Why Do Children Watch TV?" *Public Opinion Quarterly,* 18 (Fall 1954): 239–44.

[9]Alfred R. Lindesmith et al., *Social Psychology* (New York: Holt-Dryden, 1977), p. 154.

sion entered school with larger vocabularies—an advantage that was of short duration. After a period of school attendance, the language proficiency of the two groups became comparable. Also, there was little difference between them in respect to interest in class work, completion of assignments, and test performance.[10]

Exposure to fantasy may lose its beneficial effects through overexposure. A child may become "addicted" to mass media fantasy, try to substitute the "safer" world of make-believe for the real world, and actually find it difficult to separate the real from the unreal. A child or teenager watching television more than four hours a day has to do an extraordinary amount of switching back and forth between the two worlds. This oscillating existence does not contribute to his or her ability to concentrate on real problems and tasks.

A chronically disturbed youth is particularly prone to experience detrimental effects from prolonged exposure to fantasy, since fantasy can reinforce escapism to the point where a youth loses touch with reality and refuses to be bound by the rules of the social environment. Maybe the greatest danger is the possibility that the young use certain mass media images and models to formulate identities that become harmful not only to themselves but to others. Many of the television crime-busters invite emulation, although imitation of their techniques would be disastrous in real life. The world of fantasy has different rules and protects the foolhardy hero, who is pictured as invincible. If children act as though they were protected by the rules of fantasy and withdraw too often from the real world into the euphoria of make-believe, they are then headed for serious adjustment problems. George Gerbner, one of the nation's foremost TV-fare analysts, concludes in his recent research that young persons may come to view themselves in the light of fantasy and acquire a pseudoidentity that would have to be changed for everyday life.[11]

It might well have been of television's fantasy and its overexposed "addict" that the poet Gibran spoke when he said, ". . . that stealthy thing that enters the house as a guest, and then becomes a host and then a master."[12]

Another aspect of unreality concerns *pretension* about the real world. No genre of the mass media is immune from portraying reality deceptively: comedy, drama, adventure, detective stories, love stories, and the news—all have their own slant. It is this type of misrepresentation that generally is more harmful than pure fantasy. While fantasy may prove to be relatively ineffectual with respect to identification and personality formation because

[10]Eleanor E. Maccoby, "The Effects of TV on Children," in *The Science of Human Communication*, ed. Wilbur Schramm (New York: Basic Books, 1963), pp. 116–27.

[11]Reported in "Life According to TV," *Newsweek*, December 6, 1982, p. 136.

[12]Kahlil Gibran, *The Prophet*, copyright © 1961, p. 32. Reprinted by permission of Alfred A. Knopf, Inc.

the average youngster knows that it is make-believe, the pseudoreal programs seriously tempt the young to identify and select models for emulation. Movies are a frequent source of such identifiable images and models. The heroes are part of plots that range from "real-life" detective thrillers and Wild West epics to the "wholesome" swim-ski-and-surf type stories.

Grant Noble speaks of the danger of projecting mass media personalities into real life:

> These characters serve as something akin to a screen community with whom the viewer regularly talks and interacts. Viewers who feel they know these characters well may indeed compare new people they meet in real life with such characters in order to predict how these new people are likely to behave later.[13]

Books are another medium through which unreality or violence can be conveyed. One of the most typical conveyors of unreality is the Gothic novel, which presents a plot in which all the heroine need do is be beautiful as she travels through mysterious adventures and ultimately finds fame, fortune, and the man of her dreams. This type of romantic reading material seems to be still popular especially with girls. The power of imagery that reading can exert over the human mind of the young is, however, minimal when seen in the light of 1990 statistics that show that on the average young teenagers spend merely 1.8 hours on outside reading (other than homework) per week compared with 22 hours of TV viewing.

These plots, whether occurring in books or on television, purport to depict real life but actually select only certain aspects of life. They convey situations, achievements, and human relationships that have little or no validity in the real world. The heroes as well as the villains of these stories display superior strength, imagination, and achievements, making the parents seem pale and unimaginative in comparison.

And the flawless beauty of the heroine, as well as her miraculously good luck in life, is extremely difficult to match in the real life of the teenager—as one look into the mirror or stepping onto the bathroom scales may well prove. At that moment, ideas of equivalence or imitative possibilities may abruptly cease and painful frustration set in.

Violence

Violence, the other major theme, is heavily laced with unreality—both in quantity and quality. The vast majority of all types of violence in real life takes place between persons who are friends or family members. In only about 10 percent of all homicides are the assailant and the victim strangers. In the television world, the majority of violent acts occurs between strangers.

---

[13]Grant Noble, *Children in Front of the Small Screen* (Beverly Hills: Sage, 1975), p. 164.

Similarly, crooks make up 17 percent of all TV characters vs. 1 percent or less in real life.[14] Gunslingers, psychopaths, and sadists have leading roles in a significant portion of television entertainment, and their behavior is shown to millions every day. The classic content analysis by Wilbur Schramm of 100 television hours of the so-called children's hours, 4:00 P.M. to 9:00 P.M., Monday through Friday, produced an impressive list of nonhumorous (as distinct from cartoons and comedies) acts of violence:

12 murders
16 major gunfights
21 persons shot (apparently not fatally)
21 other violent incidents with guns
37 hand-to-hand fights (15 fist fights, 15 incidents in which one person slugged
    another, an attempted murder with a pitchfork, 2 stranglings, a fight in the
    water, a case in which a woman was gagged and tied to a bed, and so forth)
1 stabbing in the back with a butcher knife
4 attempted suicides, three successful
4 people pushed over cliffs
2 cars running over cliffs
2 attempts made in automobiles to run over persons
A psychotic raving in a flying airliner
2 mob scenes, in one the mob hangs the wrong man
A horse grinding a man under its hooves
A great deal of miscellaneous violence, including a plane fight, a hired killer
    stalking his prey, 2 robberies, a pickpocket working, a woman killed by falling
    from a train, a tidal wave, an earthquake, and a guillotining.[15]

The reason this study can be called a "classic" is that it established an early assessment of the *nature* of violence in American TV programs during the children's hours. While the nature has hardly changed, the *quantity* with which we bombard children with violent images has increased over the years. Mid-1980s statistics by the National Coalition on TV Violence reported a notable rise since the 1960s in the use of violent images on TV and MTV, as well as in the lyrics in popular rock 'n' roll music.

Precise figures were published in 1989 by University of Pennsylvania communications professor George Gerbner in the report, *Violence Profile 1967–1989: Enduring Patterns.* The project uses a "violence index" to compare from year to year the programs offered by CBS, NBC, and ABC. Violence is defined as explicit physical acts or threats of hurting or killing in any context. The rate of violence during weekdays' prime time has increased insignificantly, from slightly under six acts per hour before 1980 to a little over six acts after 1980. During prime time 70 percent of network programs use violence, but during children's hours 90 percent of the programs show

[14]"Learning to Live with TV," *Time*, May 28, 1979, p. 49.
[15]Schramm et al., *Television in the Lives of Our Children*, pp. 139–40.

violence. The most significant increase in violence has been found in the weekend daytime children's programs. Whereas before 1980 there were 18 violent acts per hour, after 1980 their number increased to 26.

Simple arithmetic tells us that if we count an average of six acts of TV violence per hour's watching (basing it on the more moderate weekdays' prime time), then an eighteen-year-old American, who has on the average watched 22,000 hours, has witnessed 132,000 acts of violence.

THE QUESTION OF IMITATION

Such staggering figures justify raising the question as to how violence influences the audience, especially the malleable young.

The Controversy

Representatives of the broadcasting industry claim that television has no harmful effects on the viewer. Mental health officials, social workers, teachers, and the general public are divided over the question, some believing that exposure to violence breeds violence, and others assuming that exposure has a cathartic and pacifying effect, allowing children to identify with the aggressor and in this way rid themselves of pent-up hostile emotions without harmful acting out.

The divergence of interpretations is typically exemplified by the dispute between sociologist Paul Hirsch and communication researcher George Gerbner. Hirsch, using National Opinion Research Center data, compared heaviest and lightest viewers and concluded that heavy watchers show no negative signs. On the contrary, he thinks, TV is probably more of a solution to their problems than a cause of their problems. Gerbner rebuts by pointing to Hirsch's biased sample, which was only 6 percent of those polled by NORC, including housewives and retired folks whose TVs are almost constant companions against loneliness and not agitators intent on imitation. Hirsch's study is not representative of teenage viewers, who may watch less but more violent fare and may be affected quite differently.[16]

The controversy reached the highest echelons of the American political institution. In 1990 Congress reacted to the critics of the TV industry, ranging from religious conservatives to consumer groups like Action for Children's TV, and sent a bill that would set limits on commercial time in children's programs and increase educational fare to President Bush.[17] But the modification even as mild as the bill suggested—the question of censor-

---

[16]"Are TV Addicts Healthy?" *Time*, October 20, 1980, p. 81.
[17]"Is TV Ruining our Children?" *Time*, October 15, 1990, pp. 75–76.

ing violence wasn't even raised—encountered Presidential reluctance. President Bush argued that the bill would infringe on broadcasters' First Amendment rights. Two years earlier President Reagan had vetoed a similar measure. This goes to show that American TV networks enjoy nearly unchecked license.

Experiments and Studies

Insight into the nature of media violence influence is derived from the Bandura experiments at the Stanford University psychological laboratories, which evaluated the impact of televised aggression on preschool children. Experiments tested the extent to which children copy aggressive behavior when such behavior is demonstrated by models in three different situations: in real life, on film (television), or as cartoon characters on film. The typical experiment divided the children into four groups. While three groups witnessed violent behavior under the different conditions mentioned above, the control group was not shown any violence. After the children of the three groups had watched the acts of violence, they and the control-group children were individually placed in an observation room under conditions that mildly irritated them. The observation room contained a variety of toys, including a three-foot Bobo doll that could be used as an object of aggression. Each child spent twenty minutes in the room, and his or her behavior was rated by psychologists observing through a one-way mirror. The results left little doubt that exposure to violence stimulated aggressive tendencies. Children who had viewed the aggressive adult demonstrated approximately twice as much aggression as those in the control group. The researchers concluded: (1) Exposure tends to reduce inhibition to act in a violent manner. (2) Exposure tends to shape the form of aggressive behavior. While most of the children from the first three groups sat on the Bobo doll and punched its nose, beat it on the head with a mallet, tossed it in the air, and kicked it (the exact kinds of attack they had observed), the children of the control groups rarely acted that way. (3) Display of violence on film is almost as influential as a display in real life. The child exhibits a high degree of imitation in both situations. However, the children were slow to imitate cartoon characters.[18]

The weak element in the Bandura experiments is the substitution of an inanimate object, the Bobo doll, for a real human being as the target of aggression. The substitution is understandable. In spite of certain risks involved, some other studies tried to measure aggression as it was directed at actual persons. The findings were positive. For example, one study showed

---

[18]Albert Bandura, Dorothea Ross, and Sheila A. Ross, "Imitation of Film-Mediated Aggressive Models," *Journal of Abnormal and Social Psychology*, 66 (January 1963): 3–11.

that an 11-day overexposure to aggressive cartoons led preschoolers to enact violence toward peers.[19]

A large and methodologically sophisticated study by the Huesmann team followed approximately 1000 elementary school boys and girls in the United States and in Finland for three years.[20] It provided for the examination of the larger social matrix in which the children lived, with an emphasis on family conditions. The study yielded a major insight insofar as it revealed bidirectional effects. That is, watching TV violence stimulates the child to become aggressive, and the more aggressive the child becomes, the more it selects violent programs. It is, in short, a mutually stimulating process. Another significant contribution by the study showed that aggressive behavior has multiple causes. There is a complex mesh of at least seven conditions that seems to make for a positive relationship between media violence and its enactment: (1) The child's belief that the violent show portrays life as it is. (2) The child's identification with the violent hero. (3) The child having habitual aggressive fantasies. (4) The child's mother being noticeably more aggressive than would be considered normal. (5) The child's lower socioeconomic background. (6) The child doing poorly in school. (7) The child being unpopular with peers.

What this important study shows is that TV violence is not the only cause of aggression in children; rather, it is one of the conditions in a highly complex causative matrix. Nonetheless, it appears that media violence was a salient enough condition to be called a predictor of future levels of aggression for boys and girls in both cultures.

Periodic upsurges in public concern over possible negative consequences of violence-filled TV programs have prompted a number of official inquiries. The first major inquiry was the 1972 study by the Surgeon General's Scientific Advisory Committee on TV and Social Behavior, yielding five volumes of findings. Generally, the findings linked violence on TV with aggressive behavior in young people. Here are two representative studies.[21]

Monroe M. Lefkowitz studied 900 third-graders, observing them over a ten-year period. He found that children unpopular as third-graders stayed unpopular ten years later. The child unpopular in the third grade watched TV more as he or she grew older and continued to be unpopular. There was a direct correlation between degree of violent program preferred and aggressive behavior, both in the third grade and ten years later. While the re-

[19]F. B. Steuer et al., "Televised Aggression and the Interpersonal Aggression of Preschool Children," *Journal of Experimental Child Psychology,* 11 (1971): 442–47.

[20]L. R. Huesmann et al., "Intervening Variables in the TV Violence-Aggression Relation: Evidence from Two Countries," *Developmental Psychology,* 20 (1984): 746–75.

[21]Surgeon General's Scientific Advisory Committee on TV and Social Behavior, *TV and Adolescent Aggressiveness,* vol. 3 (Washington, DC: Government Printing Office, 1972).

searchers conclude that this phenomenon illustrates the impact of TV violence on personal aggressiveness as well as its cumulative effects, the study as such does not prove its contention but merely points out a correlation.

A similar study by John Robinson and Gerald Bachman completed a longitudinal study of 2,200 tenth-graders throughout the United States between 1966 and 1970. Among the boys who initially were found to be most aggressive, preference for violent TV shows was linked to their behavior. More instances of violent fights occurred among heavy viewers of TV violence than among those who had no violent shows among their favorites. Again, it is not clear whether this finding is a correlation or a causal relationship.

Predictably, the television networks reacted defensively and, reminiscent of the parallel rationalizations by the tobacco industry, tried to capitalize on the technicality that though a *correlation* was established, there was no proof of a *causal* relationship between TV violence and aggressive behavior.

The matter was more or less laid to rest until 1982 when the National Institute for Mental Health published another notable report. *Television and Behavior: Ten Years of Scientific Progress and Implications for the Eighties* derived from a two-year review of hundreds of research studies and reached an unambiguous conclusion: Television is a "violent form of entertainment" that clearly leads to aggressive behavior by children and teenagers.

Again, network reaction to the report was quick and predictable. All three networks rejected the report. NBC felt certain that many of the report's conclusions would be challenged by social scientists conducting independent research. It also announced that it would publish its own report at a later time, showing that the NIMH conclusions about the effect of viewing TV violence are not supportable. The networks' basic argument was that, based on high ratings, the programs are giving the public exactly what it desires and the networks are therefore serving the public interest.[22]

In addition to these comprehensive reports, which integrate masses of research data, there are numerous specific studies that contribute valuable insights. For example, one study's focus dealt with gender-differentiated responses to media violence. Up to about 1970, researchers had regularly found girls to be less influenced by media violence; either they did not watch TV violence in the first place or did not respond aggressively to such violence. Boys, on the other hand, were more interested in violent shows, viewed more of them, and reacted aggressively. This gender difference has changed. Psychologist Leonard Eron's latest study shows that such gender-differentiated responses to media violence has been erased.[23] His explana-

[22]"Warning from Washington," *Time*, May 17, 1982, p. 77; also AP report, Washington, May 9, 1982.

[23]"Learning to live with TV," p. 49.

tion: TV's violent female role models have dramatically proliferated and star in such regular shows as *Bionic Woman, Wonder Woman, Charlie's Angels,* and *Policewoman.*

In spite of what appears overwhelming evidence for negative influence, some social scientists continue to remain aloof from the imitation theory. They are convinced that television is a secondary cause of real-life violence and that other factors, such as the individual's background and personality, are much more causative. Some feel that television violence may actually make viewers *less* violent by allowing them to cathart their pent-up hostility. Among those who deemphasize the imitative role of media violence are Seymour Feshbach and Robert D. Singer, who experimented with several groups of boys aged nine to fifteen and varied their exposure to media violence under controlled conditions.[24] Some groups watched aggressive programs, such as *The FBI, Gunsmoke,* and *The Untouchables;* other groups watched milder ones. The experimenters kept track of the changes in aggressive attitudes and values as well as in the number of aggressive acts in which the boys engaged during their exposure to the different fare. The findings failed to support the traditional theory. The group that watched the milder programs engaged in more than twice as many fist fights as the group that watched the rougher shows; as for angry arguments, the "nonviolent" group had 859 arguments, compared with the "violent" group's 407. Criticizing or insulting others amounted to 973 versus 456 instances, respectively, manifestations of jealousy compared 254 to 87 instances, and instances of destruction of property were equal.

The researchers arrived at the conclusion that *no* group became more aggressive as a result of viewing aggressive television programs and that some subgroups actually became *less* aggressive. Astonishingly, they found that youngsters who watched the nonaggressive television programs became *more* aggressive in their behavior. In short, they concluded, the vicarious aggressive experience is therapeutic and calming.

Another reason mentioned by social scientists for nonimitation of violence is viewers' ability to discern between fiction and fact. Robert P. Snow found children capable of interpreting acts of violence on television as taking place in a "play" setting; they were rarely tempted to reenact them.[25] If seen in this light, the experiments by Bandura lose some of their significance insofar as the children may have realized that a Bobo doll is not a real person, and beating it is therefore not to be equated with any degree of violence against another human being.

[24]Seymour Feshbach and Robert D. Singer, *Television and Aggression: An Experimental Field Study* (San Francisco: Jossey-Bass, 1971).

[25]Robert P. Snow, "How Children Interpret TV Violence in Play Context," *Journalism Quarterly,* 51 (Spring 1974): 13–21.

Examples of Imitation

The argument that media violence breeds imitation in real life can be more effectively supported by reports that clearly show its existence. Some examples (from the author's "imitation" file) include:

1. Teenage girls gang-rape a San Francisco girl in imitation of a scene from the 1974 TV movie *Born Innocent* in which Linda Blair played the victim of sadistic teenage girls.
2. An inmate escapes by helicopter from a Michigan prison; the escape was planned after seeing the movie *Breakout.*
3. Teenagers commit several inventive Chicago murders, following in vivid detail the killings depicted in the TV detective series *Shaft.*
4. Teenagers immolate a woman in a Boston street forcing her to douse herself with gasoline, in imitation of a scene in the TV police story *Fuzz* presented two nights earlier. Later that year the scene was reenacted in Miami where a derelict, as in the movie, was set on fire; three young teenagers were charged with murder.
5. A seventeen-year-old boy stabs to death a young woman, imitating a scene from the Emmy-Award-winning TV movie, *The Marcus-Nelson Murders.* The boy had memorized the movie down to the last detail and arranged the crime scene to look exactly like it did in the movie.
6. A sixteen-year-old boy kicks to death an old man after he had seen it done by the "hero" in *A Clockwork Orange* and tells the police that he remembered his act "like a scene from the film."
7. Two fourteen-year-old boys commit suicide when they imitate the mock hanging they had seen performed on TV by rock music star Alice Cooper.
8. A young man extorts $500,000 from Quantas Airlines in a pressure-bomb hoax modeled after Rod Sterling's *The Doomsday Flight,* which had just been shown on Australian TV. When the movie was shown on American TV, bomb threats against airlines went up 80 percent within a week.
9. A fifteen-year-old boy shoots to death an eighty-three-year-old woman and is defended in court as a victim of "involuntary TV intoxication" and his parents in 1978 filed (unsuccessfully) a $25 million damage suit against the three major TV networks.
10. Two California youths rob a bank in imitation of an *Adam 12* story and hold twenty-four hostages against a $1 million ransom.
11. A sixteen-year-old girl sprays a crowded San Diego elementary school with rifle fire in 1979, killing and wounding several persons. The sniper told police later that she had always fantasized about being a sniper and derived idea and technique from watching *SWAT* on TV.
12. In the movie *Taxi Driver* a disturbed cabbie, played by Robert De Niro, sets out to shoot a presidential candidate in an attempt to impress a child prostitute played by Jodie Foster. John Hinckley, after seeing the movie 15 times, so identified with the film's hero that he bought an Army fatigue jacket, took to drinking peach brandy, and sent emotional messages to Foster, as did De Niro's character. Then, in 1981, he shot President Reagan.
13. Three youths, aged fifteen, nineteen, and twenty-one, sadistically murder a Florida talk-show celebrity in 1982 by reenacting a bizarre ritual patterned after the movie *The Shining* (involving ice to suffocate or freeze a person to death and the word "redrum"—murder spelled backwards). The movie had been shown on television during the week of the slaying.

Besides such spectacular imitations, making national if not international headlines, most imitations remain local news. A sampling includes numerous TV-inspired burglaries. Among them were an eleven-year-old boy and his seven-year-old accomplice, who imitated detailed techniques of breaking into homes. A Washington youth committed burglaries by skillfully forcing skylights, a method he had observed on TV. An *Ironside* script had Jackie Cooper playing a scientist who was locked in an explosive belt by a criminal. Ten days later a young man was arrested when he tried the same method to kidnap a Hartford businessman's daughter. A four-year-old Brooklyn boy died in 1979 when he fell seven stories from a building ledge while imitating Superman. Inmates of the Florida State Hospital in 1980 armed themselves with sharp metal objects and makeshift clubs for a three-hour rebellion minutes after they had watched the TV movie *Attica*, which depicted a similar situation. Teenagers affected by the 1979 movie *The Warriors* went on a rampage and caused several thousand dollars worth of damage at a Scottsdale, Arizona elementary school.

Imitation of media violence has crossed national borders and shaken the public in other countries. For instance, a fourteen-year-old London boy committed self-immolation in 1979 in exactly the same manner as he had seen on TV the night before; the diary he left behind attested to his carefully planned imitation. This case, and others, dramatically illustrate the findings by William A. Belson, sociologist at the London School of Economics' Survey Research Center, whose six-year study of nearly 1,600 London teenage boys disclosed that long exposure to TV steeply increased their acts of violence (smashing cars, damaging phone booths, setting fires, etc.).[26]

Imitation of a peculiar form of violence took place in 1976 in the diocese of Würzburg in Germany. A 22-year-old university student, Anneliese Michel, exhibited the classic symptoms of Satanic possession after the movie *The Exorcist* had made its rounds in the local theaters. Ensconced in a Catholic environment of true believers, she attracted wide attention by what finally was officially diagnosed by the Church as genuine possession. Two priests were charged by the archbishop with the responsibility to perform the appropriate rituals—as specified in the *Rituale Romanum*—to drive out the Devil. Anneliese, unbeknownst to the priests and the family, did a splendid imitation of Linda Blair's notorious role in *The Exorcist*. Only the outcome took on a particularly macabre twist: the priests starved the girl to death. That's when the D.A. and the courts took over. Psychiatric experts posthumously diagnosed that the young woman's affliction had been a mixture of role playing and epileptic symptoms.[27]

[26]William A. Belson, *Television Violence and the Adolescent Boy* (Lexington, MA: Heath, 1978).

[27]Hans Sebald, *Witchcraft—the Heritage of a Heresy,* (New York: Elsevier North Holland, 1978), p. 233–34.

"Disturbance" Theory

Many researchers warn, however, against overgeneralizing the impact of media violence. They think that imitation occurs only under certain circumstances, as in cases where disturbed adolescents are exposed to violent fare. While this assumption has the ring of plausibility, it raises questions of definition. What is disturbed; what is normal? These definitions are not yet clear and they differ among researchers. For example, if we equate what Freud called "moral anxiety"—the entirely normal control emotions that accompany the conscience and without which a person would be a sociopath—with being "disturbed," then normal would mean being occasionally anxious and disturbed. Most research concentrating on imitators indeed finds many of them disturbed to some degree. But it would be difficult to prove that all nonimitating viewers then must be "normal." It is possible that the amount of violence imitated by viewers definable as disturbed is not significantly larger than that imitated by viewers definable as nondisturbed. We don't really know how they compare. At this time, equating disturbance with receptiveness to violence imitation remains a hypothesis.

THE DESENSITIZATION EFFECT

Another possible effect of exposure to media violence is desensitization toward violence. Habitual viewing of violence may lead to the viewer thinking and feeling that violence is a normal, everyday phenomenon. Such interpretation may ultimately induce endorsement of violence as an acceptable, tolerable, and perhaps unavoidable way of solving problems—and studies have borne out that this attitude has been engendered in children.[28] Desensitization has also been measured through physiological indicators. Comparison of boys with different histories of exposure to media violence showed that autonomous nervous system responses (blood pressure and galvanic skin response) to violent scenes were significantly stronger in the low-exposure boys than in their TV-tempered peers.[29] This simply means that boys who were overexposed to media violence were no longer upset by it.

Concern that TV-induced insensitivity may spread and become a normal part of the American lifestyle has been voiced by a number of notable writers and public figures. Barbara Ehrenreich put her finger on a tragic

[28]Joseph Dominick and Bradley Greenberg, "Attitudes Toward Violence: Interaction of TV Exposure, Family Attitudes, and Social Class," in *TV and Adolescent Aggressiveness*, vol. 3 (Washington, DC: Government Printing Office, 1972).

[29]Victor B. Cline et al., "Desensitization of Children to TV Violence," *Journal of Personality and Social Psychology*, 27 (September 1973), 360–66.

element in American civilization when she called it the "warrior culture." She thinks that "our collective fantasies center on mayhem, cruelty and violent death. Loving images of the human body—especially of bodies seeking pleasure or expressing love—inspire us with the urge to censor."[30] Norman Cousins feared that "the ability to react instinctively to suffering seems to be atrophying. Youngsters sit transfixed in front of television or motion-picture screens, munching popcorn while human beings are battered or mutilated."[31] Marie Winn felt that among the characteristics of a new breed of juvenile delinquents is their heavy exposure to violent media programs. The common strain running through these youthful criminals—many have mugged, murdered, and raped—"seems to be a form of emotional detachment that allows them to commit unspeakable crimes with a complete absence of normal feeling such as guilt or remorse. It is as if they were dealing with inanimate objects, not with human beings at all."[32]

It is difficult to determine whether or to what degree a dulling of the Americans' capacity for empathy has progressed. We can only try and interpret certain symptoms. This brings to mind a large, quarter-page picture of an adorable little boy smiling at us from the front page of Arizona State University's student paper, *The State Press* (November 14, 1985). He is holding a toy revolver in his hand and is whiling his time away on the main mall of the campus by "shooting people." The reporter and the editor apparently found this a cute pose. The caption informs us that while the child's sitter, a graduate student, was busy with paper work, "Adam spent his time shooting people." The fact that a picture of fake killing was found to be an acceptable and entertaining feature and that not one letter to the editor (from a student population of over 40,000) protested it may well document insensitivity to the dignity of human life in an environment where presumably the better values of humanity are to be protected and furthered.

CONTROL ASPECTS

Most research suggests that televised models are important sources of social behavior and can no longer be ignored as influences on personality formation. However, one must distinguish between learning and acting out. Although children readily learn patterns of social behavior, including violent acts, from television programs, their imitative behavior may be limited by at least three factors:

---

[30]Barbara Ehrenreich, "The Warrior Culture," *Time*, October 15, 1990, p. 100.
[31]Norman Cousins, "The Decline of Neatness," *Time*, April 2, 1990, p. 78.
[32]Marie Winn, *The Plug-in Drug* (New York: The Viking Press, 1977), p. 73.

1. Children ordinarily do not have access to the weapons necessary for duplicating what they have observed. If, however, they had switchblades, blackjacks, brass knuckles, and six-shooters, it is safe to predict that the incidence of harmful imitative aggression, patterned according to television stories, would rise sharply.
2. Normally, parents suppress any learning that conflicts with what they consider "proper" conduct. Often such television-produced conflicts are merely on the verbal level, and parents have no particular difficulty in correcting them. The influence of television is ordinarily checked by the standards of parents and other adults, and the full impact of television can be measured precisely only when parental supervision is removed and the children are given the instruments they need to reproduce the aggressive behavior.
3. It is often assumed that an ethical ending to a story, in which the villain is punished, will serve to extinguish what a child has learned from exposure to antisocial models and therefore keep him or her from imitating the violent behavior.

What can be said in response to these control expectations?

First, the nonavailability of instruments is a weak argument, since consumption-oriented postindustrial society provides just about any instrument, including guns and knives, that a young American desires. The public debate about curbing the sale of handguns, especially the so-called Saturday-night specials, is testimony to the concern of many citizens about the easy availability of deadly instruments.

Second, with rising employment of mothers, children increasingly associate with peers who do not necessarily endorse parental standards. It is interesting to note the paucity of concrete suggestions in the professional literature telling parents how they can curb excessive television exposure, neutralize its negative effects, and, if necessary, substitute more creative activities. One of the best methods might be to encourage the young to take up a constructive hobby rather than spend all their time in front of the television set. But for such suggestions to be effective, parents would have to apply more than verbalization: they would have to guide and join the offspring in such projects—something they often find too time-consuming. The majority of parents find it more convenient to turn their children over to the babysitting function of television and even leave the program selection up to them. Research found that 53 percent of 600 parents studied who had eleven-year-old children did not prohibit their offspring from watching any program.[33]

Third, research seems to indicate that the "ethical ending" (or the "happy ending") is a weak safeguard against imitation.

This point can be illustrated by some of Bandura's experiments. A group of nursery school children watched a television movie in which Rocky,

---

[33]P. Musgrave, "How Children Use TV," *New Society*, 13 (1969): 277–78.

the villain, took all of Johnny's toys. Clearly, the story showed that aggression pays off. Another group of children saw the same program with a different ending: as Rocky tried to seize the toys, Johnny overpowered him and gave him a sound beating. The two groups of children were then tested. As might have been expected, children in the first group, who witnessed that Rocky's aggression was rewarded, readily imitated his physical violence and his hostile remarks, while children in the second group, who saw him punished, showed little imitative aggression. Further inquiry, however, presented the researchers with a surprise: all the children were highly critical of the way Rocky behaved and called his action "mean" and children who imitated him did so because his aggression "paid off" or "worked."[34]

Another experiment testing this question found that when a fantasy sequence in a comic strip pictured a villain as relatively successful, children were more likely to identify with him or her and wanted "to be like him or her," while they were reluctant to identify with a weak hero. The children tended to admire and copy "what works" and preferred to be like the character who was successful, regardless of the method used.[35]

These studies suggest that when children see an individual punished, they are not likely to spontaneously imitate his or her behavior. However, they seem to retain information concerning the method of aggression, regardless of the punishment of the villain. There is no denying the possibility that they may put this knowledge into practice on future occasions if they are provoked, obtain access to the necessary weapons, or anticipate a sufficiently attractive reward. The ethical ending of a story functions merely as a *suppressor* of violence, but not as an *extinguisher*.

Despite ominous correlations between TV and violence, the influence of television is obviously somehow limited. The majority of adolescents grow up without ever engaging in violence, let alone the type of violence they have viewed for so many years. Apparently elements of the American ethos proclaiming fair play, kindness, and cooperation somehow become part of their personality makeup. Once internalized, they are safeguarded by the universal control emotions of guilt and shame, which in normal human beings (exceptions are sociopaths) will be aroused when one violates one's standards of right and wrong.

When television suggests values and models inconsistent with principles parents have demonstrated, there is no evidence that the influence of television is paramount. When children have internalized values on a given subject and are not suffering from anomic blanks, television models seem to

---

[34]Bandura et al., "Imitation of Film-Mediated Aggressive Models," pp. 3–11.

[35]Robert Zajonc, "Some Effects of the 'Space' Serials," *Public Opinion Quarterly*, 18 (November 1954): 367–74.

have relatively little effect.[36] "It is in the area of the unfamiliar, where parents have not yet made clear their own point of view and where the child has little real-life experience to use as a guideline, that TV influences beliefs and attitudes."[37]

OTHER FARE AND FUNCTIONS

It must be stated in all fairness that not all television material thrives on violence and unreality, and that many programs convey other images and values. In fact, some of the other ingredients may help to control or balance violence and unreality.

The Information Function

The mass media have the potential of adding to the emotional and intellectual growth of children. Selective exposure to television constitutes a liberal education: available are samplings of history, music, the arts, political science, anthropology, the behavioral sciences, and various physical and biological sciences. This encounter with the world of knowledge stimulates curiosity, communication, and verbal skills. Probably the main reason such positive effects have not been sufficiently researched is their nonproblematic nature. Positive effects are relatively inconspicuous because they are acceptable and do not arouse public concern.

The information function of television for children should not be underestimated. While children, like adults, watch television primarily for entertainment rather than for education and edification, they absorb much "incidental" information about society and the world. They become electronic cosmopolites and acquire a plethora of detailed knowledge, albeit not necessarily integrated in a meaningful manner. For example, the young television pundit may know the finer points of docking in outer space, can distinguish Picasso from Michelangelo, can become a connoisseur of styles and fashions, may understand the principle of biofeedback, and may know the latest in the world of sports. In addition, these stationary tourists become storehouses of such miscellany and trivia as the facts that whales' backs get sunburned and peel, you do not tip the stewardess on an airplane, Japan is

---

[36]The relative ineffectualness of television in trying to change a person's perception once definite images have been established was illustrated by a study with college students on election day in 1960. It was found that students with a definite image of and preference for a presidential candidate were hardly affected by the so-called Great Debate, the public television confrontation of the candidates. See Hans Sebald, "Limitations of Communication: Mechanisms of Image Maintenance in Form of Selective Perception, Selective Memory, and Selective Distortion," *Journal of Communication,* 12 (September 1962): 347–51.

[37]Maccoby, "The Effects of TV on Children," p. 125.

the size of California and has a population of over 100 million, and no one knows the cause or cure of arthritis.

One of the classic learning programs, *Sesame Street,* has had a particularly valuable function for children who are relatively isolated or culturally deprived.[38] Its entertaining format achieved success in learning complex cognitive processes as well as verbalizing them. The product of collaboration among educators, psychologists, writers, and artists, *Sesame Street* became a fast-paced variety show with humor, intelligence, and artistry. It became an international hit, winning youthful audiences the world over.

Through television, children learn about our society's division of labor and various types of occupations. The medium's "homogenization effect" breaks down complex occupational responsibilities into images children can understand. Sociologists Melvin and Lois DeFleur warn, however, that in the process of homogenization the world of work becomes stereotyped and oversimplified with superficial and even misleading cues.[39]

Promoting Social Change and Generational Conflict

Television also functions as a force for social change, since it makes social events so vivid and immediate that it creates a sense of involvement not experienced with other media. It can bring the Mideast conflict, the energy crisis, ecological disasters, and racial injustices into the living room as no other medium can. This tangible immediacy of current problems has contributed to the rise and perpetuation of youthful activism.

In fact, some media analysts believe that the power of American movies and TV programs played a primary role in bringing down the Iron Curtain and toppling Communism in Eastern Europe. People under Communist rule were able to tune into American programs and became inspired by the images that showed America radiating with freedom, democracy, and prosperity; they consequently demanded changes in their own societies.[40]

However, while the information function of TV has made youth keenly aware of social issues, it has underplayed the tedious and time-consuming inner workings of the democratic process and, instead, presented the "show business" side of the political apparatus. This reinforces the youthful activist's tendency to embark on political projects by direct intervention, demonstrations, and a variety of "the-voice-of-the-people" proclamations. Simplistic as this approach may appear, it has rendered useful functions by speeding the

[38]Gerald S. Lesser, *Children and Television: Lessons from Sesame Street* (New York: Random House, 1974).

[39]Melvin L. DeFleur and Lois B. DeFleur, "The Relative Contribution of TV as a Learning Source for Children's Occupational Knowledge," *American Sociological Review,* 32 (October 1967), 777–89.

[40]Carl Bernstein, "The Leisure Empire," *Time,* December 24, 1990, p. 56.

completion of long-overdue work on the part of legislators and politicians. The popularity of direct confrontation with the Establishment is reinforced by constant television exposure to shows of action and emotion, not words. Such conditioning leads more to action than logic or abstract negotiation.

Some social scientists are certain that the generation gap is in part perpetuated by the nature of television fare. Margaret Mead believed that television, more than anything else, brought about the confrontation between the generations by bringing actuality into the home and destroying many myths and half-truths adhered to by parents and teachers.[41] She assumed that television's reporting of reality gives youth a glimpse of the world and an orientation different from that of the parents.

In other words, children, by merit of more extensive exposure to the mass media, often are a step ahead of their parents when it comes to instantaneous information, though it may amount to mere trivia. This once more brings into focus the concept of the *halo effect*—that is, the youngster's tendency to engage in the arguable, inductive logic of starting with an isolated instance of parental ignorance and expanding it to arrive at general parental ignorance and backwardness.

There is a related dimension to this argument that should be mentioned. Realistic and often quite graphic reporting of the legions of cases of adult immaturity and incompetence—in the context of crime, drug abuse, infidelity, child abuse, and so forth—have exposed adult behavior patterns that adults have tried to hide from children since time immemorial. TV has broken up a tacit adult conspiracy to keep children in the dark about a certain range of adult behavior. This exposure is a new feature of our age. Although Margaret Mead may have overdrawn TV's role as the cause of the generation conflict, TV's contribution to the conflict is significant.

The Identification Function

Television fare can also serve as a medium for identification. While this has obvious psychological risks and can lead to aberrations of personal identity, it can also be of temporary comfort until concrete and more suitable models are found. This may be of special aid to children whose parents fail to function as adequate models. A primary task of adolescence is to consolidate one's identity and substantially answer the question "Who am I?" In order to accomplish this, the adolescent must learn something about the adult world and the appropriate roles in that world. He or she often turns to television for help.

One of the dangers of selecting models from television fare is that they are culturally stereotyped. Women on Words and Images, a special interest

---

[41]Margaret Mead, "Our Leaders Do Not Understand TV," *TV Guide*, December 6, 1969, pp. 10–15.

group of the women's liberation movement, completed a content analysis of 1974 prime-time television and found a surfeit of men among the major characters: in situation comedies, 55 percent of the characters were male; in adventure shows, men played 85 percent of the parts.[42] The diversity of male occupations portrayed was nearly twice that of females'. While men were more often depicted as confident, independent, worldly, and decisive—in short, competent—women were more than twice as likely as men to be incompetent, bungling opportunities, and making serious mistakes. In fact, approximately 20 percent of women's behavior consisted of such incompetent acts.

The study included the analysis of over 200 commercials during these shows. The stereotypes conveyed showed men working more, playing more, eating more, and getting sick more often. Women were shown to be primarily concerned with their appearance; after that, they did housework, shopped, cooked, and cared for others—including their sick males.

The "Contrast Effect"

Another imposition of TV on the female image deals with influencing the viewers' perception of physical attractiveness. Most actresses starring in movies and shows exhibit a physical beauty that—because of a highly selective process, the help of modern make-up, and skillful photographic techniques—can rarely be matched in everyday life and hence carry an element of unrealism. How do teenagers respond to this type of unrealistic beauty? For example, can the boys' normal, everyday girlfriends live up to these images? Do these images become expectations in the minds of the teenagers? Do the images inflict inferiority feelings on the girls? The question could, of course, be turned around to focus on unrealistically attractive male images. But, it seems, in American culture the burden to be beautiful weighs heavier on the female.

Psychologists at Arizona State University examined some of these questions by conducting experiments in which males were asked to rate a picture of a moderately attractive female as to dating desirability and attractiveness. Two groups of college men, depending whether or not they were watching *Charlie's Angels*, were selected in their dorms. The perceptions of the two groups were compared and it was found that the males viewing the highly attractive females on the *Charlie's Angels* series rated the photo of the moderately attractive females significantly less attractive than those who were not watching the program.[43]

---

[42]Women on Words and Images, *Channeling Children: Sex Stereotyping in Prime-Time TV* (Princeton, NJ, 1975).

[43]Douglas T. Kenrick and S. E. Gutierres, "Contrast Effect and Judgments of Physical Attractiveness: When Beauty becomes a Social Problem," *Journal of Personality and Social Psychology*, 38 (1980): 131–40.

The Arizona State University research series included situations where the experimental variable was the nude centerfold of such erotic magazines as *Playboy* and *Penthouse*. The findings showed that after having viewed the pictures college men subsequently downgraded the appearance of their girlfriends or mates. Experiments with groups of college women who were exposed to *Playgirl* centerfolds reacted similarly toward their boyfriends or mates, though not quite as strongly. Overall, psychologist Douglas Kendrick concluded, this type of mass media fare "spoils our perception of the 'average' looking person."[44]

In today's world where media exposure is at an all-time high, it seems possible that the "contrast effect," even with a limited span of effectiveness, could pose serious problems. It becomes a real possibility that an individual might reject or be less satisfied with a normally acceptable date or mate if the relationship is influenced by media exposure that conveys unrealistic levels of physical attractiveness—and possibly makes such levels the norm for everyone. This would be particularly crucial for adolescents, who are forming criteria for date and mate selection; they might confuse artificial media images with reality, seeking the former and rejecting the latter.

Similarly unrealistic are the standards of living depicted on the screen. Usually they are unrealistically high (or unrealistically low to provide contrast), and myriads of commercials are trying to engrain this as a fact in the child's perception. The basic question of "Who am I?" becomes tied to ephemeral and superficial commercialism that guarantees the viewer a front seat in the social-status circus if he or she just uses the right deodorant, mouthwash, toothpaste, flashy clothes, and stylish car. Any serious attempt to gain prestige and sincere recognition by peers on the basis of such commercial goading would most likely end in mental and social disasters of the person gullible enough to try. Fortunately, most adolescents have the ability to discern fake from fact. Nevertheless, as mentioned earlier, disappointments, inferiority complexes, and the constant effort of sorting out reality from fiction keep the young busy, while they could be spending their time more creatively.

The Modeling Function

A good deal of television fare is couched in stereotypes that suggest formulas to be emulated. This is particularly true of commercials, which advise youngsters to equate sugar with health and snacks with happiness, ignoring the lack of nutrition in most of these edibles. The television viewer is persuaded to consider him- or herself primarily as a consumer and is promised such rewards as being or looking like the glamorous, sexy female or

[44]Reported and quoted by Rob Kelton, "Skin," *State Press*, November 1, 1990, p. 3.

popular he-man who uses the product in the ads. But stereotypes presented on television lack empirical referents or are unavailable to the vast majority of viewers. While idealization can serve as a temporary comfort and an object of identification, in the long run there is the danger of frustration, especially for the adolescent who is generally hypersensitive about his or her appearance.

Reinforcing the Self-fulfilling Prophecy

One particularly insidious stereotype reinforced by television is the equation of "good looks" with "good personality." It is simple to figure out who's who in the movies and on television at one glance. The good guys are handsome, while the bad guys range from plain to ugly, and the same holds true for female counterparts. Unfortunately, the habit does not stop with the mass media—there is evidence that people tend to make the same judgments in real life. Studies by psychologist Karen K. Dion reveal that attractive children were judged less likely to commit offenses, or if they had, to repeat them in the future, and less likely to have antisocial dispositions.[45] Unattractive children, however, were regarded as more dishonest and unpleasant than their good-looking counterparts in similar circumstances. Transgressions committed by attractive children were considered less undesirable than the same acts committed by unattractive children. This prejudiced association has serious implications. First, good-looking children get away with more than plain-looking children; there is a tendency to punish and reprimand unequally. Second, reinforced stereotypes may become self-fulfilling prophecies, with the children assuming the roles ascribed to them. Evaluation by others ultimately tends to become self-evaluation: the unattractive child may grow up with an antisocial disposition simply because adults expect it.

Suppressing Creativity

Although television may be of some benefit to the culturally deprived child for whom it is a window to the outside world, it is better at contributing to existing interests than in stimulating intellectual activity. It is interesting to note that the upper-third IQ children in a study by Wilbur Schramm spent over an hour per day less watching television than the lower-third group.[46] Interviews with the more intelligent children disclosed that by the time they entered high school, television had ceased being a challenge to them and they therefore appropriated less time to viewing. Whether bright children are bright because they do not watch television, or whether they do not watch

[45]Karen K. Dion, "Physical Attractiveness and Evaluation of Children's Transgressions," *Journal of Personality and Social Psychology*, 24 (November 1972): 207–13.
[46]Schramm et al., *Television in the Lives of Our Children*.

television because they are bright, is, of course, an open question. At this time, it is simply stated as a correlation.

However, researchers are in agreement that TV viewing suppresses creativity, the ability to see new, effective solutions to problem situations, and the knack for the unique patterning of mental, physical, and artistic tasks. And this may be one of the most significant points that can be made about the nature of TV viewing. All studies that have touched on this topic have come to the same conclusion, not even exempting those programs acclaimed to be educational. Even if we allow for TV's role in enriching knowledge and vocabulary, the special quality of creativity remains negatively affected.

Why? The answer seems to lie in the fact that TV leaves strangely unstimulated the brain's capability for imagination; it fails to set into action the brain's synergetic activities, because all the action is completed on the screen: visual and auditory information complement the scene. These are information elements that must be imagined in a situation where the person reads: the printed word supplies the script, but the brain is called upon to supply the rest—the sound, the vision, the color. These demands constitute a bundle of challenging stimuli, revving up myriads of brain circuitries that now must do the job of imagining and completing the setting. Compared with this massive brain stimulation, mostly unconsciously processed by the reader, TV viewing is a dulling, ready-made, instantly consumed package that leaves no room for personal imagination and bypasses our creative faculties.

A number of dimensions that are usually thought to be related to creativity have been found affected negatively.

Critical thinking. When persons become habituated to looking at a medium that is as anti-intellectual as television largely is, they develop a noncritical attitude and a disposition to "look without seeing."[47] Stanley Stern completed experiments with 250 intellectually gifted grade schoolers, dividing them into seven groups, and exposing six of them for several weeks to cartoons, educational television, sports, comedies, and dramas.[48] The seventh group was not exposed to television. The children took a battery of creativity tests before and after the experimental periods. Only the seventh group registered consistent improvement, while the other six showed a notable decline in all areas of creativity except verbal skill. Cartoons had the worst effect, but even educational programs decreased creativity scores.

[47]Vigo A. Demant, "The Unintentional Influences of TV," *Cross Currents*, 5 (1955): 220–25.

[48]Stanley Stern, "Creativity and TV—A Depressing Picture," *Psychology Today*, 7 (November 1973): 14–16.

Attention span. Yale psychologist Jerome Singer found that children who are heavy TV watchers tend to be more restless and poorer students. Apparently they expect all of life, including the educational process, to be an instantaneous and entertaining experience. "A teacher who is going into a lengthy explanation of an arithmetic problem will begin to lose the audience after a while. Children are expecting some kind of show."[49] Neil Postman, communications professor at New York University and the author of *Amusing Ourselves to Death*, concurs by pointing out that even the beloved *Sesame Street* has reinforced the TV-inspired notion that education must be fast-paced and entertaining. As a consequence, many children like school only if school is like *Sesame Street*.[50]

Logic. A good portion of TV programs exposes children to simplistic, faulty, or no logic at all. Since TV's orientation is primarily geared toward entertainment, logical elements are of minor importance, and what few such elements there are must not burden the viewer with too much brain work, for that would violate show business's definition of entertainment.

Literacy and articulation. TV fails to exercise our capability to articulate thought and sentiment. Whatever has to be said is being said on the screen and is usually said in the simplest and most superficial language. It would be difficult to derive from it any measure of sophistication usable for articulate speech, let alone writing. This explains the seeming paradox whereby high exposure may provide a better vocabulary but still fails to inspire articulateness: processing words and putting them into intelligible sentence structures is a task that demands skill beyond merely accumulating words. Norman Cousins put it this way: "Clean, precise writing or speaking requires systematic, sequential thought. Words have to be crafted, not sprayed. They need to be fitted together with infinite care."[51]

The suppression of this skill led Pico Iyer and others to use the adjective "postliterate" to describe the modern American population steeped in TV fare.[52] According to these scholars, by means of the TV set we have reverted in our culture to becoming a population using pictographs instead of thought-sculpting language. We increasingly resemble the habit of prehistoric tribes who scratched signs and rough pictures onto rocks. But even they had a revered place for the word—in an oral tradition that called for skill in telling and listening. Thomas Dooling summed up the point:

---

[49]Quoted by Richard Zoglin, "Is TV Ruining Our Children," *Time*, October 15, 1990, p. 75.

[50]Ibid.

[51]Norman Cousins, "The Communication Collapse," *Time*, December 17, 1990, p. 114.

[52]Pico Iyer, "History? Education?" *Time*, May 14, 1990, p. 75.

And why should young people be inspired to be articulate? In their steady fare of TV "drama," they see thought expressed, not in words, but by action—usually direct and brutal—accompanied by musical conventions. No wonder they are not verbal! They often communicate in shared visual experience: they watched the same TV show in which any words that may have been spoken are entirely eclipsed by the power of the visual image.[53]

Time Away from Real Social Interaction

One of the concerns voiced by a few social scientists is not so much what television does to the young but what the young are *not* doing while viewing. Semanticist S. I. Hayakawa pointed out that the average eighteen-year-old American has lost 22,000 hours of potential interaction with other human beings, and that, for all the value television may have, it cannot teach human interaction.[54] The loss may be reflected by lack of skill in social interaction later in life when many of them "express their thoughts in form of tantrums." There simply is no substitute for human interaction, which includes misunderstandings, expressing and solving problems, and getting to know people. Excessive television viewing detracts from this experience, precludes this experience. Vigo A. Demant supported this notion, saying that a group watching television "can no more be called a social interaction than a number of monologues in the same room is a conversation."[55] Additional views and studies demonstrate that television seriously inhibits family communication. An interesting study of Australian adolescents by W. J. Campbell found that they spent less time entertaining, dancing, visiting, playing, and talking to friends three years after television was introduced into their homes compared to before they had television.[56] The interpretation here again expresses concern that teenagers misappropriate time and miss out on interaction with family and peers.

Other researchers, however, disagree with the negative interpretation and believe that teenagers learn appropriate ways of social interaction by viewing television. Self-reports by teenagers indicate that they feel they learned appropriate behavior modes from watching dating, playing football, and family stories.[57] Whether the images accepted as adequate and realistic will turn out as real and dependable in life is, of course, a question that still has to be answered.

[53]Thomas Dooling, "Glory," *Parabola*, 8 (Summer 1983): 61.

[54]S. I. Hayakawa, "Image and Reality," *The Bulletin of the National Association of Secondary School Principals*, 53 (May 1969): 35–48.

[55]Demant, "The Unintentional Influences of TV," p. 223.

[56]W. J. Campbell, *TV and the Australian Adolescent* (Sydney: Angus and Robertson, 1966).

[57]Schramm et al., *Television in the Lives of Our Children.*

SUMMARY

Exposure of American children and adolescents to television is enormous. Among the themes and values projected are violence and unreality. Unreality can be divided into straightforward fantasy and deceptive description of reality. Most experts believe that fantasy is not harmful and, on the contrary, can be beneficial by stimulating creative thought. Pseudoreality, however, can mislead the young in their search for models.

Opinions on the effects of violence are divided between those who believe that violence serves a cathartic function and those who believe that it leads to imitation. Both camps present logical thought and empirical findings in defense of their interpretations. A point accepted by both is the susceptibility to imitative violence on the part of the disturbed child or adolescent. Also, high-exposure children lose sensitivity to violence and show no or greatly reduced reactions when viewing it.

The fact that the vast majority of American adolescents, in spite of growing up with violence-laced television, fail to engage in any violence indicates that control mechanisms are operative. They may include non-availability of necessary instruments of violence, parental indoctrination, fear of an unsuccessful ending, and effects of the general American ethos of decency and fair play. Yet, there is evidence that children are tempted to imitate the villain if they profit from it and "get away with it."

To more fully understand the impact of TV on the lives of our young, we must take into consideration the total social matrix in which they are enmeshed. Few studies have achieved such completeness. Where they have approximated it, they have found that media impact is significantly modified, positively or negatively, by such family background features as mothers' disposition, education, socioeconomic background, academic achievement, and other features.

TV viewing has been found to have multifarious functions: providing information, promoting social change and stimulating generational conflict, selecting models, causing a "contrast effect," reinforcing the self-fulfilling prophecy, ushering in a "postliterate" population with minimal ability for linguistic articulation, stealing time away from social interaction, and, perhaps most importantly, suppressing creativity.

11

Etiology and Dimensions of Subculture

With this chapter we begin to shift the focus of our discussion from the individual adolescent to the youthful collectivity. The term collectivity is broad, nonspecific, and can refer to a subculture or to a counterculture or to anything in between. The following three chapters describe, first, the subculture, as it primarily pertains to mainstream-American high school youth, and, second, the counterculture, as a largely historical phenomenon of American culture that used to be carried by mostly older and politically oriented young adults.

Both are forms of youth collectivities and can be understood, at least to a large extent, as natural consequences of the adolescent experience in a postindustrial society. These collectivities provide the young with an environment in which they find fellowship, a sense of belonging, and a haven away from the world of the adults. The most important function of such belonging, temporary as it might be, consists of members dropping an emotional anchor and deriving an identity from it. Hence the youthful collectivity functions as a compensation for an adolescent experience that otherwise might be unbearably anomic.

This chapter is a general and theoretical treatment of the question of how subcultures evolve and are sustained. The dimensions that are suggested as generic to the rise of a subculture can be applied to the general teen subculture as well as to specific youth movements. To start, we present a theoretical exploration of the development and dimensions of subculture.

DEFINITIONS AND DIMENSIONS

The conceptualization of subculture is beset with at least two major problems. First, sociologists are unclear as to the specific dimensions that characterize a subculture. Although the literature reflects suggestions concerning some subcultural elements, the notions are not followed up by a concerted effort to integrate, systematize, and apply them. The second problem deals with the frustrating fact that the suggested definitions are too general and lack operationability. An example is the definition stating that subculture "refers to norms that set a group apart from, not those that integrate a group with, the total society."[1] This definition is so general that, while it cannot fail to be theoretically correct, it is practically unusable in actual research. Another example is the proposal to combine a number of factors, such as "ethnic group, social class, region, occupation, religion, and urban and rural residence."[2] Again, these factors lack operational specifications. Finally, to epitomize the sociological disregard for the concept, Fairchild's *Dictionary of Sociology* did not even have the word *subculture* as a listing.[3]

Since *culture* refers to a blueprint of behavior for an entire society, the largest human grouping, *subculture* refers to the blueprint for behavior of a smaller group within the society. This subsidiary blueprint is frequently formed without the encouragement, acceptability, or full cognizance of the "parent culture." It is a special blueprint that accommodates a number of people whose needs and desires are not provided for by the main blueprint of society. Thus, there are subcultures for narcotic addicts, longshoremen, inmates in prison, Texas oilmen, those in the world of fashion, jazz musicians—and adolescents.

A subculture can be defined by its *functions*. As noted above, the general function of the subculture is to compensate for the failure of the main culture to provide a definite status, a feeling of acceptance, and need-satisfactions unique to a certain group of people. To accomplish these functions and to make the subculture a viable process, a number of prerequisites must be met.

Eight dimensions are proposed as basic elements of subculture: (1) Relatively unique (or uniquely accentuated) values and norms. (2) In-group lingo

---

[1] Milton J. Yinger, "Contraculture and Subculture," *American Sociological Review*, 25 (October 1960): 628.

[2] Milton M. Gordon, "The Concept of the Subculture and its Application," *Social Forces*, 25 (October 1947): 41.

[3] H. P. Fairchild, ed., *Dictionary of Sociology* (Totowa, NJ: Littlefield, Adams & Co., 1968).

not shared with the larger society. (3) Distinct channels of (mass) communication not shared with or dependent on "outsiders." (4) Unique styles and fads (including grooming, dress, gesture, and other behavioral patterns) often resulting in subcultural ritual. (5) A sense of solidarity and *esprit de corps* manifested by thinking in terms of "we" instead of "me and them" (or simply the cogency of in-group versus out-group sentiments). (6) Status criteria in terms of cognizing them and adhering to them in actual peer relationships. In other words, existence of a working order of social positions—at a minimum, clarifying what makes for prestige, leadership, and follower. (7) Influence and power of leaders enhancing the identity and *esprit de corps* of the collectivity. This is the dimension of *charisma*. (8) Gratification of specific needs that the larger social structure fails to provide. The significance of this item is the subcultural institutionalization of need fulfillment.

A methodological paradigm has been proposed for consistent use of the eight dimensions in examining collectivities concerning their degree of subcultureness.[4] This design provides a tool that, if consistently applied, would promote comparability of different research findings, greater reliability in following the fluctuations of a subculture over its lifetime, and, most important, a measurement in terms of *degree of subcultural quality*. It was customary to dichotomously answer the question whether a certain collectivity is a subculture with either "yes" or "no"—a method totally inconsistent with reality and with most procedures in other matters of sociological endeavor. Qualities always exist in terms of degree, and methods of analysis must be responsive to this fact. Therefore, a paradigm measuring collectivities as to their degree of subcultural quality is necessary.

The above mentioned definitional dimensions, enumerating major functions of the subculture, must be checked against the youth subculture to see whether there is enough empirical evidence to bear out some degree of subcultural salience:

1. Young people have derived from their interaction a peculiar set of *norms and values* that no longer consists of child standards nor is part of the adult world.
2. They speak an *argot* that is not shared with adults. In fact, it is only partially understood by outsiders and is often unacceptable to the Establishment.
3. Youth's channels of *mass communication* consist of mingling in youth "ghettos" (the high schools), various "underground" media (youth newspapers), and their own programs via general mass media (radio, television, etc.).
4. Young Americans cultivate their own independent *styles and fads*, and are unwilling to share them with adults. For example, teenage grooming and hair

---

[4]The technical aspects of the subcultural paradigm are discussed in Hans Sebald, "Subculture: Problems of Definition and Measurement," *International Review of Modern Sociology,* 5 (Spring 1975): 82–89.

styles led to vehement confrontations during the late 1960s and early 1970s. The young tend to change a style as soon as adults imitate it.

5. Adolescents acquire a *primary-group belonging* in which they are accepted as total individuals. Peer involvement functions as a partial substitute for the teenagers' families, which they leave gradually to establish personal autonomy. The adolescent peer group helps young individuals in their emancipation from parental control.

6. Youths derive *status relationships* that make them predictable in peer interaction. Status criteria help to ameliorate the lack of social status during the transition from child to adult. The peer group also provides criteria and models that allow emulation during a time when such models in the adult society are either lacking or too frightening.

7. They are receptive to *charismatic leadership*. The world of the American teenager includes outstanding and famous personalities who, if not precisely leaders, function as heroes. The charismatic aura of such heroes is entirely a function of teenage hero worship.

8. Adolescents have needs, problems, and anxieties for which the adult social structure makes only partial allowance. Hence, young Americans have come to work out their own substructures over the years. This *institutionalization of patterns of need-fulfillment* is probably the most powerful indicator of how far a given collectivity has matured into a subculture—or even a counterculture. (Here we approach the study of social movements and of social change.) The highly subculturized—or counterculturized—activities of American youth during the tumultuous late 1960s and early 1970s can serve as an example. The collective behavior of youth during that period indicated a high degree of social structure. Among the behavior patterns—patterns consistent and recurring enough to justify the application of the concept of subcultural institutionalization—were how food was supplied and distributed, legal aid, entertainment, psychiatric first aid, business, education, and literature.

The most salient of the dimensions deals with the establishment of social institutions within a collectivity markedly separate from the main society. I call these internal structures—dedicated to specific need fulfillment—*subcultural institutionalization*. It is this enmeshing of persons in their own segregated social structure that is of utmost importance to sociology, since structural arrangements result in regular patterns of human behavior and relationships.

It should be added that subcultural institutionalization usually arises only when a sense of solidarity prevails. Conversely, a latent function of the new specialized substructure that fulfills needs is a reinforcement of the *esprit de corps*. Subinstitutionalization often allows for behavior that would not be permitted within the structure of the larger society. In so doing, subinstitutionalization enables relatively new forms of behavior, of which drug use is an example. Some subinstitutionalizations, however, merely establish counterparts to already available avenues in the larger society. Many forms of dating, entertainment, and recreational activities are examples. In general, the desire for exclusivity, freedom from adult supervision, and unique styling determines the contours of subinstitutionalization.

THE QUESTION OF ETIOLOGY

What are the conditions and processes that make for the emergence of a subculture? It seems that the *necessary condition* for the emergence of a subculture is the existence of a *number of persons* in society who seek solutions to common problems and who *effectively interact* with one another.

It might be added that every collective segment of society has its own problems. Certain social categories, determined, for example, by age, sex, race, ethnicity, or occupation, exhibit unique problems. "The structure of society generates, at each position within the system, characteristic combinations of personality and situation and therefore characteristic problems of adjustment."[5]

The early formative stage of subculture, before the in-group structure and the norms and values become firmly established, includes a process of "exploratory gestures." This process consists of mutual explorations and joint elaborations of possible solutions, often accompanied by mass-communicative and/or physical (crowds, mobs) interchanges during which a set of common sentiments is recognized and subsequently reinforced.

The *sufficient conditions* for the establishment of a subculture lie in the acceptance of common norms and values specifying the "proper" way of doing things. When a sufficiently elaborate corollary of symbols has become the unique property of the persons involved, a collective identity has been born. One can then speak of a subcultural or a new cultural form "because each actor's participation in this system is influenced by his perception of the same norms in fellow actors."[6]

Membership in such a group or category ordinarily functions not merely as a problem-solving device in a narrow and technical sense, but also as a source of values, which ultimately has formative influence on the individual's self-perception. The price for gaining a clearly defined frame of reference is conformity to the norms of the group. In return, the member has access to ready-made conclusions, solutions, and peer-approved actions that help to solve a number of conflicts and ambiguities. There are compelling incentives not to deviate from the established ways of the group: fear of disapproval or even ostracism by the peers and fear of an inhospitable larger culture combine to keep the member within the confines of the subculture.

A collectivity of individuals becomes subcultural only when its system of norms and values is significantly different from the main culture. The solutions to the problems of the given collectivity are embodied in the larger society neither in terms of structural provision nor, frequently, in terms of

[5]Albert K. Cohen, *Delinquent Boys: The Culture of the Gang* (New York: Free Press, 1955), p. 55.
[6]Ibid., p. 65.

cultural acceptability. The new solutions may conflict with society's traditions and may result in the collectivity being labeled deviant, thereby generating antagonism and mistrust between the larger and the smaller social systems. From the subcultural point of view, the so-called deviant-solution approach may more effectively ameliorate needs and problems than the existing solutions institutionalized in the larger society. In addition, members of the subculture frequently do not feel that their activities could harm individuals inside or outside of their group and thus see no reason to change their patterns. As a result, they tend to perceive their activities not only as effective but also as justified.

New solution approaches and the symbols of subcultural membership may, from the outsider's point of view, be perceived as relatively haphazard and undefined behavior. For the in-group members, however, it is structured and well defined. This misconception on the part of outside observers arises because of a tendency to judge unfamiliar behavior in terms of one's own values, not realizing that the seemingly nonconformist behavior actually conforms to subcultural expectations.

One of the aspects most often ignored by observers is the subculture's different criteria for ascribing prestige. Frequently the members of the subculture, prior to their joining, have encountered serious obstacles in the path of achieving status in the larger society—a condition certainly true of adolescents. Within the confines of a subculture there are opportunities for achieving status and respect. The solution for teenagers who share this predicament of unclear status in the adult world is, therefore, to gravitate toward one another and jointly establish new criteria of status that describe as meritorious those characteristics they *do* possess and the kinds of activities of which they *are* capable. This, quite obviously, is a group approach to an individual problem. If an individual adolescent tried to establish such criteria alone, he or she would probably not only fail to achieve status in the larger society, but would suffer total isolation.

The usual side effect of joining a new status system that encourages behavior frowned on by the larger social system is an inverse correlation: the more the individual gains status in the new group, the more he or she will lose status outside the group.

Belonging to and depending on a subculture usually has far-reaching effects on the personality of its follower. The influence may be strong enough to provide the nature of one's identity. Indeed, the decision to join a subculture is normally indicative of the person's need for a clear identity. The subculture, then, comes to function as an important psychological refuge.

A chapter on the development of subcultures is not complete unless it describes, at least briefly, pertinent etiological theories. Among the models purporting to explain the origin of subcultures are the psychogenic, culture-transmission, and behavioristic. Familiarity with these theoretical frameworks aids in understanding specific elements in the complex process of subcultural development. Although they represent different ways of looking at the empirical phenomenon, they are not incompatible but rather complementary, emphasizing different aspects of the process.

The Psychogenic Model

The basic assumption of this theory is that a subculture evolves from problems of adjustment that are common to a large number of persons. Emphasis is on the independence with which individuals contrive solutions. The individual is depicted as a creative innovator. Although the role of the social milieu as the genesis of the problem is recognized, its role in determining the solution is minimized. New cultural forms emerge as a *parallel* development of individual solutions, which, more or less unaccountably, merge into a collective entity. The aspect of the subcultural development that is unaccounted for in this framework is the process of social interaction as a necessary condition during the incipient phase.

The psychogenic approach views teenage behavior as an effort to solve the problems characteristic of the frustrating sojourn in adolescence. The adolescent, standing between child and adult statuses and being devoid of a clearly structured social position, may frequently ponder the agonizing question of who he or she really is and come face to face with the issue of identity. Erik Erikson, Gordon Bronson, Margaret Mead,[7] and others maintain that the major task facing the adolescent is the search for meaningful identity. This task is more difficult in the modern urban-industrial setting than in smaller folk or tribal societies. The rapid pace of social change, exposure to a confusing variety of secular and religious value systems, and revolutionary technological innovations make the world appear too relativistic and unpredictable to provide the teenager with a stable frame of reference.

Modern teenagers experience an abstract introduction to life, which results in the perception of the world as complex and ambiguous. They have difficulties in seeing just where and how they fit in. Their escape attempt leads them to other teenagers, and this subculture offers them a subcultural identity. In the process of maintaining this identity, special clothes, language, and attitudes toward the world play an important role in symbolizing belonging.

While the psychogenic model appears to accurately reflect empirical processes, it is limited in its explanatory *range*, unable to give an explanation of the exact nature of the *formative* process of the collectivity. One of the more unexplored areas in sociology remains the analysis of the bridging

---

[7]Erik H. Erikson, *Childhood and Society* (New York: W. W. Norton & Co., 1963); Gordon W. Bronson, "Identity Diffusion in Late Adolescence," *Journal of Abnormal and Social Psychology*, 59 (November 1959): 414–17; and Margaret Mead, "The Young Adult," in *Values and Ideals of American Youth*, ed. E. Ginzberg (New York: Columbia University Press, 1961), pp. 37–51.

process that leads from individual problems to the actual beginnings of subculture.

The Culture-transmission Model

This theory is concerned with the perpetuation of an already established subculture by transmission of its values and unique behavior patterns from one generation to the next. It is interested more in understanding the *learning process* whereby, for example, the younger teenagers acquire their older peers' modes of thought and actions than in understanding the *prime* origin of these subcultural patterns. The limited scope of the approach often excludes from consideration those crucial problems that render each new generation susceptible to the established subcultural form. At the most, this theory suggests a number of plausible mechanisms of subcultural transmission, such as the learning of rules that lend orientation and direction to the life of the teenager and the role of the mass media in disseminating these rules and ideas.

Mass media, especially television and teen magazines,[8] are probably the most effective mechanisms for perpetuating the teenage subculture. Mass media offer ready-made solutions to teenagers and promise to save them the effort of searching for new forms. David L. Altheide makes this point forcefully: "Youth culture is both a product and a target of the media . . . The development of youth as an idea was a by-product of media culture and the discovery that young people could consume."[9]

A specific example of this process was the rise of rock music. It actually *changed* American youth, helped to create a self-conscious teen generation, and perpetuated this self-consciousness from generation to generation of teenagers. Before the 1950s there was no music, or any other medium, that enveloped so powerfully the feelings and behavior of young Americans. Rock music spoke clearly to the interests and needs of adolescents. "It defined the correct behavior . . . and noted the irrelevance of school routines as compared with the realities of fast cars, surfing, and the exhilaration of dancing. Throughout rock lyrics there were pointed contrasts between the teen way of life and the behavioral norms imposed by adults."[10]

The idea that rock music was a significant carrier of youth culture is further developed by Bernice Martin. Rock music evolved into what became probably the most truculent vehicle, telling, as it were, the epic story of

---

[8]Charles H. Brown, "Self-Portrait: The Teen-Type Magazine," *Annals of the American Academy of Political and Social Sciences*, 338 (November 1961): 20.

[9]David L. Altheide, "Mass Media and Youth Culture," *Urban Education*, 2 (July 1979): 224.

[10]R. A. Peterson and D. G. Berger, "Three Eras in the Manufacture of Popular Music Lyrics," in Denisoff and Peterson, eds., *The Sounds of Social Change* (Chicago: Rand McNally, 1972), p. 296.

American adolescence. Rock music became a sacrament; it interpreted agonies, joys, the holy and the unholy in the lives of teenagers. Martin visualized the role of rock music as symbolizing the "sacred" in youth culture, not unlike the need to symbolize the "sacred" in primitive tribal society. The feeling of *Communitas*, belonging together, is expressed by "ritualized symbols of group identity particularly in the beat of music, in common fashions and through the star performer who acts as sacred 'totem.' "[11]

In summary, the media facilitate connections between adolescents and perpetuate certain themes. These themes dwell on solving problems of loneliness, confusion, and alienation from adult society. They are embodied in songs, the beat of rock music, TV programs, movies, teen magazines (particularly those with "Letter" departments), and the actual physical mingling of teenagers in their ghettos—the school campuses, gangs, dance places, and rock concerts. These lyrics, rhythms, programs, stories, statements, and places are the media for communicating and transmitting subcultural thought and behavior. Needless to say, these media are powerful conditioners, often commercially exploiting the need of teenagers to communicate with other teenagers.

The Behavioristic Model

Although behaviorism has neglected to apply its framework to the question of subcultural formation and to formulate a precise etiological theory, it is capable of pointing out significant steps in the process of converting adolescents into members of teenage subcultures. It would be presumptuous to attempt to present a complete picture of the behavioristic approach in this limited context; a few remarks must suffice.

Behavioristic principles to explain the rise of a subculture resemble the psychogenic model. The point of departure again is the frustrations that youths experience during adolescence. If tensions and frustrations are equated with pain, one finds American teenagers frequently exposed to it when interacting with adults who technically would be called *aversive stimuli*. To carry the process to its logical conclusion, it follows that teenagers try to avoid this type of stimulus and hence tend to withdraw from the adult world. This type of behavior is defined as *escape behavior*.[12] The reaction is common to most adolescents since the same *hedonistic principle* applies to all. On the escape route the adolescent meets other adolescents who have similar problems. Through interaction among themselves, adolescents discover that they

---

[11]Bernice Martin, "The Sacralization of Disorder: Symbolism in Rock Music," *Sociological Analysis*, 40, 2 (1979): 87.

[12]See, for technical treatment and definition, Arthur W. Staats and Carolyn K. Staats, *Complex Human Behavior: A Systematic Extension of Learning Principles* (New York: Holt, Rinehart & Winston, 1964), p. 44.

are free of stringent adult expectations, which they have found difficult to meet and accept. As a result, they experience a lessening of tension and frustration. Interaction among peers consists of stimuli that are gratifying to teenagers and can be called *positive reinforcers*, which are usually more powerful than negative reinforcers because they allow enjoyment of common activities and interests. Thus, independently from adolescent problems, normal gregarious activities help to sustain the peer culture.

In the final analysis, these two types of reinforcers, the negative (escape from frustration) and the positive (finding security and the gratification), effectively establish and perpetuate the subcultural milieu.

There is still another aspect of the adolescent phenomenon that can effectively be explained by behavioristic principles. It deals with the consequences of *inconsistent stimuli*. In one instance adolescents are told to be responsible and independent, while in another instance they may be prevented from showing responsibility. In many cases, they are expected to show responsibility and independence concerning vocational preparation, but must obtain their parents' permission in questions of finances, dating, and marriage.

Such inconsistent stimuli are also definable as inconsistent and ambivalent role expectations, as mixing a number of elements from the adult and the child roles.

Inconsistent stimuli due to such unclear role expectations tend to produce ambivalent behavior—sometimes defined as neurosis.[13] The initial reactions to such ambivalent conditioning include frustration and tension. Eventually, this frustration makes the adolescent choose the less frustrating conditioning system of the peer culture with its simpler and more consistent processes.

DISAGREEMENTS ON THE EXISTENCE OF THE TEENAGE SUBCULTURE

Although this book relies on the assumption that the teenage subculture is a real fact in life, some academics hold different views. As has been pointed out in the discussion on peer-parent conflict and the autonomy process (Chapter 8), opinions range from affirmative to negative.

Clarity of the argument is impaired by lack of a consensual definition of subculture, illustrating the dilemma mentioned in the first section of this chapter.

---

[13]Behavioristically inclined psychologists have demonstrated the effect of ambivalent conditioning in laboratory situations using animals as their subjects. They found that inconsistent conditioning can result in neurotic disturbances, possibly to the extent of a so-called nervous breakdown. See, for example, Jules H. Masserman, *Behavior and Neurosis* (Chicago: University of Chicago Press, 1943).

The criterion of subculture that appears of pivotal significance to the discussants is "unique values and norms." The proponents who assume a youth subculture feel that there is substantial indication for the existence of this dimension; on the other side, there are some academics who think that there is not enough evidence for the existence of a youth/adult rift in values.

The argument of the *proponents* can be summed up by three related assumptions:

1. The typical adolescent is characterized by symptoms that can be described as socially caused "storm and stress." These expressions stem primarily from the adolescent's uncertain position in the social structure. Some of the confusions and insecurities typical of the American adolescent arise from uncertainty of occupational choice, difficulties in identifying with adult models, inconsistencies in authority relationships, conflicts between generations, sexual frustrations because of conflict between physiological maturation and social prohibitions, and discontinuity in socialization patterns.

2. A teenage subculture exists and is powerful and widespread. The youth subculture is a social reaction to the young individuals' uncertain statuses in the adult world and eases the transition from childhood to adulthood. The subculture is particularly dominant in metropolitan areas, exerting far-reaching demands on its followers, creating a feeling of belonging and a status system that judges behavior by subcultural standards. James S. Coleman's large-scale surveys concluded that the American adolescent is progressively becoming more ensconced in secondary institutions, from nursery school through college:

> He is "cut off" from the rest of society, forced inward toward his own age group, made to carry out his whole social life with others his own age. With his fellows, he comes to constitute a small society, one that has most of its important interactions *within* itself, and maintains only a few threads of connection with the outside adult society. In our modern world of mass communication and rapid diffusion of ideas and knowledge, it is hard to realize that subcultures can exist right under the very noses of adults—subcultures with languages all their own, with special symbols, and, most important, with value systems that may differ from adults.[14]

Talcott Parsons thinks that the characteristics of the adolescent subculture include three main aspects: (a) the rebelliousness of youth against adult expectations and authority; (b) the tendency toward peer conformity, guarded by considerable in-group intolerance of differences; and (c) a romantic adherence to emotionally significant objects.[15] Robin M. Williams, Jr., contends that the social distance between generations is sometimes so great

---

[14]James S. Coleman, *The Adolescent Society* (New York: Free Press, 1963), p. 3.

[15]Talcott Parsons, "Psychoanalysis and the Social Structure," *Psychoanalytic Quarterly*, 19 (July 1950): 378–79.

that parents and children confront each other as members of vastly different subcultures.[16] Arnold W. Green believes in the existence of a teenage subculture and calls it a "world of irresponsibility, specialized lingo, dating, athleticism, and the like, which rather sharply cuts off adolescent experience from that of the child and from that of the adult."[17]

3. The concluding assumption suggests a causal relationship between "storm and stress" and the teenage subculture, implying that affiliation with peers provides a structured social environment and personal identity. The subcultural arrangement is reinforced and its survival guaranteed by the satisfaction the teenagers derive from having found status among peers.

Most of the opponents to the subculture theory have completed studies—mostly small in scale—from which they concluded that the difference in values between adolescents and adults is not large enough to call the young's attitudes a separate value system. In fact, these researchers conclude that parental values are socially inherited by the offspring and manifested in the youngsters' choices of peer affiliation and value orientation. They concede, however, that there may be differences in norms, the rules and the means of doing things and achieving certain goals (goals that are synonymous with values and presumably coincide with those of the parents). The young, hence, may sometimes resort to deviant means to achieve such basic goals as status, success, and material gains. While it is an essential purpose of the socialization process to teach the young the proper means, some researchers feel that the basic goals are "naturally" learned and imitated.

It is possible that these researchers mistakenly equate basic human needs, such as seeking security, acceptance, expression, and new experience within the peer environment, with the cultural values of American society. In other words, the equation of seeking acceptance among peers (by cooperation and sporting material accessories) with the cultural values of cooperation and materialism of the adult world is spurious. The young's seeming imitation of cultural goals is really nothing more than their way of coping with a peer situation.

Also, much of the research findings meant to deflate the subculture theory are based on highly specific and nongeneralizable samples. For example, Frederich Elkin and William A. Westley's mid-1950s study resulted in a widely publicized and often quoted dissent from the subculture theory, since they found the teenagers of a Montreal suburb more integrated in the adult society—its customs, norms, and values—than was generally thought.[18] Family ties were close, and the degree of family consensus was high. The adoles-

[16]Robin M. Williams, Jr., *American Society: A Sociological Interpretation* (New York: Knopf, 1960), p. 80.

[17]Arnold W. Green, *Sociology* (New York: McGraw-Hill, 1968), p. 113.

[18]Frederich Elkin and William A. Westley, "The Myth of Adolescent Culture," *American Sociological Review*, 20 (December 1955): 680–84.

cents acknowledged their parents' right to guide them and set rules concerning dating practices, discussed their choice of school courses and vacation plans with parents, and often engaged in joint parent-child activities, such as parties, dances, and community sports events. Parents expressed few complaints about socialization problems or peer group activities of their teenage children, and the continuities of socialization were more striking than the discontinuities. In short, the patterns of the adolescents' social lives were not significantly different from those of the older generation, and adolescents demonstrated "adult" perspectives.

Despite the highly specific character of the study the findings were widely generalized, disregarding the fact that the data were derived from interviews of a sample of only twenty adolescents and their parents and from life-history material of another twenty teenagers. This selection is by no means an adequate sample from which to safely draw conclusions about American teenagers in general—especially when the researchers themselves admitted that the sample may not have been completely representative even of the community from which it was taken. Also, allowance should be made for possible differences between Canadian and American teenagers. Montreal, heavily influenced by English and French traditions, may have a different type of teenager than most cities in the United States. Moreover, the locale of the research was a well-to-do suburb, classified by the authors as upper-middle-class, where "typically, when a girl gives a party, she sends out formal invitations, and her guest list includes those she *should* invite as well as those she wants to invite. The girls take great pains to play their hostess roles properly, and the boys strongly recognize their escort responsibilities."[19]

The formal manner of social interaction in this suburb seems to be more typical of the United States upper class than of the broad middle class. Since the present focus is more on adolescents of the broad American middle class, Elkin and Westley's study has minimal relevance.

Other advocates of nondifferentiated youth-adult culture include psychologist Albert Bandura, who has argued that the "storm and stress" of adolescents has been exaggerated and that parents and teenagers are more in agreement than in conflict.[20] L. Eugene Thomas revealed that children of highly politicized parents tend to be like their parents both in political attitude and political behavior.[21] Elizabeth Douvan and her coworkers consistently discovered harmonious youth-parent relationships.[22] Reuben Hill and

[19]Ibid., p. 682.

[20]Albert Bandura, "The Stormy Decade: Fact or Fiction," in *Issues in Adolescent Psychology*, ed. D. Rogers (New York: Prentice-Hall, 1972).

[21]L. Eugene Thomas, "Family Correlates of Student Political Activism," *Developmental Psychology*, 4 (March 1971): 206–14.

[22]Elizabeth Douvan and Joseph Adelson, *The Adolescent Experience* (New York: John Wiley, 1966), and Elizabeth Douvan and H. Gold, "Modal Patterns in American Adolescence," in *Review of Child Development Research*, vol. 2, ed. L. Hoffman and M. Hoffman (New York: Russell Sage Foundation, 1966).

J. Aldous, Jr. found that religious beliefs remain relatively stable between generations.[23] Daniel Offer et al. try to explain adults' concern about a teen subculture as a misconceived view of their offspring's growth of independence. That is, parents overemphasize the influence of the peer group and "use the peer group as an externalized object and influence that provides a reference group for expressions of dissatisfaction with their offspring."[24]

What the latter authors are trying to say is, more plainly, that parents have invented a teen subculture to use it as a scapegoat for the complaints they have about their kids. This is a surprising psychoanalytic exercise for writers who, throughout their work, vehemently dispute the validity of any psychoanalytic notion. The Offer team ostensibly relies directly on the responses they have collected from their surveys and claims that "data collected directly from normal adolescents are often significantly different from what many adults assume teenagers feel about themselves."[25] That may well be so, but what the data mean becomes a matter of *interpretation*. By taking teenagers' statements verbatim, they actually fail to make an interpretation at all. What teenagers say may not adequately reveal what they really feel and experience. To conclude that if teenagers don't verbalize turmoil (and the subcultural compensation for it), then such a phenomenon does not exist is less than insightful. In sum, it appears, the Offer team holds an a priori bias according to which there is no subculture.

THE DIVERSITY OF TEENAGE SUBCULTURES

One of the more justified criticisms of the portrayal of the youth subculture deals not so much with the basic question of whether it does or does not exist, but how diversified it is. This criticism calls attention to the fact that there is no uniform subculture for all teenagers, but a number of significantly different versions. Many sociologists deplore the blanket application of the concept "teenage subculture" because it implies a monolithic membership group for all teenagers. They remind us of important differences in peer culture based on such variables as socioeconomic class, age, race, ethnicity, and rural or urban residence. For example, a black inner-city teenager living in the slums exhibits different values, has a different outlook on life, and belongs to a different type of peer culture than a white middle-class teenager growing up in suburbia.

For the purpose of communication, subcultural diversity must be sim-

---

[23]Reuben Hill and J. Aldous, Jr., "Socialization for Marriage and Parenthood," in *Handbook of Socialization Theory and Research*, ed. D. Goslin (Chicago: Rand McNally, 1969).

[24]Daniel Offer, Eric Ostrov, and Kenneth I. Howard, *The Adolescent: A Psychological Self-Portrait* (New York: Basic Books, 1981), p. 122.

[25]Ibid., p. 121. Also see Daniel Offer et al., *The Teenage World. Adolescents' Self-Image in Ten Countries* (New York: Plenum, 1988).

plified by some arbitrary guidelines: when the unqualified terms *youth subculture* or *teenage peer culture* or a synonymous phrase appears, reference is made to the nondelinquent middle class, reaching over into the upper-lower socioeconomic stratum. The teenage groups, cliques, campus crowds, and so on of this socioeconomic range are characterized by their independence from and usually nonviolent rejection of many adult standards, their conformity to peer-group patterns, their observance of teenage fads and fashions, their romanticism, and their participation in hedonistic activities. Specific expressions may include distinct ways of dressing, grooming, and talking. Their argot, representing a relatively exclusive communication system, is not shared with adults.

The upper socioeconomic class of the American population can hardly be said to have a youth subculture. In that social stratum one would most likely encounter the type of nonadolescent youth who is integrated in his or her family and special community and who suffers little status uncertainty— often to the point where there is no need for a compensating teenage subculture.

On the other side, lower-class youths live a subcultural life that has its own ethos. Anthropologist Walter B. Miller suggested a culturistic etiology of delinquency and tried to explain youthful offenses by a particular lower-class set of values and problems that increase the probability of law violations.[26] Over years of observing and analyzing lower-class street-corner groups, Miller discovered a number of "focal concerns" of lower-class culture that set it distinctly apart from other positions in the social order. These focal concerns include "trouble," "toughness," "smartness," "excitement," "fate," and "autonomy." They should not be understood as being in opposition to the law, but rather as helping to bring about the circumstances that invite criminal behavior. For example, the search for excitement may lead to auto theft, and the stress on toughness may encourage not only verbal insult, but physical violence as a retribution for it.

Other criminologists feel, however, that a youngster's membership in a delinquent subculture is better explained by "differential opportunities." Richard A. Cloward and Lloyd E. Ohlin, for example, think that there is more than one delinquent subculture among working-class youth and that a main goal of research should be to detect how selections of delinquency adaptations are made.[27] According to the theory, these selections depend more on characteristics of community organization than on psychological differences among delinquents. In other words, types of delinquency depend on types of illegitimate opportunities which, in turn, are primarily dependent on features

---

[26]Walter B. Miller, "Lower-Class Culture As a Generating Milieu of Gang Delinquency," *Journal of Social Issues*, 14 (1958): 5–19.

[27]Richard A. Cloward and Lloyd E. Ohlin, *Delinquency and Opportunity: A Theory of Delinquent Gangs* (Glencoe, IL: The Free Press, 1960).

of the community. Cloward and Ohlin specified three major types of delinquent subculture adaptations and called them *criminal-oriented, conflict-oriented,* and *retreatist-oriented.* These types differ in activity patterns as well as in etiological conditions. In terms of behavior, the criminalistic form concentrates on systematic theft as a way of life and a major avenue for upward social mobility into the world of organized crime. The conflict form is the result of disorganized communities in which traditional institutions of control have been rendered ineffective by high population mobility or diversity. The retreatist form provides isolation from conventional values and persons, and focuses on "kicks" through drugs, alcohol, and sex. In this form, steady work is eschewed in preference to "getting by," and the art of being "cool" is practiced.

A special type of delinquency has become notorious over the past few decades: youth-ghetto delinquency in the form of school vandalism. A 1980 report shows that 110,000 teachers, 5 percent of the U.S. total, were assaulted by students, an increase of more than 50 percent over the annual rate of the late 1970s. For example, school muggings, lawsuits, thefts, and vandalism in 1980 cost Los Angeles schools over $100 million while city and school officials were stymied over jurisdictional problems.[28]

The diversity of juvenile subcultures has been summed up:[29]

The "parent" male subculture. This is the small gang, described as non-utilitarian, malicious, negativistic, versatile, and characterized by short-run hedonism. It is referred to as "parent" subculture because it is the most common and generic collective delinquency form.

The conflict-oriented subculture. This is usually a highly developed form of collective delinquency, exhibited in large gangs, the membership of which may run into the hundreds. They have an elaborate organization that often includes such roles as president, vice-president, war-chief, and armorer. They have a territorial base, a name, a strong sense of corporate identity, and a public personality or "rep" in the gang world.

The drug-addict subculture. There is usually a correlation between drug addiction and delinquency. In most cases, the addicts were already delinquent before grouping themselves into subcultures. Their delinquency is almost always of the nonviolent and income-producing type that makes their drug habit possible.

[28]"Help! Teacher Can't Teach!" *Time,* June 16, 1980, p. 63.

[29]Albert K. Cohen and James F. Short, Jr., "Research in Delinquent Subcultures," *Journal of Social Issues,* 14 (1958): 20–37.

Semiprofessional theft.   This is a loosely integrated forerunner of the subculture of professional adult thieves proficient in ordinarily nonviolent thievery. In a sense, it is a stage in the life history, a specialized delinquency before ascending to the elite thievery of the adult professionals.

The middle-class delinquent subculture.   Cohen and Short anticipate empirical exploration of a phenomenon not yet clearly developed. The traditional form of middle-class delinquency is usually of the "parent" type, but it may evolve into other forms. For example, the above-mentioned youth-ghetto delinquency (school violence and vandalism) could possibly be placed into this category. Generally, however, the middle-class delinquent subculture may not be clearly defined simply because it largely lacks empirical representation.

The female delinquent subcultures.   A female's status is largely dependent on the status of the males with whom she is identified. There are some exceptions, however, for example, when girls organize in gangs for sexual pursuits (usually prostitution), drug addiction, or as counterparts of the male hoodlum gang. Though research literature on female delinquency is sparse, there are indications that the traditional double standard has also declined in respect to delinquent activities and that girls are catching up with boys in the arena of law violations.

But, of course, not all teenage subcultures are of a delinquent nature. Many of them rally around relatively harmless and recreational fads and styles, such as the subcultures of the surfers, bikers, backpackers, athletes, punkers, religious groups, cults, and movements. Delinquent subcultures have been dwelled on primarily because they are clearly discernible as subcultures and illustrate some of the principles of the three explanatory models of subculture etiology, particularly those of the psychogenic approach in which common problems become shared problems for which the conspirators invent a delinquent solution.

ADOLESCENT NONSTATUS AND TEENAGE STATUS: A PARADOX?

Classification of certain adolescent activities as subcultural behavior introduces a theoretical problem: how can the portrayal of teenagers as confused and uncertain adolescents be reconciled with their portrayal as members of the teenage subculture, within which they have found role security and certainty? This seeming paradox is not easily resolved, since teenagers are actually characterized by *both*. The decision as to which of the two characterizations is more applicable depends entirely on the *specific teenager-other* relationship that is to be analyzed. When examining the teenager's relationship with adults, a multitude of problems are detectable that in their sum total substantiate the claim of the existence of adolescent uncertainty. Problems intrinsic to this *teenage-adult* relationship include confused communication, unclear authority definitions, generalist-specialist discontinuity, incongruous standards, and many other problems that have been discussed in previous chapters.

However, the *teenager-teenager* relationship is characterized by few, if any, such confusions and uncertainties. Among themselves, teenagers have created a relatively stable, though temporary, social structure. They know that they belong together and observe norms and values not necessarily consistent with the adult world's folkways and mores. In others words, there is a subcultural arrangement that compensates for the experience of adolescence in the adult world.

In summary, the seeming paradox must be understood as a problem of *differential analysis*. Most modern teenagers are *both* typically confused adolescents in the adult world and relatively self-assured and status-conscious members of their peer groups—depending on the interaction being analyzed.

A final word of modification should be added. Allowance must be made for the fact that not *all* teenagers are adolescents and members of teenage subcultures. It is possible to be an adolescent and not a member of some discernible peer culture. This would be the case of a youth who is socially isolated from peers and suffers from adolescent symptoms without recourse to an agemate subculture. Such a youth might lack opportunity to communicate with peers and be unaware of the commonality of adolescent problems. However, such a socially isolated adolescent would be a rarity, because almost any degree of social interaction would provide enough opportunities to communicate, meet, and share problems with peers. In general, for American teenagers the adolescent condition constitutes an ever-present latent force whose dynamics are restlessly at work to form and maintain a compensating subculture.

It is also possible to be a member of the teenage subculture and suffer minimally from adolescent tension and confusion. This relatively conflict-free situation may be due to either one or both of two circumstances. First, the teenager may be so deeply involved in the peer subculture, may carry out peer commitments and follow peer standards to such a degree that he or she derives a sense of total belonging from the subculture. Adult standards affect him or her only minimally, and he or she suffers little or no ambiguity and confusion as to where to place loyalty. Second, a teenager may be a member of the peer culture not because of basic psychological needs but rather because of proximity or coincidental acquaintances, such as neighborhood friends and school environment. This nonadolescent may be integrated in the family, have clear perceptions of a future occupation, satisfactory access to adult models that he or she emulates, and may freely adhere to the value orientation of adults. Participation in the teenage subculture is therefore merely perfunctory and of superficial significance to personality development. This type of youth is in the minority. It is safe to assume that the majority of American teenagers are both adolescents and members of peer cultures.

SUMMARY

Many social scientists agree on the existence of the teenage subculture as an empirical reality. Numerous studies and a multitude of daily manifestations seem to support the assumption.

Care must be taken in defining subculture to specify *which* type of teenage subculture is to be discussed. Generally speaking, the present discussion refers to the teenage culture within the broad American middle class.

The seeming paradox that a teenager can be both an adolescent and a status-conscious member of the peer culture can be resolved by *differential analysis*, by focusing, respectively, on the adolescent-adult or the teenager-teenager interaction.

The functions of the teenage subculture that meet the needs of the participants and enable the subculture to become a continuous process include a number of "services": (1) common norms and values, (2) a subcultural argot, (3) channels of communication not shared with outsiders, (4) unique styles and fads, (5) a sense of solidarity, (6) a status structure, (7) the charisma of leaders or heroes, and (8) gratification of specific needs through subcultural institutionalization.

Three etiological theories complement each other in explaining subcultural formation. The *psychogenic* and *behavioristic* models focus on the prime origin of subcultural evolvement and start with the problems a number of persons have in common. *Behaviorism*, with its premise of human nature as hedonistic, explains the attraction of teenagers to their peer culture as escape from confrontation with adult culture and as gravitation toward common interests. The *culture-transmission* model deals with learning and communicating. Television, movies, radio, and magazines perpetuate subcultural ways of thinking and acting.

It must be emphasized that motivation to join and maintain a normally nondelinquent teenage subculture does not stem entirely from the need to alleviate adolescent frustration and confusion. Motivation also stems from gregariousness and the enjoyment of fellowship. Teenagers enjoy engaging in activities (for example, dating) and in sharing interests that are neither entirely child nor adult. This enjoyment of peer companionship positively reinforces the subculture and operates in conjunction with the more negatively reinforcing influence of adolescent insecurity. In fact, even for teenagers relatively unaffected by adolescent disturbances, the gregarious enjoyment alone is a sufficiently powerful positive reinforcer to attract them to the subculture of peers.

12

Inside the Teen Subculture, Part I

While the preceding chapter was theory-oriented, this chapter and the next one are graphic and draw more from popular than from theoretical sources. Inclusion of popular material sharpens the illustrations of actual behavior and events in the teen subculture. The material in these two chapters is ordered into eight dimensions that are elemental to the nature of subculture. Since there is more material on the first dimension, values and attitudes of young people, this entire chapter is on this topic; the next chapter discusses the remaining seven dimensions.

These two chapters are oriented toward the general American teenage collectivity, high school students and the younger college students, rather than the older or more activistic segment of American youth. In spite of some overlap of these collectivities, the distinction may prove helpful in ordering the immense amount of material available from the overall youth scene.

The chapter following the two subculture chapters addresses itself to the question of counterculture, mostly a historical event in American civilization. It included, rather loosely integrated, a number of youth factions, such as the young intelligentsia, radical political groups, liberation phalanxes, and cultic movements.

IN-GROUP VALUES

Any group of individuals interacting over a period of time will sooner or later come to agree on a blueprint that creates predictable behavior patterns. These patterns include norms, rules concerning *how* to achieve certain values and do certain things, and values, the goals and basic attitudes concerning *what* is important.

Teen groups hold norms and values that, though not always entirely different from those of the adult community, at least reflect a unique accent. We will now explore some teen in-group standards, such as popularity, prestige, friendship, and sex.

Researchers have repeatedly noted that popularity is the most emphasized value among teenagers. The dynamics of popularity are complex and involve such features as admiration and recognition by peers. The data of the National Norms for Entering College Freshmen show that "obtaining recognition from peers" is essential to about 40 percent of beginning college students and that this proportion varies little from year to year.[1]

James S. Coleman, in his famous survey of American high schools, likewise found a strong desire to be popular. Interestingly, the desire is more intense among girls than boys.[2] The Purdue Opinion Panel supported this and showed that 60 percent of the teenage girls answered affirmatively to "want people to like me more," while 47 percent of the boys answered in the affirmative. Of the girls, 47 percent affirmed "wish I were more popular," while 36 percent of the boys did.[3] Still another study corroborated the sex-differentiated emphasis and found that girls with middle-class background showed persistent preoccupation with popularity and social success.[4]

The most pronounced emphasis on popularity was found among girls whose fathers occupied managerial, business, and professional positions commonly referred to as upper middle class. These girls daydreamed of popularity and often cited it as a source of worry. They indicated that they would like to have more social skills, be more popular, and be more accepted by peers. This preoccupation was not exclusively a result of the standards of the high school crowd, but was reinforced by the middle-class parents. Lower-class girls and boys, regardless of specific family circumstances, were markedly less concerned about popularity.

[1]National Norms for Entering College Freshmen, annual reports for 1966, 1967, 1968, 1969, 1970, 1971, 1972 (Washington, DC: Office of Research, American Council on Education).

[2]James S. Coleman, *The Adolescent Society* (New York: Free Press, 1963), p. 30.

[3]H. H. Remmers and D. H. Radler, *The American Teenager* (New York: Bobbs-Merrill, 1962), p. 85.

[4]Elizabeth Douvan and Joseph Adelson, *The Adolescent Experience* (New York: John Wiley, 1966), p. 406.

A longitudinal study shows that the importance attached to being popular in the high school crowd has changed only slightly over the years.[5] Samples taken from the same suburban high school in the Phoenix metropolitan area were surveyed in 1976 and in 1982. The 1976 responses to the question "How important is it to be liked and accepted by other teenagers?" showed that 47 percent felt it to be of "very great importance," 37 percent of "great importance," 14 percent of "some importance," and 2 percent of "no importance." The 1982 distribution was, respectively, 17, 37, 41, and 4 percent (1 percent no response). The 1982 proportions show a marked increase of the "some-importance" category. However, the "no-importance" category changed little, showing an increase of only 2 percent. When combining all categories that report "importance," comparison between 1976 and 1982 shows an insignificant decrease from 98 to 95 percent.

Likewise, the respondents in both surveys chose very similar *criteria* of popularity. Both distributions of answers to the question "What is expected of a teenager by his or her friends in order to be popular with them?" ranked the conformity principle first (doing, speaking, thinking, dressing, etc., "our way"). Second was what could be summed up as "good personality" (being friendly, cheerful, getting along with others, etc.). Third was "being yourself" or a similar reference to individualism. Fourth was taking an interest in others and helping them. And fifth was being honest and trustworthy. The rank order of these major categories did not change between 1976 and 1982.

There were, however, some changes in the gender-differentiated responses. The 1980s responses showed a diminishing of the girls' previously extremely high emphasis on conformity and now approached the proportion of the boys (roughly a third) who felt conformity was a criterion of popularity. Shifts of gender-differentiated responses were also noticeable in some of the minor categories: While anti-Establishment behavior as a criterion of popularity elicited 2 percent of the boys' and none of the girls' responses in 1976, the responses were reversed in 1982. A shift in the same direction occurred in regard to "having money": The 1970s responses showed 4 percent of the boys and none of the girls considering it a means to be popular. The 1980s responses showed 3 percent of the boys and 2 percent of the girls considering it so. "Helping and caring," previously an almost exclusive female response, attracted 8 percent of the boys and only 4 percent of the girls. Several of these changes seem to suggest a shift away from the traditional feminine role.

Nonetheless, conformity still seems to be the main price of popularity for both sexes. Other studies have corroborated this and discovered a consistent age correlation: While conformity is not particularly characteristic of

---

[5]Hans Sebald, *A Longitudinal Study of Popularity among Adolescents*, unpublished survey study, Department of Sociology, Arizona State University, 1982.

children below seven to nine years of age, it increases thereafter, reaches a peak during early adolescence (around thirteen), and then declines. Young teenagers are therefore more vulnerable to the influence of peers than older adolescents.[6]

What qualities do teenagers seek in a friend? The Douvan and Adelson research found that boys and girls have somewhat different expectations, with the former seeking someone who is first "amiable and nice" and secondly "supporting in trouble," and the latter seeking a friend who first of all is "not a gossip," secondly is "amiable and nice," and thirdly is "supporting in trouble."[7]

Another quality, considered most important in a friend, emerged in a survey by psychologist Vivian Seltzer: cleanliness. Sixty percent of the teenagers in the sample said that this was a quality to which they were particularly sensitive in their peers.[8]

Sometimes a teenager's prestige determines desirability as a friend; for a minority, it is a primary criterion for choosing a friend. It is more common, however, that such choices are made on the basis of a combination, such as desirable personality traits and prestige in the group.

The prestige of a friend can cause complications—especially among girls. There is frequent rivalry among girls for popularity with boys. A girl-girl friendship must recognize the problem of differential popularity—that is, popularity sought among boys and popularity sought among girls—and make protective adjustments. This problem has generated an interesting value orientation among girls in general. In order to avoid hostility and envy from her female peer group, the girl who is popular must learn to accept her good fortune modestly. In fact, the adolescent girl ordinarily is far more concerned about her acceptance by other girls and often uses her popularity with boys for its effect on her appraisal by her own sex-peer group.

ANTI-INTELLECTUALISM

Another teenager in-group attitude deals with anti-intellectualism. Learnedness has always been the nemesis of popularity and friendship, and it usually is laid down on the altar of peer acceptance as the sacrificial offering for "belonging." Nothing has changed in this respect, and various studies have borne this out—from the early Purdue Opinion Panel (60 percent disdained intellectualism and preferred to be popular rather than brilliant) to the

---

[6]Jane E. Brownstone and Richard H. Willis, "Conformity in Early and Late Adolescence," *Developmental Psychology*, 4 (May 1971): 334–37.

[7]Douvan and Adelson, *The Adolescent Experience*, p. 406.

[8]Vivian Seltzer, *The Psychosocial Worlds of the Adolescent* (New York: Wiley & Sons, 1989).

Goertzel survey that showed an even further increase in anti-intellectualism.[9] What are the social psychological dynamics behind this almost invariable pattern?

The young teenager must be understood in terms of *subcultural* involvement. The individual reaches adolescence conditioned in the skills of group membership, having learned how to get along with peers and to do the accepted things. Naturally other-directed and with little self-consciousness, he or she is attuned to behave in concert with others. As an adolescent, he or she enters a life phase that increasingly calls for independence. But at the same time he or she becomes even more sensitive to the security he or she has enjoyed among peers. It is now that he or she relies on the subculture most heavily—and this subculture demands conformity. Deviation from group norms would incur alienation—a dreadful punishment for any youngster. For the most part, idiosyncratic qualities among members are suppressed. Intellectual pursuits constitute such idiosyncrasies and are immediately suspect. Researchers have shown that this attitude runs through the core of secondary schooling and that "friendliness, popularity, and mediocrity" are more highly regarded than being a "good student."

Modern education often employs the self-defeating *individual* approach when learning problems arise, overlooking the fact that the teenager is essentially other-directed and marches to the drumbeat of peers. Learning problems are frequently not individual problems but are *social* problems with the intellectually negating power structure of the adolescent peer group being the hostile background. Some sociologists have suggested that we seriously explore ways of moving adolescent peer groups collectively toward intellectual interests, rather than continue the futile piecemeal attempts to correct individual students in the hope of diverting them from identifying with their peers.

REFERENCE GROUPS AND VALUES

It would be misleading to assume that teenagers look exclusively to their peer group for value orientation. There is no such uniform reference group. In some areas of decision making they align their values with peer standards and in other areas with the views and advice of adults, particularly parents. An Arizona study (Table 12–1) indicates that adolescents are selective in their conformity and in some matters are guided by the opinions of the peer group and in other matters by their parents. In still other matters they listen to both sides, and in some sectors of life they seem uncertain, lacking a definite reference group. For example, in matters of money, choosing courses at

[9]Ted Goertzel, "Changes in the Values of College Students 1958 to 1970/71," *Pacific Sociological Review*, 15 (April 1972): 235–44.

TABLE 12-1   1982 percent distribution of boys' and girls' responses to the question: If you had to decide between your friends' and your parents' opinion and feeling in the following situations, whose opinion would you consider more important?

	Friends'*		Uncertain**		Parents'*	
	Boys	Girls	Boys	Girls	Boys	Girls
1. On what you spend your money	19	2	27	38	54	60
2. Whom to date	41	47	46	40	14	13
3. Clubs you join	54	60	38	33	8	7
4. Advice on personal problems	27	53	24	29	49	18
5. How to dress	43	53	46	44	11	2
6. Courses you take in school	8	16	35	20	57	64
7. Hobbies	46	36	41	56	14	9
8. Choosing your future occupation	0	2	35	42	65	56
9. Social events you attend	65	60	27	29	8	11
10. College or not	0	0	35	36	65	64
11. Books you read other than those requested by school	38	40	49	53	14	7
12. Magazines you buy	46	51	46	47	8	2
13. How often you date	35	24	51	49	14	27
14. Whether you participate in drinking parties	46	40	35	42	19	18
15. Choosing your future spouse	8	9	57	67	35	24
16. Going steady or not	30	29	57	56	14	16
17. Intimacy on a date	35	24	54	67	11	9
18. Whom to go for information about sex	30	44	32	16	38	40

Source: Hans Sebald, "Adolescents' Peer Orientation: Changes in the Support System During the Past Three Decades," *Adolescence* 24 (Winter 1989):937–46.

*Categories include responses of "definitely" and "probably" friends or parents, respectively.

**24% of the boys and 35% of the girls modified the label of this category by writing in "myself," "own opinion," or something to that effect.

school, deciding on future careers and plans to go to college, they tend to consult their parents more than their peers. However, in matters of dating, clothing, hobbies, attending social affairs, choice of magazines, and joining clubs, they follow the opinion and advice of their peers.[10]

[10]Hans Sebald, "Adolescents' Peer Orientation: Changes in the Support System During the Past Three Decades," *Adolescence* 24 (Winter 1989): 937–46.

The teenagers express uncertainty (or, as some specified, self-reliance) in certain areas. Roughly half of both girls and boys are uncertain whose advice they would follow when it comes to reading books other than school texts (maybe the explanation is the majority's failure to read outside books in the first place), buying magazines, selecting a spouse, going steady, how intimate to be on a date, and how often to date. Uncertainties in exactly these areas prevailed among the high schoolers of six years earlier. (See Table 12–2.) But a serendipitous finding revealed that one thing had changed: In 1976 17 percent of the boys and 16 percent of the girls had amended their "uncertain" responses by saying that he or she was guided by "myself" or "own opinion." The proportions of "uncertain" responses increased in 1982 to 24 percent of the boys and an astounding 33 percent of the girls. This was purely the initiative of the respondents, since this option had not been listed on the questionnaire.

GENDER-DIFFERENTIATED VALUES

Such a response possibly signals increasing individualism and, conversely, decreasing familism of teenagers of the 1980s. It may specifically signal increasing female liberation, since many more girls than boys shifted from parent orientation to "uncertain" or self-reliant. While the 1976 girls sought significantly more parental advice than boys in seventeen out of the eighteen areas, the 1982 girls sought more parental advice in only six out of the eighteen areas. On the other side, the 1976 girls were more "uncertain" than boys in eight of the eighteen areas, while in 1982 they were more "uncertain" (or self-reliant) in eleven of the eighteen areas. (See Table 12–2.)

Sex-differentiated responses are clearly visible in a number of items. In the 1976 as well as the 1982 survey, boys significantly more often than girls, turn to friends' opinions in regard to how to spend money, whereas girls more often listen to their parents in this respect. "Advice on personal problems" has always elicited a more peer-oriented response from girls. This might be explained by the possibility that girls understand "personal problems" to include matters of feminine hygiene, a realm where girls tend to consult girlfriends more often than parents. This tendency may also be reflected by the 44 percent of girls vs. 30 percent of the boys who go to friends for information about sex. Generally, however, the 1982 survey suggests a far less gender-differentiated picture than the earlier survey.

TREND ANALYSIS

The identical eighteen questions were asked in a 1960 survey in a suburban high school of Columbus, Ohio, a school socioeconomically (largely middle class), religiously, and ethnically (largely Protestant and white) comparable to

TABLE 12-2 Comparison of 1976 survey with 1982 survey in terms of percent distribution of boys' and girls' responses to the question: If you had to decide between your friends' and your parents' opinion and feeling in the following situations, whose opinion would you consider more important?

Survey Questions	1976: Friends'		1982: Friends'		1976: Uncertain*		1982: Uncertain**		1976: Parents'		1982: Parents'	
	Boys	Girls	Boys	Girls	Boys	Girls	Boys	Girls	Boys	Girls	Boys	Girls
1. On what you spend your money	45	22	19	2	24	23	27	38	31	55	54	60
2. Whom to date	64	54	41	47	32	29	46	40	4	17	14	13
3. Clubs you join	71	66	54	60	23	25	38	2	6	7	8	7
4. Advice on personal problems	40	60	27	53	23	5	24	29	37	35	49	18
5. How to dress	63	62	43	53	31	29	46	44	6	9	11	2
6. Courses you take in school	42	22	8	16	26	34	35	20	33	44	57	64
7. Hobbies	66	54	46	36	28	36	41	56	6	10	14	9
8. Choosing your future occupation	10	4	0	2	47	31	35	42	43	64	65	56
9. Social events you attend	76	77	65	60	20	13	27	29	4	10	8	11
10. College or not	11	7	0	0	38	23	35	36	51	70	65	64
11. Books you read other than those requested by school	52	50	38	40	41	42	49	53	8	8	14	7
12. Magazines you buy	62	54	46	51	34	40	46	47	4	6	8	2
13. How often you date	62	19	35	24	26	24	51	49	12	57	14	27
14. Whether you participate in drinking parties	62	54	46	40	20	20	35	42	18	26	19	18
15. Choosing future spouse	27	9	8	9	47	49	57	67	27	42	35	24
16. Going steady or not	54	21	30	29	32	47	57	56	14	32	14	16
17. Intimacy on a date	53	33	35	24	39	50	54	67	8	17	11	9
18. Whom to go for information about sex	46	34	30	44	30	23	32	16	24	43	38	40

Source: Hans Sebald, combined material from: "Adolescents' Shifting Orientation toward Parents and Peers: A Curvilinear Trend over Recent Decades," *Journal of Marriage and the Family* 48 (February 1986): 5–13; and "Adolescents' Peer Orientation: Changes in Support System During the Past Three Decades," *Adolescence* 24 (Winter 1989):937–46.

*17% of the boys and 16% of the girls amended this category by writing in "myself," or "own opinion."

**24% of the boys and 33% of the girls amended this category by writing in "myself," or "own opinion."

the Phoenix metropolitan school.[11] Adding data from that survey to the longitudinal view introduced above enables us to compare the responses of 1960, 1976, and 1982. Scrutiny of the responses reveals that certain changes have occurred over this period and that these changes indicate how the role of parents in the lives of teenagers has fluctuated. We can generalize that 1960 was characterized by conservative, parent-oriented attitudes, 1976 by powerful peer orientation, and 1982 by a balancing of the peer and parental reference groups.

Comparing 1960 and 1976 reveals a loss of parental influence and shows a sweeping shift toward peer orientation in *all* areas. Some of the more radical shifts (amounting to at least 20 percent) away from parent orientation affected the areas of how to spend money, whom and how often to date, going steady, clothes, which courses to take at school, which social events to attend, and participation at drinking parties. However, other decreases are just as significant, especially when considering that the time-honored tradition of consulting parents in matters of personal problems and troubles declined by 15 percent. There were also declines in following parental advice in career plans, going to parents for sex information, and seeking parental advice about mate selection. (See details in Table 12–3.)

Comparing 1976 and 1982 reveals that by the 1980s parents had partly recovered the territory they had lost during the 1960s and 1970s to peer influence or to the "uncertain/self-reliant" attitude. Perhaps the pressure of the economic slump of the early 1980s prompted increases in reliance on parents: 15 percent in money spending, 23 percent in course selections, 7 percent in career questions, 5 percent in college decision, and 2 percent in book purchases. In most areas the increases were minor, and in seven areas the changes were negative, though not as drastic as in 1976. Most of the decreases took place in the social realm, including how to dress, whom and how often to date, and in the private realm, such as advice in personal or sexual problems.

From the vantage point of the 1980s, reliance on parental advice has not recovered its 1960 standing. With the sole exception of consulting parents on college plans (only 2 percent increase over 1960), all eighteen areas have experienced decreases in parental consultation. The sharpest decreases exist in social and personal affairs, with decisions about dating, dressing, and partying now being more "uncertain" or dependent on the teenager's own taste and opinion.

The generalizations of the Ohio-Arizona surveys could be refined by controlling a number of variables, among them, for example, dropout-proneness and graduation-orientation. Identifying respondents by one of the two

[11]Hans Sebald, *The Crisis of Adolescent Discontinuity*, mimeographed research report. The Ohio State University, Columbus, Ohio, 1960.

TABLE 12-3   Changes of proportions of teenagers seeking parental advice in 18 areas between 1960, 1976, and 1982. (Boys and girls combined.)

Areas	Percent of Teenagers Seeking Parental Advice			Percent Change		
	1960	1976	1982	1960–1976	1976–1982	1960–1982
1. On what you spend your money	62	42	57	−20	+15	− 5
2. Whom to date	31	10	13	−21	+ 3	−18
3. Clubs you join	23	6	7	−17	+ 1	−16
4. Advice on personal problems	51	36	32	−15	− 4	−19
5. How to dress	35	7	6	−28	− 1	−29
6. Courses you take in school	69	38	61	−31	+23	− 8
7. Hobbies	14	8	11	− 6	+ 3	− 3
8. Choosing your future occupation	64	53	60	−11	+ 7	− 4
9. Social events you attend	30	6	10	−24	+ 4	−20
10. College or not	63	60	65	− 3	+ 5	+ 2
11. Books you read other than those requested by school	20	8	10	−12	+ 2	−10
12. Magazines you buy	21	5	5	−16	none	−16
13. How often you date	58	33	21	−25	−12	−37
14. Whether you participate in drinking parties	64	23	18	−41	− 5	−46
15. Choosing future spouse	39	34	29	− 5	− 5	−10
16. Going steady or not	41	21	15	−20	− 6	−26
17. Intimacy on a date	23	12	10	−11	− 2	−13
18. Whom to go for information about sex	48	32	39	−16	+ 7	− 9

Source: Hans Sebald, based on data in "Adolescents' Shifting Orientation toward Parents and Peers."

categories might result in a polarized picture, showing the former type of student more aligned with the peer culture and the latter with parental values. Lucius F. Cervantes' study found a sharp cleavage between the two types, establishing that dropout-prone students indeed have their own peer culture.[12] This finding deserves to be verified in future studies. In the meantime we accept the Ohio-Arizona findings as showing that teenagers in general cultivate divided reference groups, selectively looking to peers and parents for advice and guidance.

[12]Lucius F. Cervantes, *American Youth Culture: Independent or Dependent?* Paper read at the Annual Convention of the American Sociological Association, Chicago, 1965.

DECISION MAKING: PARENT–TEEN CLASHES

The demand of the parents to be taken seriously as a reference group is not always obeyed. Gallup Polls found that teenager-parent arguments erupt over a number of issues. Asking parents of teenage children "What do you argue about most with your teenager(s)?," the poll found a number of major clashes: 18 percent about chores/housework, 15 percent about freedom/responsibilities, 12 percent about evening curfew, 9 percent about homework, 8 percent about money, 6 percent about where the teenagers go, and 5 percent about choice of friends and dates.[13] In general, 30 percent of the parents felt that they were not strict enough with their teenage offspring, 11 percent felt they were too strict, 54 percent thought they were just about right, and the rest qualified their responses or had no opinion.[14]

When 13-to-17-year-old teenagers were asked about the areas of conflict with parents, a somewhat different rank order emerged: (1) what clothes to wear, (2) staying out late, (3) quitting school, (4) sexual activities, and (5) drinking. The percentages of the teenagers who felt that they themselves should have the right to make decisions in these areas were, respectively: (1) 99%, (2) 85% (3) 82%, (4) 73%, and (5) 55%.[15]

VALUES AND TEENAGE SEXUALITY

Important attitudes held by teenagers deal with their sexual activities. However, these attitudes, like just about any attitude or value orientation, fluctuate and are greatly affected by sociocultural changes. During the counterculture years of the 1960s and 1970s the prevailing sexual standards were labeled the New Sexuality, evidently characterized by liberated attitudes and equally unrestrained behavior, and can be summed up by a number of characteristics:

1. *Noncommittal sexuality.* Sex was accepted as pleasure, and the fulfillment of it was not seen as requiring a commitment stipulating exclusivity, loyalty, or continuous personal care and concern. The New Sexuality implied the intention of the young to preserve as much independence and individualism as possible—and yet to enjoy sexual intimacy.

2. *Tolerance or acceptance of varying sexuality.* Sexual liberation included many of the sexual expressions previously considered deviant. It was largely to the credit of the vocal counterculture and the women's movement

[13]*Gallup Opinion Index 1978,* #156, pp. 22–23.
[14]Ibid., p. 24.
[15]Public Opinion Survey, "Big Decisions for Teens," *USA Today,* July 13, 1987, p. D1.

that homosexuality and lesbianism were looked upon as relatively acceptable alternatives and no longer as pathological aberrations.

3. *Female sexual liberation.* The most important aspect of the New Sexuality was the changing role of women. Young women became more aware of their own sexuality and sought equal satisfaction. The aspect of pleasure was possibly the most revolutionary feature in the Sexual Revolution: the female now openly regarded sex as enjoyable.

4. *Medical and technological innovations.* Probably nothing decreased inhibition and fear of sexual activities for the woman more than the availability of contraceptives. A woman freed from the old moral compunctions did not imperil her future by unwanted pregnancy and could enjoy with impunity the physical and psychological pleasures of sex.

5. *Credo of instantness of fulfillment.* Postindustrial conditions markedly fostered a belief in instant fulfillment of needs. Insistence on an instant remedy was the response to any slackening of society's ability to come to the individual's aid and provide an effective and immediate answer to any desire that was defined as a need. Frustration was blamed on society's failure to prevent such unpleasantness. Individual sexual frustrations entered the list of such societal failures. The Sexual Revolution was strongly supported by the demand for instantness and, conversely, by the rejection of the old Protestant ethic that included deference of gratification. This new credo became a part of the new psychology of entitlement. Accordingly, young Americans assumed that they had a right (not merely a chance) to self-actualization, economic security, and general comfort.

During the late 1970s the New Sexuality ran out of steam and a new tenor became noticeable. Several conditions were responsible for the decline of the liberal sexual orientation:

1. *Disillusionment.* On the basis of books, movies, talks, rumors, and pseudoacademic promises, adolescents were faced with sexually superhuman promises that sooner or later led to frustration and disappointment. From the author's counseling experiences with college students, it appeared that many young persons were disappointed by their initial sexual experience. The failure of sex to be as glamorous as expected tended to downgrade the value of sexuality. This disillusionment became crucial when it was combined with the failure to establish a secure human relationship. Inexperienced teenage lovers were left deeply disillusioned with sex as a cure for alienation and loneliness.

Such disillusionment had manifold results. Those who had been hurt sought other routes of escape from isolation and turned to drugs, suicide, creative sublimation, or a new Victorianism. The last reaction rejected the New Sexuality and turned toward a New Asceticism which was expected to heal disappointment, solve confusion, and supply missing psychological security.

This reversal pattern may actually be a *generational* experience in which most young people go through the liberated, disappointed, and finally puritanical stages, ultimately becoming relatively conservative adults. Such a pattern may well explain in large part why there always exists a mass of conservative parents who just a few years prior were rebellious youngsters. It may also explain why each adult generation continues to view premarital sex as deviant behavior.

2. *The quest for romanticism.* The New Sexuality was inimical to a sense of romanticism. Sexual realism deprived the young of the mystery of sexuality that used to include the reverent ritual, passion-amplifying delay, pulse-raising awe, ideal-inspiring imagination, and every sort of sublimation. The New Sexuality had branded these mental gyrations as dishonest and fallacious. Shooting down romantic pathos also killed the mystique of sex, and the survivors found themselves with banal physical lovemaking that soon conveyed a feeling of relative deprivation.

Combined with the heady sense of freedom was a sometimes uneasy feeling of pressure to take advantage of the new freedom. As Dustin Hoffman said in *The Graduate*: "I'm starting to feel the same way about getting laid as I did about getting into college."

When circumstances are created that are so realistic that they allow complete insight into the everyday life of the other sex, romantic feelings go out the window. Surveys found that men and women sharing coed dorms prefer to bring in sex partners from outside.

The desire for romanticism is strong and a constant in human life. Our Western civilization is permeated with romantic attitudes and promises waiting to be called upon to embellish human relationships that otherwise appear too sober and unexciting. Crass realism, in any realm of life, usually is surprisingly short-lived.

3. *The quest for psychological security.* Though the New Sexuality had fulfilled some heretofore frustrated needs and desires, new needs and problems arose. Although, for example, sexual tension was released and a source of fun and pleasure tapped, the lack of personal commitment endangered psychological security and led to anxiety. The prevalent emotional repercussion to adolescent sexuality during the era of repressive mores had been feelings of guilt and shame; the new emotional response was anxiety and a vague feeling of meaninglessness. This anomic version of the sexual relationship seemed to weigh heavily on the minds of the young. Humans display a natural need for norms and predictability—especially when it comes to sexual relationships—and a phase of liberal excursion is usually followed by a phase of reconsideration and conservatism.

4. *The tenacity of traditional values.* The old sexual mores were by no means forgotten. The liberation had not totally obscured the old "rights and wrongs," and though many young Americans spoke—and perhaps even acted —as if liberated from them, they still responded to them on an emotional, albeit unconscious level. Though it may be true that the more prevalent

modern reaction to premarital sex is anxiety (the typical reaction to normlessness), there are still many young people who react with the traditional "control emotions"—such as guilt and shame—to their violations of social standards.

5. *The academic fabrication of the New Sexuality.* There was exaggeration in the accounts of social scientists when they interpreted changes in sexual behavior. For example, Herbert H. Otto, chairperson of the National Center for the Exploration of Human Potential, forecast in 1971 that "there are 12,000 communes in the U.S. and I foresee that within five years, 20 percent of American families will be involved in them."[16] Such misextrapolation gave the impression that modern marriage, family, and sexual patterns were changing radically.

Another example of possible misinterpretation was the high premarital pregnancy rate, which was attributed to a higher premarital coitus rate. While this may have been so, this rate was not an accurate indicator since it may merely have been a function of fewer young people feeling obliged to marry because of the pressure that pregnancy exerts.

Tenuous interpretations led some social scientists to predict and even recommend changes in lifestyles. For example, well-known humanistic psychologists suggested exploring the many dimensions of monogamy, reinventing marriage by "engaging in serial polygamy" (Sidney Jourard), and trying out an "intimate network of families" for collective problem solving (Frederick Stoller).[17]

Sexologist Albert Ellis interpreted cohabitation as an intelligent decision to learn whom not to marry. It is not a "copping out" of human responsibilities. Ellis' opinion is that "anybody who marries without living with someone for at least six months is copping out."[18] He also foresaw a change in the family structure that would allow "legalized adultery"; that is, two people will marry mostly for each other but will have casual sexual experiences with others. Lawrence Casler, in *Is Marriage Necessary?*, proposed a similar restructuring of traditional marriage, allowing for "permissive matrimony."[19] The list of academics who supported the New Sexuality could be expanded.

Though many academic suggestions were based on valid insight, some were unduly generalized and gave an exaggerated picture of changed social and sexual mores. Social scientists were heavily influenced by their immediate social environment, which is relatively isolated in academia. Their students live in an artificial hothouse climate that is significantly different from

[16]"Marriage and Family," *Arizona Republic*, December 1971, p. 47.

[17]Herbert A. Otto, "Has Monogamy Failed?" *Saturday Review*, April 26, 1970, p. 25.

[18]"Noted Psychologist Is Seminar Speaker," *Arizona Republic*, June 24, 1972, p. 51.

[19]Lawrence Casler, *Is Marriage Necessary?* (New York: Human Sciences Press, 1974).

the world of working people. Their attitudes and behavior patterns tend to influence the interpretations of sociology and psychology professors, whose research more often than not samples this population, leading them to believe that what their students say and do is what *American youth* says and does.

For example, the mostly theoretical tolerance of sexual practices previously defined as deviant is not only not shared by nonacademic Americans but is often abandoned by college graduates when they enter the world of employment and family life. Much of their professed tolerance adds up to verbiage merely deemed sophisticated and liberated among college peers.

The academic factor has been discussed in order to show the intrusion of bias into the formulation of the New Sexuality. To some extent its formulation was inspired by academicians who were overimpressed by the immediacy and vociferousness of students.

These, in sum, were the main psychological, social, and cultural conditions that bore on the decline of the New Sexuality during the late 1970s. And then, during the 1980s came the final condition that sealed the debacle of the New Sexuality: AIDS, the new plague.

This fatal peril has added an entirely new perspective on human sexuality. It is too early, however, to know the extent to which it is changing sexual behavior. Again there is the danger of overassessing its actual impact. With every New Sexuality or New Peril comes the New Verbiage, the way people talk about the new phenomenon. But does this "talk" relate directly to actual behavior? Most likely not. It seems that in spite of AIDS, relatively liberal sexual practices continue—as testified by the unabated rate of premarital pregnancies of American teenagers. Rather than initiating a new asceticism or new chastity in the moral sense, the primary reaction may be limited to a new caution, as the increased sale of condoms across the nation seems to indicate.

POLITICAL ATTITUDES

The beginning of the last decade of the twentieth century saw American youth, more or less youth of Western Civilization generally, in a calmer mood and relatively well integrated into their society. No great causes or battles were being fought. The counterculture had become a historical phenomenon and young people seemed primarily directed toward work and the completion of an education so they could make it through hard economic times.

Even the war in the Persian Gulf fought during January and February of 1991 did little to alter this mood, though a rise in patriotism could be observed, especially at the victorious conclusion of the war. Compared to American youth's reaction to the Vietnam War, factionalism was at a low key. There were some relatively minor demonstrations by the "doves"; but the "hawks" carried the day. The overwhelming majority of American youth supported the Bush Administration's war effort, elated by the low casualty rate of the American forces and the short duration of the fighting.

It is worthwhile to recall that America's youth responded radically differently to the military involvement in Vietnam. Militant opposition was shown by a significant proportion of the young. A study took the Vietnam War as a test case to examine an important question about human behavior: Does knowledge about a certain issue influence or determine the attitude toward the same issue?[20] Over 400 college students were quizzed on their knowledge of Southeast Asia, the war, and their attitude toward the American involvement. The responses showed that the sample was divided into 110 antiwar demonstrators, 50 prowar partisans, and 276 students whose noncommittal attitude put them within the purview of the so-called silent majority. All of the students were given identical sets of questions relating to political, geographic, military, and historical conditions of Vietnam and adjacent areas. The "doves" did best, getting 55 percent correct; the "hawks" scored 47 percent, and the silent majority only 45 percent. Higher scores among the activists had been expected since they were the ones who had to defend their dissent, but all scores were surprisingly low. Also, the differences between the groups were not significant.

The lack of knowledge of a vital national as well as international issue was astounding: 25 percent of the students could not identify North and South Vietnam on an unmarked map; 33 percent were unable to name a single ally fighting with the United States; less than 10 percent could name a single North Vietnamese leader; and 25 percent could not even name Saigon as the capital of South Vietnam. This was at the height of the war (1970), when over 40,000 young American men had lost their lives!

The conclusion is that there is hardly a correlation between knowledge and attitude, and that emotionality about a given issue is relatively *independent* of knowledge about the issue. It seems that the genesis of an attitude does not lie at the root of knowledge or ignorance, but at the root of emotional predisposition and basic orientation—a condition to be remembered when we look at the variously expressed attitudes of youth.

ECONOMIC ATTITUDES

For generations, Americans have modeled their ideas of success after the Protestant ethic, with occupational status, money, investment, and possessions as focal points. The new generation seems to have shifted its preoc-

---

[20]Hans Sebald and Rudolfo N. Gallegos, "Voices of War and Peace—What do They Know? Attitudes and Knowledge About the War in Southeast Asia," *Pacific Sociological Review*, 14 (October 1971): 487–510.

cupation to various forms of self-fulfillment, moving psychological demands to the forefront. The new emphasis has effected corresponding changes in their sense of obligation to friends, family, employer, and community. Materialistic-competitive attitudes of old have given way to a privatism that cultivates social and political isolationism and aims at the satisfaction of personal psychological needs. The genesis of this attitude must be sought not merely in temporary reactions to political events, but in postindustrial conditions that encourage and allow exactly this type of self-service.

The nadir of the work ethic was reached during the late 1960s and early 1970s, when only about half of young Americans believed that "hard work always pays off."[21] In the meantime, with economic hardship providing motivation, the work ethic has made a modest comeback.

Nevertheless, it is surprising that young Americans remain relatively unimpressed by the economic crisis and somehow seem to assume that some satisfactory economic security will materialize for them. This is not so much personal optimism as it is a new *philosophy of entitlement*. This evolution of "social rights" feelings manifests itself in such attitudes as students assuming that they are entitled to codetermine how to run a university. The desire "I'd like a creative and enjoyable career" becomes the righteous demand that "I am entitled to a creative and enjoyable career." The desire "I'd like a secure income" becomes "I am entitled to a secure income." While the tendency to feel righteous about one's desires is natural and has been with us for a long time, the equation of desire with right has grown significantly in the current generation. Whether the equation can be solved is of course another question.

Notwithstanding the new philosophy of entitlement, careerism is as strong as ever. Concentrating on a career is a natural function of privatism, which is typical of modern youth. Careerism is particularly evident among modern young women. Increasing numbers of them put the career first and having a family second; while wanting both, they want them in this sequence.[22]

RELIGIOUS ATTITUDES

While many American teenagers have declined in traditional religiosity with and since the counterculture, a new religiosity has evolved over the past fifteen to twenty years. The new form is a synthesis of Oriental and Western beliefs. From a historical perspective, the extent to which it has reached masses of young people in virtually all Western societies is an unprecedented

---

[21]Daniel Yankelovich, *The New Morality: A Profile of American Youth in the '70s* (New York: McGraw-Hill, 1974), p. 26.

[22]"Youth on the Move," *U.S. News and World Report*, January 5, 1981, p. 76.

development. Theodore Roszak, the chronicler of the counterculture, emphasizes in his book, *The Making of a Counter Culture,* that the infusion of Oriental philosophy was the unique benchmark of the twentieth-century counterculture.

One of the bizarre outcomes of the new religious-mystic synthesis is that teenagers who think of themselves as Christians now innocuously add the belief in reincarnation to their personal belief system—notwithstanding the lack of logic or compatibility. Survey data collected and currently analyzed by this author shows that up to 20 percent of college students classifying themselves as Catholics, Protestants, or nonspecific "Christians" believe in reincarnation, karma, and other Oriental or occult notions. The most interesting aspect of this development is that the young synthetic believers fail to be aware of the disparate cultural origins of the components of their beliefs and, in the process of trying to integrate the components, create a religious credo that is neither Christian nor Oriental. The making of this religious synthesis was an integral part of the counterculture and thus will be mentioned once more in Chapter 14.

These, then, constitute some aspects of the new cultural values as they are emerging with the young generation. One of the most noteworthy discoveries of the nationwide surveys was the involvement of working noncollege youth in the new cultural trends. In many instances, the traditional and almost customary distinction in attitudes and values between noncollege and college youth has been erased. This is a new development.

This large group (seven out of ten American youths are not college educated) may experience feelings of relative deprivation. Having absorbed the new cultural values of self-fulfillment, enjoyable careers, and the liberated work ethic, they may experience difficulties implementing them in their work life. Here is an example of the disharmony between cultural promises and social-structural limitations. Their comparatively less independent work life will offer fewer psychological rewards than that of college-educated people and is bound to exacerbate feelings of deprivation. This, indeed, may lead to a split within the youth population that may be more severe and may prove to be more dangerous to American society than the split between generations. American society may soon be confronted with demands on the part of young noncollege-educated workers for the same enjoyment and privileges as the college-educated workers, and the demands may aim at earlier retirement, shorter work weeks, more generous vacations, greater participation in industrial planning and management, and other methods of reducing the traditional monotony and powerlessness of the industrial worker. The future will most likely bring clashes between the new cultural attitudes and the built-in rigidities and limitations of the industrial work place.

It is interesting that most of the new values had their genesis in the counterculture of the late 1960s, traveled the customary route through the student population, and have now reached working-class youth. The legacy of the counterculture is now becoming visible in the form of pervasive new cultural attitudes and feelings that affect nearly all segments of the young generation.

COMMITMENTS TO THE AMERICAN WAY OF LIFE

A portion of the teenage population manifests values that are harmonious with adult standards. These values are not indigenous to the teen subculture but are expressions of motivation transcending the circle of peers. Justification for discussion of nonsubcultural behavior is twofold: (1) to render a more complete picture of youth in contemporary America and (2) to provide a contrast to subcultural behavior and values.

Student volunteerism manifests itself in civic concern, political interests, and various social services all across the nation. The commitments include a wide range of voluntary public service programs: tutoring disadvantaged children, assisting the poor with tax returns, entertaining and nursing patients in hospitals, clearing slums, cleaning up ecological disasters, and offering health care for the underprivileged.

Many volunteers work through such organizations as Candy Stripers, 4-H Clubs, Boys' Clubs of America, Tri-Hi-Y, Scout and Camp Fire groups, student governments, and various school clubs. Also, many of the service programs of the religious communities have been supported by young people, including Catholic, Protestant, Jewish, Mormon, and other religious organizations. Additional examples of value commitment include teams of medical, dental, and special-education students who go into impoverished Appalachia, giving and teaching badly needed health care; architecture students in many states who design playgrounds and summer camps for underprivileged children; law students in several states who give advice to consumers and teach ghetto children to use the law rather than to fear or despise it; language students at New York high schools who tutor Spanish-speaking people; and young people in many cities who help to maintain "hot line" telephones.

Federal organizations have attracted thousands of young Americans who seek fellowship and the experience to serve others. Thousands of young Americans have served as Peace Corps volunteers in many parts of the world to bring about technological innovations, and at the same time have respected the customs and mores of the natives. The success of the Peace Corps can be attributed to volunteers who (1) put into practice the American value of helpfulness; (2) feel enthusiastic about performing vital tasks, and (3) want to learn more about others and themselves.

Participation in VISTA (Volunteers in Service to America) has been widespread and constructive. A study by sociologist David Gottlieb showed that more than 50 percent of the participating youths felt VISTA had changed their career decisions, and 76 percent said their experience had increased their commitment to solve the nation's problems.[23]

Another federal organization is the Youth Conservation Corps, which pays young Americans a minimum salary and teaches them conservation techniques, often pitching them against forest fires and other disasters. Again, the participants accrue tremendous personal benefits, learn to get along with coworkers of varying ethnic, racial, and socioeconomic backgrounds, and often develop a lasting interest in a conservation career (forestry, fish and game administration, construction, and reclamation work).

The California Conservation Corps is a successful example. Its twenty-five work centers are sworn to the work ethic and are home to nearly 2000 men and women between the ages of eighteen and twenty-three. The CCC members work all day and then, if their literacy is poor, take classes at night— 35 percent do because they cannot read beyond a third-grade level. There are no alcohol, drugs, violence, or refusals to work. A member breaking the rules is discharged immediately. For respecting the rules corps members receive $580 a month (minimum wage), but must return $135 for room and board. The skills they learn include sandbagging hillsides to stem floods, smashing boulders to repair High Sierra trails, building recreational facilities, battling forest fires, erecting solar panels, and planting trees. In the early 1980s the CCC had a nine-month backlog of requests from all over California to do work that cities and counties could not afford. According to a study, for every dollar invested in the CCC, the state benefited $1.20. As a result, several other states are considering initiating similar projects of their own.[24]

The American Red Cross attracted four million unpaid youth volunteers during the early 1980s. Young people were found to work longer hours, had more energy, and were willing to take physical risks for helping people in need.[25] Tornado-devastated Grand Island, Nebraska, benefited from youth volunteers, some of whom put in 90 hours a week. A 1980 Washington, DC, fire left 140 people homeless, and youth volunteers helped set up shelter with food, blankets, and other needs. Blood-donor centers, hospitals, homes for the elderly, and recreation centers are regular recipients of youth volunteer help.

It would burst the frame of this chapter to try and enumerate all the service projects that young people make possible all over the nation. The above examples, showing American high school and college youth lending more than a token hand in many vital services, must suffice as illustrations.

Every experience has a variety of consequences. Some of the results

---

[23]New York Times Service (May 24, 1971).
[24]"The CCC," *National Wildlife*, 20 (February/March 1982): 17–18.
[25]"Youth on the Move," p. 76.

may simply be the achievement of material goals that projects set out to accomplish, but there are also unanticipated consequences, which involve psychological by-products. In the case of youth volunteerism, these by-products include:

Integration into society.   Service work is an integral part of society and provides a status rooted in the Establishment. This bonds youth to society and alleviates youth's feelings of alienation, showing them a side of society with which they can identify.

Self-testing.   The service experience is an example of the welcome respite that Erik Erikson called a psychosocial moratorium. Not only is the youths' delay in choosing a vocation socially accepted while they are serving in voluntary agencies, but there is a simultaneous opportunity to assess one's own resources, capabilities, and interests, and thereby apply a valid test to one's identity.

Independence.   Meaningful service is a constructive expression of independence from parents and provides a sound resolution of the adolescent conflict. Peace Corps returnees reported that they appreciated the high degree of responsibility given and the extent to which they could exercise their own initiative. It seems that volunteer service helps young individuals achieve social maturity, which otherwise might be delayed or not achieved at all.

Solidification of values.   Joining volunteer service is often a symptom of experimentation with alternative values. While many choose to pursue more competitive and materialistic values, those who focus on humanitarian values are able to test their chosen values through service projects. The outcome of the test often reinforces these values, and the person achieves greater certainty and self-assurance. This last point has been supported by a survey of returning Peace Corps volunteers who overwhelmingly (75 percent of the men and nearly 90 percent of the women) reported great satisfaction with their experience. While both sexes thought they had gained in self-assurance and outgoingness, the young women were especially convinced of having gained in the area of self-determination, greater curiosity in life, and effectiveness.[26]

The reasons American youth participate in service in the adult world involve a complex mixture of motivations. While the desire for service probably is a prevalent motive, healthy self-seeking, curiosity, interest in travel and

[26]Norma Haan, "Changes in Young Adults After Peace Corps Experiences," *Journal of Youth and Adolescence*, 3 (1974), 177–93.

other people, and a patriotic desire to improve the image of the United States are other elements.

SUMMARY

This chapter started the discussion on the dimensions of the subculture, focusing on the first one: unique values and attitudes. This dimension is so important and yields so much material with which to describe the teen subculture that an entire chapter was needed to discuss it.

The various aspects included (1) in-group values and concerns, especially as they reflect teenagers' needs for popularity and status among peers; (2) anti-intellectualism as a particularly significant attitude, for it bears heavily on the outcome of teens' educational experience; (3) the different roles that reference groups play in guiding teens' preferences in life, especially as they differ between the parental and the peer reference groups; (4) distinctions between girls' and boys' attitudes, with the former holding noticeably more emancipated attitudes than during previous years; (5) the curvilinear trend of parent-orientation on the part of teenagers over the past few decades, with high degree of parent-orientation during the 1960s, extremely low orientation during the 1970s, and again moderately high during the 1980s; (6) the clashes between parents' and teens' assumptions as to who may make the decisions in a number of realms; (7) the rise and decline of the New Sexuality, with AIDS as the new great peril; (8) some political attitudes that reflect unrelatedness between knowledgeability and basic emotional disposition concerning such important national issues as war and peace; (9) the new philosophy of entitlement, departing from the old Protestant Ethic and demanding economic security and psychological gratification as a "right" that society should guarantee; (10) the new religious synthesis between Christian and Oriental ideas, as a spiritual heritage, though mostly unawarely so, of the counterculture; and (11) various commitments in the form of volunteerism that are indicative that American youth is not suffering total isolation or alienation from the traditional American way of life.

The next chapter continues discussion of teenage subcultural dimensions.

13

Inside the Teen Subculture, Part II

This chapter continues the discussion on the basic dimensions of subculture, examining how teenage behavior expresses itself through them. The first dimension examined deals with argot, the linguistic quality of a subculture or a peer group, a quality which linguists and many sociologists consider of much deeper significance to the human mind than merely being a vehicle of in-group communication; in its most significant function it conditions the mind to think in certain ways and perceive the world through linguistically predetermined categories and nuances.

ARGOT

Argot is a "special language" reflecting the idiom of a particular group or social class. It is used by persons who interact over a considerable period and share special circumstances. One example of an argot is the language of the law. In the course of their professional associations, lawyers employ a language markedly different from ordinary speech. Other examples are the ecclesiastical language, the argot of thieves, the military establishment, miners, and medical doctors.

These sublanguages are adaptations to particular circumstances; most people speak only a few of them well and have little knowledge of others. The common characteristic is the function of adapting communication to the particular needs and interests of the group. Medical students have to learn a medical vocabulary; students of this textbook must be familiar with some sociological and psychological terminology.

Acquisition of an argot means more than just learning a new vocabulary. It signifies membership in the subculture to which the lingo is indigenous. It promotes group cohesiveness and insures privacy. It also stands for new knowledge and insights, both cognitive and affective.

Teen lingo is a special language. An adult listening to typical teenagers talk is aware of being a stranger to their ways of thinking. Iona and Peter Opie, in their study of several thousand English schoolchildren and their lingo *outside of the school,* discovered a lore and terminology of the children's argot that was largely unknown to the adult population.[1] Adults in England or the United States are not familiar with many of the terms and idioms of teenagers, and consequently not capable of cognizing and reacting in the same way. Usually, the only way to acquire the meaning is to join teenagers and participate in their activities—provided they accept the adult. Of course, many adults recall their own teenage days and may be able to roughly equate terms of today's argot with similar terms they used themselves, since many of the experiences, conditions, and circumstances of the adolescent phase have remained similar throughout recent generations.

The reason teenage argots evolve and are tenaciously maintained must be sought in their functions. At least six major functions can be discerned:

Shorthand device. Many of the terms of teenage argot are designed to save time when referring to complex processes in which teens are involved. For example, to spell out the fine details and connotations of what is meant when referring to a person or an event as "cool" would take considerable time and would slow down communication. The word evokes a clear concept for teenagers, saves time and effort, and preserves their unique style of communication.

Precise reference. In conjunction with the exposure to unique adolescent circumstances and conditions, the teenager finds that adult standard language does not include a sufficient reservoir of expressions to describe many of the ensuing experiences. Teenagers meet their need by modifying the general language with a battery of subcultural words that, in effect, lead to an argot. As a result, teenagers use words that are literally untranslatable into adult language because the empirical referents are unknown in the normal adult environment.

Teenage lingo can be vivid and clever. It can be sly enough to fool the

---

[1]Iona Opie and Peter Opie, *The Lore and Language of School Children* (Oxford: The Clarendon Press, 1959).

uninitiated, occasionally describing the diminutive without bothering to use the diminutive grammatical form. Many teenagers play their lingo like virtuosos, skillfully hitting just the right nuance of pronunciation and accompanying it with studied body language.

Not all experts credit teenage slang with discriminatory acuity. Dissenting opinions fail to take seriously the claim that teenage talk is profoundly discriminatory between nuances of meaning. For example, Cleveland Amory in one of his classic columns in *Saturday Review* dissected a number of frequently, if not ubiquitously, used teenage expressions. He concluded that they were practically interchangeable since their meanings hardly differed. What differed was merely the sound between the phrases as "with it," "far out," and "right on."[2] Similarly, Norman Cousins abhorred "slovenly speech . . . drained of color and distinction; [and] chopped-up phrases, relying on grunts and chants of 'you know' or 'I mean' to cover up a damnable incoherence."[3]

Status criterion.   Ardent and masterly use of argot functions as a prestige gauge among peers. Symbolic bluffs can be played out by clever use of argot, and the degree of their skillfulness often determines leader or follower status. Not unlike other species, it is not necessarily the physically strongest of the group (or pride, flock, covey, or herd) who assumes the leadership position, but the one who impresses most. This may be the lion in a pride who consistently roars loudest and most ferociously, or the teenager who uses subcultural lingo most cleverly. In both instances, no physical test of strength is necessary; status differentiation is accomplished through the use of signs or symbols.

Group solidarity.   When teenagers use or hear their "own" words, they are strongly reminded of their peer membership. Hence the use of lingo functions as a phonetic banner proclaiming association with the peer group.

Value statement.   Argot reflects what is important to members of the subculture. The index of argot is such a sensitive indicator of peer values that it can be used to determine the type of association of a given individual. Research found that although argot, peer values, self-reports, and police contacts measure different referents, they are so highly correlated that measuring argot by itself is sufficient to determine the nature (delinquent or nondelinquent) of a teenager's peer involvement.[4] The high correlation is due to the unity of argot, values, and behavior.

[2]Cleveland Amory, "Curmudgeon-at-Large," *Saturday Review*, October 2, 1976, p. 51.

[3]Norman Cousins, "The Decline of Neatness," *Time*, April 2, 1990, p. 78.

[4]Paul Lerman, "Argot, Symbolic Deviance and Subcultural Delinquency," *American Sociological Review*, 32 (April 1967): 209–24.

Linguists discovered that the significance to a group or a society of a given thing is indicated by the number of words they use to refer to it. The classic example is Benjamin Whorf's oft-cited observation that Eskimos have various terms referring to snow, while standard English has only one.[5]

Linguistic conditioner. Once firmly entrenched, value-laden argot greatly influences (if not determines) the way members of a group perceive their social environment and, most significantly, the way it patterns their behavior.[6] It is through this linguistic process that habitual and distinctive ways of thinking and behaving of the typical teenager can be explained to a significant extent.

Teenage argot, as based on the above six major elements, does not consist of a uniform body of linguistic expression for the American teen population. Rather, it is divided into sublingos, bearing out the principle that different environments and different needs call for different vocabularies. It is therefore no surprise to hear the teenage surfers of the West Coast use a set of expressions of their own. The psychedelic drug users have developed their own lofty vocabulary. So have reborn Christians. Inner-city and black youths cultivate a version of argot closely related to racial and ethnic lingos. The lingo of athletes illuminates another side of the youth scene. And the vocabulary of cross-country skiing would excite only the aficionado of SNS (Salomon Nordic System): "tail" (rear portion of the ski), "base" (running surface), "ultra tuning" (base preparation), "waist" (midsection of the ski), "camber" (the arc in the midsection), and so forth. Some of these vocabularies overlap and are understood, although not spoken, by most teenagers; they are like different dialects of one language.

Research discovered that familiarity with subcultural phrases also varied according to age and sex.[7] Frequency of argot use increases during childhood and reaches a peak during adolescence. Some topics prompt greater increases than others, with relatively small increases used in referring to money, cigarettes and smoking, and clothes and styles. These, apparently, are issues that do not change much in significance between the years of childhood and adolescence; thus no significant changes in style of references take place. However, there were large increases for topics concerning alcohol and drinking, popularity, and (particularly among males) for cars, motorbikes, and girls. Girls tended to use more argot references concerning clothes, styles, appearance, and being popular or unpopular. Boys and girls lin-

[5]Benjamin Whorf, *Language, Thought, and Reality* (New York: John Wiley, 1956).

[6]Gary Schwartz and Don Merten, "The Language of Adolescence: An Anthropological Approach to the Youth Culture," *American Journal of Sociology,* 72 (March 1967): 453–68.

[7]Edward A. Nelsen and Edward Rosenbaum, "Language Patterns Within the Youth Subculture: Development of Slang Vocabularies," *Merrill-Palmer Quarterly of Behavior and Development,* 18 (July 1972): 273–84.

guistically accentuate those aspects of their lives in which they are more involved and interested.

Although every generation of teenagers seems to adhere to an argot, its specific content, such as particular expressions, changes from one generation to the next. What was "keen" twenty years ago changed to "tough," "boss," or "dapper," and finally back to "keen"—all referring to roughly the same phenomenon. It would therefore be futile to present a glossary of current teenage lingo, since it would rapidly become outdated. The linguist Jacques Barzun reminds us of the ephemeral lifespan of argot and slang expressions: "Only 50 years ago, in a representative novel of college life called *The Plastic Age*, the young men and women say: isn't it the darb!, that's the bean!, pike along, pash, razz, bughouse, simp, smack for him, and other mysterious remarks. The very word *plastic* in the title of that book has almost lost its original meaning thanks to the chemical industry."[8]

How do certain teenage expressions spread and become part of the argot of the national teenage subculture? Often it is the entertainment media that are responsible. The argot of the "valley girls" of Los Angeles' San Fernando Valley suburbs went national when, in 1982, parody-rocker Frank Zappa and his fourteen-year-old daughter created a record with "Val-speak."[9] Teen slang, up to that time not heard in any other part of the country, suddenly was imitated by teenagers everywhere.

On a more local scene, teen expressions spread as a result of imitating the talk of a teen hero. Ghoulardi, a Cleveland television semicomedian of the mid-1960s, invented the word *Knif* (fink spelled backward) and began offering Knif buttons. The teenage television audience immediately accepted the neologism, spread the vogue, and bought thousands of buttons. In one show, Ghoulardi coined the expression "All the world's a purple Knif." The idiom spread throughout the region and became a popular saying of the teenagers. Similarly, he named a pet crow Oxnard, and subsequently Cleveland's teenagers called each other Oxnard.[10]

A deliberate experiment to generate argot was attempted by students in a Phoenix high school communications class to study the process of word acceptance. The students invented a number of new words (*thacka, verk, greazums, shigbig,* and *bahamas*) and spread them around their school in personal conversations and in announcements on popular teenage radio stations. After two months, the experimenters visited more than fifty English classes to assess the results of the experiment. They discovered that *bahamas*

[8]Jacques Barzun, *Simple and Direct; A Rhetoric for Writers* (New York, Harper & Row, 1975), p. 38. See also two witty essays on this topic: Sam Hinton, "Moribund Metaphors Rise Again," *Verbatim,* 5 (February 1978): pp. 3–4; Lance Morrow, "If Slang is not Sin," *Time,* November 8, 1982, pp. 91–92.

[9]"It's Like Tubular!" *Newsweek,* August 2, 1982, p. 61.

[10]"What Catches the Teen-Age Mind?" *Time,* September 27, 1963, p. 55.

(meaning "underwear") was the most widely accepted. *Verk* ("punk"), *greazums* ("French fries") and *thacka* ("turn on") followed second, third, and fourth in acceptance. The reactions of the students to the invented terms were varied, but several remarked that the words were "dumb and weird." The linguistic innovations did not get a firm foothold in the community, and within two months the use of the words died out.[11]

There is notable lack of research in the genesis of argot vocabulary, and the question of etiology awaits more exploration.

CHANNELS OF MASS COMMUNICATION

Subcultures need channels of communication to maintain a sense of solidarity. Communication can proceed through various media, the simplest being direct person-to-person communication and general milling on America's high school and college campuses. Some of the communication in such situations does not need to be verbal; mere appearance is sufficient to convey a sense of belonging.

However, direct interaction within these ghettos is not sufficient to sustain the type of nationwide subculture that American teenagers form today. Various mass media come into play to accomplish that. It is no empty slogan to say that the media become the message: TV, radio, magazines, and the lyrics of music bombard the teen population with ideas and values that become singularly adolescent property. The media and their contents become the world of the teenage subculture.

The role of TV is most likely primary in encouraging conformist ideas and styles. It could hardly be otherwise, since its influence can be felt in virtually every living room.

Equally tangible is the medium of the record industry, which conveys lyrics, the ideas of teen heroes, subcultural values, and common joy and pain. Whether heard on the radio or on the stereo at home, records constitute a form of mass communication. The power of this medium is illustrated by over ninety record companies who release more than 9,000 pop records, including a total of 52,000 songs, each year.[12] Closely related are the music festivals and rock concerts where many heroes appear in person.

A medium of considerable importance to teens is magazines. Influential teen magazines are available at newsstands and drugstores. They try to attract attention by "teen"-connoting titles like *Teen World, Modern Teen, Teen Time, Teens Today, Teen Parade, Seventeen,* and, simply, *Teen.* Other magazines have taken their titles from slang vocabulary and have assumed

[11]"Students Buy, Soon Forget Slang Words," *Arizona Republic,* January 1, 1968, p. 35.
[12]R. Serge Denisoff, *Solid Gold* (New Brunswick, NJ: Transaction Books, 1975).

that such terms as *Dig* and *Flip* would appeal to teenagers. A survey revealed that most of these magazines have limited circulations. Typical examples are *Dig,* founded in 1955, with approximately 171,000 purchasers, *Teen,* with about 245,000, and *Modern Teen,* with about 221,000. One reason for limited circulation is the fact that these magazines are aimed at specific readership within the teenage population. Some of them are for young teenagers, some for girls only, some for middle teenagers, others for older teenagers including college students. Still others have a certain socioeconomic slant, as for example *Seventeen,* which caters to upper-middle-class girls. One of the variables that distinguishes one category from another is the degree of sophistication, usually reflected in the style of humor. While publications for younger teenagers appear intense and humorless, a more relaxed style emerges for older readers.

The diversity of youth publications can be illustrated by juxtaposing *Kids,* "The Magazine by Kids for Kids," and *Rolling Stone,* a newsmagazine with some political sophistication. The former addresses teenagers younger than fifteen, and in 1975 prided itself on being the "only national magazine written and illustrated totally by kids for kids." Its objective is to give children and teenagers a medium through which they can learn from each other and about each other, and at the same time enjoy working on a common communication project.

The biweekly *Rolling Stone,* however, which addresses the eighteen-to-twenty-five-year-old category, emphasizes modern music, offers views on a lifestyle that is a combination of counterculture and rock world, and publishes "personal ads" reminiscent of the style of the underground press. It is a heavily politicized publication that used to be part of the "youth revolution."

These publications are probably at opposite ends of the spectrum of youth magazines. In between lies a colorful array of printed matter, all vying for a segment of the youth population.

The factor that remains constant throughout all youth publications, and that is of foremost sociological importance, is the magazine's function of conveying a sense of collective identity. This unity function can be illustrated by the large volume of "Letters to the Editor," in which young people describe themselves, talk about their problems, and give and ask advice. In addition, the magazines organize fan club and pen pal departments. The close communication within the world of peers is strikingly illustrated by the exchange of personal views and problems.

Besides its subcultural role, the magazine market is of course also big business. A recent newcomer to the teen market, *Sports Illustrated for Kids,* began publication in January 1989; it illustrates the point. The magazine distributed 250,000 copies of each monthly issue free to 1,200 underfunded schools, presumably to encourage literacy. At the same time, it took advantage of the lucrative commercial opportunity and within the first four months sold nearly $8 million in advertising to tap the estimated $5 billion spent annually by American youngsters aged 9 to 12—who, in addition to their own spending, heavily influence their parents' annual spending, which is estimated to amount to $45 billion.[13]

FADS AND STYLES

Peer-group belonging can also be signified through clothing, grooming, music, dancing, and lingo. While these media are timeless, the specific content can be quite ephemeral. And this is where the definition of fad enters the picture. Ray Gold defines *fad* as "markedly novel, trivial, and ephemeral behavior which spreads rapidly through whatever portions of society choose to adopt it. Fad behavior involves crowd-like imitation directed toward momentary circumvention of folkways and mores; it also provides substitute ways of expressing normatively thwarted emotions, such as status yearning and sexual drives."[14]

The major elements of the definition include ephemerality, novelty, triviality, creation of status criteria, identification with the in-group, compensation (for powerlessness, alienation, and sexual frustrations), and the security of "sameness."

These elements can be recognized in the fads of American youth:

1. Almost all youth vogues are *shortlived,* one displacing the next in rapid sequence. It is difficult to determine the average duration of a youth fad; it may range from a few months to several years.
2. For a behavior style to qualify as a fad, it must introduce a relatively *new* way of doing, speaking, grooming, or dressing. It must draw attention and be clearly distinguishable from both the preceding habit in the given behavior area and the customary folkway in the adult world.
3. The significance of the fad is usually *trivial* compared with the mores of society. This implies that fads are "odd" forms of existing folkways, normally within the range of the permissible and not violating the mores. However, one can find instances where society has reacted with a severity toward teen fads that ordinarily is reserved for punishment of infractions of the mores. For example, the vogue of shoulder-length hair for boys during the late 1960s was judged so negatively by some school administrators that suspension from school was threatened or actually enforced.
4. Teenagers use fads as *status measurements.* Fads allow them to achieve prestige in the eyes of their peers by conforming and excelling in observance of the vogue.
5. Teen fads are considered in-group property. This exclusivity is both crescive and deliberate; that is, fads spring up more or less spontaneously and are imitated by teenagers without particular scrutiny of their purpose. However,

[13]Laurence Zuckerman, "Tapping the Kiddie Market," *Time,* April 24, 1989, p. 74.

[14]Ray L. Gold, "Fad," in A *Dictionary of the Social Sciences,* ed. Julius Gould and William L. Kolb (New York: Free Press, 1964), pp. 256–57.

once established, a fad is jealously guarded and deliberately kept from adults. In fact, it has been observed that as soon as adults accept and imitate a teen faddist style, teenagers reject it. The fad is part of the *identification function* of the subculture, using the uniform appearance or habit as a boundary-maintaining device.

6. Fads serve as *outlets for thwarted creativity* and as compensations for various frustrations. An example would be rechanneling of sexual aggressiveness into harmless, "safe," and culturally tolerated behavior forms (for example, teenage dancing). Also, compensatory fads may harness hostility into tolerable forms of rebelliousness.

7. There is psychological, and maybe even physical, *security* in uniformity of looks and behavior patterns. The young can feel safely ensconced in a peer group, are not only accepted but also protected by sameness, and do not suffer feelings of standing out and being vulnerable to outside forces. Apparently fad adherence serves the same universal function as the uniform: submergence of the individual into a protective body of collective sameness.

With these theoretical background remarks in mind, specific areas of youth fads and styles are now examined.

Clothing.   Clothing is a visual means of communication. Teenagers are able to identify in-group members by their appearance. Once clothing has given a teenager an idea of the social identity of a person, he or she is able to pattern his or her behavior and responses accordingly. If a teenager looks like a teenager, he or she is likely to be treated as a teenager, just as a schoolteacher who looks like a schoolteacher is likely to be treated as a schoolteacher. It can therefore be concluded that clothing influences the type of social interaction a person experiences.[15]

Clothing fads serve three additional functions beside the main functions of identification and protective "sameness." First, they serve as a medium of rebellion against the adult world; second, they often afford utilitarian comfort; and third, they allow for aesthetic expression.

Of these functions the one signaling rebellion is of primary interest here. Rebelliousness of youth has varied roots. Partly it is the age-old hedonistic resistance to being reined in by cultural dicta. Such rebelliousness becomes particularly accentuated, virtually provoked, if the culture is low in self-confidence and proceeds with diffident permissiveness in socializing its young. This condition seems to prevail, unlike in simpler societies, in most postindustrial countries. Additional roots of rebelliousness are found in the many adolescence-creating conditions that age-segregate, frighten, and confuse teenagers vis-à-vis a complex social system.

[15]Social-psychological functions of clothes have been examined by such writers as John Brooks, *Showing off in America: From Conspicuous Consumption to Parody Display* (New York: Little, Brown, 1981); Hilda M. Buckley and Mary E. Roach, "Clothing as a Nonverbal Communication of Social and Political Attitudes," *Home Economics Research Journal*, 3 (December 1974): 94–102.

It appears that the hippie movement, emerging in the mid 1960s, was originally based on just such a rebelliousness. What took form was not a mere faddist mood, but a social movement; it rejected not only conventional clothing but also middle-class art, philosophy, and values. The hippies conveyed a studiedly worn and bedraggled image, usually including regulation denim, regulation ornamentation (medallions and the popular Indian beads), and regulation hiking boots.

Occasionally, a leading member of some teenage subgroup asserts his or her ideas, or the ideas of the group, by adding special adornments to his or her clothing. Examples were (and still are) T-shirts that sported slogans and/or pictures on the front and/or the back. It was a medium through which the wearer could express serious or not-so-serious whims, concerns, complaints, political and philosophical views, and anything else he or she wanted to proclaim ("Don't Bother Me, I Can't Cope," "Fly Me, I'm Henry," "Cocaine, The Real Thing"). Major department stores, as well as thousands of small T-shirt shops across the country, are cashing in on the craze that has consumed millions of decorated T-shirts.

This again brings to mind the commercial exploitation of style-conscious youth. A fundamental rule of Madison Avenue strategy is that "the younger you reach them the more impressionable they are" and the more lucrative the return in the long run. For this purpose a large portion of American advertising aims at preschoolers, which at the beginning of the 1990s numbered approximately 23 million, the offspring of the baby-boom generation.

A typical example was observable during the early 1990s when, rather suddenly, somber black became the preferred hue of children's clothes—from toddlers to teenagers. The trendiness was quickly supported, if not instigated, by the industry which unloaded tons of black garments from black leather jackets, unitards, leggings, jogging outfits, to shirts and blouses.[16]

Vestiges of many if not all fads are still found. Perhaps no fad ever dies completely; it only slumbers to be reawakened, and often goes through fascinating metamorphoses to reappear in a slightly altered form.

Music.   Unlike clothing fads, music styles have proved of longer duration. Popular music, once primarily an adult-oriented entertainment, underwent radical changes in the mid-1950s and emerged at the end of that decade as the almost exclusive property of youth. The driving force behind this development was a combination of musical styles that fused the sounds of country and western music and rhythm and blues into rock 'n' roll. This original musical hybrid sired a number of offshoots, such as rock, soul, psychedelic, bubblegum, and even punk music. Compared with the music of

---

[16]Elisabeth Snead, "Babies in Black," *USA Today,* November 29, 1990, p. 1.

the Roaring Twenties, which lasted only about ten years, the rock 'n' roll tradition has endured much longer.

Adult reactions to youth-oriented popular music were severe and swift in coming. Frank Sinatra condemned it as a "rancid-smelling aphrodisiac"; Samuel Cardinal Stritch compared it to "tribal rhythms"; Pablo Casals publicly called rock "poison put to sound"; a group of psychologists, mindful of teenagers' frenzied response to Elvis Presley, called it a "medieval type of spontaneous lunacy"; and a United States Senate subcommittee started investigations of possible connection between rock and juvenile delinquency.[17]

Part of the reason for the virulent reaction had to do with the personality cult, the riots by fans, and the sexual innuendos associated with the new music. Elvis Presley is indelibly associated with the early history of rock 'n' roll, having helped introduce the new style to the teen world. The initiation was ecstatic and often unruly, causing numerous fan riots—not only in this country but around the world. The authorities took a dim view of this novel lack of inhibition and restraint. This was also the time when scientists started to voice concern about the physiological effects of the onslaught of the up-to-then unheard-of-decibels characteristic of the new style; they exceeded 100 decibels in front of a rock band—equal to the noise level of a moon rocket blastoff.

Chubby Checker introduced the twist in 1960. For the first time since the decline of the jitterbug, American teenagers had their own dance. But about two or three years later the twist became obsolete and taboo for connoisseurs, and such free-style versions as the "Watusi," "hitchhiker," "frug," "jerk," and the "monkey" appeared.

Versions of rock 'n' roll spread and became an international fad. Some English musicians were particularly influenced by American rock 'n' roll and began to refertilize the American mainland with their own versions. In 1964 the Beatles appeared on the Ed Sullivan Show before a television audience of almost 70 million, received one of television's biggest publicity coverages, and embarked on one of the most successful show business careers in history. With the Beatles began the actual rock revolution that subsequently defined an emerging segment of the American population, literally financed a counterculture, spawned a $2 billion industry, and gave young Americans a common means of expression—a common music, a common language, and even a common dramaturgy with roles of heroes and martyrs.[18]

Rock style has not remained uniform over the years. The folk rock of Bob Dylan was different from the more sentimental eloquence of the Beatles

[17]"The Sound of the Sixties," *Time*, May 21, 1965, p. 85.

[18]Bernice Martin, "The Sacralization of Disorder: Symbolism in Rock Music," *Sociological Analysis*, 40 (1979): 87–124.

at the height of their career; the acid rock of the Rolling Stones became more sophisticated over the years; the mid-1970s brought a gentler variety of rock sounds with soothing melodies and reconciliatory lyrics; and the early 1980s saw the spread of the cacophonous, nihilistic Punk, New Wave spinoff, and heavy metal.

It may be this flexibility that made rock the viable musical form it turned out to be and that allowed it the retention of certain basic characteristics since the 1950s.

Throughout the 1980s and into the early 1990s, American pop music hardly strayed from generic rock—be it in the form of the more sonorous and Establishment-approved Michael Jackson or in the form of the vituperously snarling Ozzy Osbourne. But what seemed to prevail in the end was an overreaction to the heavy-metal groups, such as Motley Crüe with its satanic symbolism, and the Beastie Boys and the 2 Live Crew with their studied vulgarisms. Despite the fact that the vast majority of teenagers listening to heavy metal are more enthralled by decibels and rhythms than by lyrics, the words of which they rarely hear or understand, the infuriated moral right wing of American society called for censorship of what they considered unwholesome music and lyrics.[19]

In the meantime, the opinions have polarized once more. On one side are rallying the liberal attitudes, insisting that art forms are entitled to attack and to shock and disagree with the prejudices of the powers-that-be; on the other side are the defenders of traditional values (including such voices as John Cardinal O'Connor of New York and Senator Jesse Helms) who feel that adult society has the responsibility to educate, preserve human dignity, and point the way to constructive values. No doubt this sort of confrontation and dispute will rage on as long as we have adolescents with the indomitable inclination to challenge tradition and experiment with styles purposely intended to produce shock and outrage.

It must be added that rock did not remain the sole domain of teenagers—it captured a large adult following, adults who fervently, and in a sense uninvitedly, imitated the youngsters, forming an adult fan club that was unwanted and embarrassing to the teenagers. More than 40 percent of the "teen beat" records sold in the United States at one time were bought by persons over twenty years old. Teenagers complained about adult intrusion and felt that their "sacred" domain was invaded by uninvited parents.[20]

Dancing.   Obviously, this type of music was inseparable from dancing. The simple beat seemed monotonous to the musicologist and too loud for the sensitive, but it had a kinetic effect on dancers that proved compelling to

[19]Richard Corliss, "X-Rated," *Time*, May 7, 1990, pp. 92–99.
[20]"The Sound of the Sixties."

teenagers and adults alike. As a result, the discotheques, places of sustained rock 'n' roll rhythm and performing go-go girls, multiplied throughout the nation.

Dancing itself was a private choreography, enabling the dancer to be creative in steps, gestures, and motions. A partner was not really necessary since no bodily coordination between partners was needed. In essence, the partners danced by and for themselves, most of the time paying little attention to each other. Some observers called it a kind of "fertility rite," intended to alleviate the sterility of urban-industrial life.[21] However, it was "fertility rite" minus sexual contact—a paradox. On one hand, modern dance openly displays a degree of sexual suggestiveness that no other Western dance forms have dared before; on the other hand, it cooly refrains from any bodily contact with the partner—in fact, it studiously ignores the partner altogether. It sounds like a contradiction. Why do young Americans in an age of relative sexual permissiveness choose to dance in isolation?

Several explanations are possible and probably make a stronger point in combination. One is that our age of liberation is also reflected in dancing behavior. Each dancer is "doing his or her thing," expressing rhythms and improvisations without having either to lead or follow a partner. This development has been supported, on an unconscious level, of course, by the female's general surge toward emancipation. It may be part of her general revolt against having to follow the male lead. A second reason deals with American youth's increasing presumption that instantness in all things is possible, including dancing skill. Old-fashioned dance forms required learning and effort. Dancing apart from one another required none of the initially tedious synchronization of steps and movements. Modern dancing could be achieved instantly! A third reason assumes that, insofar as today's dancing has no rules, none of the participants are held responsible for "proper" steps and movements, in fact, none care about rules—it represents a miniature model of present-day society, characterized by anomie and alienation. Dancing, then, consists of an isolated, gyrating body unaccompanied by an identity.[22] Still another encouragement for this dance style comes from the awkwardness and inexperience that many adolescents bring to a situation where they have to intimately interact with the other sex. Rock dancing largely eliminates the embarrassment of sweaty hands, missing a beat, stepping on the partner's toes, and not knowing what to say. Dancing in isolation to music usually too loud for conversation lets the adolescent off the hook.

Given these "safety" factors, inhibitions all but disappear and raw, sensual expressions can be observed, the anatomical gyrations of the dancers

[21]Samuel Grafton, "The Twisted Age," *Look*, December 15, 1964, pp. 37–38.

[22]An interesting study, examining the parallelism between dance form and civilization form throughout Western history, has been completed by Gabriele Klein, *Über die Zivilisationsgeschichte des Tanzes*, Ph.D. Dissertation, Ruhr-Universität, Bochum, Germany, 1990.

sometimes frankly suggesting copulatory motions. Judgments concerning the sexual expression of rock 'n' roll dancing vary widely. Some parents condemn it completely; others think that some of the dances are acceptable. Analytical observers conclude that this type of dancing is "safe sex" for teenagers. Harvard psychiatrist Philip Solomon sees these dances as healthy outlets for youthful restlessness and as sublimated sexual desires.[23]

Studies have revealed that the predominant feelings experienced by young dancers are *release* and *abandon,* sensations that social scientists explain by the dancers' temporary retreat from the tensions and frustrations of being status-deprived adolescents. It was also found that teenagers considered adults at a discotheque to be trespassers and intruders.[24]

It seems, then, that rock 'n' roll music meets a number of teenagers' needs—their desire to express themselves bodily without limiting coordination to another moving body, without the need to converse, and without the fear of getting out of step. Moreover, erotic expressions pass with impunity and are rendered relatively inoffensive because of the dancers' abstention from physical contact.

Explained on the basis of these various functions, the longevity of rock 'n' roll is not surprising.

Hair style. The youth style fomenting extremely hostile reactions on the part of adults and frequently jolting authorities into severe countermeasures was young males' infatuation with long hair. Of all the fads and styles of the past decades, long hair seemed to offend the mores and the aesthetic sensibilities of the Establishment most profoundly. The new hairstyle was not perceived as a fad but as a perversion.

It is not ascertainable how and why the fad of long hair for boys developed. Coincidentally or causatively, the style started around 1964, when the Beatles exhibited their trademark, long hairdos, in the United States.

The controversy over long hair applied exclusively to boys. Girls, it seems, enjoy almost unlimited license to fashion their hair in any way they wish, whether short or long, bleached or colored, ribboned or loose. To be sure, feminine hairdos go through fashions too, but since, by societal consensus, *all* of their styles pass as acceptable, deviant or "odd" fads are rarely ascribed to them. The difference between male and female hair styles is that the former are described as fads or deviations and the latter as fashions. Fashion, by definition, is a style approved or at least tolerated by the larger society and should therefore not be equated with fad.

In their own defense, boys point out that long hair has been a symbol of virility ever since biblical days and confess that they often grow luxuriant tops

[23]"The Sound of the Sixties," p. 88.

[24]Lucille H. Blum, "The Discotheque and the Phenomenon of Alone-Togetherness," *Adolescence,* 1 (Winter 1966): 351–66.

because their girlfriends admire them. They complain that a more liberal policy on hair styling is necessary to provide them with an opportunity to create more individualistic appearances to compete with girls, who traditionally are allowed more styling alternatives concerning not only hair but also dress, colors, shoes, hats, scarfs, make-up, and jewelry. Finally, some youngsters added that they wear long hair simply because they *want to* and because they want to look *different* from others, especially adults.

As the opposition grew, so did the hair—and with a fascinating display of obstinacy, the style spread, persisted, and even eventually influenced adult hairstyles to some degree.

The path of the new style abounded with innumerable clashes—many comical, others sordid, and some outright tragic. Examples from the earlier period include the action by the dean of Cardinal Hayes High School in the Bronx, who met students returning for the fall semester with a pair of scissors and shortened the locks of several boys; the refusal of the Kenosha, Wisconsin high school to admit nearly 200 boys because of their long hair; the order by Federal Judge Richard Duncan of Kansas City that a young delinquent get a haircut because "I refuse to sentence anyone I can't see"; and hundreds of teachers who apparently agreed with the judge and refused to teach students whose visibility was obstructed by a surplus of hirsute resources.[25]

Some extreme outcomes include the cases of a California father, who, after a longstanding feud over his son's long hair, shot the boy to death in anger;[26] two Texas brothers, thirteen and sixteen, who fatally shot their father, an Air Force officer, when he was asleep because he objected to their long hair and refused to buy motorbikes for them;[27] and a fifteen-year-old Rolling Stones fan who threw himself to his death under a train after he had been forced to have his long hair cut.[28]

The controversy raged between students and school administrators, employers and employees, and especially between parents and offspring. It continued long after the rebellious counterculture had ceased agitation. By the late 1970s two convergent trends seemed to resolve the controversy: the public turned more accepting, and teenagers' insistence on long hair dissipated, possibly because adults had gradually imitated it to some extent.

But peace was to be short-lived. The last decade of the twentieth century to some extent reintroduced the issue. Increasing number of children and teenagers again insisted on long hairdos, particularly the male ponytail. Again tempers flared across the nation. As mentioned earlier, in one case a Texas school barred a boy from regular class attendance because of his

[25]Reported by Hal Cooper in an AP report (New York, December 3, 1965), and by "The Unkindest Cut for Student Moptops," *Life*, August 24, 1965, p. 4.

[26]UPI Report (April 24, 1971).

[27]UPI Report (November 10, 1972).

[28]AP Report (January 19, 1966).

7-inch ponytail. The disciplinary action was appealed by the parents of the boy, but the court upheld the school's decision. The mysterious vehemence shown by the authorities, especially school authorities, against boys' "deviant" coiffures turns out to be a battle without end.

Besides fad formation in the areas discussed above, there have been many additional youth fads that were minor, regional, or very short-lived. They range from the 1960s wave of wearing Nazi medals to the 1970s "streaking" (a craze perhaps short-lived but hardly minor) to the mock violence of Punk style in the 1980s. The examples mentioned in the above discussions are just that—examples. They are not intended to catalog the innumerable fads that have delighted, dismayed, or left this nation indifferent over the past decades.

SENSE OF SOLIDARITY

The youthful sense of solidarity emanates from all the dimensions discussed so far. There is really no separate dimension by which this *esprit de corps* can be measured; it is conveyed through teenagers' attitudes, values, lingo, music, dancing, fads, styles, hero worship, status criteria, and subcultural institutionalization.

Their attempts to exclude adults from their activities and styles is one of the surest indications of youth's solidarity. This exclusion is frequently manifested by discontinuing a fad or style as soon as adults begin to accept and imitate it. The habitual reference to the impersonal third-person "they" (the adults, the Establishment) as distinct from the first-person "we" and "us" is a constant reminder of modern youth's practice of setting itself apart from the larger society.

Teen lingo in general is a good measure of how much an in-group awareness prevails and reinforces a separate identity. A sense of solidarity almost invariably results in a distinct lingo. Worshiping common heroes is another indication of solidarity. Such individuals serve as focal points for youth's need to consolidate feelings and values. Heroes are often defined as such because they represent alternative or even deviant values from the larger society and thus function as exponents of the youth collective's sense of solidarity.

Certain drugs—it used to be marijuana—served as a means of cultivating a sense of separateness. Engaging in a deviant or illicit practice is a powerful means of generating a feeling of being a distinct collectivity, a community of the "persecuted," "rejected," or "victimized." Some social scientists used to liken the typical setting of marijuana smoking and the stereotypical demeanor displayed at such times (the ritualistic passing of the "joint" around the circle of the initiated) to the passing of the Holy Eucharist among the believers to merge the participants into a common body. Such illicit, deviant, or at least unique, rituals play a powerful role in substantiating a feeling of belonging to the in-group and accentuating a feeling of alienation from the outgroup.

An unfailing sign of the youthful sense of solidarity is the fervent cultivation of the generation gap by word and deed. The frustrations growing out of the socialization process find their consolidating and consoling culmination in solidarity, using adults as scapegoats. The sense of solidarity is greatly enhanced if the in-group can identify a common adversary or "enemy," since it enables the followers to focus their dissatisfaction away from the in-group interaction and directs frustration and hostility to an out-group target. This habit also clarifies group boundaries, an important condition for maintaining cohesiveness.

A significant step toward measuring the concept of solidarity was made by James A. Cramer and Dean J. Champion, who believed that solidarity refers specifically to the *affective content* of group relations and is made up of the positive emotional elements prevailing among the members of a group, resulting in sentiments of "we-ness."[29] The researchers determined a number of items that are best suited for measurement of solidarity. These items included such statements as "Troubles and discouragements just draw us closer," "When we have a job to do, everybody pitches in," "Members are close knit, stick together through thick and thin," and "Spend lots of time together because we prefer each other's company."

STATUS CRITERIA

Just as in the case of the sense of solidarity, status criteria must be deduced from various dimensions of behavior. What is counted as status and prestige is directly correlated with success in such behavior as fads, drug use, dating, use of teen argot, and material acquisitions that reflect and enhance subcultural belonging.

Hence, a pair of faded jeans is not just clothing, it is a symbol of belonging and status; having a date with a member of the opposite sex is frequently not a human encounter based on personal attraction but on prestige derived from being seen with a popular girl or guy; flaunting possession of the latest popular hits does not necessarily mean enjoying them as personally meaningful, but means letting others know that you are up on the latest productions; participating in marijuana smoking frequently has nothing to do with the enjoyment of the elusive "high" (that is as often faked as it is actually experienced), but has something to do with the recognition by

[29]James A. Cramer and Dean J. Champion, "Toward the Clarification of Solidarity," *Pacific Sociological Review*, 18 (July 1975): 292–309.

peers that you are "cool"; fads are often enjoyed not because they gratify the youth's need for creativity, but because they achieve the necessary "look alike" and the acceptance as "one of the gang"; speaking the argot is not so much preference as coercion to live up to peer expectations; and joining in the worship of certain heroes is not always an expression of liking or respecting that individual, but an attempt to impress peers and to appear knowledgeable as to who is "great" and who is not, what is "in" and what is not, and in general to convey an air of appreciating the presumed spokespersons of their generation.

All of these behavior forms are part of the fine art of followership and correlated prestige. Beyond a certain point of following, the skill of leading emerges; that is, the teenager with the biggest achievement in these behavior patterns earns the highest prestige and qualifies for leadership status. However, to achieve true leadership requires additional personality features.

The desire for status among peers often seems to influence the choice of friends among teenagers. Boys and girls sometimes choose, or are chosen, "friends" on the basis of prestige. It appears that the prestige of a teenager carries over to his or her associates and, thus, a "friend" actually functions as a status criterion. In most cases, however, a modified process operates whereby teenagers look as much at personality features as the prestige potential of a friend-to-be.

Status criteria differ from peer group to peer group and depend heavily on the teenager's orientation. Hence, behavior that would be prestigious among delinquent youths would be rejected by nondelinquent youths. Significant items of prestige among middle-class youths might be different from those of working-class youngsters and, of course, the racial and minority groups imbue their young with still other status criteria.

However, certain items are used throughout most, if not all, groups to assess a teenager's standing. One of them is clothing and appearance. Research found that urban high school girls used these aspects in deciding whether new girls qualified as personal friends and as group members. However, when they discussed old friends, the question of appearance receded and personality, friendliness, and similar interests and involvements became more important. It followed, then, that once the appearance of a newcomer was assessed and a decision to pursue or not pursue a friendship was made, appearance was more or less taken for granted.[30]

The study also discovered that girls are able to infer socioeconomic background by the way a peer dresses. Girls in lower socioeconomic classes were found to be "improperly" dressed by more affluent girls and not accepted into certain groups. In most instances, the rejected girls were well

[30]Joanne B. Eicher et al., *A Longitudinal Study of High School Girls' Friendship Patterns, Social Class, and Clothing* (East Lansing, MI: Michigan State University Agricultural Experiment Station, 1974), p. 20.

aware of the ostracism but maintained their own ideas about clothing and appearance. They eventually formed their own groups, cultivated their own clothing styles, and thus avoided isolation.

The consequences that follow from this status behavior are of considerable significance to educators and social workers. The status criteria of clothing and appearance separated the high school girls to the disadvantage of students in lower socioeconomic classes. "The situation in the school was almost a case of 'never the twain shall meet,' so that girls were denied opportunities to learn ways different from those they had grown up with.[31] This implies that youthful status behavior reinforces and perpetuates the status quo. It is suspected that such labeling behavior contributes more to the isolation and eventual dropping out of lower-class youth than difficulties that are purely academic.

Being rejected by peers must be one of the most tragic experiences for a young person. That this occurs on the basis of "first impression" is particularly unfortunate because it means the decision of accepting or rejecting is not being made on grounds of more important factors. The moral of the story is that if teenagers from different social backgrounds want to be accepted by one another, they must learn to understand each other's views regarding dress.

There were some age differences, however, in the approach of choosing a friend. Ninth-graders considered personality as the most important basis on which a given girl would be judged. But twelfth-graders put personality in second place and considered "looks and appearance" as the first standard. These older teenagers relied more heavily on "first impression" and believed it gives them a realistic assessment of lasting reliability.

It is interesting that the opinions of teenagers concerning the criteria of popularity and what is sought in a friend have hardly changed over the past decade. The 1974 Eicher study (mentioned above) and the 1982 Sebald survey (see section on in-group values in Chapter 12) have come up with basically the same rank order of criteria.

Researchers have noted that determined status-seeking girls sometimes use sex as a means to enhance their prestige. They try to attract high-status boys for dates, and to do so they occasionally engage in rather intense petting without endangering their "reputation." The interaction consisted of a game of providing just so much sexual favor for so much prestige by association. On the other hand, boys' status behavior was found to primarily consist of drinking and dating practices through which "manhood" was tested and proved. In conjunction with the drinking behavior, a sort of daredevil approach to the problem of the purchase of beer or liquor developed, and accomplishing the illicit purchase was considered an act of cleverness and

[31]Ibid.

"having guts" that added to the status among peers. Such a purchase (with faked IDs or lying about one's age) was a battleground reserved for the courageous only, and the risk to the boys' self-esteem was great. If a boy revealed that he was afraid of showing a false ID or otherwise bluffing his way through demands to prove his age, he lost face within his peer group. This was the acid test of "keeping your cool." Any boy who failed to rise to the occasion had his claims to "coolness" ruthlessly deflated by his peers.[32]

Status expectations differ among groups. There is no *one* system with perfectly hierarchically arranged status positions for all. Studies seem to indicate that young people perceive of status as a set of ranked, slightly ambiguous prestige categories that are internally differentiated. This can be explained by pointing first to a horizontal dimension that is an array of different lifestyles heavily influenced by the teenagers' socioeconomic background. Each lifestyle differs somewhat in dress, speech, interpersonal demeanor, and prestige in the community (boys in a lower-class neighborhood, girls in a predominantly middle-class high school, college coeds, and rock 'n' roll groupies). Second, a vertical dimension can be visualized within each group according to which the members are assessed and status-ranked. While the horizontal dimension is qualitative, dividing teenagers into distinct categories that might be judged delinquent or nondelinquent, lower or upper class, the vertical dimension is a quantitative measure ascribing more or less popularity to a member of the group.

The process of status attribution is complex. Status does not simply derive from objective talents and characteristics, such as a boy's athletic ability or a girl's physical attractiveness. Teenagers acquire esteem in a variety of contexts and obtain subcultural validation by adherence to their group's standards. An element that seems to run through all modern peer groups is the presentation of oneself as "cool." To the extent that "coolness" becomes a part of a teenager's behavioral routine, peer acceptance and admiration will rise—and that, after all, is what status among teenagers is all about.

HERO WORSHIP

Most identifiable subcultures come equipped with leaders. Yet, when we look at the teen subculture in America on the national level, we find leadership conspicuously absent. Instead, heroes abound who are idols of the masses, passive figures of the world of entertainment, whose ability to lead is negligible and whose vision is myopic. With rare exceptions, they are profiteers cashing in on fads and styles that they have not created. Many of them

---

[32]Schwartz and Merten, "The Language of Adolescence," *American Journal of Sociology*, 72 (March 1967): 453–68.

become millionaires not because they are particularly talented or have something to say but because they were lucky enough to get into the limelight of the world of entertainment. This individual becomes the target of the teenagers' emotional accolades and their need for heroes. The result is hero worship—which is not to be confused with following a leader.

There are, however, certain segments of the youth population that have, or had, leaders. Among them are the spokespersons of the counterculture, the political activists and radicals (Joan Baez, David Harris, Jerry Rubin, Pete Seeger, Bob Dylan, Jane Fonda, and others) who stood up against the Establishment and in some cases became martyrs for their causes. There are also the leaders of the local teenage scene: the leaders of cliques, gangs, and crowds who rally their followers in the community, neighborhood, or school.

The present discussion focuses on the general, nationwide teen subculture and, because of the peculiar hero-orientation of the American teenagers, deals more with heroes from the entertainment world than leaders in the real sense of the word.

Hero worship is a timeless indulgence. It appears to be such a deep-seated need that if no real heroes are available, supernatural ones tend to be invented. This need is observable in both adults and teenagers. Depending on the cultural milieu, the hero may be a military figure, a political personality, an outstanding athlete, or a popular entertainer. Commensurate with the American ethos, which cherishes popularity more than Spartan values, teenagers in the United States exhibit special admiration for entertainers, singers, actors, and musicians. The worship of these popular heroes often proceeds in overt demonstrations. At concerts, cheering crowds manifest their loyalty; in teenagers' bedrooms, pictures on the wall silently testify admiration; in record stores, sales reveal listeners' adoration; and dress and hair styles often imitate popular idols.

The attractiveness that heroes have for the masses is composed of a number of complex elements. Some of them have been verified by research, and some have been assumed by theory. Major gratifications American teenagers derive from hero worship include:

Romanticism. Romanticism refers to emotions and attitudes that usually are insufficiently based on facts. The appeal of romantic emotions lies in the heroic, remote, mysterious, and idealized. This emotional disposition can be related to a number of areas in life, but it is most frequently observed in connection with attitudes toward love relationships. Teenagers are particularly prone to adhere to romantic perceptions of the male-female relationship because they lack the experience of the older generation and are reluctant to accept adult standards. As a result, teen heroes can easily capitalize on the romance hunger of their followers, reinforce unrealistic perceptions, and become tangible foci of romantic identifications.

Teenagers see in their heroes the incarnation of many of their fondest dreams and desires. Since the unrealistic nature of the dreams makes imple-mentation in the life of the individual teenager impossible, they are trans-ferred to a person whose popularity seems to attest to their success in materializing such dreams. Popularity is perceived by the teenage followers as the *carte blanche* of all dreams and hopes.

Sex and fetishism. Expressions of hero worship have frequently been interpreted as substitution and sublimation of sexual desire whereby some material aspect of the popular hero, such as his or her clothing or hair, becomes a fetish. In other words, a fetish is a tangible substitute for the coveted person that provides a degree of erotic gratification. A mild, usually socially acceptable, and widespread fetishistic practice is collecting and/or pinning up pictures of heroes. Expressions of this romantic adulation can be gleaned from almost all teen magazines, which provide fan departments, print pin-ups, and advertise "real photos of rock stars."

American teenagers have established by now an impressive history of fetishistic pursuits (often exploited by business). Frankie Avalon, an earlier rock 'n' roll balladeer, was attacked by his fans numerous times. Once, teenage girls pulled the shoes off his feet; another time, a crowd of excited teenagers trampled him and sprained his back in an effort to touch him and tear off pieces of his clothing.[33] On their 1966 return to the United States, the Beatles were beleaguered at their hotels by hundreds of shrieking girls. A teenager who let it be known that she had a lock from the head of one of the Beatles was mobbed by the other girls who wanted to touch and kiss it. At numerous performances, the Beatles' music and lyrics were completely drowned out by the screaming teenage audiences, who were more interested in seeing than hearing their idols. Several hotels at which the Beatles slept turned the teenagers' fetishistic desires into lucrative business by cutting up and selling square inches ($1.00 a piece) of the bed sheets used by the heroes.[34] A similar fate awaited the sheets used by the Rolling Stones at a 1973 stopover in New Zealand, where businessmen purchased them to make them into souvenir handkerchiefs and shirt panels.[35]

Some sexual expressions are less substitutional and more direct. Paul Dean of the popular rock group Loverboy was asked how it felt to be a sex idol for youngsters who aren't old enough to drive a car. "Well, I've got to laugh when a 13-year-old is crying, 'I love you, I love you, I love you.' I say, 'No you don't.'" According to Dean, then she screamed even louder, "Yes, I dooooo!"[36]

[33]Thomas B. Morgan, "Teen-Age Heroes: Mirror of a Muddled Youth," *Esquire*, March 1960, pp. 65–73.

[34]UPI Report (Chicago, August 13, 1966).

[35]AP Report (Auckland, New Zealand, March 22, 1973).

[36]Lynn Pyne, "Rock Group," *Phoenix Gazette*, December 7, 1983, p. G1.

Dean added an observation of sociological acumen: "But I understand what's going on, because they don't have anything in their lives and they have this fantasy that they built up that we are superhuman and the perfect person, you know: 'This guy is unbelievable, how could I love anyone else?' "[37]

The scene is reminiscent of the so-called groupies, who constitute a special institution of teen subculture and are hero worshipers who, according to the simple definition of Frank Zappa (leader of the rock group called the Mothers of Invention) are "girls who go to bed with members of rock 'n' roll bands."[38] These girls are also known as "rock geishas" and engage in sexual activities with rock stars and their immediate entourages. Groupies cultivate numerous relationships, and it is not uncommon for them to extend sexual favors to several members of a group within one night. An internal status system has developed among the groupies that largely depends on which famous bands they can list as their "friends." Many of them travel with bands, staying with one for a week, then changing to another. These girls are a small minority. For the rest of the masses of teenagers, their heroes remain more distant, romantic figures with whom they stay in touch by various fetishistic practices.

Crowd ecstasy.   Heroes often serve as catalysts for the type of mass behavior that allows abandon and release. Youthful rambunctiousness and excitement find an outlet when heroes perform in front of large teen audiences. Concert settings give the young an opportunity to physically express exuberance by screaming, touching, and moving rhythmically. Being in a mass of peers is a visceral experience, not unlike dancing, and offers an outlet for tension. The behavior at teen concerts is governed by completely different rules (and maybe needs) than that at adult concerts. While the heroes perform, the audience is not expected to remain silent and motionless; band members are not usually disturbed by the noise their appreciative audience makes.

A good part of the behavior at such rallies is not intended as listening but as a testimony of *belonging.* A number of physical expressions of "worshiping," such as screaming, jumping, and even "fainting," have a mutually reinforcing effect in a crowd situation. The reinforcement is due to the rewards derived from the prestige assigned to such peer-approved and peer-encouraged actions. It is interesting that many vociferous teenagers are not looking at their heroes on such occasions, but at each other, apparently to make sure that they are seen screaming. Back rows usually do not scream,

---

[37]Ibid.
[38]"Manners and Morals," *Time*, February 28, 1969, p. 48.

but, merely applaud conventionally, since they are outside of the field of observation.

An interesting example of crowd-reinforced imitation comes from the early days of the rock 'n' roll era. Frankie Avalon's presence and singing would always induce some girls to faint—or to pretend to. It became the thing to do. During a Milwaukee presentation by Avalon, twenty-one girls ostentatiously fainted. At another performance on television, when Avalon sang "Boy Without a Girl," the camera showed a number of sobbing teenagers. *From then on,* this behavior became a routine and was imitated whenever Avalon appeared and sang that particular song.[39] Avalon's record was broken in 1975 when 250 young girls fainted ritualistically at a concert given by a Scottish group, the Bay City Rollers.

Michael Jackson exerted similar magnetism when he caused "fainting" on an international scope. When, in 1988, he performed in Vienna, Austria, approximately 130 girls (not one boy) fainted in homage to the U.S. superstar at a concert attended by 50,000 devotees.[40]

The fascination with the bizarre and the absurd.   Humans of any age category can be turned into a captive audience by the bizarre and the absurd. The heroes of modern American teenagers cultivate this fascination by a freak style that during previous epochs was confined to the semiunderground adult theatres à la Marquis de Sade. Today's teenage version is carried out by some (heavy metal) rock groups, wallowing in the macabre and the ghoulish. A particularly virulent form of combining the bizarre with the violent was the Punk style. Another version that never seems to lose its popularity, and one not totally deprived of humor, was/is the Rocky Horror Picture Show, a midnight movie of delight to young aficionados of the bizarre.

Such mid-1970s freak heroes as Alice Cooper, Mick Jagger, and Elton John devised freak gimmicks to win teen attention that included transvestic, surrealistic, sadomasochistic, and macabre appearance and performance. Among the most notable acts was Cooper's ritualistic suicide fake in front of shrieking teenage audiences with the tragic consequence of a number of imitations that proved fatal to teen fans.

Many teen aficionados are attracted to the freak shows because they find them "scary," "weird," and they make their skin "tingle" with excitement. Is the type of teenager attracted to the freak style an exceptional youth, characterized by deviant tendencies, or the quite normal youth who simply responds to the unusual, the bizarre, and the grotesque? The best one could do at this time is to reiterate that attraction to the bizarre is a phenomenon universal to all humans regardless of personality tendencies. However, one might hypothesize that persons with serious personality problems may go a

[39]Morgan, "Teen-Age Heroes," p. 65.
[40]"Jackson-Spannung war zuviel," *Eifeler Volkszeitung,* June 4, 1988, p. 5.

step further than merely enjoying the "weird and tingling" sensation that the vision of such fare induces and try to imitate the grotesque in their personal lives.

Identification.   A hero is a ready model for imitation. He or she provides the "worshipers" with an image to which they can aspire. It must be noted that the first-class teen hero is a recording star and not a politician, business-man, or intellectual. Compared with the entertainer, even the top athlete is only moderately admired. It has been suggested that the reasons for this preference are the similarity in age and ability of many entertainers to the crowd-oriented teenagers. It seems easier for teenagers to identify with someone who is crowd-oriented like themselves, and is mediocre, "humble," and nonserious. Teenagers, due to the adolescent experience, need collective protection within which they feel safe from and invisible to adults. They are afraid of exposing themselves individually to evaluation and criticism, and they project this negative feeling onto personalities who are outstanding. Their aversion is aimed at the politician for his or her *principles,* the busi-nessperson for his or her *enterprise and success,* and the intellectual for devotion to the *hard truths*—all representing values that tend to separate the individual from the crowd, expose him or her, possibly make him or her unpopular and therefore insecure. Teenagers try to escape exposure and seek the security of the crowd. They prefer virtues of conformity, mediocrity, and sincerity. Through their heroes, songs, and dances they can express them-selves without leaving the secure environment of the group.

The Beatles, for example, were admired for their simplicity and sin-cerity. When asked whether they liked being idolized, they answered "we just like the money." Another important element that made the Beatles loved and admired heroes was the fact that they conveyed a nonserious image. By doing so, they enabled their fans to relax and meet them as equals. The Beatles admitted publicly that they did not think much of their own music but that they had "fun" entertaining and getting paid for it.

Another condition that induces identification with many of the teenage heroes is based on the subtle rivalry that girls introduce between the idols and their boyfriends. Directly or indirectly, boyfriends are frequently urged to look and act like teenage heroes, and they are rewarded, if they are successful in a certain degree of imitation, with some of the type of admiration that is ordinarily reserved for popular idols.

Heroes as "messengers."   Heroes are significant others who have influ-ence on teenagers' thinking and value-orientation. However, of all the func-tions American teen heroes perform, extending values is probably the least effective. The need to express and release emotional dispositions and the use of the hero as a catalyst for that purpose by far supersede the need for more rational formulations and value-orientations.

Nevertheless, one could classify some of the early "folk rock" heroes as advocates of certain values of adolescents—probably of the *older* and more intellectual adolescents. One of the best known was Bob Dylan, a young poet-songwriter who achieved popularity with such songs as "Tambourine Man," "Subterranean Homesick Blues," and "Like a Rolling Stone." His songs criticized social conditions and focused on civil rights, the threat of nuclear war, and the war in Vietnam. Although his singing made him a millionaire, he maintained an image that teenagers found acceptable and imitable. To his fans, the scruffy hair, wrinkled shirt, and faded jeans meant that he was one of them.

Others like Joan Baez, Judy Collins, Joni Mitchell, and Peter, Paul and Mary followed the lead of Dylan, expounded social commentary, and showed talent in distilling the moods of their time. The recurrent themes in their creations were justice for all, peace, brotherhood, love, sensitivity and the condemnation of urban-industrial conditions. Their collages pieced together images of tension between the generations, the loneliness of the young in an anomic society, the bittersweets of young love, the search for a stable and secure reality, and the fear of the fleeting and blurred meanings of our age.

While the charisma achieved by these heroes made their message credible to many, the majority of young teen fans approached the message more from the visceral, musical, and hero-worship angle, and the folk-rock following was never as broad as the rock 'n' roll enthusiasts in general. The political and philosophical messages of the protest heroes, however, made an impression on the older and more serious young population and contributed to countercultural development.

The early heroes of the American youth scene, especially as they were part of the counterculture, are ancient history to today's teenagers, who are much more interested in the immediacy and the sensateness of entertainment figures. If one would distill the late-twentieth-century American-teen-hero phenomenon to its core, the final essence would be that it must be "fun." And "fun" is antithetical to a serious value statement, because it would require thinking, self-examination, and it would set up demands of standards of behavior. Such demands are a threat to most teenagers. "Fun" is non-threatening because it leaves hedonism undisturbed. (The "fun syndrome" in American society is, of course, important to both teenagers and adults. Curiously enough, it has escaped serious analysis by behavioral scientists, though its exertion on American life is powerful.)

SUBCULTURAL INSTITUTIONALIZATION

All societies institutionalize the functions deemed necessary for taking care of basic needs. This means that behavior aimed at satisfying such important needs as sex, reproduction, training of the young, trading, protection, order, and leadership is not permitted to occur at random or by idiosyncratic preference, but is prescribed by the cultural blueprint, and is implemented, respectively, by marriage, family, education, business, police or the military, and government. Members of society must comply with specific structures, such as the monogamous relationship, the family group, the organization of public schools, and so forth.

If the main culture fails to provide an institutional framework for the gratification of a certain need, subcultural institutionalization may develop to facilitate fulfillment of the need. Subinstitutionalization is probably the most telling indicator of how far a collectivity has matured into a subculture. These new structures may or may not be in conflict with the larger society, may or may not totally replace the Establishment's procedure, and may be seen as deviant or as merely supplemental.

American adolescents have begun to develop several institutions of their own. By doing so, they manifest, more convincingly than by any other means, their attempt to be independent of the adult world. The manifestations can be recognized by regularities in behavior that indicate a surprising degree of organized social structure within the youth collectivity. It is the enmeshing of young people in their own segregated social structure that is of utmost sociological pertinence, because a structural proviso makes for regular patterns of social behavior.

Some subinstitutionalizations have already been mentioned. The whole area of youthful entertainment, including music, songs, dancing, and festivals, can be called institutions of the young. Of similar nature are teen magazines that promote hero worship and, most importantly, serve as channels of mass communication. A few more subinstitutions are:

Dating. Dating is an example of a supplemental institution that is not necessarily in conflict with adult norms and institutions but rather defines the culturally accepted meeting ground between boys and girls and patterns their interaction. To a large extent, however, the specific norms and expectations are defined by the young people themselves, and certain aspects of the subinstitutional behavior border on the "forbidden," such as heavy petting and premarital sexual intercourse. Such behavior adjuncts exemplify the need fulfillment of young people who cannot find a legitimate outlet for sexual desires within the institutions of the Establishment, since such participation is reserved for adults and presumably limited to the institutions of marriage and the family.

Cohabitation. We call it cohabitation when a boy and a girl or a man and a woman live together without being married. Generally, American society frowns on this type of arrangement, and, technically speaking, several states have laws against it. The nature of cohabitation differs on a wide spectrum; it can range from an ephemeral to a lasting relationship; from a noncommittal to a committal relationship. Since the U.S. Bureau of the

Census defines as cohabitation already such a short episode as living together for one weekend, a significant portion of American teenagers have had cohabitational experiences before they get married. In a sense, this amounts to subinstitutional behavior and falls far short of the approved main institution of marriage.

It has been speculated that one of the reasons increasing numbers of American youth experiment with cohabitation is their reluctance to make marital commitments in the face of perennially witnessing the breakups of adult marriages, possibly including those of their own parents.

Another reason, probably a more common one, is the young's fear of losing their independence and having to assume responsibilities. Such a loss would be out of line with the preponderant fun-morality that generally governs sexual activities. To many, whether they admit it or not, cohabitation is primarily a convenient sexual relationship that lasts as long as there is "fun" in it.

This is not to deny the benefits of a premarital moratorium that young people can use to get to know each other and to eventually base a more committal decision on such knowledge. The subinstitution of cohabitation can be used or abused as can any other institution; its most dismal abuse stands out when partners enter it with different motivations and objectives, so that sooner or later one or the other party gets hurt.

Social scientists who have foreseen the modern trend and the need for a marital-halfway institution have suggested the usefulness of an arrangement that provides the secure framework of a dyad without the presumedly absolute commitment of a marriage. Margaret Mead, for example, long ago proposed two different types of marriages, one for people who want to enjoy each other's company without children and the other for people who want children and plan the conventional marriage-family.[41] Under the "individual marriage," young people could enter and leave the unions relatively freely with a minimum of obligations to each other. In a sense, the modern cohabitational arrangement represents this idea (except that Mead had some contractual and legal agreements in mind) and provides sexual gratification, companionship, and, assuming the woman is employed, two contributors to the household expenses.

Commune.   A substitution for traditional family life was and, in a few instances still is, the commune. This subinstitutional structure experienced an upsurge during the counterculture years, but has noticeably receded since then. Similarly to cohabitation, there used to be a wide range of different types, but all had one thing in common: the legal and emotional commitments were at a minimum, with no legal pressure to enter or stay. The

---

[41]Margaret Mead, "Marriage in Two Steps," in *The Family in Search of a Future*, ed. Herbert A. Otto (New York: Prentice-Hall, 1970), pp. 75–84.

commune is a subinstitution ideally suited to accommodate young people who prefer a moratorium on marital and familial commitments and yet desire some of the benefits of the equivalent adult institution such as: (1) the experience of human intimacy, (2) a feeling of belonging, (3) a feeling of security, physical as well as psychological, (4) a chance to satisfy curiosity about other people, and, most prominently, (5) sexual gratification on a regular basis.

In summary, the subinstitutions of dating, cohabiting, and communal living meet the needs of modern youth who shy away from total self-surrender and hesitate to enter into the symbiotic fusion found in traditional marriage. Many apparently are no longer willing to give themselves completely to one person and no longer expect to get all of the emotional satisfaction they need from a single lifelong partner.

Business.   Ever since the counterculture, young Americans have been trying their hands at their own business ventures. They are establishments run by youth for youth; some are legal and others illegal. The former include stores dealing in clothes, jewelry, candles, records and tapes, posters, and antiques. In the vicinity of college campuses can be seen book exchanges, small boutiques, food co-ops, vegetarian restaurants, and often small workshops manufacturing furniture, leather goods, glassware, ceramics, and art work of all sorts.

Hovering between legality and illegality are shops that sell drug paraphernalia. The 1980s witnessed an onslaught of legislative bills which outlawed the sale of articles ostensibly meant to accompany or facilitate the use of illegal drugs.

Clearly illegal is the subinstitution that procures and often grows or manufactures illicit drugs, including marijuana, heroin, cocaine, and so forth. An intricate subterranean network, with well defined roles at various levels of procurement (including the roles of producing, smuggling, transporting, and retailing), caters to the desires of young and not so young Americans — desires not covered by the legitimate institutions of society.

The automobile.   The role of the automobile in the lives of American teenagers has been cited by some writers as another example of subinstitutionalization. While having or needing a car is, of course, not an exclusive youth syndrome — on the contrary, it is typically an adult pattern — the *purpose* for which teenagers use and desire "wheels" defines it as subinstitutionalized behavior. Teenagers use the car not so much as a utilitarian appliance but to promote status, as compensation for the feeling of powerlessness, and to make dating possible.

The role of the car can be best understood in terms of its functions for the teenager. Besides providing transportation to school and work, the car usually serves additional functions:

1. Owning or having regular access to a car is *prestigious* in the eyes of peers. The newer or more customized the car, the higher the prestige. A teenager may spend all savings on customizing and maintaining a car according to what his or her peers consider admirable.
2. The car is of great *instrumental* importance for dating and related activities. For the teenage boy, having a car is not only prestigious but usually imperative when asking a girl for a date. It allows for mobility and privacy, providing American teenagers with the most frequent setting for sexual experimentation.
3. For some boys a car is a *hobby*. In fact, researchers discovered that the most frequent hobby of high school boys was "working on their cars."[42]
4. Driving an automobile can provide a *sense of power*. Since the adolescent experience includes a feeling of restriction and powerlessness, some teenagers use the car as a symbol of freedom and escape from adult control. Psychiatrist J. M. Murray hypothesized that driving a powerful automobile allows teenagers to express frustration and hostility with a minimum of risk of punishment and often with complete anonymity.[43]
5. In some communities, *cruising* has evolved as a ritual on wheels, whereby hundreds of cars parade down a main street on certain nights, usually weekends. It is a noisy and odorous show of subcultural strength, whereby prestige can be measured on the basis of type and look of car, contacts/dates established, and a general sense of solidarity enjoyed. In some instances it has involved so many cars and generated so much noise and trash that local authorities tried to ban it, as, for example, in California's Alameda County. Phoenix tried a different solution by negotiating with the young cruisers, trying to persuade them to abandon the main avenue and change to a less congestable loop. In reaction to legal restrictions, the Bay Area's cruisers in 1984 declared a "National Cruise," which attracted 3000 cruising cars, additional thousands of onlookers, and 100 police in riot gear trying to disperse them.[44]

There are a number of additional behavior patterns among young Americans that can be defined as subinstitutionalized behavior, but they tend to prevail among older youths who have achieved some degree of political and philosophical sophistication and countercultural stature. Advanced youth or countercultural institutions include legal aid, "hot line" telephone centers, underground press, free schools, psychiatric "first aid," and many others.

SUMMARY

This chapter completes the discussion of eight dimensions of subculture. The first dimension, values and attitudes, was discussed in Chapter 12, and the remaining seven were presented in this chapter. The illustrations were

[42]James S. Coleman, *The Adolescent Society* (New York: Free Press, 1963), p. 12.

[43]J. M. Murray, "Emotional Problems in Relation to Driving," *Action Achievement Report*, 8th Annual Massachusetts Governor's Highway Safety Conference, Boston, May 25, 1954.

[44]Jonathan Alter and Richard Sandza, "Cruising Through California," *Newsweek*, September 10, 1984, p. 31.

usually interpreted in the perspective of structural-functional analysis in order to introduce the reader to the often-hidden meanings of behavior forms.

1. Teen argot is as puzzling to adults as it is functional to teenagers. Its functions include phonetic ease, relevance to the adolescent experience, maintenance of a sense of solidarity, provision of a status criterion, reflection of values, and a system of linguistic conditioning.

2. Subcultures depend on channels of communication for survival. The simplest and most direct communication center is the high school campus, where young people have ample opportunity to share ideas and attitudes. Other media include television, radio, teen magazines, the record industry, and rock festivals.

3. Teen fads and styles come and go. Their intentional as well as unintentional functions include status measurement, group identification, a relatively harmless expression of rebelliousness, security in uniformity of looks and behavior, and communication of belonging.

4. A sense of solidarity is reflected in almost all forms of teenage behavior. It becomes conspicuous in teenagers' effort to retain exclusivity of style and behavior forms, to preserve group authority and cohesiveness, and thereby maintain boundaries that clearly indicate the in- and the out-group. Solidarity is greatly enhanced by the identification of a common adversary and the common modes of defense and attack.

5. Status criteria must be deduced from various behavior forms within the peer group. Group members learn early what makes for prestige. Prestige depends on the type of friend, the type of clothes (especially for girls), the show of bravado (particularly for boys), the popularity of one's date, adherence to peer style and argot, and convincing demeanor of "coolness" in everyday life.

6. The American teenager is more oriented toward entertainment heroes than toward true leaders. The functions of hero worship include the fueling of romanticism, various sex-substitutions (including fetishism), cathartic crowd behavior, attraction to the bizarre, identification with youthful heroes, and the need for values.

7. Teenagers have devised structures for gratifying needs and desires not sanctioned by the Establishment. Subinstitutionalization centers on desires for sexual expression, drug use, the use of the automobile, and the world of entertainment. Subculturally institutionalized behavior is probably most indicative of the strength of a subculture. It is also a useful approach to understanding a counterculture or social movement.

We now move to a discussion of the more serious, goal- and action-oriented youth movements.

14

Activism and Radicalism: The Making of Movements and Countercultures

Most of this chapter is history. The lessons taught by history must not be forgotten — whether they are contained in the history of the nation or specifically in the youth scene. Examination of these lessons may prepare us to anticipate and better cope with recurrences of similar conditions and events.

DIFFERENCES BETWEEN SUBCULTURE AND COUNTERCULTURE

The general teen and pop subculture is to goal-oriented youth movements as a cops-and-robbers game is to a military battle. Differences between the teen subculture and the counterculture can be illustrated by a number of contrasts: static quality vs. dynamic quality; faddist-orientation vs. goal-orientation; entertainment vs. action; coexistence vs. intolerance; not intent on changing others vs. intent on proselytizing.

While this juxtaposition gives the impression of two radically different phenomena, the differences should be understood as differences in degree, with the typical subculture and counterculture occupying opposite poles,

298

thus allowing for modified versions. For example, it is quite possible for a relatively passive subculture to undergo significant changes over time and to emerge as a militant counterculture (or vice versa). It seems helpful, therefore, to look at the definitions of these two types of collectivities in the Weberian tradition of *ideal types* that facilitate communication and research. This kind of definition has been encouraged by other students of collective behavior, such as Milton J. Yinger, who contrasted subculture and "contraculture."[1]

It is possible to operationally implement the idea of a continuum by applying the eight dimensions discussed and gauging them to determine the degree of solidarity achieved. A counterculture would reflect sharper goals, clearer subinstitutional (or counterinstitutional) structures, and a keener sense of solidarity.

Another problem in sorting out the countercultural lifestyle from that of the subculture is that there are no concrete contours distinguishing membership between them. The teen subculture has absorbed many countercultural characteristics, and vice versa; for many practical purposes, the two collectivities largely coincided in sentiment and preference. Yet the true bearers of the counterculture were those called "youth" by Kenneth Keniston: the older-than-eighteen adolescents who made a serious attempt to change the American social system. These young adults were concentrated in the colleges and universities, claimed to be the youthful intelligentsia of the country, were politically radicalized, and came from the ranks of the psychedelic movement and other nonconformist groups. They coalesced into the "melting pot" of the counterculture.

ADOLESCENCE AND ALIENATION

The incentive to participate in social movements may spring from a variety of sources. Sociologists have suggested such major reasons are relative deprivation,[2] the mass society,[3] social class aspiration,[4] personal pathologies,[5] the

---

[1]Milton J. Yinger, *Countercultures* (Riverside, NJ: Free Press, 1982).

[2]C. Y. Glock, "The Role of Deprivation in the Origin and Evolution of Religious Groups," in *Religion and Social Conflict*, ed. Robert Lee and Martin Marty (New York: Oxford University Press, 1964).

[3]William Kornhauser, *The Politics of Mass Society* (New York: Free Press, 1959).

[4]D. E. Morrison and A. D. Steeves, "Deprivation, Discontent, and Social Movement Participation: Evidence on a Contemporary Farmers' Movement," *Rural Sociology*, 32 (1967): 414–34.

[5]Hans Sebald, *Momism: The Silent Disease of America* (Chicago: Nelson-Hall, 1976); Bruno Bettelheim, "Obsolete Youth," *Encounter*, 23 (1969): 29–42.

search for meaning,[6] and alienation.[7] In life, many of these factors overlap and combine. For example, an exaggerated need to depend upon and be approved by an outside authority may combine with the attempt to satisfy the search for meaning, or the frustration suffered from relative deprivation may intensify the sense of alienation. The success of a movement in attracting followers depends therefore on the problems and sentiments of people and on how a movement's objectives relate to them.

American adolescents form a population that is hyperreceptive to countercultural ideas and radical suggestions because they look for an escape from the alienation caused specifically by adolescence and by anomic society in general. Hundreds of thousands of modern American youth struggle to overcome alienation and to supplant anomie by meaning or a cause.

The concept of alienation is probably the most fitting single description of the motivating power that drives modern youth to pursue countercultural objectives or join True-Believer movements. A cause, a sense of destiny, and the accompanying benefits of belonging to a community of peers are strong attractions for the masses of inexperienced youth who seek to alleviate meaninglessness.

Alienation, in degree as well as kind, strikes no two persons the same way; it assumes a multitude of types and hues. It is the favorite playground of sociologists, political scientists, philosophers, and theologians. To simplify things, our discussion focuses on only a few of these types.

1. Probably the most important source of alienation for young persons has to do with the process of *developmental estrangement*—a sense of loss that comes as childhood ways are discontinued and adult ways not yet assumed. From this perspective, adolescence and alienation are inextricably bonded. The young feel rejected by a system that does not give them a productive and egalitarian place and puts them in ghettos for an ever-lengthening period before they are released to enter the labor force. They feel like aliens in the system, fail to establish a sense of belonging, and develop a rejective mood in return.

2. Rapid and uneven social change inflicts alienation through an acute sense of loss of tradition. The rapid chain reactions with which social, as well as technological, innovations succeed each other undermine the feeling of being anchored in acceptable and predictable customs. The supertechnologi-

---

[6]Hans Toch, *The Social Psychology of Social Movements* (New York: Bobbs-Merrill, 1965); Orrin E. Klapp, *Currents of Unrest: An Introduction to Collective Behavior* (New York: Holt, Rinehart & Winston, 1972) and *Collective Search for Identity* (New York: Holt, Rinehart & Winston, 1969); Eric Hoffer, *The True Believer* (New York: Mentor Books, 1951); Pitirim A. Sorokin, *The Crisis of Our Age* (New York: Dutton, 1941); Erich Fromm, *Escape from Freedom* (New York: Holt, Rinehart & Winston, 1941).

[7]Karl Marx and Friedrich Engels, *The German Ideology* (New York: International Publishers, 1947).

cal dynamics of postindustrial society create flux, unpredictability, and a sense that something is being lost. This flux-prone lifestyle imposes strain on the nervous system, which normally prefers routine. Institutions, among other functions, serve the purpose of reducing nervous strain through predictable and routine procedures in everyday life.

3. Anomic society provides unwanted freedom. The young have a natural aversion to ideational vacuums and demand orientation and direction. The search for meaning is a powerful desire that often leads to participation in collectivities that promise a definite credo. Eric Hoffer, in *The True Believer,* and Erich Fromm, in *Escape from Freedom,* have called attention to the susceptibility of anomic populations to the persuasiveness of radical slogans.

4. Alienation of the poor, the jobless, and the victims of racial or ethnic prejudices is nothing new. What is new and has proved difficult for many to understand is alienation among segments of our population whose reasons for feeling estranged are obtuse, abstract, and have little to do with poverty, exclusion, oppression, or cultural deprivation of any kind. In fact, the most vocal of the alienated come from socioeconomically advantaged backgrounds. They are a vociferous minority of privileged middle- and upper-class youth who dissent from the established order. Richard Flacks surveyed activist youth and found that the student movement represents the disaffection not of an underprivileged stratum of the student population but of the most advantaged sector of the students, with most of the activists coming from high-income families.[8]

There is no simple reason why this should be so. A major cause probably originates in the affluent and comfortable background that prevents many offspring of well-to-do parents from earning their own livelihoods and working their way through college. The ensuing leisure time can be spent on more abstract activities such as philosophizing about possible reasons why one is bored and cannot find meaning in life. Life has started them out without a struggle—thus, they invent one: the reform or overthrow of a system shot through with injustices and social ills, none of which is personally relevant to them. This is not necessarily a denigration of this type of youth; one could interpret their motivation as either a romantic fancy born out of pampered, unrealistic, and bored lifestyle, or an exquisite vicariousness that, observing the suffering of others, instills compassion and incites activism.

A related insight that came from the same study by Flacks was that

---

[8]Richard Flacks, "The Liberated Generation: An Explanation of the Roots of Student Protest," *Journal of Social Issues,* 23 (July 1967): 52–75. See corroboration in Hans Sebald, "The Waxing and Waning of a New Age Commune. From Nudity to Business Suit," *Humboldt Journal of Social Relations,* 15 (Fall/Winter 1987–88): 1–27; Mike Brake, *The Sociology of Youth Culture* (Boston: Routledge & Kegan Paul, 1980).

activists' parents were decidedly more liberal than the parents of other youth. This held true even when socioeconomic backgrounds were held constant. Only 6 percent of nonactivists' fathers described themselves as "highly liberal" or "socialist," whereas 60 percent of the activists' fathers described themselves in such terms. The implication of this is that activism, at least to some degree, runs in the family and thus is a familial rather than a generational phenomenon.

5. For many young Americans, the reason for their alienation was more identifiable: They rejected the protracted war in Vietnam as immoral on the part of their nation and consequently refused to be drafted, preferred to go into exile, or joined antiwar organizations—activities that in turn, as a collectivity, became part of the countercultural movement. Was the alienation of many young Americans truly based on antiwar conviction? This is still an unanswered question, especially in the light of earlier-mentioned research that discovered striking ignorance about the facts, figures, and circumstances of the war, not only among the "hawks" but also among the "doves." The conclusion seemed plausible that alienation is prompted more by basic emotional orientations rather than specific and objective assessment of the circumstances.[9]

The generalization growing out of this discovery suggests that the search for an alternative lifestyle may be based more often on bias and powerful emotion rather than on a rational and cognitive approach.

6. Finally, the process of undergoing socialization in a complex society is enough to cause frustration to the adolescent, creating a rejective mood toward the Establishment. Only romanticists and a few anthropologists whose explorations never exceeded the horizon of a couple of idyllic islands might venture to suggest that socialization is fun—for the young as well as for the elders. In plain words: most of the time it is not! Given the American ethos of instantness and the technological promises of ease and pleasure in life, it is understandable that America's young find themselves frustrated at having to go through a tedious introduction that includes the learning of a myriad of things which to them appear trivial, trying, and tiring.

Four qualifications should be added.

First, a certain degree of alienation is not to be judged as entirely negative. A society with some youthful alienation can profit from the converted energy and channel it in creative directions. Without any conflict or alienation there would be little motivation to search for improvement. Anthropologists have noted that in societies in which the status of the young is well defined and integrated into the social structure (thus eliminating adolescence), change and innovation tend to be low. On the other hand, in societies

---

[9]Hans Sebald, "Voices of War and Peace—What Do They Know? Attitudes and Knowledge about the War in Southeast Asia," *Pacific Sociological Review*, 14 (October 1971): 487–510.

in which youth's roles are uncertain and adult responsibilities and privileges are delayed, there is a predisposition to change, innovate, and experiment. The frustration caused by such confusions and delays generates a readiness to respond to new ideas and to try out alternatives to existing institutions.[10] The nature of the social structure thus determines at least in part the degree of youth's activism. Karl Mannheim elucidated the functionality of youth as a potentially deviant population when he described them as not committed to the status quo and thus free to push for change and innovation.[11] For this function, as we have discussed in an earlier chapter, we must pay the price of intergenerational conflict.

Second, alienation is not a phenomenon that applies uniformly to the youth of a nation. It is usually only a minority that feels alienation keenly enough to express it in the form of agitation and noteworthy opposition to the Establishment. For example, at the height of the counterculture in 1970, most students went along with the system and did not actively work toward abolishing or radically changing it. Harvard sociologist Seymour M. Lipset found in a worldwide study of collegiate political views that despite a season of well-publicized protests both in the U.S. and abroad, the vast majority of university undergraduates were either apolitical or supporters of well-established parties. Lipset claimed that, for example, the leftist, militant Students for a Democratic Society had only 7000 members among the 6.5 million American university students. In contrast, the Young Republicans and the Young Democrats had an enrollment of nearly 250,000. Lipset also believes that during the 1930s far more students were activistic, both on the right as well as the left, than during the counterculture years.[12]

These moderates were the young who probably distanced themselves from the counterculture and other radical movements, but who nevertheless took part in the general youth subculture with its fads, styles, hero worship, argot, norms, and values. For many young, then, there existed a division between the general subculture and the radical counterculture. One might be safe, however, in assuming that countercultural youth most likely were part of or grew out of the subculture, whereas the converse was not necessarily true. This is a good example of the blurring and diffusion that are characteristic of the amorphous youth population.

Third, not all countercultural participation grew out of adolescent alienation—or any alienation, for that matter—but rather out of insight, information, and loyalty to America as a nation, wanting to influence and

[10]Frank Musgrove, *Youth and the Social Order* (Bloomington, IN: Indiana University Press, 1965), pp. 126–27.

[11]Karl Mannheim, *Essays on the Sociology of Culture* (New York: Oxford University Press, 1956).

[12]Seymour M. Lipset and Gerald M. Schaflander, *Passion and Politics: Student Activism in America* (Boston: Little, Brown, and Company, 1971).

deflect the direction of national policies and to contribute to a stronger and saner country. Hence, not out of alienation but out of dedication may a minority have decided to promote the countercultural cause.

Fourth, it must be realized that the counterculture was not an entirely exclusive youth movement and that many adults were actively involved. In fact, some segments of the movement were pioneered primarily by adults and only later taken over or joined by youthful activists. For example, the psychedelic movement started with adult psychologists and writers (Huxley, Leary, Alpert, Metzner), and the civil rights movement had been borne by adults before youth adopted it.

THE SEARCH FOR ALTERNATIVE LIFESTYLES

Apart from the exceptional motivations of small splinter groups, alienation seems to be the driving force behind many youth's agitation and search for new lifestyles.

A collective identity search is a symptom of modern society's depriving its young (as well as old) of certain psychological benefits, the lack of which prompts mass groping for activities and symbols in which to anchor a new identity. Young individuals in such situations grope because they are not fully aware of what is wrong and causes them discomfort—especially since they only too obviously cannot blame material or cultural deprivation as the source of their discontent. And yet they feel somehow cheated. When movements become concerned with identity, they develop certain characteristics, such as "style rebellion," self-ornamentation, concern with emotional gestures rather than pragmatic goals, hero worship, and cultism. Such a symbolic stance indicates that what is sought is not satisfied by ordinary economic and political solutions, but instead, basic questions of meaning and direction.

Youth's sense of being cheated cannot be explained in economic terms because the perception has its roots in our civilization's shortcoming in providing a convincing ideation. It is ideational alienation that is at the heart of modern youth's groping.

There are vast differences in the individual's response to the alienating elements of society. Some youth compensate by sublimation and by making positive contributions to the Establishment. Others see no way to work within the established order and are prone to march down deviant and militant avenues. In the process they generalize their rejection from specific elements and direct their wrath toward the entire social system, seeing justification in wanting to supplant it totally with a new, "just," and "beautiful" society.

Utopias have always held a fascination for humans. It is their grand promise to abolish suffering and injustice that attracts humans one generation after another. It is an endearing and comforting thought, enhancing hope and courage, that there might be an ideal solution and that the dim light at the end of the tunnel will reveal itself as a bright and shining light that will safely guide and protect.

Still other youths manifest alienation by withdrawing from society as a whole. Some of them suffer deep and silent despair, apathy, and nihilistic attitude, and find no outlet or compensation for their frustration and confusion. Many of these end up receiving psychiatric care because they turn their pain inside and direct hostility at themselves. The masochistic Punk style of the 1980s seems to be representative of this type. Others direct hostility outward in such an uncontrolled and vehement form that their actions assume brutal criminality.

An increasing proportion of youth over the past decades has tried to alleviate alienation from American society (or Western civilization in general) by engaging in a search for alternative lifestyles. They have turned to meditation, Eastern religions, and the occult, or they have become ensconced in aesthetic or artistic pursuits, making art, poetry, and music a way of life. They may have retreated to the "simple and natural" life of living with "the earth" by plowing the proverbial Idaho soil; or retreated to the symbiosis of communal life. Retreatisms of these various sorts were and are cultivated individually or communally.

The inclination of American youth to embrace a cultic solution to alienation and anomie has become legendary during and since the counterculture years. Cults that promise to provide a total and absolute meaning for life have multiplied in America (and Western Europe) and are seeking the conversion and allegiance of the young. Conway and Siegelman described the youthful epidemic of cultic conversions in their book *Snapping*.[13] The twofold motivation of wanting to substantiate a personal identity and wanting to find a solution to all personal problems has created a profound vulnerability to the promises of various exotic and esoteric cults. "To snap" means experiencing a sudden personality transformation, being transformed from a seeker to a true believer, becoming totally filled with a new life-orienting meaning, and usually confusing wishful thinking with reality. The unrestrained yearning of youth for an omnipotent and omniscient guru often plays a portentous role in the process of "snapping" and tends to elevate charlatans to charismatic leaders.

The cultic retreat from mainstream society is a particular form of retreatism (the "sacred" type) and has become widespread.

Retreatist youth has by now established a tradition in American life. The hip bohemians of the 1950s were among the colorful founders of the tradition. They constituted a leisure-time and unaffiliated intelligentsia fol-

---

[13]Flo Conway and Jim Siegelman, *Snapping: America's Epidemic of Sudden Personality Change* (New York: Lippincott, 1978).

lowing the European tradition of coffeehouse philosophy, attic art studios, and some peripheral drug experimentation. Two meccas were San Francisco's North Beach[14] and Greenwich Village in New York. These retreatists engaged in relatively coherent and philosophically mature critiques of modern society and had literary flair. However, they soon attracted a lay following that infiltrated their ranks and wreaked a metamorphosis of the whole movement. The beatniks evolved in the late 1950s, and were a far less talented and sophisticated circle, though still fairly literate.[15] They, in turn, were the immediate forerunners of the hippies, attracting ever-younger and increasingly unsophisticated followers, including runaways, drug derelicts, and generally very confused teenagers, with Haight-Ashbury becoming the epitome of a movement that had no direction and went nowhere.[16] One offshoot of the hippies was the communards who tried a semiretreatist life in the company of the like-minded. A later retreatist development coming in the wake of the debacle of the hippie experiment was the street people, who were relatively indistinguishable from the hippies, except that they seemed to be less gregarious, less prone to affiliate with like-minded peers, and even less sophisticated.

The great upheaval of the counterculture more or less swallowed up these splinter groups, temporarily unified them in a common cause, and later (during the calmer late 1970s) regurgitated a metamorphosis: the New Age movement.[17] The New Age people were the true heirs of the counterculture and synthesized into a philosophical core the best of the unique aspects that the counterculture had to offer. These counterculture scions of the 1980s had a predilection for communal living, vegetarianism, and a mixture of the occult and Oriental religions. They no longer had the political militancy of their predecessors, but preferred a more philosophical-religious retreat. The economic vision was the Jeffersonian dream, consisting of independent farmers and small craftspersons who would revive the ancient personal bartering system instead of continuing the impersonal industrial lifestyle.

It is among New Age people that we see the clearest evidence of subinstitutionalization. Communes or communities of New Agers specialize in different services, from fruit growing to wilderness survival schools to holistic health centers. A participant-observer study by this author spanned several years during which he saw the rise and fall of a New Age commune settled around paradisal thermal springs in the Arizona desert.[18] The spe-

---

[14]Jerry Kamstra, *The Frisco Kid* (New York: Harper & Row, 1975).

[15]Bruce Cook, *The Beat Generation* (New York: Scribner's, 1971); Jack Kerouac, *On the Road* (New York: The Viking Press, 1955).

[16]Sherri Cavan, *Hippies of the Haight* (St. Louis: New Critics Press, 1972).

[17]Hans Sebald, "New Age Romanticism: The Quest for an Alternative Lifestyle as a Force of Social Change," *Humboldt Journal of Social Relations* 11 (Spring 1984): 106–127.

[18]Hans Sebald, "The Waxing and Waning of a New Age Commune," op. cit.

cialty of this commune was to provide alternative healing (as opposed to modern medicine) through exposure to the presumed energy flow from the earth, meditation, a vegetarian diet, and fasting. The central idea of the commune was to be "conscious" of all surrounding life and energy—a canon this group shared with all New Age people. But the specialty, the subinstitution within the movement, was healing. This service was offered to in-group members as well as to outsiders (those from the "straight" society)—to the latter primarily in order to derive an income that would assure continuous existence of the commune. Alas, as appears to be the fate with most, if not all, New Age communes, the "Commune at Healing Water" disintegrated after a few years of attempting to carve out an alternative lifestyle and offering the service of a subinstitution.

To be sure, there has been no consistent cultivation of a philosophical or social sophistication that would culminate in a historical precedent of significance for youth the world over. Instead, serials of unorganized and largely unremembered trial-and-error experiments went in circles and ended up nowhere. The counterculture reached its height about 1969–70 and was sparsely remembered five years later by American youth—though it was better remembered by adults. Obviously, history begins for the masses of American young around eighteen years of age; events and happenings prior to that age recede into a broad blur. The current generation of young Americans has entered a new era, and the counterculture is only known through occasional lectures or reading assigned by compulsive professors. There seems to be truth in the statement that one year's freshmen are likely to be oblivious to the causes, heroism, and battles of last year's seniors.

This reminds us that learning and the acquisition of wisdom is an ever-new process, and that the upheavals and sacrifices of one generation have little pertinence to the next. It means that each generation is predisposed not merely to new but to repetitive trials and tribulations. Social maturity is thus not learned in a unidimensionally ascending way, but through repetitive experimenting to come to grips with the contingencies at hand. The best one can say, then, is that besides their follies, humans may also repeat the noble and the dignified.

Hence, the following discussion of the 1965–72 counterculture as a movement aspiring to an alternative lifestyle is largely an exercise in history.

FROM THE COUNTERCULTURE TO THE NEW AGE MOVEMENT

The counterculture was a prime example of the search for an alternative lifestyle. It was a collective attempt to change the system. Arising in the early 1960s, peaking around 1969–70, and gradually ebbing in the early 1970s, the movement was all but dead by the mid-1970s, and only the last, slight ripples could be felt in 1976. Nevertheless, some discernible impressions, maybe lasting ones, have been left on the shores of the Establishment.

That the counterculture indeed represented a weighty force in social change is convincingly argued by Robert Wuthnow.[19] Derived from Mannheim's theory,[20] the concept of "generation unit" allows Wuthnow to illustrate that a certain age group can be far more than merely a statistical cohort. In a sense, a generation unit is a "cultural unit" in which the members (1) are bonded together by a specific range of experiences, which predispose them to a typical mode of perception and behavior; (2) feel a "common destiny" or interest just as forcefully as a socioeconomic class; and (3) manifest "identity of responses," that is, they act or react in similar, if not identical, ways to the contingencies of life. This generation unit acts as an agent of rapid social change by challenging existing norms, values, and traditional behavior modes. Hence the theory that social change is a steady, evolutionary process must be modified in the face of the generation unit.

The counterculture was a prime example of a challenging generation unit. It exhibited all the vital characteristics of a cultural unit, particularly a separate identity (as strong as a "social-class consciousness") that pitted it against the rest of society. The broader impact far exceeded the assumptions of the slow-evolutionary-change theory. Robert Nisbet, in criticizing the theory, put the significance of the counterculture into perspective when he said: "Change in any degree of notable significance is intermittent rather than continuous; mutational, even explosive, rather than the simple accumulation of internal variations."[21]

The discontent of the counterculture generation was indeed explosive. Foremost among reasons that the young gave for their anger and alienation was their opposition to *technocracy*—a lifestyle presumably dominated by technology, instead of the other way around. This phrase became a catchall concept for everything the young found wrong with American society and Western civilization in general. It included a pervasive rejection of a number of aspects, such as the military-industrial complex, which they accused of profiteering and chicanery; the impersonality of urban-industrial life, which they felt had lost the human touch; insensitivity toward human needs and human dignity, injustices of various types, inequality of racial, ethnic, sex, and age groups; the specific inhumanity and authoritarianism of the authorities; the abusiveness of the power structure; ecological disregards resulting in devastation of the natural environment; the capitalistic-materialistic world

---

[19]Robert Wuthnow, "Recent Patterns of Secularization: A Problem of Generations?" *American Sociological Review*, Vol. 41, October 1976, pp. 850–67.

[20]Karl Mannheim, *Essays on the Sociology of Knowledge* (New York: Oxford University Press, 1952).

[21]Robert A. Nisbet, *Social Change and History* (New York: Oxford University Press, 1969), pp. 281–82.

view, which they saw as a means to dehumanize; and the futile "objective consciousness" typical of Western inquiry into the riddles of life and the universe.

How pervasive can a rejection be? Literally, no building block of Western civilization was left untouched, and not one passed muster!

Complaints and rebellion against the power hierarchy, and against material destitution and social oppression are an old history story that has recurred many times and, in fact, has been a constant in American society (and Western civilization in general). The significant new feature of the counterculture was its condemnation of the very method that has contributed to combat material wants and social problems: the scientific world view. Appraised as "objective consciousness," this world view was now condemned as being too impersonal and superficial and as leading to nowhere but disaster. The alternative groping for a lifestyle and a way to gain knowledge became a form of *mysticism* that consisted of a conglomerate of largely misunderstood Eastern thought,[22] immature hedonism straight from Haight-Ashbury, and some thoughts of appreciable sensitivity and insight.

The counterculture had its prophets and literary heroes. Some of them, had they been asked, would probably have declined candidacy for such status. For example, Hermann Hesse's novels were adopted variously as a door to Eastern peacefulness and mysticism (*Siddhartha*) and as a visionary example of psychedelia (*Steppenwolf*),[23] but there is serious doubt that Hesse wrote any of his works with a countercultural concept in mind. As he cautioned in his 1963 foreword to *Steppenwolf*, his perspective was artistic and psychoanalytic, and varying interpretations were outside his literary responsibility. Nonetheless, the counterculture boosted the sale of his books; of the 30 million sold worldwide nearly 12 million were sold in the United States by 1977.

Psychologist Timothy Leary gleefully grasped the nomination, became a prophet and, in fact, a martyr of the psychedelic wing of the counterculture. Fired from Harvard in 1963, along with Richard Alpert, because of unauthorized psychedelic experiments with students, he became guru of the drug culture that joined forces with the counterculture. His style, however, literary and otherwise, was so phantasmagoric and unbecomingly egotistic, even to most of the young drug users, that his role of psychedelic guru was limited to the inner circles of the newly founded International Federation for Internal Freedom and never penetrated into other segments of the counterculture. His autobiographical works, *High Priest* and *The Politics of Ecstasy*,

---

[22]Authoritative assessment of what American youth's adaptation of Hindu elements means was presented by Gita Mehta, *Karma Cola: Marketing the Mystic East* (New York: Simon & Schuster, 1981).

[23]Hermann Hesse, *Steppenwolf* (New York: Random House, 1963) and *Siddhartha* (New York: New Directions, 1951).

add up to an unintentional caricature of countercultural themes delivered in an embarrassingly egomaniacal style.[24]

The counterculture selected Allen Ginsberg its poet. His style, a combination of protest, lament, and mysticism, appealed to sentiment-hungry youth who welcomed a poetic manifesto reflecting their dissatisfaction.[25]

Alan Watts, through his televised lectures, books, and private classes, became the foremost popularizer of Zen Buddhism.[26] Though his background was associated with erudite studies of Oriental religion, the popularized version of his work crystallized into a naive cult that enhanced and reinforced the adolescent knack for rationalizing hedonism, "dropping out," and the inability to be articulate. With its commitment to "wise silence," for example, Zen provided a convenient camouflage for the inarticulateness of adolescents. Although adolescents talked about it and made it a significant entry in their argot, "satori" (the achievement of inner peace and bliss) remained far from the American coast.

The wide acceptance of Carlos Castaneda's works signaled the passing of the age of ideology and the inauguration of the age of mystagogy. His works deserve this distinction on the basis of their astonishingly widespread acceptance and the religious fervor with which the young adopted his ideas, replacing the scientific world view with Castaneda's "magical view" of life. In such books as *The Teaching of Don Juan: A Yaqui Way of Life* and *Journey to Ixtlan: The Lessons of Don Juan,* he tried to persuade the young that the psychedelic vision is a way of life that is vastly more profound than the knowledge obtained through the traditional "objective" approach.[27] The setting of his presumedly factual observations was a Yaqui Indian's Sonoran environment. Although Castaneda's lore remained unverified (he refused to introduce anyone to the characters or places described, and his depiction of life in the desert creates a credibility gap for those who know it), the teachings of the shaman, Don Juan, were accepted with a singular ferocity by masses of young Americans as if they were truly verified and opened the door to a truer, albeit magical, world. This was the time for college instructors to be nonplussed by the noncritical acceptance of such "magical" and "mystic" credos. It was not until Richard de Mille's publication of two critical tomes, *Castaneda's Journey* and *The Don Juan Papers,*[28] that Castaneda's credibility was

---

[24]Timothy Leary, *High Priest* (New York: World, 1968) and *The Politics of Ecstasy* (New York: Putnam, 1968).

[25]Allen Ginsberg, *Empty Mirror: Early Poems* (New York: Totem Press, 1961).

[26]Alan Watts, *This Is It, and Other Essays on Zen and Spiritual Experience* (New York: Collier, 1967).

[27]Carlos Castaneda, *The Teaching of Don Juan: A Yaqui Way of Knowledge* (Berkeley, CA: University of California Press, 1968) and *Journey to Ixtlan: The Lessons of Don Juan* (New York: Simon and Schuster, 1972).

[28]Richard de Mille, *Castaneda's Journey* (Santa Barbara, CA: Ross-Erickson, 1976); *The Don Juan Papers: Further Castaneda Controversies* (Santa Barbara, CA: Ross-Erickson, 1980).

seriously questioned—and even then fanatics tried to ignore evidence that strongly suggested Castaneda's tales to be hoaxes.

A degree of political sophistication was derived from reading the works of socialist and political scientist Herbert Marcuse, who compared Marx and Freud, accomplished amazing theoretical combinations, and offered scathing criticism of the capitalistic system.[29] Such reading of political philosophers, including Marx and Engels, was reserved for the college-educated and politically radicalized wing of the counterculture and remained esoteric matter to other segments of the movement.

Then there were writers who were proponents and evaluators of the counterculture, largely applauding it, and praying for its longevity. Theodore Roszak's *The Making of a Counter Culture*[30] became the counterculture's little book of thoughts and prophecies, supplemented by such manifestos as Charles A. Reich's *The Greening of America*[31] and Philip E. Slater's *The Pursuit of Loneliness.*[32] These books reiterated the counterculture's assaults on American civilization, gave it a literary platform, and became part of the movement proper.

It would tax the frame of this chapter to discuss all the important writers and contributors who promoted the cause of the counterculture. Suffice it to say that they included personalities who offered political philosophy, religious orientation, educational reform, poetic protest, the psychedelic approach, utopian constructs, and a rejection of Western science.

The diversity of these contributions is correlated with the diversity of the countercultural population itself, which consisted of an amorphous body with diverse motivations, orientations, and interests. Yet on one basic goal, all seemed to coalesce: to supplant Western technocracy by a "humane and just" system that would reintroduce (the question of "re-" from what and where was never clarified) sensitivity and humanity. Another agreement was the antiwar stance directed against American intervention in the political and military processes of Southeast Asia. More than any other element, this issue added cohesiveness and some degree of organization to the movement. It is a good question whether or not the counterculture would have had a chance to evolve had the U.S. not been involved in the war.

Two other basic agreements seemed to run through the counterculture. One was prodrug and the other was promysticism. A majority of radical

---

[29]Herbert Marcuse's writings are too prolific to be listed here; the interested reader is directed to an anthology, *The Critical Spirit: Essays in Honor of Herbert Marcuse,* ed. Kurt H. Wolff and Barrington Moore (Boston: Beacon Press, 1967).

[30]Theodore Roszak, *The Making of a Counter Culture* (Garden City, NY: Doubleday, 1969).

[31]Charles A. Reich, *The Greening of America* (New York: Bantam, 1970).

[32]Philip E. Slater, *The Pursuit of Loneliness: American Culture at the Breaking Point* (Boston: Beacon Press, 1970).

youth accepted drugs (psychedelics and marijuana) as a life-enhancing medium. A vast majority sympathized deeply with a mystic (vs. "objective") approach to life and knowledge. While youthful political activism was not an entirely new thing in American history, a novel dimension became an integral part of the counterculture: the infatuation with the occult, magic, and exotic ritual.[33]

The craving for the mystic and occult spread and took root outside the counterculture and has been growing ever since. Future historians may define this development as a significant turning point in the religious orientation of Western people. It was with the counterculture that a singular religious-philosophical syncretism arose that blended elements of Hinduism, Buddhism, Christianity, and various and sundry aspects of the occult into a new panmysticism. Illogical and romantic as it may appear to "objective" outsiders, this mixture seems to endure and give meaning to many modern youths, particularly to those identifying with the New Age movement. However, identification with the movement is not a necessary condition for embracing the new syncretic "consciousness." For example, college students, many of whom are hardly familiar with the phrase "New Age," reflect a high degree of occult-mystic inclination. Inquiring into this question over a three-year period resulted in the information presented in Table 14–1. Accordingly, in 1981 nearly 30 percent of college students believed in reincarnation, with the same proportion undecided but allowing for its possibility, and only 40 percent not believing in it. At the same time, 75 percent believed in a personal God. Half of the respondents either believed in astrology or allowed for its validity. Only 8 percent of the respondents refused to believe that we are visited by UFOs directed by intelligent beings from outer space. (See details in Table 14–1.)

Apart from prodrug and promysticism, the diversity of the counterculture was remarkable. The counterculture incorporated the psychedelic movement, the peace and protest movement, the various liberation movements (women, homosexuals, ethnic and racial groups, etc.), radical professional groups (the radical therapists, liberal clergy, progressive academicians and educators, etc.), the New Left movement and possibly some religious-mystic movements (Hare Krishna, meditators, Jesus movement, etc.). A conglomerate of numerous intertwining movements and organizations either totally or partly, lastingly or temporarily pursued countercultural objectives.

How did the activism manifest itself in the actual behavior of young Americans? A part of the outward expressions of the counterculture included protest demonstrations, sit-ins, riots, occupations of buildings on campuses, taking hostages of university administrators to force consent to political and social demands, destruction of government property, disruption of classroom

---

[33]Roszak, *The Making of a Counter Culture*, p. 124.

TABLE 14-1   Percentage distribution of religious/occult beliefs held by college
students, 1979, 1980, 1981

Belief In		1979 (N = 100)	1980 (N = 157)	1981 (N = 106)
Reincarnation	yes	20	23	29
	no	47	44	42
	undecided	33	33	29
Astrology	yes	14	12	12
	no	57	58	50
	undecided	29	30	38
UFOs from outer	yes	39	52	59
space directed by	no	20	16	8
intelligent beings	undecided	41	32	33
Personal God with	yes	65	73	75
whom you can	no	17	12	9
communicate	undecided	18	15	16
ESP, including	yes	54	58	66
clairvoyance,	no	16	20	6
psychokinesis, etc.	undecided	30	22	29

Source: Hans Sebald, Surveys at Arizona State University, Tempe, Arizona, 1979, 1980, 1981.

procedures, ritualistic burning of draft cards, militant confrontations with law enforcement personnel (such as culminated at Kent State University), and widespread draft evasion and desertion from the armed forces.

Though some of these mass expressions were organized and reasonably constrained, many of them sprang from impulse and were destructive, failing to serve the nobler causes of the movement. Among the masses of protesters were many adolescents who were not trained in abstract thought and not honed in political sophistication. They were primarily attracted by excitement, the personality drama at elections and other political exhibitionisms, and the sensate experience of being bodily engulfed in the excited mass of a mob or riot. Maybe Dr. Andrew Weil's notion that the human brain, old and young, needs to be "blown" or "stoned" once in a while to clear the neurons of congestive tension is valid to such scenes.[34] Such ecstasy, presumably natural to the brain, can find implementation in the context of a mass of protesters or rioters. (Weil, who was sympathetic to the counterculture, saw in psychedelic drug use only one avenue—one he warned against—to achieve this beneficial ecstasy.) This brings to mind Gustave LeBon's classic treatise on mass psy-

[34]Andrew Weil, *The Natural Mind* (Boston: Houghton Mifflin Company, 1973).

chology, which proposed that individuality is absorbed and suppressed by the crowd's raptures and action-oriented surges.[35]

Not all countercultural expressions assumed a mass character. Part of the activities consisted of rational negotiations and legitimate political campaigns, especially at election time to promote sympathetic candidates and to publicize new ideas.

A large portion of activities took place *within* the counterculture, in interaction with like-minded peers. Many of the styles and patterns of interaction deserve to be defined as subinstitutions or, as Richard Flacks called them, "counterinstitutions."[36] Examples include the commune movement that stirred within the counterculture;[37] publications such as *Rolling Stone* and *High Times* (particularly slanted toward the psychedelic movement) and the flamboyant underground press; musicals or rock operas such as *Hair, Jesus Christ Superstar, Godspell,* and *Tommy;* free schools; childcare centers; people's parks; credit unions; tenant organizations; "hot-line" phone services; "first-aid" psychiatric service centers (such as Terros); rock music festivals; organic food co-ops; illegal drug traffic, including growing, manufacturing, smuggling, distributing, and consuming illegal drugs; business enterprises marketing books, clothes, psychedelia, jewelry, candles, incense, posters, and so on; therapeutic networks and free clinics helping youngsters with such problems as abortion, VD, drug addiction, and mental health; and peace centers serving as bases for the planning of protest actions.

The pursuit of these functions and the adherence to structures to carry them out had an interesting consequence: *it territorialized the counterculture,* reinforcing youth ghettos, forming youth communities, and establishing exclusive channels of communication. The creation of jobs in subinstitutions and the sharing of economic responsibilities in collectives suggested viable means to becoming absorbed by conventional social structure. Examples of youth's territorializing were rural communes established in an effort to live off the land, and to live cooperatively and maximize self-sufficiency. It was hoped that in the process the pressures of competitive work, police, pollution, crowds, and the corruption of technocratic affluence could be shut out.

The movement can thus be understood first as activism directed outward, aiming at changing and reforming the "system," and secondly as an attempt to regulate interaction and to satisfy desires not met by the parent society's regular institutions. The former function distinguishes the movement from an ordinary subculture; the latter, dealing with internal structure, operates to varying degrees in both subcultures and countercultures.

---

[35]Gustave LeBon, *Psychologie des Foules* (Paris: F. Olean, 1895).

[36]Richard Flacks, *Youth and Social Change* (Chicago: Rand McNally, 1971), pp. 110–20.

[37]Keith Melville, *Communes in the Counter Culture: Origins, Theories, Styles of Life* (New York: Morrow, 1975).

These two major functions tended to conflict with each other. In fact, they deflected the main goals of the counterculture and sidetracked the whole movement. This happened because the counterinstitutions developed ever-greater exclusivity, grew into rigidity, and preserved territoriality—conditions that blocked the proclaimed goal of reforming the larger society and transcending it with the subinstitutions. In other words, the counterinstitutions and the internal organization got in the way of revolution. It is the old story of an initially revolutionary movement becoming immobilized by preoccupation with internal functions and the structures that go with them.

Not all interpretations of the counterculture were as positive and supportive. Unlike Roszak or Reich or Slater, psychologist Bruno Bettelheim, historian Lewis S. Feuer, and essayist John W. Aldridge, for example, interpreted the movement not as an expression of rational and informed youth combatting a "sick society," but as a symptom of irrational, destructive, and even pathological personalities who rebel against a society that is reluctant to accept their hedonism. To some degree, the disagreements between these assessors stem from a failure to fully recognize the diversity of the counterculture and to distinguish among different kinds of activists.

Feuer uses psychoanalytic theory to debunk the assumption that the youth movement was based on idealism and altruism though he allows for minor degrees of such motivations. Rather, he sees the movement as an expression of largely unconscious hostility against parents in specific and adults in general.[38] Despite individual variations, history has revealed a consistent similarity among all youth movements (specifically student movements): in motivation; the social conditions that provoked them; and the course the movements run. Youth movements are characterized by largely nonmaterialistic motivations that are rarely invited by conditions of daily life but are rooted in "deep, unconscious sources" that essentially deal with a conflict of generations. Feuer overlooked a very concrete source of motivation for rebellion: the war in Vietnam, which was extremely unpopular with an appreciable proportion of the young as well as the old. The refusal to risk one's life or health and the refusal to kill or maim others (the so-called "enemies") were certainly rational, conscious, and, in a sense, "materialistic motivations."

Bettelheim's assessment of the counterculture was even more negative.[39] He explained it as rebelliousness growing out of "permissive" child rearing, particularly in upper-middle-class homes, and the result of protracted adolescence that subjects youth to a moratorium that is boring, degrading,

---

[38]Lewis S. Feuer, *The Conflict of Generations* (New York: Basic Books, 1969); also see "Anti-Science. The Irrationalist Vogue of the 1970s," *Free Inquiry* 4 (Winter 1983/84): 36–46.

[39]Bruno Bettelheim, "Student Revolt, The Hard Core," *Vital Speeches of the Day*, 35 (1969), 406; see also D. Dempsey, "Bruno Bettelheim is Dr. No," *New York Times Magazine*, January 11, 1970, p. 22.

and infuriating. In addition, he believed that a sizable segment of American adults is caught up in a youth cult that has the wrong effect on young people. The cult tends to reinforce youth's rebelliousness, since its followers feel that their youthfulness not only makes them admirable but also endows them with impunity to do whatever they wish. Many adults are in awe of anything that is youthful and are therefore hesitant to react negatively toward young people. What the public often overlooks, Bettelheim feared, is that radical youth are basically "fixated at the age of temper tantrum." Needless to say, Bettelheim's claim that the "pathology" against which activists presumably fight lies in their own personalities rather than in society has as much pleased and appeased the conservative audience as it has disturbed and displeased the liberal audience.

Aldridge, the most eloquent of the critics of countercultural activism, warned against dignifying it by calling it a "culture" of any sort, feeling that if we do, we would pay homage to the infantile hedonism of youth.[40] Western societies tend to give credence to youth's complaints as if they were legitimate matters and rational propositions, whereas actually they are largely bluffs—which often succeed because of society's pervasive guilt complexes and its pursuit of youth cult. Youth must learn that real life is not to be confused with an encounter group session, that status interaction is not necessarily bad, and that clear and hard functional work without disruption by *ad hominem* arguments is an indispensable prerequisite for society.

Sociologists Ken Keniston[41] and Richard Flacks[42] take the middle ground—seeing mature as well as immature aspects of countercultural activism—and they take a scientific stance in describing their findings. They have found activist youth more intelligent, independent, sensitive, concerned with moral values, idealistic, and emotionally secure than nonactivist youth. Rather than rejecting youthful activism and dissent by references to psychopathology or, on the other hand, accepting it uncritically as the dawn of a new millennium, these sociologists encourage the public to be responsive to what is legitimate and reasonable in the dissent. By engaging in a dialogue, the older and the younger generation as well as the radicals and the conservatives could help each other obtain insight and understanding. Radical youth, in the opinion of these sociologists, points the way to improvement because they react against a society that may need alternative or modified values to improve a materialistic-capitalistic civilization.

Where has the counterculture gone and what has it accomplished?

[40]John S. Aldridge, *In the Country of the Young* (New York: Harper's Magazine Press, 1970).

[41]Kenneth Keniston, *Young Radicals: Notes on Committed Youth* (New York: Harcourt, 1968) and "Student Activism, Moral Development, and Morality," *American Journal of Orthopsychiatry*, 40 (July 1970), 577–92.

[42]Richard Flacks, "The Liberated Generation."

First, the youthful counterculture is not an ephemeral moment in history; it is an ongoing process that will linger to some degree as long as there exists an adolescent population that possesses the potential for rebellion, deviation, and innovation. (This argument, discussed earlier, is also advanced by Mannheim and Musgrove.) The countercultural potential is an intrinsic element of the adolescent collectivity, and, in a sense, there is a correlation between the degrees of adolescence and the degree of potential. In sum, one may say that adolescence provides for some degree of perpetual counterculture. The virulent upheaval of the 1965–72 counterculture is therefore merely a sharp upward fluctuation of the seismograph that measures adolescent unrest. Its extreme expression was probably triggered by the unusually vulnerable climate surrounding the war in Vietnam; and, interestingly enough, countercultural activism dissipated as the war declined and finally came to an end. The potential for renewed explosion remains, and the triggering of new unrest depends on processes occurring in the larger society as well as in international relations.

Second, the counterculture left impressions that will not soon be deleted. "Straight" society, in absorbing them, has been bent. Student activism, a core aspect of the counterculture, has largely abolished the old *in loco parentis* authority and promoted a clearer transition into adult status. It is largely to the credit of the agitation and demands of the counterculture that federal legislation fixed the legal adult age at eighteen. A new morality reflects the impact of the counterculture: Yankelovich's survey during the mid-1970s revealed the emergence of new cultural attitudes and the decline of some old ones. To reiterate, the postcounterculture generation is characterized by: (1) a less sex-stereotyped view of human interaction, (2) a more sensitive outlook on war, the military, and national policy, (3) a "self-actualizing" career motivation, (4) a psychology of entitlement that takes economic security and other privileges for granted, and expects the government to provide them, (5) resistance to the old Protestant ethic, and (6) skepticism toward the scientific world view.

The last point was illustrated by a 1989 international survey. In response to the question whether they believed that scientific progress will be beneficial to humanity in the long run, only 23 percent of the young people polled in Japan were affirmative, 33 percent in West Germany, and 37 percent in France. Women showed significantly higher skepticism than men in regard to the role of science in making this a better world; differences between members of liberal or conservative political parties were insignificant. It is noteworthy that Japanese youth, belonging to one of the world's most scientifically advanced nations, felt most pessimistic.[43]

---

[43]The German Research Service, "International Comparison," *Special Science Reports,* 5 (October 1989): 4–6.

Most importantly, the counterculture has silently spawned the New Age movement. Because the movement refrains from militancy, missionary zeal, and representation in public life, its growth and significance have largely escaped public attention. While it is unlike its progenitorial counterculture in manner and in the amount of decibels used to express an alternative lifestyle, it resembles the counterculture insofar as it lacks coherent organization, definite leadership, and a uniform platform. The core followers of the New Age are withdrawn communards who prefer a gentle and "natural" way of life and "doing one's own thing." Their lifestyle is a conscious and uncompromising result of the counterculture, and their guiding star is a philosophy that has little use for the traditional American materialism and capitalism.

Core characteristics of the counterculture and perpetuated by the New Age included a blending of Oriental philosophy and Judeo-Christian theology, as pointed out in Table 14-1. Substantial proportions of young Americans believed in occult and pseudoscientific assumptions, as revealed by surveys during the 1970s and 1980s. The proportions of Americans believing in these assumptions have shown surprising stability over the years; 1990 Gallup surveys have yielded comparable data.[44] Beliefs in ghosts, telepathic abilities, horoscopes, and UFOs continue unabatedly.

But there are several aspects of the more recent findings that are noteworthy. First, when asked "Have you read or heard about the New Age?" only 29 percent said yes, 69 percent said no, and 2 percent weren't sure. Second, when those who were familiar with the term were asked about their opinion about it, 18 percent expressed favorable and nearly 50 percent an unfavorable opinion. The rest had no opinion.

What is so interesting about the lack of knowledge about the New Age and the high proportion of unfavorable attitude of those familiar with the term is the historical fact that every young generation since the counterculture years has perpetuated New Age core concepts, mostly without knowing it, it seems. The most outstanding feature of the counterculture continued by the New Age is the peculiar combination of Oriental philosophy and Judeo-Christian theology. Findings of surveys carried out by this author in the 1970s and 1980s, showing that at least 20 percent of the young generations believed in reincarnation and the Christian God *at the same time,* were corroborated by 1990 Gallup figures:

> One out of five Americans (21%) believe in reincarnation—the "rebirth of the soul in a new body after death"—a concept significantly different from the life-after-death belief that forms the central component of mainstream Protestant and Catholic theology in this country.
> Despite this, belief in reincarnation cuts across all of Gallup's traditional

[44]George H. Gallup and Frank Newport, "Belief in Paranormal Phenomena," *Skeptical Inquirer,* 15 (Winter 1991): 137–146.

religious measures: it is believed in by 24% of Catholics, 19% of Protestants, 21% of church members, 18% of those who attend church regularly, and 22% of all those who are "born-again" Christians. About one in ten Americans, in fact, go as far as to say that they themselves feel that they were here on Earth in a previous life or existence in another body.[45]

It is for future historians to more fully evaluate what the impact of these synthetic belief patterns—once countercultural, then New Age, now popular—will be upon American society, or indeed upon Western Civilization in general.

THE TRUE-BELIEVER MOVEMENTS

The escape routes from alienation and meaninglessness during the 1960s and 1970s jutted out into many different directions. Where they arrived depended not so much on youth's sense of direction as on three related factors: (1) the intensity of alienation, (2) the basic emotional predisposition of the individual, and (3) the coincidence of exposure. Most likely it is the basic emotional makeup of the individual that is the major prompting force to join radical and totalitarian groups.

For example, young persons who have been consistently conditioned from early years to depend on outside authority to guide them and make decisions for them are more interested in affiliations where they again can play a subservient role. If their sense of alienation and loneliness is strong enough, they may lock into a movement that calls for following and obeying rather than for independent thought. Conversely, youths whose upbringing equipped them with a sense of self-confidence may either stay aloof from radical affiliations or seek out groups that provide opportunities for independent thought.

Pitirim A. Sorokin's theory of historical phases forms a cogent background for this discussion. The theory assumes that we have left an idealistic era, are currently groping in a sensate age, and are about to enter a new ideational phase. Our current unrest, symptomized by youth's search for identity, signifies the advent of an ideational civilization that will satisfy the need for an unambiguous world view.

Apparently our traditional ideational forces have declined and become meaningless for the young generations, whose alienation drives them on toward alternative realities. The old scientific reality, the "objective consciousness," is no longer sufficiently powerful to capture the imagination of youth and dispel their existential anxiety.

No movement other than the religious-totalitarian provides so complete

[45]Ibid., p. 143.

a gratification for youth's ideational search. It is in this perspective that a number of powerful religious youth movements must be understood. The revival of mystical religion, primitive lore, spiritualism, ritual occultism, astrology, and the preoccupation with meditation is beyond a mere fad—it is youth's attempt to expand awareness beyond the limits imposed by modern science and the objective approach to life. This reaching out for new meaning is the great adventure of our age.[46]

While the search for meaning is of course a natural part of every individual's life, the followers of the True-Believer movements distinguish themselves from ordinary searchers insofar as

1. they use their lives to serve the belief instead of the reverse;
2. they make proselytizing their duty;
3. they claim that their belief is the only valid philosophy in life;
4. they use radical means to accomplish the vision of the True Belief;
5. they subordinate themselves to a totalitarian-radical organization and to leaders who demand absolute loyalty.

These characteristics illustrate that the psychological climate of the general counterculture was different only in degree and not in kind. The True-Believer movement must also be understood in terms of the *ideal type*, which means that some of the movements discussed do not meet all criteria or meet them only to some extent.

All radical youth movements have a religious core. It is the integrating, meaning-giving function at the heart of the definition of religion (from *religare*, "to bind together") that youth seek. Such movements typically possess *creed, cult,* and *code*; that is, they proclaim a basic meaning, provide ritual and sensate implementation, and present guidelines for everyday life.

The cultic is instrumental in creating a sense of transcendence, the feeling of merging into a wholeness of existence, being related to others, and being integrated meaningfully into the universe. This feeling can be strong enough to envision a freedom from conventional rules of language and logic—ultimately of freedom from all the rules of society. Some movements exhibit these characteristics more explicitly than the general counterculture, and that is why we present some examples:

The Jesus movement.   A movement that has amassed many followers and much publicity is the Jesus movement. It was a revival of a fundamentalist version of Christianity, the brunt of which was carried by the fervor of

---

[46]See detailed discussions in David G. Bromley and Anson D. Shupe, Jr., *Strange Gods: The Great American Cult Scare* (Boston: Beacon, 1981); Ken Levi, ed., *Violence and Religious Commitment* (University Park: Pennsylvania State University Press, 1982); and Herbert Richardson, ed., *New Religious and Mental Health* (Lewiston, NY: Edwin Mellen Press, 1980).

thousands of young Americans who proclaimed a revolution in Jesus' name.[47] Their message was that the Bible is absolutely true and that miracles do happen. They proceeded to spread the message with the zeal of revolutionaries, relying on otherworldly powers. Their activism followed a timetable that was announced by Bill Bright, the founder of Campus Crusade for Christ, who forecast the saturation of America with the gospel of Christ by 1976, and that of the world by 1980. He allowed, however, that the Lord might prefer a slower pace.[48]

Studies have shown that many of the young zealots had gone through serious personal difficulties prior to their conversions, and many of them engaged in a May-December marriage of the rebellious counterculture and conservative religion.[49] Many of them switched from the fraudulent promises of drugs to the promises of Life Eternal and Life Meaningful. They replaced the situation ethics with the Ten Commandments, expecting greater psychological security from an ensconcement in a totalitarian world view. Many of them switched from being flower children to children of the Lord. In letters to editors teenagers repent their past "dope" habits, find Jesus far more rewarding to be "stoned on," and approve of Him as a "far-out guy," who works miracles.[50]

The emphasis of the New Christian movement was on the *personal relationship* with Jesus, who enters the lives of individuals and manifests Himself in miracles that still occur today. The commitment of many adolescents to the new Christianity was total and they burned all bridges behind — though they didn't have that many to burn.

This was not a uniform movement. There were the well-dressed collegians, the Campus Crusaders for Christ, maintaining booths on campus malls and taking every opportunity to speak to classes and groups. Then there were the more spontaneous and younger converts who chanted hymns, swayed to musical rhythms in ecstasy, crowded beaches for mass baptism, and proclaimed their newly found identity with jubilation, love, and eternal promises. They were also known as Street Christians, Jesus Freaks, or Evangelical hippies, and it was they who blended conservative religion with the counterculture. Their beginning is usually traced to the 1967 flower era in San Francisco, but there were simultaneous stirrings in other parts of the U.S. Many of the converts, though by no means all, affected the hippie style; many others, however, foreswore it as part of their new lives. And finally

---

[47]Flo Conway and Jim Siegelman, *Holy Terror* (New York: Doubleday, 1982). A less analytic and more personal account of confronting the Jesus cult is by Steve Allen, *Beloved Son: A Story of the Jesus Cults* (New York: Bobbs-Merrill, 1981).

[48]"The New Rebel Cry: Jesus is Coming," *Time*, June 21, 1971, p. 56.

[49]Fred L. Whitam, "Peers, Parents, and Christ," *Proceedings of the Southwestern Sociological Association*, 19 (1968): 154–58.

[50]"Letters to the Editor," *Look*, March 23, 1971, p. 6.

there were the dead-serious Children of God who foresaw doomsday for America, retreated into farm communes, adopted biblical aliases for their members, pursued proselytizing with fanaticism (they were accused of brainwashing), and spread to become an international movement.

The mass-behavior aspects of the movement would have provided a laboratory for testing the Durkheimian theory of the origin of religiosity: the contagious chanting, singing, dancing, swaying, and the reinforcing corollary of testimonials, oratory, and ritual seemed to produce in many participants a degree of ecstasy that was interpreted as religious experience by the transfixed. Durkheim's theory maintains that religiosity is predicated not by cognitive search but by the ecstasy-arousing participation in group rituals and mass excitement. The French sociologist called attention to the power of the group in bringing forth social products which could not be explained through individual physiological or psychological process.[51]

The Unification movement.   Another radical religious movement that recruited followers primarily from the young was Reverend Sun Myung Moon's international Unification Church and its college chapters, the Collegiate Association for the Research of Principles. The youthful followers were inspired by the idea of changing the world and making it a better place. The method for achieving this, according to the movement's spokespersons, is a "unification of thought" that, more than being merely a religious creed, consists of a total lifestyle. It aspires to unite the world on a spiritual basis. To pursue the conversion of college youth, the movement maintains communal living centers in the vicinity of most large universities. Just as the Krishna movement (discussed below), Moon's circle was a haven for ex-hippies who fled confusing anomie to embrace an ascetic and absolutistic lifestyle that provided security and direction.[52]

The endurance of the movement is astounding. It has weathered difficulties on all fronts, including the 1982 federal conviction of Reverend Moon on tax offenses, restrictions by local authorities, and the relentless pursuit of "deprogrammers" over several decades. Instead of diminishing, membership has grown steadily and by the early 1980s far exceeded the reported 30,000 of the mid 1970s.

At the Unification Church Training Center at Barrytown, New York, Moon's young missionaries are being prepared for a World Plan to rid the world of Satan, who is believed to be very much alive and active—in fact, among other things, causing possessions. From the very beginning believers

[51]Emile Durkheim, *The Elementary Forms of the Religious Life* (New York: Macmillan, 1915).

[52]Berkeley Rice, "Messiah From Korea: Honor Thy Father Moon," *Psychology Today*, 9 (January 1976): 36–45.

assumed that Moon is the messiah, hence entitled to command absolute devotion. In 1990, Moon finally affirmed this belief personally.

Cases of youthful followers' alienation from their parents have been reported and the movement was accused of brainwashing young people. Press and TV reports described mental breakdowns as a consequence of intense indoctrination and the resulting conflicts and anxieties. Some parents, realizing that they had lost control over their offspring, conspired to have them kidnapped.

The movement declares the world ripe for spiritual change, for spiritual revolution. This finds a receptive audience among adolescents who long for peace and clarity and can identify with the goals of the movement. The slogans of "spiritual revolution," "replacing America's materialistic values," and "new values of love and brotherhood"—ancient as they may sound—function as the promise for deliverance, particularly for those youths who are in extreme need of "spiritual" (speaking more correctly, emotional) guidance and deliverance.

The Divine Light Mission.   Also during the 1970s, the Divine Light Mission, headed for several years by the teenage guru Maharij Ji, rallied thousands of young Americans around the belief that there is always a Perfect Master on earth and that Moses, Jesus, Buddha, and Krishna are now succeeded by Maharij Ji, who is in charge of spreading the Divine Word to initiate modern humans into the full knowledge of God. This was fervently believed by an estimated 60,000 young Americans.

Young people's need for a totalitarian meaning and for a spiritual leader was met by the charismatic mystique the young Oriental guru seemed to possess. This charisma was apparently powerful enough to make palatable— if not plausible—the conspicuous discrepancy between the lifestyle of the guru and that of his followers. The former included airplanes, expensive real estate, mansions, a Rolls Royce, two Mercedes Benz automobiles, and so forth, whereas the latter approached the nonmaterialistic level of the countercultural people. Rennie Davis, of Chicago Seven fame and the most celebrated of the guru's converts, explained the discrepancy by pointing out that Maharij Ji was divine, the Lord, and that his followers gladly wait on him.[53]

Again, the movement used the elements of mass behavior to inspire followers. There were secret rituals, pageantry (e.g., the three-day "Millennium 1973" that attracted 25,000 devotees to the Houston Astrodome), public commitments, and an uncomplicated, grandiose World Plan for deliverance from all problems. That masses of young Americans found credence in

[53]David Snell, "Goom Rodgie," *Saturday Review*, September 2, 1974, p. 19.

something so unoriginal and simplistic is testimony to the depth of their starvation for meaning and identity.

The Krishna movement.   Youth's search for meaning and order has found Krishna a source of bliss.[54] The American public has become somewhat accustomed to the chanting head-shaven, saffron-robed youths found standing and swaying as if in a blissful trance in public places. Accustomed is not the proper way of describing the public reaction, however, since it usually consists of a mixture of uneasy emotions, including a vague embarrassment that is usually reserved for something slightly repulsive and untouchable— such as the primitives' awe of the insane. Be this as it may, the Hare Krishna disciples exhibit a singular courage to openly behave in a way so radically different from that of the Western churchgoing believers.

The Hare Krishna movement takes its strength from asceticism and, simple as it may sound, from chanting and dancing. Its participants conceptualize "the illusion" that the physical world reported by our senses is real as *maya*. This assumption offers to the Krishna devotee the same challenge that sin offers to the revival preacher. Krishna, to the believer, is the name of God in His highest manifestation. Chanting His name drives away this illusion and is the source of absolute bliss.

The personality cult of the movement used to focus on Swami Bhaktivedanta, the spiritual master and inspirer of the International Society of Krishna Consciousness. His death in 1977 did not slow down the movement. Instead, it continued to grow (nationally and internationally) since then, manifesting its vitality by completing in 1980 a "Palace of Gold" on a 2,000-acre spread in the hills of West Virginia, winning a New York State Supreme Court judgment in a deprogramming case, untiringly soliciting in airports and other public places, which netted them injunctions by various local authorities, and producing out of their own ranks effective new leadership.[55]

Few of the thousands of followers, including full initiates, part-time chanters, and temple worshippers, are over 30, and a large proportion are in their teens. Their lives include vegetarianism; abstention from drugs, alcohol, and sex (except for purpose of reproduction within the marital relationship); adoption of Sanskrit aliases; up to 12 hours of daily chanting and dancing in public places; and what modern Americans would call an outspokenly sexist philosophy. Females (or as they would put it, "living entities that assume the female organism") are always considered inferior to males. The female devotee's only purpose in life is to serve her husband.

During and right after the counterculture years, many of the Krishna

---

[54]J. Stillson Judah, *Hare Krishna and the Counterculture* (New York: Wiley-Interscience, 1974).

[55]"Religion," *Time*, September 15, 1980, p. 71.

devotees drifted over from the hippie movement, where they lived in communes, were into drugs (many admit to LSD trips during that stage), and lived promiscuously. Conversion to Krishna Consciousness radically reversed the latter two aspects and led to the condemnation of Leary and others as false prophets and to a new "puritanism" unmatched by any other current movement.

The power of conversion was illustrated by a participant-observation study by Joseph Damrell, who describes the unintentional conversion of a commune to the Krishna creed: a typically drug-infested (dealing and "tripping"), hedonistic hippie commune tried to pass itself off as a religious group using marijuana as a "sacrament" (thereby intending to gain impunity before the law) and in the process of charading became serious about Krishna ideas, ultimately converted, refashioned the commune into a temple, and radically altered their former ethics.[56]

The Meditation movement.   The most powerful and numerous among the different meditation groups is the Transcendental Meditation movement. TM practitioners increased by leaps and bounds during the 1970s, starting with perhaps 100,000 at the beginning of the decade and ending with about 800,000.

TM's student branch, Students International Meditation Society, addressed itself to college students and established a chapter on nearly every large campus in the U.S. The founder, Maharishi Mahesh Yogi (again the focus of personality cult), has control over the vast network of teachers and initiators and has established a business enterprise that would do honor to a successful industrial magnate. From the angle of most devotees, however, it is not business (notwithstanding the relatively high initiation fee, costs for "retreats," "residence courses," teacher's training, etc.) but a True Belief and the answer to all problems. Again, we notice the all-encompassing solution that meditation promises. Given that there is little doubt that transcendental meditation can function as hygiene for the human brain, leading to relaxation and thus to a more comfortable and healthier life, the philosophy of transcendental meditation has been expanded to visualize "levels of consciousness," the highest of which is God Consciousness—which brings us straight back to Krishna Consciousness.

Like the Krishna chant, transcendental meditation uses the medium of a repetitive word to induce trance and relaxation—called "bliss." This time, however, the word is called a *mantra* and is repeated silently in one's mind, usually without the benefit of an immediate group (though group meditation is a favorite, too).

[56]Joseph Damrell, *Search for Identity: Youth, Religion and Culture* (Beverly Hills: Sage Publications, 1978).

Unlike the Krishna devotees, meditators keep cult and ritual at a minimum (though there are Hindu rituals and prayers at the time of initiation), do not base communal living on it, and essentially adapt meditation to the fast pace of American life without retreating to it more than twice daily for 20 minutes each time. In general, meditators exhibit a more adaptive attitude, make meditation serve other functions in their lives, are not radically oriented, and, unlike members of other movements, they meet the earlier mentioned characteristics of the True Believer movement only in a few aspects. This Oriental import has in fact been adapted to scientific and Puritan values because "it makes you *work* better."[57]

This exercise in brain hygiene, however, has assumed more and more the nature of a totalitarian philosophy that claims to possess the solution for all of humankind's problems. In line with this assumption a World Plan has been prepared, according to which every population center should have a World Plan Center and enough teachers (ultimately one per 1000 population) to bring transcendental meditation to everyone. Maharishi International University (formerly Parsons College) has a hefty enrollment of devotees studying the Science of Creative Intelligence and forming a potential pool for teachers of meditation.

It must be emphasized that the benefits of meditation seem to have a sound scientific basis insofar as they include relaxation and the consequent freeing of extra nervous energy.[58] The attributes of a True Believer movement come into sharper focus only when the theology of God Consciousness is added—a level of consciousness that presumably can be achieved through consistent meditation and that will mean the deliverance of humankind from all evil.

The psychedelic movement.   Close to the core of the counterculture, the psychedelic movement could be singled out as a True-Believer movement because it tried to make converts, assumed to have found a lifestyle of bliss and superior insight, and practiced ritual and cultism to provide the emotional solidarity of the like-minded and the persecuted.[59] Presumably, its essential *raison d'être* was the pursuit of internal freedom and the exploration of the inner reaches of the human mind. This ideology of the mystical experience must be understood against the background of what was perceived as an insensitive and overobjectified civilization; it was a withdrawal from Western objectivism to the inner dimensions of visions and beatitude.

---

[57]A simple in-group statement of what TM is was presented by Denise Denniston and Peter McWilliams, *The TM Book* (New York: Price, Stern, Sloan, 1975).

[58]The psychosomatic benefits of TM were extolled by psychiatrist Harold Bloomfield et al., *TM* (New York: Delacorte, 1975).

[59]Orrin E. Klapp argues cogently the appropriateness of defining the psychedelic wave as a social movement in *Collective Search for Identity* (New York: Holt, Rinehart & Winston, 1969), pp. 170–76.

The movement, which started in the late 1950s and early 1960s, had its major prophet in Aldous Huxley,[60] soon found its gurus in such figures as Timothy Leary and Richard Alpert, not long thereafter acquired armies of "martyrs" (including Leary and Alpert), founded the International Federation for Internal Freedom with its short-lived esoteric quarterly, *The Psychedelic Review*, and established centers for research and the psychedelic experience. The movement gradually spilled over into the masses of unprepared adolescents, attracted followers who were less interested in research and insight than in the thrill of the new and forbidden and in the benefits of belonging to an in-group. Soon the movement became coterminous with the hippie movement. What attracted the adolescent followers was more the identity derived from submerging into an underground movement than a serious interest in finding the doors to higher levels of consciousness (including the elusive "cosmic consciousness" promised by the earlier and more serious pioneers of the movement).

There was also the promise—mostly fraudulent as it turned out—of *instant* gratification and insight through such drugs as LSD, mescaline, and psilocybin. The philosophy of instantness was perfectly suited for the adolescent mind whose hedonism was not yet harnessed by the experiences of life. This attitude was a natural extrapolation of society's philosophy of "better living through chemistry" and the habit of taking recourse to chemicals for almost any conceivable problems or ailments. The psychedelists based their mystical pursuits on chemical promises.[61]

Insight and knowledge, alas, defy chemical instantness. Nonetheless, the movement continued, vociferously covered up its abortive experiment and, instead of the mystical function of psychedelics, increasingly accented the gregarious bonds among the followers. By the mid-1970s, the psychedelic movement was largely dissipated, at best an empty shell that was merely sporadically inhabited by stragglers who had not yet reconciled themselves with the historical fact that the hippie-psychedelic movement had largely become defunct. We can thus see that this movement, from its inception in the 1950s to its demise in the 1970s, has gone through the fervor of a religious movement, the rebellion associated with the counterculture, the indiscriminate following of masses of unsophisticated teenagers, to merely sporadic and individual experimentations.

Archconservative movements.   It would be misleading to assume that a True-Believer movement must always be revolutionary and threaten to overturn existing mores and institutions. A True-Believer movement may consist

---

[60]Aldous Huxley, *Doors of Perception* (New York: Harper & Row, Publishers, 1954).
[61]Hans Sebald, "The Pursuit of 'Instantness' in Technocratic Society and Youth's Psychedelic Drug Use," *Adolescence*, 7 (Fall 1972): 343–50.

of archconservatives who defend the status quo and who, if necessary, are willing to do so by radical means. Though their motivation is not so much a search for identity, it is the defense of an identity they already have, want to keep, and feel is the only true source of wisdom. They are similar to the radical searchers for meaning insofar as they try to convert others; have some sort of a World Plan, a vision of salvation that applies to all humans regardless of whether they know or like it (in the first instance they have to be told, in the second instance, persuaded or coerced); subordinate their personal lives to the goals of the True Belief; become obedient followers of charismatic leaders, and, most significantly, share a common perception of a Great Conspiracy or Great Peril.

This kind of movement is usually carried by adults, which is only logical, for in order to conserve something, one first has to have something. Youth, by age limitation, are not in a position to be conservative about their own values; they can only adopt values and join other conservatives. This, of course, is done every day in the U.S. and around the world. Were this not true, no established organization, sect, or cult would survive. There is an ongoing process of recruitment from the ranks of the young, and a sizable proportion of American youth throws in with the meanings and premises of such conservative groups—be they Pentecostalists or the Moral Majority— and find their identity in such fashion.

COMMON FEATURES

Although the labels differ, the functions of the various True-Believer movements are very similar, if not identical. All of them present a total meaning of life; provide the emotional succor of belonging to a community of the destined, elect or persecuted; make possible a transcendental feeling that opens the cage of self-isolation; make ecstasy possible through rituals and group raptures; define evil; suggest a World Plan that spells out the way to salvation; engage in a personality cult and make idols of their leaders; and strongly proselytize, often winning converts who have already a history of search or affiliation with radical or deviant groups.

TRENDS AND OUTLOOK

Since the 1970s, the waves of youthful activism and radicalism, once of shattering power, have calmed. Resignation and privatism have set in. The Establishment has once more withstood the onslaught of youth's restlessness, rebellion, and demand for meaning. Neither side has won the battle; the larger society has been affected by the counterculture and has bowed to some of its criticisms; and the younger generation, before as after, finds itself ensconced in an essentially postindustrial system that keeps them in the youth ghettos of adolescence. Provided that no new national or international crises disrupt the relative calm of the 1980s, American youth most likely will, though grudgingly, stick to books and lectures to get an education and will pursue careers with "self-actualizing" potential. To ameliorate banal existence and appease the worst of the craving for a sense of destiny, they will be attracted to a range of pop mysticism, including the occult, astrology, and spiritualism—unfailing signs of alienation from existing institutions.

The cultic experiences will continue, but will not necessarily become more prevalent.[62] It appears that with the 1980s a stagnation period has set in, with youth having settled on a tolerable plateau of alienation and separatism.

Sooner or later, the vast majority of rebellious youth will be swallowed up by the social structure of society and find positions that will soothe the hurt of adolescence and make them miraculously forget all about it. In fact, soon after they anchor their personal identities in the adult social structure, *they* in turn will be the older generation against which the resentment of the younger generation (including their own offspring) will be directed. So much for the erstwhile countercultural youth!

This illustrates the power of the Establishment's social structure, the arrangement of positions, which, once entered, have a way of surreptitiously and imperceptibly changing attitudes and outlook to convert countercultural individuals into members, even defenders of the "system."

However, the reentry principle fails to apply to a minority of counter-cultural people. Certain young adults appear unable to fully reenter the mainstream of American society. Not addressing herself so much to bonafide activists, Amira Wallach completed 105 follow-up studies of persons who, during the 1960s and 1970s, had identified themselves as hippies and had been heavily into drugs (an average of thirteen different kinds, including daily marijuana).[63] She discovered that by the late 1970s the subjects could be categorized into three groups: reentry, semireentry, and nonreentry into mainstream American society. The young adults were assessed on six variables—drug use, occupation, education, residential stability, interpersonal relationships, and therapy—and had to meet the norms and expectations of the dominant society on at least five variables to be considered reformed. The forty-three persons who were considered as having reentered came from large, stable families and felt more attached to their families. Of the sample, they had been the lightest drug users and largely nondelinquent. The thirty-five semireentries were least competent in establishing an economically

[62]Andrew J. Pavlos, *The Cult Experience* (Westport, CT: Greenwood Press, 1982).

[63]Amira Wallach, "Straggling Back: Yesterday's Flower Children are Growing Up," *Human Behavior*, Vol. 7, February 1978, p. 36.

independent lifestyle; one third of them were on welfare. They had consider-able personality problems and came from families where role models had been unstable. The twenty-seven nonreentries were, unlike the other two groups, almost all males. They were lowest in educational achievement, with most not having completed high school. Their drug use was heaviest (includ-ing opiates) and their employment record highly unstable. These people stayed in the hippie subculture, or in a substitute thereof. To Wallach, "the hippie movement seems like a prolonged adolescence that some participants outgrew and some didn't."[64]

Focusing on a sample of young adults who had been sophisticated activists rather than mere hippies, James M. Fendrich traced the socio-economic careers of the former over ten years.[65] He found that almost all of them gyrated toward the public sector of the job market, where the largest proportion of them were concentrated in university teaching positions (pri-marily social sciences). The second largest concentration was found in the social service and creative occupations. They became social workers and freelance writers. These positions allow them the role of societal critics and many of them continue to express political concerns as they attempt, espe-cially as teachers, to influence young people. Their new style of activism is less raucous. Being more subtle, it often claims immunity from criticism by merit of the traditional sanctity accorded the role of the educator.

The integration of erstwhile dissident youth into the adult structure is highlighted by "reform" of such notorious counterculture figures as Abbie Hoffman and Jerry Rubin. They changed to channel their fervor into the business world of America, intent on making money, intent on becoming "successful." Hoffman was a leader of the 1960s underground Yippie move-ment, preaching revolution against the American Establishment, dealing in drugs, being convicted, escaping from justice and going underground for seven years. With opportunistic flair, he timed his reappearance in 1980 to coincide with the publication of his autobiography, *Soon to be a Major Movie Picture*, with the movie rights sold to Universal for $200,000.[66] When he died in 1989, he was a well integrated citizen of the American system. Rubin, another leading figure of the Yippies, mocked the U.S. political system in 1968 by trying to run a pig for President. As one of the Chicago Seven defendants, he was convicted of inciting the riots at the 1968 Democratic Convention. By the 1980s he had changed into a businessman's suit, drew an impressive, nonproletarian salary as a securities analyst in a respectable New York firm, and proclaimed what would cheer the Moral Majority as well as

[64]Ibid.

[65]James M. Fendrich, "Activists Ten Years Later: A Test of Generational Unit Continu-ity," *Journal of Social Issues*, 30 (Fall 1974): 95–118.

[66]"A Yippie Comes in from the Damp," *Time*, September 15, 1980, p. 22.

the Republican Convention: "The challenge of the '80s is to bring back the entrepreneurial spirit."[67]

There are additional examples. Rennie Davis, another revolutionary who rejoined middle America, took to managing a high-tech finance firm in Colorado. Bobby Seale, tired of rebellion, changed to researching a cookbook on barbecuing. Former rebel Tom Hayden, with substantial support from his movie-actress wife, changed his political manners and in 1982 decided to run for the California state assembly. In 1988 he published *Reunion: A Memoir* and thereby followed the example of other ex-counterculture celebrities in beating a capitalistic fortune out of his anticapitalistic past.

The list of famous persons whose rebelliousness once made headlines across the nation and who now lead bourgeois lifestyles could be continued.

The immediate reaction of young adults who have suffered (or at least witnessed) the defeat of their counterculture usually is retreatism and renunciation of the world, and the pursuit of personal salvation. Even younger youths, not knowing what it was all about, tend to follow their example for awhile, imitating their privatistic ways and what is "in" until in the years ahead a new mood may arouse them to a new cause. And what that will be, no one can safely predict.

No observer of youth should make the mistake of believing that a countercultural upheaval will not recur. The motivation for it continues to exist and is only temporarily anesthetized by privatistic diversion. If there is any truth in Sorokin's historical-sociological theory, our sensate age screams for a resolution, and demands may again be couched in a countercultural framework.

SUMMARY

While the general teen and pop subculture is fad- and entertainment-oriented, the counterculture is action- and goal-oriented.

Alienation is probably the most generic concept for understanding youth's unrest and dissatisfaction. Youth is vulnerable to the elusiveness of tradition, an elusiveness caused by rapid sociocultural changes; to the ideational void imposed by anomie; to the meaninglessness derived from upper-middle-class youth's satiation of material needs; and the frustrations that naturally come with socialization.

Youth radicalism in our age essentially is a search for alternative realities that offer clearer identities than the present system. The response to alienation differs widely: utopias, countercultures, True-Believer movements, and retreatism.

[67]"Rubin Relents," *Time*, August 11, 1980, p. 23.

The prime example of the search for an alternative lifestyle was the counterculture, a composite of various movements which agreed on a stance that was antitechnocratic, antiwar, prodrug, and promystic. The evaluations of the counterculture ranged from enthusiastic endorsement as a presumably mature and sensitive collectivity to clinical rejection as a presumably immature and pathological expression; a number of sociologists took the middle ground, encouraging a dialogue that might benefit American society. The movement's activities can be divided into activism directed outward and into internal maintenance functions that regulate interaction and the subinstitutions—with the latter tending to interfere with activist functions.

The New Age movement of the 1980s is a more philosophical, more retreatist, and nonmilitant extension of the counterculture. It is putting to actual test an alternative lifestyle that the counterculture largely only talked about, as well as synthesizing Oriental religion with a small-community philosophy.

The True-Believer movements provide a radical and often religious environment, ideally suited for youths with extreme identity needs. The True Believers use their lives to serve the belief instead of vice versa. They proselytize, assume they possess the only true philosophy, use drastic means to achieve their goals, and give unquestioned loyalty to leaders. Examples include the Jesus movement, the Unification movement, the Divine Light Mission, Krishna Consciousness, the Meditation movement, the psychedelic movement, and archconservative movements. All offer a total meaning of life, provide a community, induce transcendentalism, use group ecstasy, define evil, have a World Plan for salvation, engage in personality cults, and pursue conversions.

Although the counterculture has subsided, the potential for renewed youth upheaval is immanent in the adolescent condition, the anomie of Western civilization, and the thirst for a total ideation.

15

A Range of Challenges

This book does not specifically address social problems. Rather it looks at structural and functional conditions, analyzes them, and presents information accordingly. The information can then be utilized by the experts of social engineering—social workers, correctional officers, educators, and policy makers—in their work to mend weaknesses in the social fabric.

Nonetheless, the central concept of this work, adolescence, is so obviously associated with a range of social problems that at least some of them should be briefly mentioned. It would, however, be futile to look in these pages for elaborate statements spelling out how to solve them; such ambition would require discussions far beyond the framework of this book. All that can be offered here are some short discussions sensitizing the reader toward a few of the prime examples of adolescent problems. They include the high-school dropout, the transition into the labor force, drug abuse, teenage sexuality, premarital sex, and teenage pregnancy.

THE HIGH-SCHOOL DROPOUT

The extent of the problem.   The term "dropout" is applied to everyone who leaves high school without a diploma. Dropping out is usually interpreted as an indication of a youngster's unwillingness or inability to learn.

The reason authorities and the general public consider the act of dropping out with as much dismay as they currently do emerges from the fact that outside high school there is no appropriate place for the high-school-aged youngster. Putting it crudely and yet fittingly, quitting school prematurely messes up the social structure. The failure to provide an alternative status to that of a high-school student is as much a function of the general value orientation of the culture as it is of modern economic conditions that pattern social structure.

Some statistics documenting the scope of the problem are misleading. It is true that the number of dropouts has increased over the past decades. The *rate* of dropouts, however, has not increased, and has, in fact, decreased. If there are *more* dropouts today than previously, it is because there are many more teenagers to start with. It has been estimated, for example, that nearly 10 million teenagers were dropouts during the 1980s—a figure unprecedented during any previous decade. On the other hand, the dropout rate was around 30 percent, which constituted a notable decrease from the rate of nearly 50 percent during previous decades. The public concern about the dropout problem is thus due to the increase in the sheer number of dropouts.

In general, it appears that the dropout rate will change less dramatically than during previous decades. The small changes that will take place will further reduce the rate—probably to about 20 percent during the 1990s.

The dropout incidence is not evenly distributed throughout the high-school population, but differs among communities, socioeconomic classes, and ethnic and racial minorities. The highest dropout rate occurs in urban high schools that draw their students from neighborhoods composed predominantly of lower socioeconomic classes and minority groups. The prevailing value orientation as well as the trying economic conditions among slum or semislum dwellers are not conducive to value education. Youngsters from such neighborhoods are known for their chronic truancy and tendency to drop out of school as soon as they reach age sixteen. Little serious official effort is made to persuade them to remain in school, because they usually have established a record of being problematic, if not delinquent, and are considered a "bad influence" on peers.

Rural environments also present a temptation to leave high school prematurely. Youngsters may prefer, or actually be asked by parents, to join the family's agricultural enterprise. Unlike in an urban slum setting, a job is waiting for them, and success in the agriculture vocation does not, in their or their parents' opinion, depend on schooling beyond the eighth grade. Although most farm families see to it that the children fulfill their legal requirement and stay in school up to sixteen years of age, they may consent to, or even suggest, withdrawal after that age. The farm people's rejection of schooling beyond the three basic "Rs" was strikingly illustrated by the Amish refusal to send their children to high school.

Probably the lowest incidence of premature termination of high school is found in the middle-class suburb. Value orientation as well as long-range professional plans keep the youngsters in high school until graduation. For a sizable proportion of the youth of suburbia, high school is preparation for college. In fact, a number of upper- and middle-class youngsters prefer to attend special prep schools rather than general high schools.

Who are the dropouts? Major characteristics of dropouts are embedded in socioeconomic conditions, family interaction, peer association, and school life. In addition, idiosyncratic problems play an important role.

Socioeconomic status. Dropouts coming from lower socioeconomic strata constitute a significantly higher proportion of the dropouts than those from middle and upper classes. Sociological research, as early as August B. Hollingshead's study of high school youth in *Elmtown's Youth*, has consistently indicated correlation between socioeconomic background and academic achievement. For example, Hollingshead found that, regardless of intelligence, one-third of the lower-class pupils as opposed to only 5 percent of the combined middle- and lower-class pupils received failing grades.[1] The social-class position of the teenager's family is of great influence in patterning the youth's orientation to education, and the middle-class student has advantages over lower-class peers. Home conditions of middle-class students conducive to academic success include the following:

1. Their parents are usually better educated and hence can tutor the offspring.
2. The parents' language facility is more proficient and enables the child to read, comprehend, and respond faster.
3. The parents instill motivation for learning in their children by being able to point to careers that can be achieved through academic effort. Homework, otherwise devoid of practical projection, takes on purpose; and exercises in English composition, arithmetic, and social studies make sense to the child.
4. The child's educational trajectory includes college education, possibly as a family tradition that gives the child an academic identity and the psychological assurance that he or she is cut out for a career in higher education.
5. There is usually a coordinated pressure of parents, relatives, friends, and neighbors that reinforces the child's academic self-view and sustains motivation to work toward scholastic success.

The vast majority of lower-class children do not enjoy the benefit of such conditions. Their value orientation shuns the academic way of life and focuses on issues tied up with everyday life in the inner-city or working-class neighborhood. Anthropologist Walter B. Miller has identified the typical lower-class preoccupations by the concepts of trouble, toughness, smartness, excitement, fate, and authoritarianism—all of which have an anti-intellectual tenor.[2]

---

[1]August B. Hollingshead, *Elmtown's Youth* (New York: John Wiley, 1949), p. 173.

[2]Walter B. Miller, "Lower-Class Culture as a Generating Milieu of Gang Delinquency," *Journal of Social Issues*, 14 (1958): 5–19.

The negative correlation between social class and dropout rate has been confirmed by sociologists Starke R. Hathaway and Elio D. Monachesi, who used more than 15,000 Minnesota high school students in a study spanning several high school generations. They found that among day-laborer families, 38 percent of the boys and 32 percent of the girls dropped out of school, whereas among professional families only 5 percent of the boys and girls left school prematurely.[3]

A 1970s study by the U.S. Department of Health, Education, and Welfare found that nearly 5 percent of America's school children aged twelve to seventeen cannot read at a fourth-grade level, and hence are defined as illiterate.[4] This segment amounted to about one million children, who came mostly from lower-class families. The study found that in low-income families, 10 percent of white youths and 22 percent of black youths were illiterate. If parents had little or no formal education, 22 percent of the whites and over 30 percent of the blacks could not pass the literacy test.

Racial and ethnic minorities.   Overlapping the above lower-class characteristics, black and Spanish-speaking youth make up a high segment of the dropout population.

A much larger percentage of Spanish-speaking persons than either whites or blacks have dropped out before graduation. During the early 1970s, the proportion of the youth population of Chicanos and Puerto Ricans who had dropped out was more than twice that of white: 34 percent compared to 14 percent; for the black population it was 21 percent.[5]

The high rate for the Spanish-speaking minority reflects two handicaps: lower socioeconomic class and language barrier. Parents of many of these youths are immigrants to the United States and in their native countries had limited educational opportunities. They were unskilled labor, and their young often have to drop out of school to help support the family. The young of these families also face a language problem that automatically puts them behind Anglo children in scholastic competition.

It is the language barrier that distinguishes the Spanish-speaking minority from the blacks who, otherwise, resemble them in socioeconomic conditions. The black inner-city youth, deprived as he or she may otherwise be, and despite the use of a nonstandard English dialect, has no such drastic drawback as having been brought up speaking a foreign tongue. Though figures for Spanish speakers were not included, a study for the U.S. Department of Health, Education, and Welfare revealed the consequences of the

---

[3]Starke R. Hathaway and Elio D. Monachesi, *Adolescent Personality and Behavior* (Minneapolis: The University of Minnesota Press, 1963).

[4]Associated Press Report, May 4, 1974.

[5]Anne M. Young, "The High School Class of 1972: More at Work, Fewer in College," *Monthly Labor Review*, 96 (1973): 26–32.

black-white socioeconomic differential in terms of literacy. Of the twelve-through-seventeen age group, 5 percent of the white males and 2 percent of the white females were found to be illiterate, compared with 20½ percent of black males and 10 percent of black females.[6] There was a double effect when the lower-income variable was added to the racial variable.

The "pushouts."   The term has been used to explain a variety of drop-outs. Some writers use it to refer to exactly the same reasons as described above, primarily the depressed socioeconomic conditions. They prefer the term because they feel it more honestly describes the process whereby a youth quits school not because of disinterest or low intelligence, but because poverty or family circumstances lead to having to quit school. So, harsh reality pushes the youth out of school.

Another application of the term focuses on mental or physical disabil-ities not recognized as such by teachers or parents, hence resulting in either expulsion from school or the child's inability to adequately meet academic work.

The economic pushout was at the bottom of the 1975 Children's Defense Fund report that indicated how short the United States falls of implementing the promise of universal education and equal opportunity.[7] The report charges that the U.S. census figures of nonenrolled children underestimates the real numbers and fails to note that the burden of exclu-sion from school falls heavily on the poor, the blacks, the non-English-speaking—in short, those who are "different" and do not fit the white, middle-class mold. In a large number of cases, the reasons for nonenrollment are simply a matter of economics: the inability to pay for books, fees, lunch, transportation, and adequate clothing.

In other cases, nonenrollment was due to specific learning disabilities that were either not discovered by school officials or were disregarded by them. Again, the children involved were not dropouts in the sense of not wanting to be in school, but were *pushed out* because of a range of handicaps: from poverty to special mental, emotional, or physical needs for which adequate provisions were not available.

An example from the range of physiological conditions conducive to pushing a youth out of school is hyperactivity, which has been estimated to affect 4 percent of children, appearing eight times more frequently in boys than in girls.[8] Traditionally this condition was interpreted as unruliness, lack of proper training, and many a parent has felt guilty for having failed in child rearing. It finally was diagnosed by a brain-imaging technique (positron

[6]Associated Press Report, May 4, 1974.
[7]*Children Out of School in America* (Cambridge, MA: Children's Defense, Fund, 1975).
[8]Philip Elmer-DeWitt, "Why Junior Won't Sit Still," *Time*, November 1990, p. 59.

emission tomography) as a malfunction of brain metabolism, particularly affecting the premotor cortex and the superior prefrontal cortex, which are responsible for regulating attention and motor control. Knowing the physiological defect now makes effective medication possible and ultimately reduces the child's misfortune of becoming a pushout from the educational process.

Family interaction.   Quality of interaction in the adolescent's family has definite influence on school behavior. A typical study found that dropouts expressed less rewarding relationships with their fathers, suffered from lower acceptance by their fathers, and consistently tried to avoid their parents more than in-school youths did.[9] Another study has shown that the degree of intrafamily consensus is significantly related to the school success of the sons. Boys who were well-adjusted in school came from families with high consensus, boys consistently underachieving in school came from families with lower consensus, and boys known for aggressiveness came from homes with the least family consensus.[10]

Parents' education is frequently reflected in their children's school accomplishment: the higher the education of the parents, the lower the dropout rate of the children. Typical findings come from a Maryland study showing that 70 percent of the mothers and 80 percent of the fathers of the dropouts had never finished high school.[11]

A definite relationship was discovered between family size and achievement motivation, and thus school attendance. Children of larger families consistently exhibited lower motivation to achieve than did children of smaller families. This finding might have been expected, for larger families are typical of lower classes, and studies have shown that lower classes have a low valuation of education. But even *within* the same social stratum large families tend to produce lower achievement motivation in their children.[12]

The broken home is strongly associated with dropping out of school. Children whose parents are divorced or separated are likely to drop out at roughly twice the rate of their peers from intact families. These dropouts amount to more than one-third of all the teenagers from broken families.[13]

Particularly strong dropout-proneness was found related to those teen-

[9]M.S. Tseng, "Comparison of Selected Familial, Personality, and Vocational Variables of High School Students and Dropouts," *Journal of Educational Research*, 65 (July 1972): 462–66.

[10]Barbara G. Myerhoff and William R. Larson, "Primary and Formal Aspects of Family Organization: Group Consensus, Problem Perception, and Adolescent School Success," *Journal of Marriage and the Family*, 27 (May 1965): 213–17.

[11]Percy Williams, "School Drop-Outs," *NEA Journal*, 52 (February 1963), 10–12.

[12]Bernard C. Rosen, "Family Structure and Achievement Motivation," *American Sociological Review*, 26 (August 1961): 574–85.

[13]Hathaway and Monachesi, *Adolescent Personality and Behavior*, pp. 93, 94, 181.

agers who suffered abuse at the hands of family members. A Minneapolis study conducted by Linda H. Harris discovered that 67 percent of the students flunking or dropping out of high school (but only 27 percent of the control group) had been victims of severe beating, sexual assault, and/or incest. One-third of the dropout-prone girls (vs. 9 percent of the other girls) acknowledged having been forced into incestuous relations with a father, stepfather, uncle, or grandfather. Besides being dropout-prone, the abused teenagers manifest symptoms of delinquency and/or mental distress, such as running away, drug use, self-mutilation, and suicidal tendencies (30 percent of the abused teenagers vs. only 1 percent of the control group had attempted suicide).[14]

The power of the home environment in forming academic attitudes and determining the scholastic success of the young seems strong enough for some researchers to conclude that the quality of the school has little to do with how well students learn. Harvard sociologist Christopher Jencks, basing his conclusion on a survey of 4000 public schools, including 645,000 students, believes that the quality of a school's output depends largely on a single input: the quality of the entering children.[15] Everything else—the school budget, its policies, the teachers—were found to be irrelevant. Schools seem to serve primarily as selection and certification agencies, whose task is to measure and label individuals, and only secondarily as socialization agencies, whose capacity is to change and mold individuals. The most important factors in the lives of the young, heredity and home environment, cannot be controlled by schools.

Jencks' findings constitute a poignant rebuttal to the cliché blaming schools for failing to socialize, change, and educate the young. According to his study, the school is merely a limited receptacle of youth whose prime socialization takes place elsewhere.

Peer involvement and delinquency. Some sociologists have found that the peer group has such a strong influence on the teenager that in many situations it overrides the advice of parents and teachers.[16] Sometimes, the pressure of the peer group and the contagion of collective behavior introduce a teenager to delinquent activities.

There is reason to believe that if a dropout is deeply involved in peer

[14]Linda H. Harris' paper was presented at the 1980 convention of the American Association of Psychiatric Services for Children and summed up under "Adolescence," *Psychology Today*, December 1980, p. 102.

[15]Christopher Jencks, *Inequality: A Reassessment of the Effects of Family and Schooling in America* (New York: Basic Books, 1973).

[16]Examples: Hans Sebald and Becky White, "Teenagers' Divided Reference Groups: Uneven Alignment with Parents and Peers," *Adolescence*, 15 (Winter 1980): 979–84; James S. Coleman, *The Adolescent Society* (New York: Free Press, 1963).

activities, they are most probably delinquent activities. The bulk of dropouts are lower-class youths who have severed most ties with formal adult institutions. Unless this teenager has a job, he or she is almost totally absorbed in activities revolving around the gang. What the high school and the clique are to in-school youth, the gang is to the jobless dropout, that is, a bridge device to span the gap between childhood and adulthood. The gang commands the dropout's loyalty and he or she, in return, obtains security, belonging, and adventure. Most middle- and upper-class youth do not form gangs, since they have transitional institutions, such as advanced education and family-social-class sponsorship in jobs.

The delinquency-proneness of the dropout is supported by a Minnesota study employing the Minnesota Multiphasic Personality Inventory (MMPI) to assess the dropout's characteristics.[17] The findings revealed considerable overlap between the students who dropped out and those who were delinquent. In fact, 39 percent of the boys and 31 percent of the girls who dropped out had a delinquency rating. The delinquency rate for the male dropout was only 1.62 times the base rate for all males, but for the female dropout it was 2.98 times the base rate for all females. This indicates that dropping out and delinquency are more closely related for girls than for boys. It was also noticed that delinquent teenagers tend to drop out most frequently during the early years of high school, suggesting that their causes for dropping out reach peak intensity in the eighth grade or earlier. Thus, remedial measures should be initiated at early school levels.

Further support for the assumption that a correlation exists between dropping out and delinquency comes from a study of working-class youth in six metropolitan areas. This study attempted to clarify whether the youth culture in the United States is independent of or dependent on parental control, that is, whether youth choose parent or age-mate influences.[18] The findings discovered a decided cleavage between responses of dropouts and the matched high-school graduates. The dropouts operate within an independent subculture. This is reflected in their responses to questionnaires concerning intergenerational mutual understanding and in their attitudes toward their parents' disapproval of their choice of friends. On the other hand, the graduates' value orientations indicate that their subculture is characterized by greater harmony with parental values.

One may be certain that dropouts form an independent subculture, are involved in delinquent activities to a larger extent than their in-school peers, are cut off from adult institutions, and reject parental advice.

---

[17]Hathaway and Monachesi, *Adolescent Personality and Behavior.*

[18]Lucius F. Cervantes, *American Youth Culture: Independent or Dependent?* (a mimeographed paper read at the Annual Convention of the American Sociological Association, Chicago, 1965).

School violence and vandalism.   The nation has been appalled by the extent of crime, delinquency, and destruction committed by students in their school facilities. There has been no letup of such behavior.

The relationship between the potential dropout and school crime is sparsely researched. But it seems safe to conclude that those who become dropouts carry the major responsibility for the destruction. The major problem is that compulsory school attendance laws force young people to be in school whether they like it or not. Most states set the age ceiling at sixteen, but some states have expanded it to eighteen. One of these states, Ohio, has suffered from increasing numbers of hostile and aggressive youths who during recent years have committed more serious acts of violence than in the past seventy-five years.[19] A major cause of this increase is seen in Ohio's having extended mandatory school attendance to age eighteen (although provisions are made for some students to leave school at sixteen if they have a job). This necessitates the presence in the school system of young people who, unable to achieve and not receiving any preparation for future employment, are continual behavior problems. Ultimately, violent and destructive students tend to quit high school before graduation, but before their demise they demonstrate unwillingness to be in school by destruction that costs the taxpayer too much for the small gain of retaining the dropout just a little longer.

Learning disabilities.   Closely overlapping with violence and vandalism and perhaps partly explaining them, is the problem of learning disability. Often school officials define disruptive or truant behavior as delinquent, unaware that the underlying reasons may be physiological, including such conditions as auditory and visual defects, memory impairment, and aphasic symptoms. As mentioned earlier, victims of such disorders often become "pushouts." Their true problems are not recognized. While not all children with such disabilities become juvenile delinquents, they meet with constant failure in school and as a means of establishing a minimum of self-assertion they often resort to delinquent or deviant behavior.

Chester D. Poremba, chief psychologist at Denver's Children's Hospital, estimated that 70 percent of juvenile delinquents committed to institutions suffer from learning disabilities.[20] Paul Broder and Noel Dunivant at the National Center for State Courts classified 37 percent of the delinquent boys as learning disabled whereas only 19 percent of the nondelinquent boys were so classified. The proportions remained the same even when age, social class, and ethnic background were taken into account. A new insight of the

[19]UPI Report, June 19, 1975.

[20]Chester D. Poremba, "Disability is Linked to Delinquency," *Arizona Republic*, March 8, 1975, p. 28.

study was that the delinquency of learning-disabled youth is often defined on the basis of a peculiar linguistic inability to describe simple events—a disability all too often interpreted by judges and attorneys as recalcitrance or acting "smart."[21]

If victims of learning impairments indeed make up such a high proportion of delinquents, courts and the entire correctional system are wasted on many offenders. What is needed are medical and physical therapy, not legal correction. Dr. Poremba warns that although it costs $3000 a year to educate a learning-disabled child it costs several times that much to deal with such a child if he or she turns criminal. He estimated that it costs about $24,000 to educate a learning-disabled child from kindergarten through twelfth grade. The average criminal, however, costs the taxpayer $40,000 a year; it costs about $7000 to incarcerate a juvenile for the first year, and this figure increases to $10,000 in the fourth year.

Learning disability is tied up with the whole gamut of physical and mental health. Such problems are difficult to recognize and are frequently characterized by unwillingness to learn, adjustment problems, and a variety of neurotic expressions, including depression, agitation, inability to concentrate, withdrawal from social contacts, and inability to communicate. Often there is confusion in distinguishing between emotionally troubled students and delinquent students; the two types of expression are not necessarily identical and one does not automatically lead to the other. In fact, the earlier-mentioned MMPI study discovered that neurotic, socially introverted, and schizoid adolescents are likely to drop out of school, but do not become delinquent.[22]

Academic performance and attitude.   Probably the most conspicuous feature of dropouts is their lack of interest in school work. Of the dropouts in the Minnesota study, one boy in three and one girl in five cited disinterest as reason for dropping out.[23]

The usual grade distribution of *all* youth in school runs as follows: 45 percent have Bs or above, 51 percent have Cs, and 8 percent have Ds or lower. Dropouts deviate significantly: 15 percent have Bs or above, 46 percent have Cs, and 39 percent have Ds or lower.[24] The same study found that of the in-school youths, only 16 percent had to repeat two or more grades. In contrast, 26 percent of the dropouts had to repeat two or more grades.[25]

The decision to promote or not promote a pupil to the next grade is

[21]Paul Broder and Noel Dunivant, "Problems in Learning Breed Problems in Court," *Psychology Today*, June 1981, p. 92.

[22]Hathaway and Monachesi, *Adolescent Personality and Behavior*, p. 93.

[23]Ibid.

[24]Bertrand, "School Attendance and Attainment," p. 231.

[25]Ibid.

most vexing to American teachers. On one side beckons the democratic ethos of keeping all educational avenues open and giving the student every conceivable opportunity to advance. On the other side, no one profits from promoting a youth who simply does not do the work. American public schools, almost without exception, refrain from forcing students to languish year after year in the same grade, even though they may be extremely poor readers and may almost qualify as illiterate. Except in rare cases, students are held back no more than once in elementary and once in junior high school. Those who repeatedly fail to meet eighth- and ninth-grade standards will nonetheless eventually be admitted to high school.

Many school systems try to solve the dilemma by spending extraordinary amounts on individually prescribed programs based on the students' deficiencies and needs. Noble as such attempts are, they usually have an ironic ending when slow or unwilling students decide to drop out of school anyway. Funds, extra classrooms, and skilled teachers are often wasted on a dropout. Some skeptical educators feel that such costs and extra provisions could be more fruitfully applied to the school in general and to the better students in specific.

More often, however, school authorities' response to poor performance is to acquiesce and even lower the academic expectations. A New York panel investigating declining test scores made discoveries exemplifying this pattern. Homework assignments had been cut nearly in half during the period from 1968 to 1977. Students often simply refused to do them. Uncooperative students' attitudes were usually blamed on overexposure to TV, which presumably reduces attention span.[26]

IQ scores show that the average dropout is by no means uneducable. Although, on the average, he or she tends to score lower than his or her in-school peers, a nationwide study by the U.S. Department of Labor discovered that 70 percent of the dropouts in the sample had IQ scores above 90. A six-year study in New York disclosed that 13 percent of the dropouts had IQ scores above 110.[27] In a Maryland study, almost 50 percent of the dropouts had average or above-average intelligence.[28] Thus, for the majority, the decisive factor in dropping out is attitude.

The attitude responsible in many cases is rebelliousness. Of the many forms that rebellion can take, underachievement is probably the most subtle. It is rarely recognized for what it is. Thus, consistent underachievement of an otherwise bright youngster may seem inexplicable. By the time the rebellious undercurrent is recognized, it may be too late to salvage a career. What is commonly termed laziness, lack of will power, or poor attitude is at heart

[26]"Help! Teacher Can't Teach!" *Time*, June 16, 1980, p. 59.
[27]Daniel Schreiber, "School Drop-Out," *NEA Journal*, 51 (May 1962): 51.
[28]Williams, "School Drop-outs," p. 11.

often a resentfulness expressed by refusal to do anything demanded by authority.

Gender differences.   Although the dropout population is divided almost equally between the sexes, some of the reasons for dropping out differ between them. Boys who drop out frequently list military service or a job as reasons; a survey showed that one in four had dropped out for military service, one in seven to work. Few boys quit school because of marriage. On the other hand, the majority of females quitting school do so because of marriage or illegitimate pregnancy.[29]

Personality characteristics.   Comparison of a group of dropouts with a group of high school graduates, matching individuals of both groups with one another on as many important demographic variables as possible, used the TAT projective technique to identify a number of personality attributes typical of the dropout. The following sums up the major points.[30]

The dropout can be characterized as an individual feeling relatively helpless in mastering or coping with the environment. Such persons are preoccupied with basic physical and security needs rather than with self-improvement or achievement, and focus on immediate contingencies rather than on aspirations and abstractions. Their value orientation is loose and unstructured, with few principles to guide their behavior other than those momentarily dictated by the environment itself. Their thought processes follow stereotyped matrixes rather than original ideas.

In personal relationships, dropouts are more peer- than family-oriented and relatively unresponsive to authority, parental or otherwise. Their attitudes are self-centered and narcissistic, possibly reflecting their alienation from the family. They lack warm, affectionate bonds, withdrawing into themselves and becoming preoccupied with gratification of immediate needs.

The analysis found also personality parallels between the delinquent and the dropout. This is not to say that the dropout will become a delinquent, but rather that the two groups share common features—especially the inadequate family relationships. In both groups the background of a weak or absent father figure is prevalent, and in either case the children, especially males, have difficulty establishing adequate sex-role identifications and clear self-concepts. Such boys tend to develop hypermasculine symptoms, most likely to overcome uncertainty in the area of male identification.

[29]Hathaway and Monachesi, *Adolescent Personality and Behavior,* p. 94.

[30]A. Barclay and Lucius F. Cervantes, "The TAT as an Index of Personality Attributes of the Adolescent Dropout," *Adolescence,* 4 (Winter 1969): 525–40.

Thus, on a statistical level, the personality of the dropout and the graduate differ significantly, the differences manifesting themselves particularly in the former's poorer capacity to adapt successfully to the social demands of his or her environment. The study lends support to the assumption that the academic dropout is a product of the social milieu—that the underachiever is made, not born.

THE YOUNG AND THE WORLD OF WORK

When they leave high school, both the graduate and the dropout face the awesome question: What now?

When dropouts abandon school, they face a labor market in which they command little bargaining power. One of the first facts they will have to learn is that unemployment among youth is of epidemic proportions. The unemployment rate of young Americans is roughly twice the general rate. Dropouts will also have to realize that they contribute disproportionately to the ranks of unemployed youths because they are undereducated and generally fall into the unskilled-worker category. This category is characterized by an unemployment rate twice as high as the rates of all other job categories.

Graduates are equipped with a wider range of options: they can enter college *or,* like the dropouts, search for a job. One out of three decides to go on to college; the other two try to settle in the labor force. While they are provided with better prospects to obtain a job than their dropout peers, it is well known that unemployment of the young—all young—is notoriously common; the 1982 percentage of unemployment of the U.S. teen population was 22 percent; for black teenagers the rate reached 50 percent.

A number of high-school systems across the nation have decided on a novel approach to encourage employers to hire young graduates. School districts in Maryland, Massachusetts, Missouri, Illinois, Colorado, and New York have started to provide each employer with a sort of one-year "good quality" warranty for every graduate hired.[31] The innovation allows employers who find that a graduate is deficient in reading, writing, or calculating, to return the young worker to school at no cost to employer or student. The worker stays on the job but enrolls in evening remedial classes run by the boards of education. School authorities want to assure employers that a graduation diploma is a meaningful document. Whether this innovation will help to reduce youthful unemployment remains to be seen.

The correlation between increasing industrialization and the increasing unemployability of youth can also be noted in other parts of the world. Youth

[31]Susan Tifft et al., "Our Student-Back Guarantee," *Time,* February 11, 1991, p. 74.

unemployment in the industrialized nations of the West and in Japan has steadily risen during the 1980s. Italy is hit hardest, with 30 percent of the fourteen-to-twenty-four age group unemployed. In West Germany youth unemployment grew from 3.7 percent in 1979 to about 10 percent in the 1980s. Similar conditions are reported from England and France. Limited demand for the largely unskilled young workforce is also becoming a problem in developing nations, where we witness an alarming growth in unemployment of recent high school graduates and a simultaneous scarcity of skilled laborers.[32]

Dropouts will usually begin, and in most cases stay, at the bottom of the job pile. They will experience surges of unemployment whenever there are declines in business activities, in the labor demand, or in general economic conditions. As a consequence, they tend to become members of the hardcore jobless, among those last hired and first fired. At least two-thirds of the jobless have less than a high school education.

Dropouts will find it increasingly difficult to obtain jobs, because the kinds of positions they can suitably fill are becoming more and more obsolete. Also, many of the factors which have influenced young persons to leave school, such as poor academic skills, discontent with programs offered, health problems, trouble with authorities, or unwillingness to concentrate on work are also likely to be a hindrance to employment. Add to these factors the dropout's relative youth and inexperience—most are sixteen or seventeen—and employment prospects grow ever dimmer.

Years of education and level of income are directly correlated. Those dropouts holding jobs earn an income substantially lower than high-school graduates. The high-school graduate at peak earning power makes at least 25 percent more than the person who dropped out of school.

Figures published by the U.S. Department of Education reveal the distribution of low-paying and mostly manual jobs typical of the dropout. (See Table 15-1.) Following up the 1980 dropouts, a national survey found that a few years later 14 percent of the males and 23 percent of the females were working as waiters or waitresses; 12 percent of the males and 8 percent of the females were working at gas stations; and 11 percent of the males and 8 percent of the females were factory workers. Barely 14 percent of the males and only 3 percent of the females had skilled trades.

To find a satisfactory job—or any job at all—more education and longer training are required. On the average, the professional or technical workers of today have more than four years of college; clerical workers have training and education in excess of their high school diploma. These academic requirements and specialized training programs will increase in importance in the

[32]"Unemployed Youth," *World Press Review*, May 1982, p. 54.

TABLE 15-1 Job Distribution of 1980 Dropouts
Three Years Later (in percentages)

	Male	Female
Yard work or odd jobs	6.0	2.9
Waiting tables	14.1	23.0
Child care	0.1	14.0
Farm work	8.7	1.5
Factory work	10.9	8.0
Skilled trade	13.9	2.8
Gas station	12.1	8.1
Store clerk	5.9	15.2
Office clerical	1.2	10.2
Other manual	8.4	1.9
Military service	5.8	2.4
Other jobs	12.9	10.0

Source: U.S. Department of Education, 1983.

future. Automation, mechanization, and other scientific advances are responsible for the decreasing number of unskilled jobs. The school dropout of the future may well become a dropout from the usable labor force.

But this does not mean that the high-school graduate garners particular usability in the labor market. Both are poorly prepared for a vocational career. And this brings into focus America's public high school dilemma: the dual attempt to prepare some students for higher education and at the same time and within the same curriculum to prepare others for the immediate entry into the labor market. The dilemma deals with making the American high school truly comprehensive (universal), offering programs geared to the diverse needs of *all* students in secondary education. This formidable question has not yet been solved—indeed, may not be solvable given the structure of American education.

In the meantime, the other question—what to do with the dropout?— has not fared much better, though numerous salient efforts at remedy have been made. A common approach is to see what can be done to ease the dropout into the labor force. One way is thought to be via returning them to high school, having them complete the degree, and *then* integrating them into the labor market. However, a return to regular high-school life, even if the dropout were willing, is usually not advisable because of the lapse of time and the consequent age difference. More adequate means appear to be night courses, adult education programs, or correspondence courses. Nonetheless, some cases are exceptional. For example, high school girls who get pregnant are invited back to school as soon as possible. Even during pregnancy, some schools set up special classes that enable expectant mothers—wed or unwed—to continue their education without interruption. Some high schools in Phoenix, Arizona arranged for the pregnant girls to withdraw from regular classes before their conditions become apparent and to attend separate, accredited classes.

Alternative ways of completing secondary education are limited, take longer, and are available in only a few localities. Sometimes dropouts may complete the requirements for a high-school diploma while in the armed forces, and a comprehensive standard examination after adequate study may belatedly furnish a high school degree. Another institution enabling completion of high school was established by the Encyclopaedia Britannica Company in Chicago, offering evening high school primarily for dropouts and applying advanced techniques of teaching. Generally speaking, the once rebellious adolescents showed excellent performance results.

Regardless of these attempts, the principal solution of the dropout problem lies in absorbing the dropout into the labor force. Thus, remedial action calls for expanding job possibilities for these out-of-school adolescents. This is a complex and trying enterprise, for placement possibilities are narrowed by the dropouts' lack of marketable skills, their underdeveloped academic ability and social immaturity. There are a number of possible methods, however, to reduce the oversupply of untrained dropouts.

First, existing job opportunities for which dropouts qualify must be made known to them. New channels of publicizing such positions must be initiated. The typical dropout from the lower class lacks occupational contacts and role models within his or her immediate environment. In contrast, the middle-class teenager's parent knows a manager or other high-placed worker, who can give advance information about job openings. Considering that only a small fraction of jobs are obtained through such formal channels as employment agencies and newspaper ads, it becomes clear that the lower-class lack of occupational "connections" is a formidable barrier to employment. Role models, which are the natural bridge to adult careers, are largely absent in the lives of youth from deprived inner-city areas.

The need to promote a more intimate acquaintance between the world of the lower-class child and the world of vocations and professions is echoed in many research findings. Lower-class children and dropouts have been found to have minimal knowledge of occupations and their differential prestige. Such deficiencies in information may partly account for the dropouts' high degree of uncertainty about future occupations and their low motivation to achieve.

A second remedial program consists of selectively stimulating the rate of new job creations, thus increasing the demand in those sectors of the labor market where there is oversupply. This approach is obviously severely limited by the natural growth of the modern economy, which simply does not call for as many unskilled workers as are available.

A third remedial approach would involve expanding job training programs and moving the dropouts from areas of heavy oversupply of labor to
areas with moderate supply, thus giving the youngsters greater assurance of
lasting employment and, while the period of training lasts, keeping them out
of the saturated labor force. Programs such as the Job Corps and the Urban
Youth Service Corps are promising.

An ambitious proposal was debated in 1989 in the U.S. Senate, envi-
sioning a new Citizens Corps that would enlist one million young high-school
graduates to spend at least a year working for $100 a week in places like
hospitals and homeless shelters within their local communities. After serving
two years, the young volunteers would qualify for educational stipends:
$10,000 vouchers for each year of Citizens Corps service to go to college. A
draconian measure added to the proposal, and becoming effective by the mid
1990s, would abolish federal aid for higher education for those not having
served in the Citizens Corps.[33] Whether this proposal for a national service
for the young will indeed materialize awaits to be seen.

In any case, these living-training-working arrangements have a number
of useful functions: (1) they prepare dropouts for jobs they could otherwise
never obtain; (2) they enable completion of interrupted education and open
up opportunities for further, higher education; (3) they teach adolescents
how to carry out work responsibly, developing in them the ability to enter a
successful career in the labor force; and (4) they relieve the labor market of
the oversupply of unskilled youth.

Carefully planned job training programs might correct situations in
which a number of job positions go begging in the face of high unemployment. This is an old problem in the United States. In the 1960s, New York
City suffered from 75 percent youth unemployment in the slum areas while
there were only five qualified persons for every seven skilled positions, with
serious shortages in auto mechanics, stenography, and nursing.[34] The 1980s
reflected similar incongruities. Figures released by the Department of Labor
showed at least two dozen occupations with wide open employability. Filling
them would have depended on training persons for certain skills. In some
cases only minimal skills were needed, skills that could have been acquired in
work training programs. (See Table 15-2.) Selective training of high-school
graduates as well as dropouts and their adequate placement into the labor
force would go a long way toward reducing unemployment and hardship
among underprivileged adolescents as well as improving the overall economic
structure of the nation.

[33]Walter Shapiro, "The Gap Between Will and Wallet," *Time*, February 6, 1989, p. 32.
    [34]*A Proposal for the Prevention and Control of Delinquency by Expanding Opportunities*,
2nd ed. (New York: Mobilization for Youth, Inc., August 1962), pp. 95–96.

TABLE 15-2 Occupations with Openings and Growth Rates during the 1980s

Job Titles	Annual Average Openings	Percent Growth in Total Jobs, 1978–1990
Industrial assemblers	77,000	43
Blue-collar–worker supervisors	69,000	16
Bookkeeping workers	96,000	12
Cashiers	119,000	50
Receptionists	41,000	28
Secretaries and Stenographers	305,000	45
Bank clerks	45,000	50
Typists	59,000	19
Building custodians	176,000	20
Cooks and chefs	86,000	32
Waiters and Waitresses	70,000	18
Licensed practical nurses	60,000	67
Registered nurses	85,000	50
Nursing aides, orderlies, attendants	94,000	52
Local truck drivers	64,000	18
Retail-trade sales workers	226,000	33
Wholesale-trade sales workers	40,000	14
Soil conservationists	46,500	27
Industrial-machinery repairers	58,000	66

Source: U.S. Dept. of Labor, 1980.

SEX AND THE TEENAGER

No one wishing to achieve a realistic understanding of adolescents can afford to ignore the powerful role sex plays in their lives. Cultural meaning, social norms, the teenagers' needs, and their sexual activities form an interrelated complex responsible for typical adolescent experiences, including reactions of guilt, shame, anxiety, joy, and pleasure. Such consequences as premarital pregnancy, marriage, divorce, and venereal disease are so prevalent among adolescents that at times they resemble epidemics.

This section sketches a limited picture of the American teenager's involvement in the activities and consequences of sex. No presumption of completeness is made. The discussion focuses primarily on premarital heterosexual activities and leaves out homosexuality and other activities popularly considered to be deviant.

Traditional Sex Codes

Codes and customs concerning sexuality form a blueprint that purports to control the sexual activities of society's members. The relationship between the blueprint and actual behavior may show considerable incongruence. This very incongruence creates emotional reactions that are often central issues in the lives of adolescents. Frequent reactions include feelings of guilt and shame, which, in essence, are assaults on the teenager's self-respect. It is therefore important to understand the cultural norms that are supposed to govern sexual activities before investigating actual sexual patterns. Comparison of the "official" norms and the "unofficial" behavior helps in understanding psychological reactions.

The cultural heritage of American society includes principles of the Judeo-Christian tradition, which dictate ascetic standards for single people and forbid premarital coitus as well as other sexual activities. The only approved sexual activity consists of marital coitus. Although these dogmas are gradually giving way to more secular and sensate-oriented views, hardly any young American can avoid exposure to views that equate premarital sex with sin or evil. Many teenagers come under the influence of such religious and moralistic evaluation in their association with parents, relatives, church, and school.

Inconsistent with this general negative pronouncement is the legacy of the double standard that has been part of informal religious tradition as well as folk culture. In effect, it called for strong condemnation of female sexual transgression, but relative tolerance of male sexual adventure. The excuse for the male prerogative was based on the assumption that the male has different sexual needs and drives than the female. His sex drive was conceived as being stronger than hers and therefore in greater need of fulfillment. Her sexual involvement was mainly seen as an altruistic act satisfying her husband's needs and serving reproductive purposes. A girl's premarital chastity was of immense importance. First, by her chastity she had to live up to the man's image of her as relatively disinterested in sexual matters. The discovery of premarital unchastity would destroy this sexually pure image of the female. Second, in the patriarchal tradition, a woman was regarded as unequal to a man and, in a sense, his "property" that no one else should ever "possess." The worth of a woman decreased sharply if virginity was not brought along to the wedding.

The double standard led to an interesting conflict. How could the man find full satisfaction with a chaste and sexually disinterested woman? As in numerous aspects of life, man found a suitable rationalization to resolve the conflict by dividing females into "good" and "bad" women. This belief had profound psychological effects on both men and women. Whereas a man could find sexual gratification outside, and to some extent inside, the marital bond and still retain self-respect, any personal sexual gratification on the part of the wife resulting from marital, let alone extramarital coitus, could lead to guilt feelings. Any overt indication that she enjoyed sex might arouse the husband's suspicion that she was not a "good" woman.

This belief was part of the patriarchal syndrome introduced into the

United States by early Protestantism and, it should be added, maintained by Catholicism as well. In Christianity's view, sex before or outside of matrimony was sinful for both sexes, but far more sinful for the woman. She was constantly reminded to resist evil and the "temptation of the flesh." If a woman was discovered by a Puritan community to have indulged in premarital coitus, a public confession had to be made before the entire congregation. This constituted a much more painful sanction than the secret confessional of the Catholic Church, which the Puritans had repudiated.

Although elements of the patriarchal syndrome still persist, modern trends have largely supplanted them with less dogmatic views permitting, more or less tacitly, some premarital expression for both males and females. The change in basic attitudes has come about over a relatively brief period of time—a period so brief that some social scientists feel justified in calling it the Sexual Revolution.

The Sexual Revolution

The social and technological innovations that took place during the first half of the twentieth century were profound enough to change basic perceptions of the functions of sex and the role of women. The label Sexual Revolution is thus not out of place as a description of these changes. Traditional sex codes as correlated to religious dogma came under severe attack and were undermined by important new developments. Several major forces of social change can be discerned:

Female emancipation.   Most noteworthy has been the liberation of women from the traditional description of being sexually passive. The so-called Sexual Revolution applies in fact more to women than to men, with the male sexual behavior remaining relatively unchanged—except in areas where it would interfere with the female's rising demands and sexual expressivity. The game of seduction is largely replaced by more equal participation in mutually desired sex. Most of America's young women will no longer retreat to coyness and a false facade, but will take the Pill and destroy once and for all the illusion of female passivity.

The female no longer pretends. She now admits that she enjoys sex as much as the male, knows as much as or more than he, and believes that males and females represent physical but not emotional or psychological differences. The male has been made aware of past chauvinism and of its vestiges in institutional arrangements. Vast changes and adaptations have followed, and studies indicate that women have largely dispatched the sexual double standard to history.

Sexual equality diminished women's dependency on marriage and on males in general. Formerly indispensable for her sustenance, the male figure had shifted directly from father to husband. Now she is able to remove herself from the influence of the father and yet not enter immediately into a dependency relationship with a husband. This interim provides the woman with a period of freedom and independence heretofore unknown.

Secularism. There has been a general shift in the perception of the institutions of marriage and the family. These primary institutions had been viewed as sacred, inviolable arrangements. The secular philosophy and attitude, in contrast, saw such institutions as arrangements that should be changed when human needs and desires call for such changes.

The decline of familism correlated with the rise of secularism: the focus of concern shifted from the family to the individual. Modern American life grants to both males and females the right to seek personal pleasure and satisfaction without the impediment of control by the parental family. Another way to characterize secularism is to note the modern preference for sensate pleasures over ascetic and orthodox religious principles. Gratification of personal needs has become a major goal. This social change is greatly relevant to the female who, for example, can now easily obtain a divorce if she feels that a given marriage fails to meet her personal needs, sexual and otherwise.

Legal reorientation. A by-product of secularism was a new trend in legislation concerning sexual behavior, marriage, divorce, and family matters. New laws granted the individual more personal choice and greater independence. For example, sexual behavior previously defined as law violations, such as adultery, sodomy, and homosexuality, were decriminalized. Safeguards were also established to protect equality of the sexes in such areas as jobs, income, sexual expression, and education.

Significantly, birth control became legal, as did availing oneself of pertinent means and devices. The 1972 *Baird vs. Massachusetts* conflict reached the U.S. Supreme Court, which struck down as unconstitutional the state's ancient prohibition of the distribution of contraceptives to *unmarried* people. The high court's decision rested on the 14th Amendment's guarantee of equal protection before the law. This meant that whatever the rights of individuals to access to contraceptives may be, the rights must be the same for unmarried and married. As a result, other states voided similar discriminatory laws.

Broadening adolescent period. Improved medication, sanitation, and nutrition led to earlier onset of puberty. At the same time, the progressively more complicated expansion of the division of labor and the social structure in general caused delay in reaching fully acknowledged adult status. The sum effect of the two developments is a longer span of adolescence. During these years, the youth is physiologically mature and characterized by fully developed sexual needs.

It is unrealistic to expect that the adolescent can or will defer gratification of sexual needs until completing schooling, which may extend into the twenties if college is attended. As long as youth are affiliated with an educational institution, it is difficult to accord them full adult status. Not until establishing themselves occupationally and earning a living do they achieve major criteria of adult status.

Despite the prolonging of the period between child and adult statuses, no socially acceptable provisions have been made to allow sexual needs to be fulfilled outside of marriage. To some degree, premarital chastity still is a social value. Technically, *any* form of sexual gratification during adolescent years constitutes a deviation from the blueprint. Whatever sexual gratification does take place—autoeroticism, hetero- or homosexuality—is defined as illicit, or at least improper, and burdens the majority of adolescents with negative self-feelings. Prolonged adolescence is in part responsible for the increased rate of premarital sexual activities over the past few decades.

Titillating mass media.   Ubiquitous American mass media also weakened traditional norms. The sexual stimuli presented in various media grossly contradicted traditional values of chastity and asceticism. Female "sexiness" became an established value, attracting emulation by the teenage girl and fervent endeavors of conquest by the teenage boy. Considering the sexual insecurity that is normally an important part of adolescence, it is hardly possible to overestimate the sex-encouraging influence of movies, TV, advertisements, and a vast range of reading material.

The cult of instantaneousness.   Modern technology has indeed given us a wide range of services and items that instantaneously solves problems and fulfills desires—from the computer to instant coffee and Polaroid pictures. The demand for instant solution has spread to the sexual realm, with the pill being a prime example. Though, as we mention later, there is the striking paradox of increasing premarital teenage pregnancies, the trust in instant solutions has permeated every aspect of teenage life. Perhaps it is exactly this blind trust that eroded the fear of or precaution against pregnancy—trusting that even if you got pregnant, somehow there will be an easy and quick solution to it too. And, of course, there is—depending on the state, abortion is legal and easily available.

In any case, idolization of instantaneousness has given the green light to also seek it in the area of sexual desires. An indication of this expectation was reflected over recent years on many campuses by students demanding the dispensation of the pill through college health facilities. In the 1990s the wish list was augmented by the condom—an instant precaution against AIDS.

Modifications of the Sexual Revolution

The need for emotional security.   The sexual revolution may have provided increased sexual pleasures, but it decreased the type of emotional security that comes with limited and exclusive sexual involvement. It also reduced the romantic aura that used to go with an intimate relationship. Most of all, it eroded the feeling of belonging together, getting to know each other's joys and sorrows, and being able to rely on the type of emotional support that comes with an explicit or implicit declaration of loyalty.

Soon, therefore, the revolutionary overtones of sexual expressions changed into the big quest for romanticism, and the 1980s saw unexpected restraints in sexual activities among young Americans.

Casual sexuality was being gradually replaced by older monogamous rules. As a college woman put it: "It's all right to live with your boyfriend, but to sleep around isn't all right." There was a lessening of the endorsement, if there ever was one, of promiscuity. Apparently, noncommittal sex made gratifying intimacy difficult. Young people wanted more than sexual relief; they wanted human relatedness that was difficult to derive from ephemeral episodes, and they even seemed to have been willing to sacrifice some of their cherished independence to regain some of the benefits of the old-fashioned twosome.

Attitudes versus behavior.   Many people are tempted to equate a verbal statement about behavior with behavior as such. The New Sexuality consisted to a large degree only of the New Verbiage—a greater outspokenness, a greater willingness to express and look at the fact of human sexuality. Symptomatic of this new expressiveness were pornography, four-letter expletives, and coed dorms.

But, alas, the actual implementation of the verbal liberality may have been slightly different. Though change in attitudes is quick and seemingly radical, behavior neither follows at the same pace nor to the same extent. Insofar as it concerns *attitudes*, the New Sexuality represented indeed a new and somewhat radical change, but actual sexual behavior still had a way to go before matching the verbal openness.

The legacy of tradition.   Though it is probably true that sexuality is now more acknowledged and accepted, it does not follow that young people choose no restrictions at all. Those growing up with a religious commitment tend to disassociate themselves from the New Sexuality. Religious commitment is still the strongest foe of the New Sexuality. Another obstacle to sexual liberality is the traditionally greater sexual conservatism of girls, which still is not entirely abolished. Although girls may now be more liberal with their boyfriends and fiancés, most still frown on casual sex.

The new plague: AIDS. By the beginning of the last decade of the millennium, the danger of sexually transmittable lethal AIDS was well known, and some writers prematurely wrote of a "new morality" brought on by it. However, all that may have happened was a slight reinforcement of the already existing romantic restraints. Rather than speaking of a new morality, it is probably more realistic to speak of mere attention paid to medical information. Whether this caution is going to turn out to merely be an initial shock reaction or whether it indeed will initiate a long-range change in sexual practices awaits to be seen.

In the meantime, the first nationwide statistical information collected by the U.S. Center for Disease Control in Atlanta shows that the incidence rate of AIDS infection on the nation's college campuses is one student in 500. This amounts to a total of 30,000 college students infected, with the vast majority of them being male.[35] College students, it should be noted, at this time do not belong to such high-risk groups as homosexuals and drug abusers.

Unabated Sexual Practices

In spite of the peril of AIDS, teenagers' sexual practices appear to have proceeded nearly unabatedly, though there has been a slight drop in the proportion of sexually active teenagers between the 1970s and 1980s, amounting on the average to 5 percent for boys and girls. Nationwide surveys in the mid 1980s have shown that by age 14 over 10 percent of the boys (including all racial/ethnic groups) and over 3 percent of the girls had had sexual intercourse. By age 18, these proportions had increased to 65 percent and 51 percent, respectively.[36] (See Table 15-3.) Highest proportions among

TABLE 15–3 Cumulative Percentages of Adolescents Having Had Sexual Intercourse. (Interviews Conducted 1983/84.)

	Total		White		Black		Hispanic	
Age	Male	Female	Male	Female	Male	Female	Male	Female
14	10	3	7	3	30	5	10	2
15	17	8	12	8	44	13	18	6
16	29	18	24	17	61	24	32	15
17	48	33	43	31	79	46	50	29
18	65	51	61	49	87	64	68	42

Source: Family Planning Perspectives, 20 (May/June 1988): 130. Reprinted by permission.

[35]Helene D. Gayle et al., "Prevalence of the Immunodeficiency Virus Among University Students," *New England Journal of Medicine* 323 (November 30, 1990): 1538–41.

[36]Frank L. Mott and R. Jean Haurin, "Linkage between Sexual Activity and Alcohol and Drug Abuse among American Adolescents," *Family Planning Perspectives* 20 (1987–88): 130.

the racial/ethnic groups were found among the blacks, where by age 14 over 30 percent of the boys and 5 percent of the girls had had sexual intercourse. By age 18, the proportions increased, respectively, to 76 percent and 64 percent.

A study concluded in 1989 and focusing on college women supported the suspicion that the peril of AIDS had very little impact on their sexual practices—with one exception: their use of condoms rose sharply.[37] A series of successive surveys, conducted in 1975, 1985, and 1989 found no significant differences over time in the proportion of college women who were sexually active, the active women's average number of male partners, or in the proportion of women engaging in high-risk sexual practices. The overall proportions of the respondents who were sexually experienced were nearly constant among the survey dates: 88 percent in 1975, 87 percent in 1985 and 1989. Also nearly constant was the number of accumulative sex partners the sexually experienced women reported: 22 percent of the 1975 respondents had had six or more partners, 20 percent in 1985, and 21 percent in 1989. Equally constant over time were the proportions of women who reported that they engaged in fellatio (over one-third regularly), cunnilingus (one-third regularly), or anal intercourse (about 10 percent occasionally). Likewise the proportion who had had a lesbian relationship did not differ among the three survey years.

All that seemed to have changed were the methods of birth control used by the sexually active women: the proportion using condoms rose sharply over the study period, from 5 percent in 1975 to 14 percent in 1985 and 25 percent in 1989. The proportion of active women not using any method of birth control or protection rose from 1 percent in 1975 to 8 percent in 1985 and then dropped to less than 1 percent in 1989.

PREGNANCY AND THE TEENAGER

Modern teenagers' sexual ardor is not matched by knowledge and caution. One of the consequences can be unplanned and undesirable premarital pregnancy. Statistics reflect that these consequences appear to be of epidemic proportions in American society. Teenagers are responsible for over 40 percent of the illegitimate births in the United States, and their illegitimacy rate has more than doubled over the past few decades. The annual number of children born to mothers under 17 years of age amounted to 500,000 during the late 1980s.

The primary reason for the high rate seems to lie with teenagers' lack of

---

[37]F. Althaus, "High-Risk Sexual Behavior Remains Prevalent among College Women," *Family Planning Perspective* 22 (August 1990): 185–86.

caution and insufficient information concerning conception and contraceptive methods. Among youth aged 17 or younger when they became sexually active, more than 1 in 10 whites and 1 in 5 blacks reported that they either didn't think about pregnancy or didn't care whether a pregnancy would happen. It seems to be this carelessness of American teenagers that explains why American youth have a higher rate of pregnancy than youth in any other industrialized democracy.[38] Nationwide statistics show that after a steep increase in the 1970s, the teen pregnancy rate continued and rose from 9.9 percent to 11 percent in the 1980s. Since levels of teen sexual activities in most Western societies are comparable to levels in the United States,[39] the explanation for the higher pregnancy rate seems to lie with poorer knowledge or practice of contraception. Only about two thirds of unmarried and sexually active teenagers report that they are using a birth control method (usually the pill).[40]

The reasons for the epidemic of teen pregnancies are many and complex. Only a few can be listed here.

Most likely the primary reason is ignorance about the reproductive aspects of sex. American society lacks openness about sex in general and about birth control in specific. According to international studies, societal differences cause drastic differences on the personal level of teenagers as to their sophistication in matters sexual. In Sweden, for example, teenagers are sexually active even earlier than in the United States and they are exposed to even more explicit television. But schools follow curriculum guidelines that ensure that, starting at age seven, children receive thorough education about reproductive biology and are gradually introduced to the various types of contraceptives. "The idea is to dedramatize and demystify sex so that familiarity will make the child less likely to fall prey to unwanted pregnancy and venereal disease."[41]

Another interesting reason seems to deal with American teenagers' demand for sex having to be "romantic." If one has to take precautions, it's no longer romantic. Romantic is apparently equated with impulsive. Guilt feelings prevent many American teenagers from preparing themselves ahead of time for sexual intercourse. They feel less guilty and perceive it as more romantic if it takes place in an impromptu manner.

A 1976 study discovered that not one girl in a sample of unwed teenage mothers had used contraception even though most expressed some knowl-

[38]Kristin Moore and J. Peterson, *The Consequences of Teenage Pregnancy: Final Report,* Washington, DC, Child Trends, Inc., 1989.

[39]Elise Jones et al., "Teenage Pregnancies in Developed Countries," *Family Planning Perspectives* 17 (1985): 53–63.

[40]Christine A. Bachrach and W. Mosher, "Use of Contraceptives in the U.S., 1982," *Vital and Health Statistics* 102, Washington, DC 1984.

[41]Claudia Wallis, "Children Having Children," *Time,* December 9, 1985, p. 82.

edge for its need. Typical explanations were: "Getting ready for sex makes me guilty"; "We'd been screwing for months and I hadn't gotten pregnant"; "I just didn't think I would get pregnant"; "We only screwed when I couldn't get pregnant—in the middle of my cycle."[42]

Perhaps many of these reasons are but rationalizations which pay homage to the ethos of *instant gratification,* a pervasive modern attitude. The "now" attitude refuses to tolerate deferment and tedious preparation.

Some teenage girls actually want to get pregnant, a desire that can derive from a number of personal conditions in the girl's life. Some of them want to prove to their mothers that they are equal and capable of producing life and controlling it. Some of them seem to choose pregnancy to exert the time-honored pressure on the lover to marry her. And increasing numbers seem to decide on pregnancy to create a baby that will give, so they hope, essence and meaning to their lives, a center of existence, and the mystery of having an extension of one's own being. This motive is found most frequently among the very romantic and also among the very insecure who seek a solution to loneliness, an unpleasant home situation, and their inability to cope.

Many more reasons could be discussed, applying to specific groups of teenagers, but the above-mentioned ones seem to come up time and again in various studies.

The Consequences of Pregnancy

The consequences of premarital pregnancy can include a hasty and unplanned marriage, putting the baby up for adoption, keeping the baby and being an unwed parent, or having an abortion. All of these consequences are poor solutions—there are rarely good solutions to an unplanned or unwise pregnancy. Some of the solutions may appear easy and thus contribute to the carelessness responsible for the pregnancy in the first place.

Correlated with the new ease with which unwed mothers can keep and raise their babies is a rejection of the traditional option to have the baby adopted. There has been a marked decline in adoptions since the 1970s. Single-parent families headed by never-married women have increased, approximately five out of ten decide to keep their babies.

Many teenagers solve unwanted pregnancies by abortion. The exact number is unknown, but undoubtedly huge. A 1973 U.S. Supreme Court ruling made abortion legal during the first twelve weeks of pregnancy. No state may interfere in the abortion decision during that period, but states may demand that females have the abortion at a hospital after the initial twelve

---

[42]Mona Lee Thomas, *Initial Feelings of Teenagers on First Realization of Premarital Pregnancy,* paper presented at the annual meeting of the Pacific Sociological Association, San Diego, 1976, p. 8.

weeks. States differ about the age at which young people may have an abortion without parental consent. Most states put the age at eighteen; below that age the consent of one parent is needed. The new legislation makes it relatively easy for a girl to obtain a legal abortion. In fact, to start the process, all a teenager needs to do is dial the number of one of the teen hotline telephones in a metropolitan area, and she will receive free counsel and referral to a Planned Parenthood Center or a clinic.

The extent to which unmarried teenage girls choose to solve their unwanted pregnancy through abortion was reflected in the statistics of the Clergy Counseling Service for Problem Pregnancies in Phoenix, Arizona, where eight out of ten chose abortion and not more than one in twenty opted for an early marriage.[43]

More recently, nationwide statistics show that between the mid 1970s and the mid 1980s the proportion of all teenage girls aged 15 to 19 who had an abortion increased from 2.7 percent to 4.4 percent. This increase explains why the actual rate of giving birth to babies for this age group decreased from 5.8 percent to 5.1 percent, while at the same time the pregnancy rate rose from 9.9 percent to 11 percent. (See Table 15-4.)

While in most cases the medical aspects of a legal abortion are perfectly safeguarded, the psychological repercussions cannot be foreseen and are often detrimental to the self-concept of the young woman.

The best approach to the issue of premarital pregnancy is therefore preventive.

The question of what to do about increasing premarital pregnancies is of longstanding concern to welfare and juvenile authorities. The attempts to cope with the problem branch into two avenues, the *preventive* and the *adjustive*, that is, efforts to reduce premarital pregnancies in the first place and efforts to help reduce the hardships that ensue once an illegitimate birth takes place.

The preventive approach is primarily educational in nature and tries to remind parents of their responsibility for their teenage children and to

TABLE 15-4 Percentage of All Females Age 15-19 Who Became Pregnant, Had a Legal Abortion, or Gave Birth, per Year

Behavior	1974	1976	1978	1980	1982	1984	1985
Became pregnant	9.9	10.1	10.5	11.1	11.0	10.9	11.0
Had a legal abortion	2.7	3.4	4.0	4.3	4.3	4.3	4.4
Gave birth	5.8	5.3	5.2	5.3	5.3	5.1	5.1

Source: Brent C. Miller and Kristin A. Moore, "Adolescent Sexual Behavior, Pregnancy, and Parenting: Research Through the 1980s," *Journal of Marriage and the Family,* 52 (November 1990): 1030. Copyrighted 1990 by the National Council on Family Relations, 3989 Central Ave. N.E., Suite #550, Minneapolis, MN 55421. Reprinted by permission.

[43]Lori Rabinowitz, "High VD Rate," *Arizona Republic* (Phoenix), April 5, 1975, p. C-1.

remind teenagers themselves of the risks of premarital sexual intercourse. The parents' role, however, in respect to the sex education of their offspring is poorly defined, lacks consensus, and is largely inactive. Who should function as the sex educator has by now become a perennial game between teachers and parents. Most of the few existing sex education programs are usually incorporated marginally into other high school courses, frequently into biology. Conspicuous regional differences abound concerning the legality, extent, and quality of such sex education. In some communities, it is shunned as a classroom subject, considered a moral and not an instructional issue. In other places, teachers include sexual information vaguely and evasively in general biology courses; and still in other places, teachers pass the issue to parents as the presumably proper agents of sex instruction. The effect of this indecision, circumvention, and neglect is to victimize the teenager, who is left to learn by hearsay, trial-and-error, and sometimes by irreversible experience.

As a result, the social apparatus needed to provide the necessary adjustment in cases of illegitimate birth has grown into a complex, expensive institution, consisting of social welfare agencies, homes for unwed mothers, and adoption agencies.

DRUGS AND THE TEENAGER

We are in the midst of a pharmacological revolution, and the belief in the cure-all of a myriad of pharmacological products are characteristics of our age. Postindustrial society with its chemical promises has opened a Pandora's box, and the citizenry greedily participates in the presumed comforts, healings, joys, and miracles of its drug contents.

The term drug is vague. If equated with chemicals, just about everything we ingest could be called a drug. But arbitrary distinctions have been drawn, and by definition we understand drugs to be those chemicals of which we expect extraordinary effects beyond the life-sustaining function of ordinary food and drink. We expect a definite reaction, such as being healed or put to sleep, made alert, elated, relaxed, inebriated, "high," or achieving sudden insight and mystical episodes.

Society assigns different statuses to different drugs. Some are openly and widely permitted, others are permitted only at certain places and for certain age groups, and others are prohibited for everyone. The assigned statuses are not based on rational or scientific assessment, but on tradition that makes very little sense from a scientific or medical perspective.

Youth tends to challenge traditional dicta and often refuses to adhere to the traditional categorization of drugs. Not that their categorization is based on more scientific grounds; it is based on rebelliousness, curiosity, ignorance, and the expectation of achieving something instantaneously.

What we experience these days is thus the clash of two irrational systems of drug categorizations. How else could we understand the confrontation between the Establishment that promotes a multi-billion dollar business in tobacco that is known as enormously dangerous to human health, on one side, and condemning marijuana that is still not fully known as a health hazard, on the other side; or the defense of LSD on the part of many young, a drug known to have resulted in numerous and often prolonged psychotic episodes, while society indulges in alcohol that every year causes unspeakable damage to property and life.

It is clear: the young as well as the old do not make sense in the way they view, legislate, and use drugs. It would be of great comfort to believe that such irrationality is a function of nothing but the lack of proper information—and, indeed, in many cases this is true. But if that were normally the explanation, we would have a relatively propitious basis for an information service that could eliminate all unwise drug use in short order. However, the motives for using drugs apparently spring from deep emotional needs or perhaps from physiological craving.

This discussion looks at a few aspects of youthful drug use, among them the clash between the irrational preferences of the Establishment and the equally irrational preferences of the young. By merit of social power, the preferences of the Establishment pass as the acceptable and "normal" ones; those of the young which deviate from these preferences are called delinquent.

The framework of this discussion is too limited to delve into all controversial drugs with which youth is involved. We shall therefore limit discussion to alcohol, opiates, hallucinogens, marijuana, "uppers," "downers," tobacco, and glue- or spray-sniffing. Below are brief sketches of the characteristics of the substances.

Alcohol.   A frequent misconception about alcohol is that it acts as a stimulant. Actually, it is a protoplasmic poison with a depressant effect on the nervous system. Taken in sufficient quantity, it can render a person unconscious by functioning as a general anesthetic. In fact, before other methods were developed, alcohol was sometimes used medically as an anesthetic. It had one major drawback: the dose rendering a person unconscious was also very close to the lethal amount.

The official opinion (The National Institute of Mental Health and the U.S. Department of Health, Education, and Welfare) is that alcohol can be addictive and that drinkers may develop a tolerance so that the same amount of alcohol produces progressively less effect and they crave larger and larger amounts. Eventually they keep on drinking to avoid the severe and painful symptoms that result from withdrawal of alcohol. The end phase is the alcoholic who experiences deterioration of his or her organism.

Opiates.   The group of drugs loosely called opiates are pain-killing and euphoria-inducing chemicals derived from or equivalent to opium. The best known are morphine and heroin; others are codeine, meperidine (Demerol), and methadone (Amidone, Dolophine). The term narcotics is often used synonymously with opiates.

A popular misconception concerning opiates is that the drugs' effects make a person dangerous and violent. Opiates, however, are depressants and lower the user's level of nervous and bodily activities. Effects include analgesia (relief of pain), sedation (freedom from anxiety, reduction of motor activity, muscular relaxation), hypnosis (drowsiness), and euphoria (a sense of well-being and contentment). The relationship between narcotic addiction and criminality is *indirect*. When addicts commit criminal offenses, it is usually in order to obtain the means of continuing to use the drug.

Opiates are addictive, leading to a dependence that has nothing to do with mere habit or the satisfaction of emotional craving. The morphine or heroin addict's organism depends on a regular supply of the chemical and reacts adversely if the supply stops. Addiction, then, is a physiochemical reality in which a drug changes the body chemistry to the degree that functioning without it is difficult.

Heroin addicts acquired lethal notoriety during the last decade of the twentieth century, since infection through shared needles made them a high-risk AIDS group.

Hallucinogens.   The most commonly known psychedelic drugs include LSD (lysergic acid diethylamide), mescaline (extracted from the peyote cactus), and psilocybin (the active ingredient of the so-called sacred mushroom). These substances directly influence the brain's chemistry, affecting synaptic functioning and the coordination of perceptual or memory material. The symptoms of such interference are hallucinations, alterations of perceptions, and reinforcement of certain moods. Such distorted perceptions have been variously acclaimed to be mystic experiences, profound insights, fun, therapy, and psychotic episodes (some were psychoses that needed institutional care). Case histories show that the outcome cannot be safely predicted. It has been found that mentally disturbed persons can sometimes benefit from LSD. On the other side, persons with mentally stable histories may terminate their LSD trips screaming in horror in the emergency ward of the state hospital. Each time an individual ingests hallucinogenic substances, he or she is experimenting with brain chemistry, the delicate balance of which is not yet fully understood.

Interesting effects of this group of drugs may include synesthesia, a cross-over between senses, so that subjects "hear" colors, "smell" sounds, or "see" ideas and thoughts. At times there is sharp amplification of memory and subjects become able to remember minute details of events long since passed. (The benefit of recall can of course turn into detriment and anxiety if the recollection includes material that is unpleasant, frightening, and had been repressed as a defense mechanism.) The mood-intensification of the drugs can be of variable consequence; though a Beethoven symphony may produce rhapsodic joy in one set of mind, it can create suicidal grief in another.

Psychedelic drugs are not addictive. Under certain personality conditions, they may, however, be habit-forming. The more powerful drugs of this group can cause "flashbacks," periodic recurrence of the drug-induced perception without retaking the chemical.

This group of drugs was sacramental to the core of the counterculture of the late 1960s and early 1970s. Its ritualistic role was part of the pervasive syndrome to abjure "objective consciousness" and reintroduce a mystical quality to human life. Since then the publication of scientific information about the human brain had a sobering effect on the metaphysical interpretations, ushering in more objective biochemical explanations of what happens when hallucinogenic molecules reach the brain.

Marijuana.   Some people, among them knowledgeable chemists, are tempted to classify cannabis as a hallucinogenic drug. Insofar as they speak strictly of the active ingredient, tetrahydrocannabinol (THC), they have a point. In concentrated form, THC has qualities similar to the psychedelic drugs. But THC does not come naturally in concentrated form. It comes as marijuana or hashish, both derivatives of the cannabis plant, and as such the effects are mild and in fact sometimes imperceptible to the uninitiated who have not yet learned to recognize a slight reaction. Indeed, there is justified suspicion that many marijuana smokers merely ape the role of the "high" without really experiencing a noteworthy physiological reaction.

The effect varies from user to user, but generally is a slight and light-headed form of inebriation, often accompanied by moderate alteration of perceptions; for example, time and space may assume novel qualities, music may be heard as more resonant, colors may appear brighter, and thoughts believed to be more clear and meaningful. But these are only perceptions. When it comes to personal performance under the influence of marijuana, such as playing the piano or writing an essay, the perception of superior quality usually proves totally unfounded and remains what it is — merely an exaggerated or distorted perception of a normal or even inferior performance.

Medical experts generally believe that marijuana is not addictive.

"Uppers" ("speed").   Cocaine and amphetamines are stimulants of the central nervous system. They promise to instantaneously provide qualities which American society admires: seemingly untiring energy, restless motion, optimism, and, for some, weight loss to assume a slim and trim look. Of these

effects, it is the euphoric high, the feeling of energy and well-being, that attract teenagers to the drugs. Taken orally or snuffed (snorted), they markedly alleviate fatigue and create a lofty sensation of confidence and alertness.

There are significant differences between cocaine and the synthetic amphetamines, with the latter vastly more dangerous than the former—a fact that has been disregarded or even turned around by authorities, medical and otherwise.[44] Cocaine, derived from the South American coca plant, is a complex substance containing several alkaloids, vitamins B and C, and other elements. Coca users tolerate their habits well and experience few, if any, noticeable side-effects. Also, coca leaves contain a highly diluted quantity of cocaine. One should no more equate the potency of coca with cocaine than one should equate the potency of marijuana with pure THC.

Cocaine was undoubtedly one of the drugs President Bush had in mind when, in the late 1980s, he declared a "War on Drugs." In its common street form it was known as "rocks," and in a purified form as "freebase" or "crack." While cocaine is not physiologically addictive, it can lead to powerful psychological dependency, and it is highly toxic to the organism. Heavy doses can lead to irritability, anxiety, paranoia, hallucination, even death.

Amphetamines are no less dangerous; indeed some experts think they are more dangerous because the drugs' effect last 5 to 6 hours, twice as long as that of cocaine; they create various toxic side effects (with occasional deaths resulting) and they rapidly increase the tolerance level of the users, which forces them to take progressively higher and higher doses. Though the latter symptom is usually indicative of an addictive drug, amphetamines are not truly physiologically addictive; they are psychologically habit forming. The depression following use—the "crash"—is almost unknown among cocaine users, but is severe after an amphetamine high wears off. Continued heavy usage may cause impairment of judgment, violent behavior, motor incoordination, hallucinations, extreme irritability, and paranoid disposition (typical of the so-called "speed freak").

Whereas amphetamines are relatively easily available (billions of pills are legally manufactured every year in the United States), cocaine remains an almost totally prohibited drug and is incorrectly classified as a narcotic, like heroin (which is not a stimulant, but a depressant).

"Downers." Barbiturates have come to be called "downers" because of their sedative effect on the central nervous system. These depressants produce an initial euphoria that, again, is perceived as a "high." Some persons combine "downers" with alcohol, another powerful depressant, to achieve a

---

[44]Lester Grinspoon and Peter Hedblom, *The Speed Culture: Amphetamine Use and Abuse in America* (Cambridge, MA: Harvard University Press, 1975); Robert Byck, M.D., ed., *Cocaine Papers by Sigmund Freud* (New York: New American Library, 1975); Richard Ashley, *Cocaine: Its History, Uses, and Effects* (New York: St. Martin's Press, 1975).

faster and longer lasting effect. The danger of such habits is evidenced by frequently fatal "trips," where the depressant effect was so profound that it stopped the vital functions of the organism.

Barbiturates are addictive. The effects of overuse are intellectual impairment, self-neglect, slurred speech, tremor, defective judgment, drowsiness, emotional lability, and bizarre behavior.

Contrary to popular opinion, the withdrawal symptoms of barbiturate addiction are even more acute than those of heroin addiction. Withdrawal symptoms (especially in abrupt withdrawal) include nausea, fever, delirium, hallucinations, and most dangerous of all, convulsion and coma that may lead to death.

Tobacco.   Nicotine, the active ingredient of tobacco, is addictive. The ability of the heavy smoker to be able "to stop whenever I want" is a myth. The drug alters the metabolic chemistry of the smoker to render him or her dependent on the drug, and the withdrawal symptoms are acute.

The research findings concerning the toxic and fatal consequences of smoking have been described so profusely in the mass media that it is unnecessary to repeat them here. Suffice it to say that they range from higher risks of heart attack to gum diseases and cancers of all sorts. Careless smoking involves the additional hazard of fire, and the press frequently reports accidental blazes that destroy property and kill or injure.[45]

Unlike other drugs, smoking often forces nonsmokers to inhale polluted air or "secondhand smoke" that contains nicotine and other toxic substances (at least eleven chemical agents that cause cancer in laboratory animals have been identified in cigarette smoke). A 1975 press release by the American Lung Association warned that "there is four times as much carbon monoxide in side-stream smoke (from the burning end of the cigarette) as in mainstream smoke (inhaled by the smoker) and this is true also for several of the other harmful constituents in cigarette smoke."[46] The report warned further that carbon monoxide levels in the blood of nonsmokers exposed to "secondhand smoke" have been found to exceed federal safety standards.

Glue-, paint-, or spray-sniffing.   In the search for the elusive "high," teenagers have discovered that all sorts of evaporative agents are suitable material. In glue, spot-remover solvents, various paints, paint thinners, and aerosol cans teenagers have found a way to go on a "trip." The variety of chemicals (including benzine, toluene, acetone, and methylene) used to achieve a "trip"

---

[45]The Metropolitan Life Insurance Company reported that among their policyholders 16 percent of the deaths from fires and burns were caused by smoking: "How Fatal Accidents Occur in the Home," *Metropolitan Life Insurance Bulletin*, 40 (November 1959): 6–8. Another study set smoker-caused burn deaths at 18 percent: *Home Accidents Fatalities* (mimeographed report, table 12, National Office of Vital Statistics, U.S. Public Health Service, Washington, DC, 1956).

[46]UPI Report, New York, March 31, 1975.

defies simple classification of their effects on the human organism. But in most cases they are hydrocarbons, which diminish the oxygen supply to the brain so drastically that the user feels light-headed and giddy. As in the case of extreme alcohol ingestion, the depressant effect and the deprivation of oxygen may have deleterious effects, cause irreparable damage to the brain, and even result in death. Other effects may include poisoning and permanent damage to liver, kidneys, and lungs. The chemicals used for such experimentation can hardly be controlled; they are legal and easily accessible, facilitating one of the most lethal teenage fads of the century.

Scope and Trends

The scope of the adolescents' involvement with drugs includes a quantitative as well as qualitative aspect; that is, how many of them use the various drugs and to what degree? Information answering these two questions is difficult to obtain and consists only of estimates.

Alcohol is the most widely used of the chemicals under discussion. The National Council on Alcoholism has estimated that between 70 and 80 percent of all adult Americans drink alcohol, that 20 percent of the drinkers are problem drinkers, and that 10 percent of the drinkers are alcoholics.[47] (This would put the figure for alcoholics at over 10 million during the late 1970s.)

Only a small proportion of alcoholics are teenagers. Alcoholism is a problem that ripens with time and requires the cultivation of a heavy drinking habit. Nonetheless, teenage alcohol consumption is widespread and sometimes a prelude to alcoholism in later life.

Teenage drug use is subject to historical fluctuation, strongly influenced by what is "in," and ruled by fad. Drinking has gone through such fluctuation. Before the onslaught of the late-1960s-to-early-1970s counterculture, alcohol was the standard drug for teenagers, serving as medium for the "high," the traditional test of manliness for boys (and for permanent adolescents), and a means through which to rebel against the Establishment. With the rise of the youth movement, alcohol's preeminence waned and marijuana's popularity rose; for a number of years it was "pot," "dope," or "grass" that attracted youth's primary attention. During the 1970s, the pendulum swung back to alcohol and again became the preferred drug of American teenagers. A survey showed that high-school administrators agreed that the marijuana fad was fading and the use of alcohol was increasing.[48]

But with the 1980s the pendulum swung again, and marijuana regained its popularity. In addition, a vastly more dangerous drug spread across the

---

[47]Linda Lamb, *A Summary for Parents and Students on Alcohol Abuse* (New York: National Council on Alcoholism, 1972).

[48]Ibid.

nation: cocaine in its various forms. The last decade of the twentieth century sees an unabated—some would say a losing—battle between the authorities and the drug users. The latter have become participants in a subinstitution of international dimensions, including the roles of producer, shipper, dealer, and consumer. The authorities had to create new technology, institutions, and law-enforcement agencies in their attempt to stem the unceasing tide of the demand for illicit drugs.

However, apart from marijuana, teenagers in general are not the prime customers of cocaine and heroin. These drugs are more a part of inner-city life or of specific subcultures (such as prostitution, for example).

A combined survey by the National Institute on Drug Abuse and the University of Michigan Institute for Social Research, spanning the decade from the mid 1970s to the mid 1980s, sampled each year's graduates enrolled in public and private high schools across the United States. Here are the major findings concerning the teenagers' 1975–1986 drug use (see Table 15-5):

1. *Marijuana* use surged during the late 1970s and reached its peak during 1979–1981, when approximately 60 percent of the teenagers reported having used it. During 1986, the last year of the survey, it dropped to 51 percent.
2. *Inhalants*, on the other hand, climbed from 12 percent to 16 percent.
3. *Psychedelics* declined, especially LSD, which dropped from 11 percent to 7 percent.
4. *Cocaine* showed the highest gain, rising from 9 percent to 17 percent.
5. *Heroin*, on the other hand, dwindled from 2.2 percent to 1.1 percent.
6. *Alcohol* held its own, hardly changing, starting with 90 percent and ending with 91 percent.
7. *Cigarettes* experienced a marked drop from 74 percent to 68 percent. It is interesting, however, that a higher proportion of girls than of boys started to smoke during the 1980s. A related insight came from a team of Arizona State

TABLE 15-5   Percentage of U.S. High School Students Who Ever Used Drugs, 1975–1986. (Figures rounded for 1975–1981)

	1975	1978	1981	1985	1986
Marijuana	47	59	60	54.2	50.9
Inhalants	NA	12	12	15.4	15.9
LSD	11	10	10	7.5	7.2
Cocaine	9	13	17	17.3	16.9
Heroin	2	2	1	1.2	1.1
Alcohol	90	93	93	92.2	91.3
Cigarettes	74	75	71	68.8	67.6
Stimulants	22	23	32	26.2	23.4
Sedatives	18	16	16	11.8	10.4

Source: National Institute on Drug Abuse and the University of Michigan Institute for Social Research. Reprinted by permission.

University psychologists who had followed the smoking habits of nearly 6000 6th-through-11th-grade students over a period of four years. Girls try earlier, many before the 7th grade, whereas boys tend to wait until their sophomore year before smoking their first cigarettes.[49]

In sum, the following changes between 1975 and 1986 have been found among 19 different drugs in question: (1) By 1985 only 3 of the drugs, inhalants, cocaine, and opiates other than heroin, increased slightly. (2) By 1986 only inhalants had increased further. All other drugs showed decreases, though only small ones, over the previous year. The largest decrease was 3.3 percent in the use of marijuana, followed by 2.8 percent in stimulants, 1.4 percent in sedatives, and 1.2 percent in cigarettes.

More recent surveys have shown a further decline of teenage drug use. Does this look like the War on Drugs is about to be won? Not at all. A distinction must be made between the very occasional *user*, such as the majority of high school kids, and the heavy, almost daily *abuser*, who usually is not the typical high school kid. So, what the above figures really show is that high school students have slightly cut back on their use of drugs—a use that has mostly been casual to begin with.

What these figures do not show is that heavy use, that is, abuse, has increased dramatically, probably involved more older than younger persons. This is the group that uses drugs regularly and should be called abusers. In sum, this means that a large population of young, casual, experimental users is slightly decreasing, whereas a smaller population of heavy abusers is increasing.

A 1988 survey conducted by the Department of Health and Human Services showed that 862,000 people used cocaine once a week or more, compared with 647,000 in 1985. (Discussion of this heavy-use group is outside of this book's domain, simply because it normally is not a part of the adolescent scene.) HHS Secretary Louis Sullivan warned that the decrease in casual use "is encouraging, but should not be viewed as a declaration of success in the nation's anti-drug abuse efforts."[50]

What the trend demonstrates is a novel *polarization effect*: either you do or you don't do drugs, with diminishing middle ground.

And perhaps this polarization effect is the only real effect that the War on Drugs has had so far. Political bias can, of course, manipulate the statistics and present them in a way to either show progress or failure of the War, depending on whether one points to the receding casual use or the increasing heavy abuse.

In any case, a victory is still a long way's off—perhaps farther off than at

---

[49]"20% of Teenagers Smoke," *Arizona State Insight*, 4 (November 13, 1984): 7.

[50]Quoted by Carron M. Sherry, "How High: To Combat Drugs," *Future Choices, Toward a National Youth Policy* 1 (Fall 1989): 19.

the beginning of the War on Drugs. Studies by the National Institute on Drug Abuse conducted in 1988 showed that

> the highest rates of cocaine use were among young adults aged 18 to 25; the studies also showed that 30% of all college students will use cocaine at least once before graduation and 80% of all Americans will try an illicit drug by their mid–twenties.
>
> The United States consumes 60% of all the illegal drugs produced world-wide. In economic terms, the sale of illegal narcotics total $100 billion annually, more than the total net sales of General Motors, more than American farmers take in from all crops. The Research Triangle Institute determined the economic costs of drug abuse to society in 1983 to be $60 billion. The Department of Justice estimates the figure to have risen to $100 billion in 1986.[51]

Solutions?

It is no wonder that a chorus of desperate voices can be heard across the nation, each voice urging action to solve the problem. But the chorus fails to sing in unison and seems unable to agree upon one tune. Various suggestions have been advanced; they can be ordered into three categories:

Education. The Americans have an undying trust in the power of information, assuming that once you provide information about a subject, rational action will naturally follow. It is this blind trust that led some people to believe that, if American society would provide drug education, rational and cautious drug behavior would automatically ensue. We came across a specific application of this assumption earlier in the chapter when it was concluded that the difference between the rate of teenage pregnancies in the U.S. and Sweden was due to the difference in sex education programs. This, of course, is a simplistic interpretation of statistics, ignoring additional variables, such as a sense of responsibility. No amount of information is worthwhile unless it is coupled with a sense of responsibility. Drug use is no exception to the rule.

Some might argue that the concept of education is broader than merely giving information, that it includes the moral command for responsible behavior. This may be true, at least on the conceptual level, but it sidesteps the question how a sense of moral responsibility is to be infused into teen-agers exposed to a society that has erected hedonism and a distortion of the concept of self-actualization as idols to be worshipped. The problem of drug abuse cannot be separated form the larger fabric of the sociocultural context; it belongs to the broader syndrome of abusing the vast freedom enjoyed by American citizens.

Nonetheless, information is, of course, better than ignorance, and the

---

[51]Ibid., p. 20.

more thorough the information, the better. Parents and teachers have a responsibility to prepare children for the chemical powers that are available at a street corner or during lunch hour at the high school so they can exercise caution and make wise decisions. But few parents sit down with their children and go through the list of major drugs, legal and illegal ones, explaining their properties and their effects on the user. Institutions of educations are not doing much better. (This glaring lacuna motivated the inclusion into this chapter of short descriptions of some of the major frequently abused drugs.)

Schools, and the authorities in general, often make the mistake of warning against drugs but failing to spell out the medical or scientific reasons for the warning. An authority-sponsored TV ad of the early 1990s tried to jolt the viewer by threatening "Do drugs, do time!" to the sound of a prison cell slamming shut. This tells the teenager nothing new; after viewing the ad, he or she knew as much as before. Such pronouncements are not information, they are monosyllabic threats, stimulating not inquisitiveness, but arousing rejection and rebellion.

One of the first things that needs to be done is to educate the educators and parents. Sparse efforts are made in this direction. The *Journal of Drug Education* is one exception, bringing helpful information, insights, and methodologies that can be implemented in real-life situations. Many workshops arranged by law enforcement agencies and financed by the government in its War on Drugs leave a lot to be desired in objectivity and accurateness. Incredibly, they sometimes perpetuate basic confusions concerning the properties of different drugs.

The irony is that many teenagers *are* informed about the properties of the drugs—perhaps more objectively so than the law enforcement agents lecturing at a workshop—and *still* use, even abuse, them. And now we are back at the beginning: giving information is an extremely limited approach—though, of course, an indispensable one—to the drug problem America faces today. Drug abuse is, besides possibly a problem of knowledge, a moral problem as well.

Stronger law enforcement. Not surprisingly, after witnessing the apparent futility of the so-called drug education, many voices called for draconian measures. Billions of taxpayers' money have been expended during the past two to three decades trying to eradicate drug abuse. The expenditures range from specially equipped surveillance planes patrolling our southern border, to the controversial meddling in the internal affairs of South American nations, to mandatory urinalysis of employees and athletes, and to the training of drug-sniffing canines.

Severe penalties have been imposed for possession of the slightest amount of such substances as marijuana; California, for example, imposes a fine of $100 for one ounce of it. The penalties for trafficking, that is, dealing, are much stiffer. Starting with 1990, Federal penalties for less than 50 kg of marijuana can be up to 5 years in jail and up to $250,000 in fines. A second offense doubles these measures. Cocaine incurs higher penalties—a pound or more results in a minimum of 5 years in jail and up to two million dollars in fines—that's for the first offense; second offenses double the penalties; higher quantities of cocaine double the penalties once more. Identical penalties apply to heroin, amphetamines, LSD, and other forbidden drugs.[52]

None of these punitive measures seem to have made much of a difference.

Even the more remedial and less punitive measures have failed to make a difference. During the early 1970s, mandatory cure programs were set up for teenage addicts. Once officially defined as a narcotic addict, the teenager was placed into a mandatory cure program. The best-known Public Health Service hospitals for that purpose were those at Lexington, Kentucky, and Fort Worth, Texas. The help offered at these places included safe withdrawal, vocational and recreational activities, and limited psychotherapy. But the volume of recidivism (close to 80 percent) and the continued increase of narcotics abuse was so discouraging as to render the services of these institutions meaningless, and, after several decades of operation, they closed their gates to addicts in the mid 1970s—a glaring defeat in the war against drug abuse!

An even greater failure rate was discovered by the Columbia University School of Public Health, finding that of a group of 147 adolescents discharged from Riverside Hospital in New York 91 percent returned to regular daily use of drugs.[53]

Legalization of drug use.   Not surprisingly, some voices have called for the legalization of the forbidden drugs, rendering them taxable commodities and subject to government control.[54] This suggestion has been variously received, spanning a spectrum from outright moral condemnation to welcoming it as an enlightened way out of the infeasible morass we are currently in. Proponents point out that we are again fighting a losing battle, comparable to the historical Prohibition. Furthermore, they claim that if we want to be true to the democratic principle of individual freedom of personal choices of what to ingest, then we should give in to the demands of hundred of thousands of Americans who insist upon using certain drugs; we should make them available for a good capitalistic price, control them medically and

[52]"Federal Penalties," *Federal Register* 55 (August 16, 1990): 33588.

[53]Alfred M. Freedman, "Treatment of Drug Addiction in a Community General Hospital," *Comprehensive Psychiatry* 4 (June 1963): 199.

[54]See examples: Ronald Hamowy, ed., *Dealing with Drugs, Consequences of Government Control* (San Francisco: Laissez Faire Books, 1990); Steven Wisotski, *Beyond the War on Drugs* (San Francisco: Laissez Faire Books, 1990).

hygienically as well as we can (just as is done in the case of other commodities under the control of the Federal Food and Drug Administration), and collect revenues from the sales. We are hypocritical, they would add, when we sell alcohol in just about any grocery store and put up vending machines that make cigarettes available to any child or teenager with a few coins in his or her pocket.

Many observers feel that American laws have not only failed to eliminate addiction, but further compounded and complicated the problem by stimulating additional delinquent acts, deepening the addicts' immersion in addict subcultures, and encouraging the formation of huge underground drug operations.

This discussion is not prepared to submit anything as presumptuous as a solution to this monstrously huge and vexing problem. As admitted at the outset of the chapter, the purpose of discussing the various problems is to sensitize the reader toward their complexity, encourage further acquisition of pertinent knowledge, and stimulate the American genius for creating solutions to seemingly insurmountable tasks.

SUMMARY

Growing up in American society is a long journey on which teenagers encounter many hurdles and perils. Many of them stumble temporarily, and some become permanently lost. This is the arena of social problems, and many adolescents detour into it. Nonetheless, adolescence as a whole should not be thought of as a social problem. The purpose of this chapter was merely to point to some frequent detours associated with young people.

1. One of the detours is dropping out from high school. Estimates put the number at 10 million during the 1980s—an unprecedentedly large number—a function of the increased teen population over the past decades and not of the rate, which has actually decreased and stands at less than 30 percent. Dropout proneness is significantly influenced by background conditions: lower socioeconomic class, racial and ethnic minorities, quality of family interaction, peer involvement, and delinquency. Some observers use the term "pushout" to refer to the identical conditions, but especially to learning disabilities not recognized as such.

2. The labor market is not hospitable to the young, particularly if he or she is a dropout. In times of economic depression the high school dropout is hired last and fired first. To alleviate the problem, national youth projects have been suggested. A recent one, the Citizens Corps, tries to encourage teenagers to complete high school then invest two years in national service, in the process earning vouchers to go on to college.

3. The incongruence between traditional morals and the actual sexual behavior of teenagers has produced a Sexual Revolution. Contributing condi-

tions have been: (a) female emancipation, (b) secular attitudes toward sexuality, (c) legal reorientation, (d) prolonged adolescent period, (e) titillating mass media, and (f) the cult of instantaneousness. The Sexual Revolution has come to be modified since the 1980s because of (a) the need for emotional security in an intimate relationship, (b) the discrepancy between verbalization of liberality and the actual behavior, (c) the legacy of traditional norms, and (d) the new plague, AIDS.

4. In spite of the availability of contraceptive information and devices, the premarital pregnancy rate has increased over the years. Because of the equally increased abortion rate, the actual rate of teenagers giving birth has slightly decreased.

5. Drug use by the nation's teenagers, in the sense of occasional and experimental usage, has slightly decreased, whereas abuse, in the sense of heavy and regular usage, has increased and caused a polarization effect which now more sharply defines between nonusers and abusers. As a consequence, statistics can be prepared selectively, possibly to serve political ends. Three solution approaches can be observed: (a) *Education*. But whether "drug education" alone can prevent drug abuse is not yet known, for no information will do much good unless it is wedded to responsible morality. (b) *Stronger law enforcement*. The proponents of the War on Drugs call for draconian measures; indeed, the Federal penalties are substantial, even for relatively small quantities of illegal drugs. (c) *Lifting the prohibition*. Some voices call for legalization of the forbidden drugs, bringing them under government control, and taxing them like other commodities. They feel that the present laws not only fail in their purpose to prevent drug abuse but, in addition, define large numbers of Americans as delinquents or criminals, and drive them into huge underground drug operations.

16

Adolescence in Perspective—
An Overview

ADOLESCENCE—A NEW STAGE IN THE LIFE CYCLE

In almost all modern societies adolescence has evolved so extensively that it appears to be an inevitable component of the human life cycle. However, adolescence is an invention of urban-industrial life and not a universal constant such as infancy, childhood, adulthood, and old age.

The epitome of adolescence evolved in postindustrial society, which has generated armies of adolescents who, even into their twenties, march to their own tune and maintain a moratorium on a range of adult characteristics.

Adolescence has received various interpretations—from enthusiastic welcome to clinical condemnation.

Sociologist Frank Musgrove felt that adolescence is one of the least efficient inventions of modern industrial age, for it wastes a resource which society cannot easily do without—the imagination and energy of its youth. Adolescents are potentially mature, creative human beings who differ from their elders largely because they are not allowed to participate in adult activities. The resulting frustrations make them rebellious and often destructive inverts who join ranks to confront the Establishment with seemingly illogical dissent. Sociologist Karl Mannheim, concurring to some degree, visualized a useful, if not indispensable, function in adolescent dissent: a force checking society's follies and blind spots, and a perennial challenge to seek more just and complete ways of meeting personal and social needs. Adolescents thus form a catalytic element in society.

But many others equate adolescence with "teenagerism," consider it a disease without which the young as well as the old would be happier. This interpretation is fostered by a number of factors: first, by the extensiveness of adolescence, stretching into the twenties and making large numbers of youth appear useless and parasitic; second, by the intensity of adolescence, bringing out disturbed, confused, and searching behavior; and third, by the collectivization of adolescent disturbance, advancing a dissentful, alienated, and alienating culture of its own.

This does not fit the traditional view that youth should be a preadult stage and that young people are apprentices going through an awkward yet learning and preparatory phase before taking their places in the adult world. Long, drawn-out adolescence and millions of cultist members of the teenage subculture seem to defy this view. Indeed, most teenagers no longer possess this preparatory feeling. They behave as if they have arrived, bearing testimony to the fact that adolescence has evolved as a phase in its own right within the life span of the modern individual. The ingredients of the youth subculture assume a semipermanent quality, particularly since much of it is adulated and imitated by the rest of society, including adults. The heroes, songs, music, styles, and fads appear more all-American than the world of jobs and professions looming somewhere out there—the encounter with which is continually postponed.

ADOLESCENCE AND THE PROBLEM OF IDENTITY IN MODERN SOCIETY

Whatever one might say about adolescents, it must be clear that it was not they who determined adolescence as the interim phase between childhood and adulthood. The forces combining to forge the conditions that gave rise to adolescence include the peculiarities of urban-industrial society's social structure and the generally anomic culture of modern Western civilization.

Two fundamental causes of adolescence can be identified. One can be traced to the original fissure in the social structure, which opened during the Industrial Revolution because of increasing requirements for education and training. Having eliminated the direct transition from childhood to adulthood, the fissure broadened over the years into a new phase, bringing along a generation gap. This break in the passage between statuses is the social-structural cause of adolescence, laying down the *necessary* cause. The *sufficient* cause arrived with the increasingly secular and anomic lifestyle of most industrialized societies, which deprived the young of cultural meanings that traditionally proved helpful in achieving orientation in life. Without these cultural meanings, the individual's reliance on the social structure, especially on the adult division of labor, for personal identity increased acutely— ironically, again affecting the young most disadvantageously, since they found themselves in preadult-structural circumstances.

The deriving of personal identity from a specific position within the social structure is a relatively recent innovation and is correlated with the weakening of cultural control. This means that as the persuasiveness of the cultural ethos decreased and became too nonspecific for life-orienta- tion, the importance of the vocational or professional position for meaning and behavioral orientation increased—identity-genesis and identity-rein- forcement shifted from the general cultural ethos to the vastly more specific and discrete social position. This shift constitutes an attempt to reanchor identity and can be understood as a natural reaction to unstructuredness and uncertainty. People need clearly defined norms and expectations that enable them to engage in meaningful, predictable, and in fact, viable behavior. Clearly, a life situation offering noncompelling cultural guidelines and highly diversified and discrete adult positions must be frustrating to young people, and it is prone to create a hotbed of unrest.

It follows from such conditions that adolescents form a pool of vulner- able individuals who starve for new (vs. the outgrown familial) object fixation, and that as such they are convenient targets for demagogues. Modern history is replete with examples in which newly dedicated youth were drawn into devastating causes, "serving" their country or their True Belief, and were exploited literally to the last drop of blood—theirs as well as their adversaries'.

In a sense, part of the responsibility of a democratic society is to refuse to give into its youth's constant pressure for deliverance from anomie and to reject infusing them with absolutistic credos, giving them collective causes, involving them in totalitarian programs—in short, to reject dominating their lives. Anomie unintentionally curtails that temptation. But, of course, in the process it conjures up a host of other problems.

This thought will be briefly pursued later. Here, we are interested in the causal backdrop of adolescence. The two major causes—one structural and the other cultural, one operative by commission and the other by omission— contain interrelated conditions.

Some of the conditions arise from the combined impact of social- structural discontinuity and cultural nonspecificity, exerting adolescence- generating influence, and should be briefly reviewed.

With the rise of urban-industrial conditions, the division of labor in- creased in specificity to the point where common cultural ground was ob- scured. An alienating factor was introduced. Young people no longer inti- mately witnessed the work of adults; the place of residence and the place of work were separated.

The conditions of postindustrial life further deepen the adolescent experience. As an important factor, the labor market repulses early entry. Mechanization and automation have made production and service possible with a minimum of labor. Young people are not needed—a fact cloaked by rhetoric dignifying prolonged education and bemoaning the dropout rate. But the gimmick is flimsy, and most adolescents cannot help but feel that they are not needed or wanted. They recognize high school, and increasingly college, as holding pens and see little meaning in them. This puts undue strain on educational institutions, which find it difficult to motivate and inform at the same time.

Postindustrial ability to cater to liberal consumption patterns and render an abundance of service unheard of during previous generations has resulted in a peculiar mental state among the young, particularly among the middle class. Called the psychology of entitlement, it not only expects instant gratification but also assumes that society owes one a financially secure and psychologically happy ("self-actualized") life.

The postindustrial conditions of delayed entry into the labor market and liberally offered consumption in fact allow the vast majority of American youth to remain preadult for so long, and thus to form a pool of potentially dissenting individuals.

American culture has been accused of lacking compelling ideation that would provide meaning and a cause for the young, and of thereby contributing to the sustaining cause of the interim between child and adult status. This accusation should not, however, be understood as denying the existence of all or any cultural values. The American culture *does* suggest a number of strong values, but not in the form of an integrated ethos that is as totalitarian, action-oriented, and cause-suggestive as the kinds of ethos experienced by teenagers in other countries or in different historical periods. The very nature of the American ethos stresses individuality and democracy; the burden of deciding on a cause, on life meaning, and on goal aspirations is thereby placed in the hands of the individual rather than in the action programs of a nationwide *Hitler-Jugend, Komsomol,* or Red Guard. A noncompelling and individualistic ideation such as the modern American ethos taxes the imagination and creativity of youth to a far greater extent than the totalitarian regime that presents ready-made programs and identities. The price paid for the freedom of self-exploration and unique identity is a longer search—a prolonged adolescence.

In addition to the noncompelling nature of the American ethos, several values are beset with negative or ambivalent elements; for example, the cultural view of pubescence is largely evasive, semitaboo, and often negative. Another cultural dilemma is the disjunction between biological maturity and social maturity: the adolescent period between pubescence and the accordance of adulthood is lengthened because of the progressively lower age at puberty. Furthermore, American culture does not offer a rite of passage in the form of a public ceremony proclaiming the transition into adulthood.

Other confusing elements of American culture are value schisms requiring the young to determine which norms and expectations apply in what situation and at what time. American culture is diverse and inconsistent enough to offer for each value an opposing one. These include the polar values of competition versus cooperation, work versus leisure, piousness versus free-thinking, individualism versus conformity, sexuality versus chastity. Another schism includes such adult-child polarities as responsibility versus nonresponsibility, sex versus sexlessness, unrealism versus realism, and dominance versus submission.

American culture is also characterized by anomic elements that fail to specify norms for achieving culturally suggested goals. Thus a lower-class teenager may be exposed to values such as material success, but may lack feasible, legitimate norms for attaining the goal. The reaction to the unstructured condition is a gravitation toward a subcultural environment with norms and values the adolescent can meet.

The greater the amount of technological innovation, the greater are the modifying effects on social life. This principle affects the relationship between generations, because rapid technological and sociological changes constantly alter conditions and render the adjustments of one generation at least partially invalid for the next generation. One could thus say that the faster the rate of sociocultural change, the greater the degree of intergenerational conflict. This conflict can be seen in the differences between the norms and values held by the older and younger generations.

THE CHANGING PARENT-OFFSPRING RELATIONSHIP

Besides suffering from a general cultural lag, parents also suffer from specific knowledge lags, for it is virtually impossible for them to keep up with the latest information provided by fast-moving science and technology. Children and adolescents, who keep abreast of the latest knowledge under the intellectual guardianship of teachers and experts, are better informed than their parents in many aspects.

Cultural and knowledge lags are not the only negative experiences of modern parents. Social scientists and educators have voiced doubts concerning the pedagogic qualifications of American parents and have even ascribed to them the responsibility for typical teenage behavior. If one adds the threat of population explosion to this parent-deprecatory syndrome, then parenthood appears no longer as an asset but as a liability to society. One parental reaction to this realization was an apologetic *mea culpa*, and parents, desiring to establish rapprochement between the generations, resorted to communication, information, and equality. This idealistic approach largely failed, for it neglected to assess realistically the nature of socialization, which is not conducive to an equalitarian relationship between socializer and socializee.

Another reaction was to reassert traditional authority. This reaction came with the awareness that teenagers, in spite of their up-to-date technological knowledge, lack insights into life's problems—the mature solutions of which require more than classroom learning and technical know-how.

Significant in intergenerational friction is a clash of psychological dispositions that has been called the "clash of inferiority complexes." On one side, parents are constantly exposed to the American "youth cult" that creates feelings of inferiority in the face of declining strength, prowess, and youthful appearance. On the other side, young people feel inferior in the face of many restrictions that limit activities and privileges. The interplay between the complexes results in a cumulative, mutually reinforcing cycle that perpetuates reciprocal resentment.

The shift to the small nuclear family created a drastic reduction of concrete adult models. It also brought about a reduction of familial peers. Clan association was replaced by association with peers whose background experiences and attitudes frequently differed greatly. Over time, this body of peers evolved into an influential collectivity forming a corporate identity apart from, and often opposed to, the family. Association with nonfamilial peers thus encourages modern youth to maintain independent subcultures.

The contemporary vagueness in cultural precepts and the emphasis on individual freedom have burdened marriage and the family with a heretofore unknown intensity of personality functions. Gratification from marital and familial affiliation, however, is often curtailed by individualism and secularism, which tend to neutralize the beneficial effects of familism. The effects of individualistic and secular philosophy are also observable in the abrogation of the placement function of the family: the adolescent is now largely on his or her own in determining career and social standing. There is even suspicion that the primariness of group interaction of the modern family has shifted slightly toward secondariness.

For the adolescent, the combined effect of these changes in family structure and function is the tendency to become involved in peer subcultures, to make family-independent career decisions, and to become engaged in nonfamilial career preparation—all circumstances that place the youth in subcultural environments and make his or her transition into adulthood more complex. The function of the peer group, however, also includes bridging the gap between childhood and adulthood, learning to get along with others, testing one's wits, and establishing autonomy from the family.

Modern family life has also given rise to a perversion of motherhood defined as Momism. In this situation, frequently characterized by a father who is remote or absent from the socialization process, the mother seeks fulfillment of neurotic needs through the child. A prevalent mode is the "perfect" mother who tries to make motherhood a "success"—and in the process produces a personality condemned to lifelong adolescence.

The converse is also true. Dadism is the child-rearing style whereby a father molds his daughter into the "little girl" she is going to be for the rest of her life. The socially significant difference between Momism and Dadism is that the former shows up as a personality defect in the boy because it undermines the personality stereotype of masculinity, whereas the latter creates the nurturing and dependent role of femininity still widely found acceptable and nonpathological in Western Civilization.

THE POWER OF THE MASS MEDIA

Modern mass media are powerful socializers of young people. Among them, TV has become the most ubiquitous influence. By age eighteen, young Americans on the average have spent more time watching the screen than attending school. This makes more than merely academic the questions of TV's ingredients and their effects on the audience; we are dealing with impingement on human nature.

The style of communication and socialization via TV is vastly more symbolic and abstract than the style that prevailed in the traditional family. The new qualities are highly susceptible to the presentation of the unreal and the violent. These two themes worry many parents, educators, and social scientists because, unlike the educational and informative functions of the medium, they are suspected of stimulating immature and possibly even violent imitation. But the definitive verdict has not yet been reached. Research is still trying to come up with unambiguous conclusions. What can be said with some degree of certainty is that certain control forces act to curb unwise imitation of TV fare: parental influence and socialization measures, the limited availability of the means necessary to carry out violent plots and images, the influence of other American norms and values balancing the more destructive ones, and the conditional arousal of anger and hostility that would motivate the imitation of violence. Imitation of violence or unrealism does, however, occur in situations where absence of all control variables coincides—situations that do not arise frequently.

TV reinforces the teenage subculture by catering to it through adoption of teen standards, tastes, and fads. Many programs, in fact, are specifically aimed at the teen population and are part of the business syndrome capitalizing on the youth cult.

TV has functions that undeniably further the knowledgeability of young people. Information covering a vast spectrum is offered. For example, events that happen somewhere in the nation or the world are almost instantly communicated, potentially enhancing youth's understanding of life and the world. The instantness and realism of witnessing happenings from around the globe may in part explain youth's quick arousal to action and political protest. However, here again looms danger. The sensational aspects seen on the screen often obscure more complex and hidden political reasons and maneuvers that lie behind the reported action, and the young are led to engage in naïve political activism.

CHANGING SOCIAL BEHAVIOR: FROM ROLE TO "FRAME ANALYSIS"

Timeless difficulties are associated with youth's unfolding into culturized human personalities: roles have to be learned and an identity established.

But are we here expressing a slightly antiquated bias? Some of the recent writing in social psychology suggests a different formula—one that has presumably resulted from a vastly changed social milieu and that has displaced formulas conducive to developing relatively stable roles and a core identity. Erving Goffman in his latest works abandoned role concepts previously applied to understanding human relationships, in favor of infinitely ephemeral, symbolic, and ritualistic etiquette that regulates human encounters on a situational basis.

He coined the phrase "frame analysis" to describe the character of modern social interaction that seems to narrowly focus on one situation at a time, a "frame" in an ongoing film strip, as it were, whereby the individual tries to understand the situational contingencies, instead of trying to bring rigid role approaches into the picture.

If this is true, the younger generations learn to become human beings in a significantly different way, one based not on lasting or semipermanent role definitions, but on principles of efficiency and expedience. This would replace traditional human intimacy with anonymity, sharing with exchange, and the sense of social communion with self-actualization.

Perhaps the difficulties and disturbances in the interaction between the sexes is a symptom of the new style of self-development: it is no longer based on pervasive cultural blueprints, but on individualistic characteristics. Roles are abandoned to make room for idiosyncratic makeup. The brunt of this development (or revolution) was, of course, borne by females. Underlying the activities of women's liberation is the more fundamental attempt to achieve a different concept in personality development. That we witness it first in the case of women is due to the antiquated limitations inherent in the stereotypical status.

As a result of respecting personal uniqueness and abstaining from imposing a priori roles on others, the ritual of encounter must necessarily be nonspecific, nonintrusive, and nonpersonal. If it is too specific or personal, it may violate a person's unique self-definition. The old role concepts run that danger. The new impersonal rituals steer clear of it.

Modern adolescents therefore learn a different style of human interaction, with a premium on communication and efficiency, and pay the price of increasing interpersonal alienation.

FROM THE INDIVIDUAL ADOLESCENT TO THE SUBCULTURE

The foregoing points attempted to summarize the major antecedent conditions of adolescence and to explain why the second half of the twentieth century is characterized by acute adolescent symptoms.

Continuation of the analysis of adolescence leads logically to the next point: the *consequences* of adolescence. The major sociological consequences of adolescent discontinuity expresses itself in collective behavior and presents a relatively novel social problem. It seems safe to conclude that there has never before been so massive a recession of the young from the adult society into their own subsociety, which is not only different but opposed to adult standards. Manifestations of their subcultural life are manifold and can be observed in distinct and recurrent fads, styles, hero worship, attitudes, values, argot, and material implementation. Many of these subcultural expressions have been insufficiently researched, and the only sources of information are often popular media through which teenagers express themselves directly, such as songs, dances, fashion, and teen magazines.

More seriously, youth has made a decisive impact on the political lifestyle of the nation. The counterculture was the epitome of modern adolescence—with its follies as well as its good points. It contained both senseless rebelliousness and valuable commentary, attacking valuable traditions as well as corruptions and perversions of the Establishment.

RESEARCH NEEDS

Sociological research into adolescent behavior reflects uneven tendencies, with great coverage of some sectors and little coverage of others. Teenage marriages, for example, have received extensive attention, and sociologists have prolifically described when, where, whom, and why teenagers marry. On the other hand, there has been neglect of inquiry into advertising and attempts to form the opinions of children and teenagers toward purchasing. In view of the affluence of young Americans, this question is of more than academic value.

A conspicuous lack of knowledge exists about collective behavior. Its study calls for scrutiny of the development and fluctuations of subcultures, fads, crazes, and hero worship. For example, such fervent activities as teenage dancing have not yet been systematically studied. The precise dimensions of the teen subculture, or of the subculture generally, are still a mystery to most social scientists. Exactly what takes place at the dawn of subcultural formation, when teenagers engage in so-called "exploratory gestures?" What mechanisms operate as younger teenagers learn subcultural norms and values from older peers? What exactly are the channels and processes of subcultural transmission?

Also needing research is the relationship between teenagers and the various mass media. What is the social corollary of teenagers who expose themselves to certain fare of the mass media? How does it affect them? How do teen tastes affect the producers of mass media fare? Although some of the questions have been researched, more investigation is needed, especially concerning the influence of teen tastes on the media's productions. A mass medium largely ignored by research is the teen magazine. Not until content analyses have been applied is there any way of knowing whether we have missed a source of insight into teenage life.

Among the unanswered questions concerning teenage affluence are questions not so much of *what* they buy—there are exhaustive itemized lists on teen consumptions—but of *why* and *how* they acquire certain items. Answers to the "why" might provide a link to the understanding of subcultural reinforcement and the nature of peer standards. Answers to the "how" would provide information on how much and by what means teenagers acquire financial power.

The issue of intergenerational conflict has been presented here more on the basis of hypothesis, inference, and nonsystematic content analysis than on the basis of reliable studies. There is enough *general* evidence to safely allow the assumption that intergenerational conflict does in fact exist; but *specific* correlations, social variables, and accentuating circumstances are relatively unknown.

How does a "generalist" teenager decide on a "specialist" future career? The questions surrounding this issue are multitudinous, and its specific aspects, such as how the transition is affected by the home or educational institutions, should be investigated.

Whereas research has paid ample attention to the circumstances that obscure the lower-class child's intelligence, it has neglected the fact that upper-class upbringing often obscures a child's low intelligence. Inquiry might reveal that the adolescent's display of socially approved manners and conformity to etiquette tend to be defined as intelligent behavior.

A question that has seldom been asked concerns the kind of social institutions that administer the *coup de grace* to the adolescent period and the manner in which they effect the transition to the adult status. The adult-initiating and adult-reinforcing roles of such institutions as the military, the labor force, marriage, civic clubs, political parties, and community organizations should be examined. It could be hypothesized that the degree of involvement in these institutions is directly correlated with changes in self-perception. Correlations should be checked against such intervening variables as time of entry into institution, personal motivation, kind of program offered, and institutional responsibilities assumed. Knowledge accrued could be used to restructure programs and activities to increase their effectiveness in helping older adolescents make the final transition into adulthood and to reinforce his or her adult identity.

The problem of identity is intricately connected to virtually all the above issues. Inquiry should focus on youths who experience generational mobility when they enter into careers different from those of their parents and face discontinuity of familiar patterns. Considering that a majority of boys and girls take up jobs or careers dissimilar to those of their parents', this becomes a timely research objective. Also to be examined is the role of the family of orientation as a value-instilling agency in the face of weak and nondescript cultural premises: Under what familial, peer, school, or religious circumstances does family influence balance cultural anomie? Under what family conditions does either peer or parental identification prevail? Which familial conditions make the young vulnerable to indoctrination by mass media, and which give the young immunity against imitation or internalization of mass media models?

Finally, there are questions concerning the diversity of the adolescent experience. Though some minority groups, such as blacks and lower-class teenagers, have been researched fairly exhaustively, other groups such as the Chicanos of the southwest and the Puerto Ricans of the east coast have been neglected. Also, more social psychological research is needed to fully understand the culture shock American Indians undergo on, near, and away from the reservation.

These research suggestions do not exhaust all needed inquiry. They are meant primarily to alert the student to research possibilities and to stimulate formulation of research propositions.

OUTLOOK

Nothing will stop the continued forays of adolescence into the purviews of the Establishment—unless a radical reversal of urban-industrial conditions commands a halt and turns society back to earlier forms of technology and commerce. But this is improbable and would happen only if the world should tumble into an unprecedented holocaust that destroyed the technological achievements forged by many generations.

In societies with advanced adolescence, like the United States, unrest will continue, though it will periodically seem deceptively peaceful. Societies that have not yet felt the rebellious power of their young will soon taste the bitter fruits of what the elders thought were the sweet seeds of increasing industrialization and long-awaited affluence. Countries surprised by what they may deem uncalled-for dissent and ungratefulness will especially include the developing countries where, until now, most youth have made swift transitions from childhood to adulthood.

It will also include some nations in which totalitarian and doctrinaire oppression has obscured chronic youth disaffection. Youth's sense of relative deprivation will break through and symptomize itself through demands and deviations that society can no longer roll back. The 1990s have already witnessed these symptoms in erstwhile Communist countries where newly acquired freedoms and adolescence-generating conditions of urban-industrialism have combined to hurry entire nations onto the path of adolescence-characterized societies.

In developing countries, youth participation will come to be particularly significant. On one side, it will represent tremendous political opportunities to raise countries to new levels of achievement and national growth; on the other side, it will mean a recurrent political threat for governments whose records of achievement may not be to the liking of the younger generation.

The generation gap will continue, and no bridges are in sight. If we give credence to such expert prognosticators as Urie Bronfenbrenner (a founding father of Head Start and consultant to Washington), the generation gap will be reinforced by continued, if not increased, age segregation. On the basis of widespread studies (including international comparisons) he contends that age segregation poses problems of great magnitude for the Western world in general and for American society in particular. If the institutions of our society continue to remove parents, other adults, and older youths from active participation in the lives of children and if the resulting vacuum is filled by the age-segregated peer group, "we can anticipate increased alienation, indifference, antagonism, and violence on the part of the young generation in all segments of our society—middle-class children as well as the disadvantaged."[1]

Bronfenbrenner discusses a five-point reform or prevention plan, believes that the family by itself can do little to bring the necessary change, and that other institutions in our society must be activated to break the vicious isolation of our young in their subcultural environment. Institutions such as school, government, business, and church shut out the young and relegate them to an amoral, antisocial milieu, which breeds rebellion and dissent.

Unfortunately, statistical trends suggest that age segregation will continue. Teenage work, early marriage, and traditional ways of assuming adult responsibilities are declining. Instead, formal education has become the norm—and a way of life shutting off the young from productive participation in the mainstream of American society. The number of young people remaining in school has increased, the steepest rise occurring among eighteen- and nineteen-year-olds, a development that is probably linked directly to the proliferation of community colleges during the past decades. Though formal schooling has almost entirely preempted other more traditional routes to adulthood, it does nothing either for those who have dropped out or for those who graduate but gain little from school.

---

[1]Urie Bronfenbrenner, *Two Worlds of Childhood: U.S. and U.S.S.R.* (New York: Russell Sage Foundation, 1970), pp. 116–17.

Teen fads and styles will continue to be exploited by business and industry to establish brand loyalties and to predict collective moods. Predictably, the American economy is bound to stimulate artificial wants, and adolescents will continue to compensate for psychological insecurity by material possessions. Material implementations create status, enhance personal significance, and build social power within one's peer group. Due to national economic difficulties, the spending behavior of youth in the 1990s appears slightly subdued when compared to the affluent behavior of youth during preceding decades. Whether youthful spending will regain its previous fervor depends on further national and international developments.

ADOLESCENCE: CRUCIBLE AND DELIVERANCE

Adolescence is a many-splendored thing. Like a kaleidoscope, it takes on different colors and designs depending how one looks at it. And each appearance bears its own truth.

The list of differing perceptions of adolescence is endless, but some of the major interpretations include a modern pathology, the tyranny of immature tastes, the happiest and freest time in life, the most depressing and unhappy period, a time of trial-and-error experimentation, a primarily delinquent period, the most creative phase, the age of conformity to the peer group, a subcultural existence, a moratorium on adult responsibilities, the age of rebellion and dissent, the time of sexual prowess and exuberance, the time of learning and training, the time of serving one's community, the time of being with one's parents, the time of insecurity and search, and the crisis of identity.

Adolescence is all of these things! Not to obscure the manifold nature of the adolescent experience dictated the open framework in which this book was couched. It allowed recognition of the many aspects of adolescence and avoided distortion of its portrait by refraining from undue theoretical encapsulation. Nonetheless, some critics might lament the fact that the book eschewed a unitary theoretical approach—as perhaps would have been reflected in a Freudian, behavioristic, problem-oriented, or lifespan-oriented framework. But the Procrustean bed is a maiming gift, and this author is unwilling to give it.

Whatever the kaleidoscope shows, all images have one thing in common: the transition to adulthood. And as such, the crisis of identity functions as the crucible out of which the young will emerge, hopefully intact in mind and body and ready to assume a productive life.

To those who worry excessively about modern adolescence, nostalgically reciting past and presumably adolescence-free days and wishing to replace adolescents with a "cause"-oriented national youth, let them be reminded of the perennial folly of the sorcerer's apprentice, who conjured up a phenomenon that could not be called back.

It is easy to point to cultures which have been spared the affliction of adolescence. They seem to fall into two categories, and in each the adolescent-free members pay a substantial price for their privilege. (1) The dictatorship does not allow selectivity in identity and thus minimizes the struggle of the young to acquire an identity. Identity comes in a ready-made package, neatly labeled and often attractively wrapped. These youths function well, at least as far as the society and its leaders are concerned. (2) The primitive or tribal society has traditional roles that are handed down unaltered from generation to generation, removing the responsibility from the young of creating unique identities.

On the other side, the democratic ethos grants to each member of society the right to and the responsibility for one's identity, as long as it does not jeopardize others. This freedom undoubtedly places a gigantic burden on the adolescent as well as on those who live with him or her. But all the trouble may pay off. In fact, it usually does: the troubled adolescent of yesterday turns out to be the responsible, integrated adult of today. The freedom for self-search begets the patience and generosity to encourage others to do likewise. And a chain reaction is established that becomes part of the democratic tradition, a tradition that is as irksome as it is imperative for the preservation of a democratic ethos.

Imposed alternatives for the process of adolescent self-search would mean a regression to some sort of mental servitude that is secure—but secure too soon.

Author Index

390

Subject Index